On Risk and Disaster

On Risk and Disaster

Lessons from Hurricane Katrina

EDITED BY
RONALD J. DANIELS,
DONALD F. KETTL, AND
HOWARD KUNREUTHER

Foreword by Amy Gutmann

PENN

University of Pennsylvania Press

Philadelphia

Publication of this volume was assisted by a generous grant from the Board of Trustees of the University of Pennsylvania Press

10   9   8   7   6   5   4   3   2   1

Published by
University of Pennsylvania Press
Philadelphia, Pennsylvania 19104-4112

A Cataloging-in-Publication record is available from the Library of Congress

ISBN-13: 978-0-8122-1959-3
ISBN-10: 0-8122-1959-7

Contents

Foreword

Amy Gutmann

> *The problems that exist in the world today cannot be solved by the level of thinking that created them.*
>
> —*Albert Einstein*

More than four months have passed since Hurricane Katrina struck. We now know that our affluent country failed both to take adequate precautions against the hurricane's deadly impact and to respond effectively to its devastation of New Orleans and other Gulf Coast areas. We do not yet know what lessons will be learned—or heeded—from one of the greatest catastrophes our country has ever experienced.

As the suffering grew ever more alarming in the hurricane's immediate aftermath, we at the University of Pennsylvania rapidly mobilized our community to help survivors rebuild their shattered lives. We invited 100 displaced students to take their fall classes at Penn. And as generous donations poured into relief agencies, students and staff volunteers traveled to the Gulf Coast to support efforts on the ground.

At the same time, we began to confront the problems that contributed to making the devastation of Katrina so troubling not only in its breadth and depth but also in its unbalanced effects across different segments of the population. Katrina's aftermath raised perhaps the most profound and disturbing moral question that our society has yet fully to confront: How willing is the United States to compensate for the increased risks to life and health associated with poverty, race, growing economic inequality, inadequate emergency preparedness, and antiquated urban infrastructures? This overarching question cannot be answered by one person thinking alone or by a single institution acting alone.

Nor can the underlying social, economic, and environmental problems that have been magnified by Katrina be solved by the level of institutional thought and action that created them. A shocking amount of shoddy thought and action—from the denial of scientifically manifest risks to the disavowal of morally apparent official responsibility—will need to be transcended to resolve the problems that have victimized hundreds of thousands of Americans.

We must find a way to distribute risks equitably in order to push our democracy closer to its promise of liberty and justice, not only for the affluent but for all. Rising to this challenge demands that the public and private sectors collaborate to develop effective prevention strategies and coordinated responses to natural disasters, industrial accidents, terrorist attacks, and pandemics.

We at the University of Pennsylvania pride ourselves on being one of the world's major research universities. But we cannot rest on our laurels. Institutional contributions to effective prevention and response are a matter not only of technical expertise but also of moral and social responsibility. Collaborating with others, we have the capacity and expertise to develop a framework within which to address such daunting and urgent challenges. We are committed to embracing our civic responsibilities to help inform public debate and discussion.

For all of these reasons, Penn Provost Ron Daniels took the lead in organizing a symposium on Hurricane Katrina in Washington, D.C. on December 1, 2005. The symposium brought together approximately 250 policymakers, public and private sector leaders, and scholars from many disciplines to raise the level of thinking on risk management issues and develop more effective strategies that can save lives and speed recovery when disaster strikes.

At the core of these discussions were two recurring questions:

- How can—and should—the nation come together to rebuild the storm-ravaged Gulf Coast?
- What broader lessons does Hurricane Katrina teach about the public and private sectors' role in helping citizens and firms deal with the inevitable large-scale risks we all face in the twenty-first century?

This book represents the first attempts to answer these questions. As this book goes to press, we are already planning a second Katrina conference—organized by the Penn Institute on Urban Research—that will build on the analyses and strategies contained in this volume. I am thankful to Provost Daniels, Professor Donald Kettl, director of the Fels Institute of Government at Penn, Professor Howard Kunreuther, codirector of the Wharton Risk Management and Decision Processes Center, and the many eminent scholars and policymakers who are doing their best to bring a higher level of thought and action to bear on the many profound problems of societal response to risk that Hurricane Katrina put into high relief. Our thanks go also to the University of Pennsylvania Press for so quickly bringing the symposium's findings to the attention of a wider public.

Introduction

RONALD J. DANIELS, DONALD F. KETTL, AND
HOWARD KUNREUTHER

The 9/11 terrorist attacks made it clear to Americans that we are living in a new world of geopolitical risks. Hurricane Katrina has shown the world how vulnerable the United States is to natural disasters. A widely predicted Category 3 hurricane left more than 1,300 people dead and hundreds of thousands displaced in New Orleans and throughout the southern part of four states. It was the most expensive natural disaster in the history of the United States, but its true cost to the region and the nation cannot be measured in dollars alone. It brought a great city to its knees and focused large questions about the nation's ability to prepare for and respond to natural disasters and other large risks.

While much-needed investigations will highlight specific failures at local, state, and national levels, Katrina raises a set of much deeper questions about how we address risk in our society. Could our current policies and infrastructure be as vulnerable in our complex modern world as the levees that were designed to protect New Orleans? What public and private initiatives will be needed to increase security and mitigate losses in an increasingly insecure and inherently risky world? Who—government, market or the third sector—is and should be responsible for taking these actions? As a catastrophic failure, Katrina presents an opportunity to look at the entire public-private systems for addressing risks, and perhaps build better ones. As Stanford Professor Paul Romer has said, "a crisis is a terrible thing to waste."

Issues of risk and responsibility for natural disasters are of interest not only to researchers and policymakers but also to those affected directly or indirectly by these tragic events. In the aftermath of Hurricane Katrina, disaster preparedness and recovery are now at the forefront of the public policy agenda. On the one hand, the devastation of Katrina raises fundamental questions about the strengths and frailties of the existing institutional, legal, and policy landscape governing the risk management of natural disasters in American society. Does the damage inflicted by Katrina imply that the

United States is vulnerable to other types of natural hazards that could impose similar, if not greater, damage on its citizens? If so, what types of reforms are required in order to mitigate the risks faced by individual citizens or communities, particularly where there is evidence that these risks are disproportionately borne by the least advantaged members of society?

On the other hand, the avowed determination of the country's political leadership to rebuild the Gulf region raises vexing questions about how best to use public money. Should governments focus on rebuilding adversely affected communities or on providing targeted assistance to adversely affected individuals? This issue of instrument choice is particularly salient because there is no assurance that individuals who receive targeted subsidies will necessarily decide to remain in those communities devastated by Katrina. Politicians who favor assistance to individuals may face onerous political consequences from local interest groups committed to rebuilding their communities—even at extraordinary public cost.

The commitment to rebuilding communities in the face of devastation is powerful testament to the indomitable American spirit. No one wants to admit defeat in the face of adversity. Most citizens and their elected officials want to take advantage of new opportunities to craft a new sense of community. And national sympathy in the face of large catastrophes often opens up the governmental purse strings wider than is the case in normal politics. No one wants to let a chance like that slip by. This attention is likely to be short-lived unless a set of concrete steps is taken to develop a long-term plan that has a good chance of being implemented.

Katrina has proven to be much more than the kind of catastrophe that has afflicted parts of the nation in past years. It hit with a fierce power, in the area long identified as most vulnerable to hurricanes. It raised tough and fundamental questions for which officials in both the public and private sectors had few good answers. Some citizens had insurance against such risks, but many did not. Much of the region's infrastructure—from telephone and electric lines to gas and water systems—was still not functioning months after the event. Some residents who wanted to rebuild returned to discover that their homes had been leveled, or that they simply could not find them at all.

As the first private insurance dollars and public relief checks started to flow, everyone discovered a new problem. Especially in New Orleans, it was impossible to begin recovering from the last catastrophe without preparing for the next. The levees have remained vulnerable to even modest storms, and everyone wants to know: Will new levees be built? What kind of storm could they withstand? Might we pour tens of billions of dollars into the city only to risk having it wiped out again? Housing is the biggest need, but no one in Mississippi or Louisiana wants to rebuild without thinking hard about how best to protect the investment.

Katrina is thus proving to be a story about both recovering from and managing risk. Private insurers are contemplating how best to structure insurance for natural disasters and whether to provide more comprehensive levels of coverage in one omnibus policy. Insurers also recognize that they have an opportunity to encourage families and businesses to protect themselves by making their buildings more disaster resistant, but also that they cannot do this alone. Other stakeholders from the private sector need to play a role in complementing government risk mitigation and risk insurance objectives by, for example, enforcing building codes.

With the federal government's commitment to pay large amounts of disaster relief, a puzzle naturally emerges. Is the message from Katrina that there is little economic incentive in reducing risk and limiting losses in advance of a disaster—what experts in the field call mitigation— because the government will act as the insurer of last resort? If that is the case, it is possible that enough people will respond in ways that guarantee that the next event will be even more catastrophic—that victims will not have insured themselves voluntarily against risk, that they will not have done what they could to reduce their exposure and limit their losses, and that taxpayers will incur an even bigger price tag than after Katrina.

This dilemma is nothing new. Students of risk have increasingly come to understand a fundamental problem in our policy toward managing disasters. All such catastrophes are, inevitably local. When money pours in, the benefits—from new homes to new businesses and roads and a refreshed civic life—are local as well. But given the propensity of the federal government to provide *ex post* assistance to affected citizens, the costs of disaster become nationalized, borne by all taxpayers. Economists have long argued that sensible planning begins by linking the expected benefits of taking action with the costs, recognizing that the actions taken prior to a disaster should be coupled with the response following the event. It is important to link so-called *ex ante* planning with *ex post* recovery. However, our policies have increasingly disconnected the expected benefits from the costs of disasters and the advance planning to reduce risks from the financial consequences of the disaster.

The dilemma would be serious enough if it applied just to Katrina, or just to Katrina-like disasters. However, a complex set of forces is conspiring to translate the same problem into many other realms. As our population grows, more of the nation's citizens live in areas prone to natural disasters, from floods and tornadoes to earthquakes and hurricanes, and some states have taken action to encourage this development for immediate economic gain (in the form of a larger tax base and other benefits). That means the consequences of such events are exacerbated. We also face significant perils from other exogenous risks like public health threats, such as avian flu. And we now must confront the threat of terrorism, on many different scales and from many different fronts, which raises additional issues about our national security.

Many of these risks are highly interdependent. Weak links in any supply chain for food and rescue equipment can prevent key materials and personnel from playing a useful role. Katrina raises both short- and long-term issues, both political and normative, of evacuating victims to other parts of the country and the impact this will have on rebuilding the Gulf Coast. A poorly designed levee system can have devastating consequences to the residents in the areas that were viewed as being protected against flooding.

Hurricane Katrina is thus not only important in its own right. It also raises a new class of problems that demand rigorous analysis, prudent planning, and courageous political leadership. Further compounding these challenges is the fact that neither the public nor the private sector can, on its own, appropriately protect the country's citizens from a range of devastating risks. Robust policy demands well-designed private-public partnerships to address these issues.

A Framework for Learning?

This book builds on a framework that recognizes the importance of risk assessment and risk perception as a basis for developing meaningful hazard management strategies. To reduce the potential losses from future disasters and aid the recovery efforts after a catastrophe occurs requires both private and public sector involvement.

The conceptual framework for investigating issues of risk and responsibility requires inputs from many different disciplines. Engineering, medicine, and the natural sciences provide data on the nature of the risks associated with disasters of different magnitudes and the uncertainties surrounding them (*Risk Assessment*). Geography, organizational theory, psychology, sociology, and other social sciences provide insights on how individuals, groups and organizations perceive the risk and make decisions (*Risk Perception and Choice*). Economics, insurance, health care, public policy, and other disciplines form the basis for alternative disaster management strategies (*Risk and Crisis Management*). Political science and law underpin important issues related to public and private responsibilities about how to develop a program that allocates resources before and after a disaster efficiently, while taking into account distributional issues and incentives for appropriate preparedness (*Implementing Public-Private Partnerships*).

Experts in risk assessment have long argued that policy makers ought to base their decisions on assessments of risk—the chances that specific events might occur and the consequences that are likely to flow from them. Just how probable is another hurricane of Katrina's force? Or of a nuclear power plant accident, a smallpox outbreak, a major terrorist explosion, or the spread of a new flu pandemic?

Producing good estimates of the direct impacts of a disaster—such as physical damage, injuries, and loss of lives—is difficult enough. The field of risk assessment, however, has expanded to include a careful look at indirect losses (such as business interruption, political disarray, and personal stress). Moreover, some activities have an impact on other actions, so analysts increasingly need to consider feedback effects when they propose a particular program. For example, new development projects can increase water runoff and, hence, hurricane flood damage. On the other hand, better mapping of areas especially susceptible to hurricane damage can alter development plans.

Better risk assessments, if heeded by public and private decision-makers, can reduce the losses from future catastrophic disasters. For example, improved weather forecasts may lower the number of deaths or injuries by providing early warning, which can help residents evacuate threatened areas before a storm arrives. Better forecasts can also eliminate unnecessary evacuations.

When undertaking risk assessments for a specific disaster, experts are likely to seek more precise information to help define the event. Consider the chance of another hurricane like Katrina occurring in the United States in the next ten years and its potential consequences. Ideally, experts will want to know the geographic area that would be affected by the hurricane, what individuals (and communities) are at risk, and how easily they will be able to evacuate the area if there are warnings far enough in advance. They will also want to know the design of the structures in the hazard-prone area and the resulting direct damage and indirect impacts, such as evacuation and relocation of victims and business interruption losses.

In the case of Katrina's devastating strike on the Gulf Coast, experts had forecast much of what actually occurred. The Department of Homeland Security, for example, had identified such a storm, along with a terrorist attack on New York City and an earthquake in California, as the three biggest threats the nation faced. *National Geographic*, almost a year before the storm struck, published an eerily accurate story on the damage a big storm could inflict.[1] The Federal Emergency Management Agency "Hurricane Pam" exercise in 2004 also gave clear warnings about what could happen. Yet, despite the advance plans and warnings, government officials were woefully under-prepared.

Risk assessment requires that one not only specify the likelihood and potential consequences of disasters of different magnitudes and intensities but also undertake systematic benefit-cost analysis to prescribe a set of actions that should be taken in response to those risks. Ideally, such an analysis would reveal the *expected* costs and benefits of different public policy strategies. For instance, should government invest in large public infrastructure projects such as dams and levees, and, if so, how elaborate should those projects be? Alternatively, should the risks of disaster be addressed by private investors in the form of safer building design and construction (perhaps motivated by more stringent building codes and municipal approvals)? Or, when measured against the up-front costs of mitigation, are the expected risks of certain hazards economically unavoidable, and, therefore, best addressed by insurance?

The precise form of insurance also raises complex design issues. Is there a need for publicly provided (or, at least, subsidized) insurance? If so, how can this insurance be supplied in a way that does not subvert economically desirable investments in risk mitigation? Further compounding the challenge is identifying the citizen groups likely to be affected by disaster. For instance, special treatment may have to be given to low income residents who cannot afford to purchase insurance or undertake protective measures that will reduce losses from future disasters.

It is one thing to assess the risk. It is quite another to estimate how people—whether individual families, private sector executives, or elected officials—perceive them. Whereas traditional risk assessment focuses on losses most frequently measured in money, risk perception incorporates the psychological and emotional factors that have an enormous impact on behavior.

In path-breaking studies begun in the 1970s, psychologists such as Paul Slovic and Baruch Fischhoff began measuring laypersons' concerns about different types of risks. These studies showed that for some technologies (like nuclear power) and activities (like storing radioactive waste) there was a wide disparity between the views of ordinary citizens and experts. This important finding raises important questions about policies for dealing with risks. Elected officials often face conflicting imperatives: citizens demand attention to some risks due to fear, dread, or catastrophic potential while experts feel the risk is not worth considering because of the small chance of its occurrence. On the other hand, experts may focus on other risks for which there is little public concern. And, of course, there is the challenge of how elected officials will mediate between these conflicting imperatives in the context of political cycles.

Compounding the problem is the difficulty individuals have in considering the probabilities when making their decisions. It is not easy to assess low-probability events, and people often disregard them. There is ample evidence that people often do not want to consider data on the likelihood that an event might occur, even when the information is available to them. Only after a disaster do most people pay attention to it, and then they overestimate its likelihood. For example, when a single, rare disaster attracts a great deal of media attention, individuals focus on the consequences of the event and behave as if it will happen again in the future. Following the terrorist attacks of September 11, many people refused to fly. They believed the chances of being on a hijacked plane were extraordinarily high, even though it could be argued that the probability of such events occurring in the future was extremely low given increased vigilance and added protection by the federal government.

This pattern spills over into natural disasters and has raised especially difficult questions in the aftermath of Katrina. Even people living below sea level in New Orleans did not consider their vulnerability to a major storm and failed to purchase flood insurance or invest in loss reduction measures with respect to their property. When the disaster struck, they quickly demanded federal help.

More generally, demands for protection and insurance often increase only after disasters hit—and long after it is too late. In California, insurers note surges in demand for earthquake insurance after a quake occurs, when the risks became more salient in everyone's minds. When asked whether the probability of a future quake is more likely, the same or less likely than before the disaster, most people correctly respond by saying "less likely."

The issue of risk perception thus compounds the puzzle of risk assessment. It shapes both the help that individuals expect after a major disaster—and how they shape the way that individuals prepare for the risks that lie ahead. It also raises challenges with respect to how one communicates risk so as to encourage individuals to take steps to reduce the losses from future disasters and to act appropriately after a catastrophe occurs.

The way that individuals perceive risks—and behave in dealing with them—often creates enormous disaster management problems. When crises do occur and individuals are not ready to meet them, they naturally demand that public and private institutions rise to the challenge. And that, in turn, poses big issues for these organizations. In developing risk and crisis management strategies that have a chance of being implemented, there is a need to incorporate the data from *risk assessment* and the factors that have been shown to influence *risk perception and choice*. A risk management strategy should reflect the likelihood and tangible impacts that are likely to occur following a disaster but also taking into account other dimensions that concern the public such as fear and dread and the types of heuristics that are utilized for making choices.

Consider a person living in a flood-prone area who believes that the likelihood of a future disaster is so small that it is not worth worrying about. A strategy of providing highly subsidized flood insurance premiums will not induce such a person to purchase a policy. Coverage may have to be required as a condition for a mortgage. The federal government resorted to such a strategy on federally insured mortgages after observing the low sales of highly subsidized flood insurance. However, this policy has not been well enforced, as evidenced by the large number of homeowners in flood-prone areas of New Orleans who did not have insurance against rising water.

Complicating the government's response is the fact, which Katrina made all too clear, that disasters do not respect the boundaries defining governmental or organizational missions and responsibilities. Almost by definition, these disasters fall outside normal routines, and they typically require extraordinarily rapid response to reduce loss of life and to minimize property damage. Government thus needs to do more than shape different policies to deal with the mismatch of risks and perceptions. It needs to devise different structures and processes to improve the coordination of public services.

Moreover, just as individuals tend to ignore disasters until the costs are all too clear—and then to overact—there are powerful incentives for government to postpone action until crises hit and then to respond with strong, but often not more than symbolic, action. These crises demand resilient organizations that are able to cope with surprise such as an unexpectedly large scale disaster.

Devising more effective organizations is one challenge, but the vast scope of Katrina-like natural disasters and September 11–like terrorist attacks makes it clear that no one organization, no one level of government, or indeed government on its own can possibly cope with the impact. An effective strategy demands effective public-private partnerships, coupled with better information, balanced economic incentives, reformed disaster insurance, and better regulations and standards. Yet the task of harnessing the strengths of different private and public actors and devising a coordinated risk control and insurance strategy is a daunting exercise.

Because people have difficulty processing data about low-probability events, the nation needs better *information provision*. Most people feel small numbers can be easily dismissed, while large numbers get their attention. Communicating information on the risk in different ways may influence individuals to behave differently with respect to the actions they take before and/or after a disaster.

Positive and negative *economic incentives* can encourage individuals to take cost-effective protective measures prior to a disaster based on risk assessments. How people process information on the costs and benefits of reducing the risk can play an important role in whether they decide to make decisions to reduce those risks. One needs to understand what role the status quo (e.g., inertia), budget constraints (e.g., the behavior of people who live from paycheck to paycheck), and short time-horizons (e.g., individuals who seek a return on their investments) play in the process of designing sound policies.

Suppose people and businesses think only about the potential benefits of these protective measures in reducing risk over the next year or two. Then they are unlikely to view these mitigation measures as financially attractive if there is a large upfront cost associated with the investment. Had they considered a longer time period in their evaluation, the proposed measure may well have been viewed as worthwhile. Economic incentives, such as long-term loans, may be helpful in overcoming this resistance to investing in mitigation measures.

Insurance helps individuals who, before a disaster, reduce their risks and invest in policies to help them recover from any losses they suffer. For insurance to be effective in both these roles, those who are at risk must bear a substantial portion of the costs of residing in hazard-prone areas. Otherwise they will have limited economic incentive to take protective actions and will rely on others to bail them out after the next disaster. Insurance can play a key role in determining who should bear the costs of making hazard-prone communities safer and who should pay for the losses caused by disasters. If private insurance is to play a central role in a hazard management program, then those in hazard-prone areas need to bear a substantial cost of making their communities safer and should be responsible for most of the losses after a disaster occurs. The larger the subsidy provided by the general taxpayer, the less important the role private insurance will play in signaling through premiums how hazardous a particular region is and inducing individuals residing there to adopt risk reducing measures in advance of a disaster.

If the government anticipates it will have to step in to pay a large share of the costs, it might increase its regulatory role. Hence, well-enforced *standards and regulations* are an important part of a hazard management strategy. Building codes may be desirable when property owners would otherwise not adopt cost-effective mitigation measures because they either misperceive the benefits from them or underestimate the probability of a disaster occurring. When a building collapses, it may create negative externalities in the form of economic dislocations and other social costs that are beyond the financial loss suffered by the owners. Losses from these and other externalities are normally not covered by an insurance policy. A well-enforced building code would help reduce these interdependent risks and obviate the need for financial assistance to those who would otherwise suffer these uninsured losses.

Principles for Shaping Hazard Management

These issues shape the way that policy-makers, in both government and the private sector, must think about the issues raised by Katrina. But behind these issues lie basic principles about fairness and efficiency that must provide the foundation for policy makers' decisions. The searing images of New Orleans residents marooned at the Superdome without food or water provide an inescapable lesson about the importance of setting broad principles to shape these policies.

Equal Treatment. In developing a strategy for minimizing risk and responding to disasters, all Americans should be treated equally regardless of sex, race, ethnicity, and class.

Risk Analysis. Public and private organizations should consider the likelihood of disasters—including alternative strategies to minimize risks and reduce costs—in developing emergency preparedness and recovery plans, as well as plans for economic growth and development.

Cost-Benefit Analysis. Public and private organizations should assess the relevant costs and associated benefits of alternative policies. The review of benefits should include social and psychological effects as well as the direct and indirect economic impacts.

Samaritan's Dilemma. Federal disaster assistance creates a Samaritan's dilemma. If individuals and organizations assume that the federal government will provide significant assistance after hardship—that the government will be insurer of last resort—there will be fewer economic incentives for those in hazard-prone areas to reduce their risks before the next disaster and to purchase adequate insurance coverage.

Uninsured Losses. A policy by both government and the private sector that implicitly anticipates high rates of uninsured losses should not be tolerated unless one explicitly acknowledges that the public sector will respond with financial assistance after the disaster.

Assisting Low Income Residents. Subsidies should be provided to low income residents in hazard-prone areas so they can afford to protect their property and to purchase insurance in advance of a disaster. Such a program would reduce the need for disaster assistance following the next catastrophic event.

Mitigation Measures. A disaster management program should encourage those at risk to adopt mitigation measures. However, disasters inevitably involve complex and interdependent risks, and policy makers need to carefully examine public programs to avoid unintended consequences.

Loss Distribution. The disaster management strategy must consider who is most likely to suffer losses and how the costs are distributed: victims (residents and private organizations), businesses in the private sector that cover some risk (including financial institutions, insurers, and reinsurers), all levels of government (local, state and federal), and the impact on taxpayers.

Relocation of Residents. In determining strategies for relocating residents to other areas following a disaster, policy makers need to consider the economic, psychological, and social effects on victims. The same careful consideration should drive strategies for rebuilding the region (especially the Gulf Coast and New Orleans in the aftermath of Hurricane Katrina).

Governance. Policy makers should devise effective public policies that avoid creating large bureaucracies, establishing complex programs, or incurring excessive costs. The governance system should be transparent, effective, and responsive.

Appropriate Roles for the Public and Private Sectors

Even after struggling with the basic issues and the broader principles noted above, a fundamental question remains as to which sectors of society ought to tackle which of these problems. On one hand, all solutions must be closely coordinated through new partnerships. On the other hand, even effective partnerships require some sorting out of responsibilities. Everyone cannot be responsible for everything and, as the government's stumbling response to Katrina showed, someone has to be responsible for each important step. We often try to sort out the roles of the public and private sectors by creating bright-line tests—a tripwire that would limit government's role. These issues are so complex and important, however, that government inevitably plays a role in setting the rules of the game: how to set the right incentives and sort out the roles of private players.

Perhaps nothing illustrates this point better than the tale of one relief worker in Mississippi. A wheelchair-bound Mississippi senior citizen had lost her home in the hurricane. After weeks of misery and waiting, a trailer from FEMA finally arrived. But she took one look at it and recognized her dilemma. She was confined to her wheelchair and the trailer's door was a foot or more off the ground. She simply could not get into the door of her new home. Separate institutions working separately had produced an answer that failed to get her any closer to a solution. Fortunately for this senior citizen, a coalition of faith-based organizations was working the area. They located her, listened to her problem, and got a wheelchair ramp built. It took a complex coalition of different organizations, public, private, and nonprofit, to solve her problem by building bridges between existing institutions. Without this intervention, the relief worker would have been stuck, tantalizingly close to an answer but no better off than she was before.

We cannot, in this volume, sketch out all the solutions to the issues we face and strategies in mitigating losses from future disasters and facilitating the recovery process following a mega-catastrophe like Hurricane Katrina. However, the outline of a strategy emerges clearly from many of the chapters. Far more important is understanding the problem. Such storms—as well as other disasters like them and other catastrophes we dare not imagine—are inevitable. Katrina revealed a large gap between the capacity of our policies and institutions and our needs, as individuals and as a society. We need a fresh understanding of the problems and new and creative solutions to tackle them. That is the most important lesson of Katrina, and if we fail to learn it, Katrina's legacy will not be "bigger and better." It will be "bigger and worse."

Notes

1. Joel K. Bourne, Jr. "Gone with the Water," *National Geographic* (October 2004), at   http://magma.nationalgeographic.com/ngm/0410/feature5/?fs=www3. nationalgeographic.com

Part One
The Challenge of the Gulf

On Their Own in Battered New Orleans

PETER G. GOSSELIN

Laurie Vignaud faces a double dilemma: If she rebuilds her wrecked ranch house at 1249 Granada Drive in the great suburban expanse south of Lake Pontchartrain, will her neighbors do the same? And even if they do, will that guarantee their Gentilly neighborhood does not end up an isolated pocket in a diminished, post-Katrina New Orleans?

Nothing in Vignaud's 46 years, not even her job as affordable housing vice president with Hibernia Bank, the region's biggest financial institution, prepared her for this problem. From her relocated offices in Houston, she recently confessed, "It's scary." "I don't know when I'll ever go home."

Double dilemmas abound in this deeply damaged city, and represent considerably more than the start of the slog back from disaster.

Lost amid continued talk of billions in federal aid is the fact that most homeowners and businesses are being left to make the toughest calls on their own. Lost is that New Orleans' recovery—which President Bush once suggested would be one of the largest public reconstruction efforts the world had ever seen—is quickly becoming a private market affair.

"My constituents have pretty much concluded that it's up to us to put our neighborhood back together and get on with our lives," said Republican city council member Jay Batt, who represents the Lakeview neighborhood just west of Vignaud's.

To market advocates, this is the way it should be. Rugged individuals settled the American West in the nineteenth century and can resettle the Crescent City in the twenty first.

But the risks that individual New Orleanians must shoulder in such an on-your-own recovery appear staggeringly large.

"There is no market solution to New Orleans," said Thomas C. Schelling of the University of Maryland, who won this year's Nobel Memorial Prize in Economic Sciences for his analysis of the complicated bargaining behavior that underpins everything from simple sales to nuclear confrontations.

"It essentially is a problem of coordinating expectations," Schelling said of the task that Vignaud and her neighbors must grapple with. "If we all expect each other to come back, we will. If we don't, we won't.

"But achieving this coordination in the circumstances of New Orleans," he said, "seems impossible."

The situation in which residents find themselves is an extreme example of a trend underway for a quarter-century, a shift of economic risk from business and government to working families, and an increasing reliance on free markets to manage society's problems.

Safety nets such as unemployment compensation, employer-provided healthcare insurance and pensions, and, recently, effective disaster relief have been reeled in or removed. Increasingly, families from the working poor to the affluent are left largely to buy and sell their own way to safety even when their individual efforts seem utterly outgunned, as they do in the case of Katrina.

"There are classes of problems that free markets simply do not deal with well," Schelling said. "If ever there was an example, the rebuilding of New Orleans is it."

Promises, Then Reality

Prospects for a quick municipal comeback peaked 17 days after the hurricane and flood, when Bush stood before St. Louis Cathedral in historic Jackson Square and told a national television audience that "there is no way to imagine America without New Orleans, and this great city will rise again."

The hopes thus raised were kept alive in the first two months following Katrina. The president sought first one, then two emergency spending bills totaling $62 billion. The Army Corps of Engineers quickly signed contracts to rebuild the city's protective levees to their pre-storm condition. The Federal Emergency Management Agency announced it would award 60,000 households the maximum allowable relief of $26,200. A steady stream of planning conferences by architects, urbanists and political leaders spread the good word that major metropolises never die.

But in recent weeks, a new reality has settled in as the agencies that were stepping up to help guide the city's comeback have stepped back down again.

FEMA said it would stop covering the hotel costs of more than 50,000 households at the beginning of December—later extended until Jan. 7—even while acknowledging that many, especially in New Orleans, would have trouble finding alternative accommodations.

Despite repeated pleas, the Corps and the White House refused to promise any strengthening of the levees beyond what was underway. Investigators, meanwhile, concluded that several of the protective walls that failed did not meet corps-approved standards, a discovery that raised doubts about the safety of the entire levee system.

Emergency spending slowed sharply. The national flood insurance program temporarily suspended claims payments for Katrina, and program officials hinted broadly that they would tighten eligibility requirements to get coverage for the next storm.

Even the tiny agency charged with gauging the elevation of America's ground added an unexpected hurdle. It quietly announced that New Orleans and environs had sunk more than anticipated, forcing it to replace all of its measuring sticks. The result is that New Orleanians will have to build higher to escape future floods. With so many new strikes against it, the city's recovery, already grindingly slow, has ground still slower. Three months after the storm, Entergy New Orleans, the bankrupt utility that serves the city, said that 55,000 of its 190,000 customers had resumed electrical service. Municipal officials estimate that less than one-third of the population has returned to live.

To an extent almost inconceivable a few months ago, the only real actors in the rebuilding drama at the moment are the city's homeowners and business owners. To be sure, Washington is offering many relief payments, tax breaks and FEMA trailers. The city is speeding the approval of building permits. But for the rest, individual New Orleanians are struggling to come back largely under their own power, using mostly their own resources and negotiating their return substantially on their own terms.

While that might seem perfectly reasonable to outsiders, local and state leaders say that it overlooks the crucial fact that most of what people need to make such a one-at-a-time, free-market recovery work was demolished or severely damaged by Katrina, including about two-thirds of the city's 145,000 homes.

"What's missed is that it wasn't a single house or business that was destroyed, but an entire region," said Rep. Richard H. Baker (R-La.), chairman of a House financial markets subcommittee and author of one of the few comprehensive rebuilding proposals.

"It does no good to stand up just one person or family, because there's nothing left where they once lived—no schools or grocery stores, doctors or banks, police stations or firetrucks," Baker said.

"We've got to go into the business of restoring whole communities."

A Family's Challenge

Among the communities are ones that Laurie Vignaud helped finance and others that her father, 74-year-old Leroy Vignaud, helped build.

The younger Vignaud grew up a few miles from Granada Drive, the only daughter among four children of a plastering contractor and his wife. Laurie Vignaud and her brothers have lived most of their lives no more than a 10-minute drive from their parents.

In the mid-1960s, Leroy Vignaud began snapping up buildings to repair, then rent or sell, and has now gone through 20. By the mid-1970s, he was landing top-dollar jobs like restoring the ornamental plaster inside St. Louis Cathedral.

With the money he made, Vignaud was able to move his family into a big house with a circular staircase in a then largely white section of town. "I busted some ground there," he said proudly of his economic and racial climb. His daughter had a debutante party when she turned 18.

But the elder Vignaud kept largely to his own. It was left to his daughter's generation to learn to move effortlessly across the racial divide. By now, they have; black, professional and rising, they are widely seen as the future of New Orleans, the people—perhaps more than any other—who must return after Katrina for the city to rebound.

After a marriage to an Air Force officer that produced two daughters—Ashley, now 20, and Lindsey, 16—and ended in divorce, Laurie went to work for black-owned Liberty Bank. By the late 1990s, she had moved over to historically white Hibernia and was responsible for helping the bank comply with federal requirements that it reach out to poor and segregated communities.

Her job gave her the wherewithal to drive a Lexus ES 300 sedan, keep a second car for the girls and hire an interior decorator to help renovate the house on Granada Drive.

Her first project for the bank was an 18-house development called Delery Square in the poor, mostly black Lower 9th Ward. She put together a program to help ensure that New Orleans police officers and firefighters could buy in the city. She put together another to help cash-poor jazz musicians afford homes. She crisscrossed Louisiana and Texas, promoting affordable housing and doing deals.

Until Katrina.

Besides wrecking Laurie's Granada Drive home, the storm damaged or destroyed virtually every one of her projects in New Orleans. In the case of Delery Square, the houses are still standing, although flooded. Almost every structure around them had been crushed or washed away.

Katrina also drowned the five properties that Leroy Vignaud had kept for retirement income—at least three of them irretrievably. He and his wife have spent most of the time since the storm sharing a three-room apartment in a Houston senior center with Laurie and her daughters. He is reluctant to go out in an unfamiliar city because he is legally blind and has diabetes. So he sleeps mostly, watches a little TV and, his daughter fears, broods about his losses.

To get some sense of the problems that confront property owners, start at 1249 Granada Drive.

Inside Laurie's house, floodwater flipped the black upholstered sofa with the white highlight, snapped her roll-top desk and deposited the washing machine on top of the dryer. Moisture got up under the glass of a hallway poster, making it almost impossible to read "Turning Point. The Harlem Renaissance." Humidity caused the wooden blades of her ceiling fans to wilt like dead leaves.

The only thing orderly is the mold, which covers every surface. Each spore sends out spoke-like tentacles called hyphae that bloom at regular intervals into furry "fruiting bodies." The result where a single colony has won dominance on a wall or overhead is a startling black bull's-eye.

"Conditions are optimal for the fungi," said University of Colorado mycologist Mervi Hjelmroos-Koski, in New Orleans recently to take samples. "They are just doing their job" of digesting whatever they land on.

Back outside, look in any direction. Every structure for miles and miles is in essentially the same shape.

City Was Ailing

New Orleans looks substantially less resilient than other American cities that have come back from disaster. Chicago at the time of the Great Fire of 1871 and San Francisco after the 1906 earthquake were boomtowns. New York after 9/11 was largely intact. By contrast, much of New Orleans' economy had been stagnating for a generation before Katrina. What had not been stagnating either contributed little to overall growth or was damaged by the storm and flood.

The ports of New Orleans and nearby South Louisiana, the largest in the nation, were largely spared by Katrina. State and local officials pass up no opportunity to describe them as gateways to the Mississippi River basin and linchpins of the American economy.

But asked about inferences that the city is equally important, Gary P. LaGrange, president of the Port of New Orleans, said, "That's bull."

Most of the steel, rubber, plywood, grain and frozen poultry handled by the ports flow straight through without stopping to be processed or purchased. "New Orleans is the biggest through-put port in the country," said LaGrange. "It doesn't need the city. The value added here is very minimal."

By contrast, the city's hospitals and universities, which provided New Orleans with 17% of its private sector employment, lie in ruins with little chance of quick recovery.

Tulane University is expected to slash its graduate programs, which now number 44, when its board of trustees meets. Among the most painful decisions will be putting off for at least the rest of the academic year, and perhaps substantially longer, returning its medical school from Houston, where most of it is now temporarily housed.

Louisiana State University, which manages the city's two biggest hospitals, Charity and University, has furloughed all but 275 of its nearly 4,000 New Orleans employees, and will shortly have to permanently lay them off.

"I'm going to run out of cash by Christmas," said Donald R. Smithburg, chief executive of the LSU hospital system. "Without some fast financial help, I don't know how I'll ever get the pieces put back together again."

With such top-down elements of its economy as these damaged or isolated, New Orleans appears almost entirely dependent on a bottom-up process of one individual's decision to rebuild piling atop another's until recovery becomes self-sustaining.

In theory, such a virtuous cycle is at the heart of every market economy, and, once underway, should revive the city. But a look at some of the uncertainties facing individual New Orleanians—rich and poor, black and white—suggests that this is where matters turn truly daunting.

Levees Hold the Key

According to Schelling, the key to making almost any kind of human activity work is "credible commitments." Buyers must make them to sellers. Governments must make them to citizens. Nations must make them to each other.

The credible commitment that virtually every resident of New Orleans wants more than any other is a pledge from the Army Corps of Engineers to rebuild the levee system bigger and better than before Katrina.

"If they put back good levees to the [Category 3] level authorized before Katrina and we can get a commitment to build them slowly up to Category 5, people will come back," said Walter Isaacson, a News Orleans native, former editor of Time magazine, former chairman of CNN and co-chairman of the Louisiana Recovery Authority, a new state board appointed by Gov. Kathleen Babineaux Blanco to oversee reconstruction. "It won't be a purely rational decision, but they'll come."

But the corps has made it clear that it has no intention of making any such grand commitment soon.

In part, the problem is cost; estimates of what it would cost to bring the city's levees up to Category 5 range from $4 billion to more than $30 billion. In addition, the corps' budget is perhaps the most closely controlled of any in the federal government, with Congress ear-marking almost every dollar to particular projects, leaving the corps little maneuvering room.

But there also appears to be a sense among senior corps officials that local demands for greater protection, if indulged, would be unceasing.

"It's of interest to me," New Orleans district commander Col. Richard P. Wagenaar told the *Los Angeles Times* several weeks ago, "that all the political leaders, all the business leaders and all the homeowners were all perfectly comfortable with the system on Aug. 28," the day before Katrina made landfall. "They knew full well it was being built to Category 3, and everybody was fine with that," he said.

But when a storm of greater strength struck and overwhelmed the levees, Wagenaar said, people "suddenly wanted to look back and say, 'Hey, what happened?'" The implication: When would calls for still more ever end?

In the weeks since Wagenaar made his comments, state investigators discovered that sheet pilings along floodwalls that failed on 17th Street and London Avenue near Granada Drive extended to barely half the depth that Corps designs called for, and that the walls themselves were of a weaker design than what the corps had recommended. On Wednesday, corps engineers partially confirmed the findings.

The news has opened a new front in New Orleanians' fight for outside help in rebuilding. In effect, they argue that while what happened to much of the city was a natural disaster, what happened to many of the suburbs south of Lake Pontchartrain was the result of a failure of the corps and therefore something for which Washington should compensate them.

"We're talking about the negligence of man, not an act of God," said Republican state Rep. Emile "Peppi" Bruneau, who represents the area.

"Our citizens are showing the spirit to survive, but it is unfair to ask people to pump their already damaged savings back into their homes and businesses without a demonstrated commitment from the federal government to protect us the right way this time," New Orleans Mayor C. Ray Nagin said.

The problem for residents is that years will pass before all of the investigations are complete and the decisions made. In the meantime, the discovery of flaws along the two canals has caused fear to spike about the safety of the entire levee system and produced the opposite of the "credible commitment" New Orleanians need.

"You have to wonder whether the same flaws exist in places that didn't breach," said King Logan, a marketing executive whose home in the tony Country Club Gardens neighborhood took on 6 feet of water, despite being considered on high enough ground to be safe from flooding.

"I'm certainly not going to rebuild," he said, "until somebody convinces me the rest of the system isn't as poorly built."

Such transparent lack of confidence represents a huge strike against chances for the kind of free-market recovery on which city now depends.

Flood Insurance Woes

If city residents aren't getting what they need from the Army Corps of Engineers, they are having even less luck with the government's national flood insurance program.

In theory, the FEMA-run program should make decisions about whether to rebuild easier because it assumes some of the financial risk involved by promising to cover up to $250,000 in flood damages.

And because FEMA requires that the buildings it insures be built above the projected level for a once-in-100-years flood, the program seems to provide protection against the actual physical risk of flooding as well.

But flood insurance has turned into a morass in the wake of Katrina, with many homeowners and business owners finding it nearly impossible to collect for the just-passed storm or to figure out what coverage they'll be eligible to get for the next one. The disarray represents a second strike against hopes for a go-it-alone rebuilding.

Part of the problem is that while Washington provides basic flood insurance, the government depends on private insurance agents to sell it as part of a standard homeowners' policy. Interviews, lawsuits and complaints filed with the Louisiana insurance commissioner's office suggest that many agents are underselling the flood portion of policies while overselling the company-provided homeowners' part.

Some homeowners, like Louis J. Gentry Jr., who together with his wife, Kim, just finished rebuilding their Lakeview home two years ago and insured it through State Farm, have discovered themselves financially "upside down" without enough flood coverage to pay off their mortgage. Others, like Vignaud, who insured through Travelers, said that they were assured the homeowners' portion of their policies would cover their house's contents even in case of flood, only to learn otherwise since Katrina.

Spokesmen for State Farm and Travelers refused to comment.

But problems with past coverage are nothing compared with the confusion over future coverage. Homeowners are worried—apparently with good reason—that the rules are about to be changed so that many will have to literally raise their houses in order to qualify for flood insurance. For tens of thousands like Vignaud, whose post-World War II suburban homes were built on concrete slabs rather than above the ground on piers, that's a near impossibility.

New Orleans now requires owners to comply with a 1984 map that divvies the city into dozens of districts, each with a different base flood elevation that's dependent not just on where a structure is relative to sea level but also on how good local drainage and the city's pumping system are in that area.

Michael K. Buckley, deputy director of the national flood insurance program, said in an interview that FEMA was about to announce that it thought the city would need to raise those flood elevations 1 to 3 feet.

Buckley cautioned that the increase was only advisory; Washington is at least a year away from requiring the city to adopt higher elevations. City officials have promised that anyone who rebuilds in the meantime will be grandfathered under current rules. But sooner or later, many New Orleanians are going to have to raise the elevations of their buildings, or go without flood insurance.

In a final perverse twist, a separate federal agency that certifies the measuring points that are used to gauge buildings' elevations recently withdrew hundreds of its benchmarks for the New Orleans area, saying that they had sunk as the ground had subsided and were no longer accurate.

The National Geodetic Survey replaced the old benchmarks with nine new ones. State and local officials said the new benchmarks effectively raised by as much as a foot the zero mark, or starting point, for measuring whether a building meets the elevation required to qualify for flood insurance.

"People have got to realize New Orleans is sinking," said Roy K. Dokka, a geologist and director of LSU's federally funded Center for GeoInformatics. "It can be made safe if the proper steps are taken, but it's a vulnerable place to live."

Chalk up a third strike against free-market reconstruction

Who Will Come Back?

Even after learning to live with their fear about the levees and solving their flood insurance problems after wrapping their minds around the idea that their homes may have to be raised and the land under them is sinking, New Orleanians still have another hurdle to cross.

That's the double dilemma of whether if one person rebuilds, will his neighbors, and, even if they all do, will that be enough to ensure their neighborhood's survival?

As a work crew gutted 1249 Granada Drive on Monday, heaping appliances, sofas and sheetrock in a 6-foot pile on the curb, Laurie Vignaud suddenly realized her only evidence that any of her neighbors had returned since Katrina was similar heaps outside their houses.

But do those piles mean that Granada Drive residents are ready to rebuild, or simply are picking through the wreckage and trying to buy time by stopping the mold's spread?

"I keep looking at all this stuff and wondering whether they're coming back or not," said Vignaud. "It's crazy, like a riddle I can't solve."

In fact, a few neighborhoods appear to have solved the riddle, or at least to have taken a good run at it. But the ways in which they have says much about the daunting dimensions of the problem facing the rest of the city.

On the northern edge of the city is New Orleans' Greek Orthodox community and its church, Holy Trinity Cathedral. As warnings about Katrina grew darker in the days before the storm, community leaders matched up families to whisk the elderly and infirm out of danger. In the days immediately after, they mobilized to come back again.

"We ran it like a business," said John D. Georges, the parish council president and chief executive of Imperial Trading Co., a regional supplier of convenience stores.

Father Anthony Stratis worked the phones and sent out e-mails to find parishioners. Parish council member Dr. Nick Moustoukas followed up by wiring money to the neediest. Ten days after the storm, Georges and council member Christ Kanellakis helicoptered in to rescue the church's chalice and tabernacle.

By acting in concert, members of the Greek community have in effect provided each other with an immense self-insurance policy, guaranteeing that if one family rebuilds, others will. And, should more enticement be needed, the church, according to Georges, Moustoukas and others, is providing returning families with thousands of dollars of cash aid, has organized bulk purchases of new appliances and has arranged for crews that repaired the cathedral to be introduced to people whose houses are in need of work.

By the time the cathedral reopens for its first full service in two weeks, its marble interior walls will have been repaired, its lawn will have been resodded and Holy Trinity will be back in business.

Without ethnic and religious ties like the Greek community's to bind them, other neighborhoods are turning to what's been described as the great new binder of people: the Internet. Dozens of neighborhood websites have popped up since the storm. Quietly, almost by accident, the city is emerging as a test of the Internet's power to let people organize themselves.

When 28-year-old Cherie Melancon Franz and her husband, Arthur, 32, used the website Rebuild Lakeview (http://groups.yahoo.com/group/rebuild_lakeview/) to organize a "back to the breach" gathering at a levee break along the 17th Street canal in early October, they expected 50 people. Instead, they got 500. When the couple, who lost their home at 5837 Milne Blvd., subsequently arranged a $6,500-a-house group rate for demolition, they got 15 takers in a matter of hours.

Others, realizing that they face the double dilemma of not knowing what their neighbors will do or whether their neighborhood will reach the critical mass needed to survive, have tried to use the website to solve the problem.

"One of the difficult parts of going to Lakeview," one resident said in a message posted last week, "is that it is impossible to know who is staying and who is leaving . . . I suggest that all those that are staying, hang a Mardi Gras flag on their houses to show their neighbors that they are coming back.

"Wouldn't it feel good to . . . see these flags popping up all over the place? Do it!"

Still, "Rebuild Lakeview" and similar sites have left many residents with the same aching questions about when will it be safe to return and what their neighbors will do.

"I read it every few days, and there's some good information," said Lou Gentry, whose house at 6622 Louisville St. is about 10 blocks from the Franzes'. "But until they tell me something definite about the levees and the insurance and who's coming back, I'm keeping my money in the bank."

Little Choice But to Leave

When Laurie Vignaud was in town last week, she registered the car she purchased to replace her drowned Lexus, and renewed her Louisiana driver's license—two inexpensive ways to maintain her connection with New Orleans.

But when the work crew gutting 1249 Granada Drive hauled the last load from the house, she told them to board it up after it dried. Then she and her daughters headed for Houston and a newly rented three-bedroom town house in a gated suburb.

"It would just break my heart if I lose that house," she said. But with so much up in the air about the levees, insurance, her neighbors and the city, she said, "there's no way I can do anything now."

Vignaud's employer, Hibernia, was acquired recently by Virginia-based credit card giant Capital One Financial Corp. and is aggressively expanding in Texas. The bank's Houston-based executives have asked her to stay, according to Hibernia Executive Vice President Willie Spears. Next week, she expects to be in Brownsville to hire a new employee, then fly on to Dallas for more hiring.

Meanwhile, Leroy Vignaud is trying to get FEMA to put a trailer next to his house with the circular staircase. He has purchased a small pickup truck and a few tools.

Legally blind and on unfamiliar terrain, he has asked his wife to drive him home to retrieve what he can.

"I can't walk away from my resources," he said.

26   Peter G. Gosselin

Note

Reprinted from the *Los Angeles Times* (December 4, 2005).

Using Risk and Decision Analysis to Protect New Orleans Against Future Hurricanes

DETLOF VON WINTERFELDT

After hurricane Katrina struck New Orleans in 2005, many questions were raised about the decisions that were made, mostly in the 1970s and 1980s, to develop a system of levees and flood walls to protect the city from hurricanes. These structures were designed to withstand a category 3 hurricane with wind strengths of 111 to 130 mph and a flood surge of 14 m (see U.S. Army Corps of Engineers 1984). Hurricane Katrina was a category 4 hurricane at landfall with higher wind speeds of up to 140 mph and a higher flood surge of about 20 m, which eventually caused several breaches of the levees. Several researchers and emergency managers had predicted the magnitude of the catastrophe for hurricanes stronger than a category 3 (see Laska 2004; Maestri 2002). Yet decisions on construction of the levees, even at the category 3 protection level and investments for flood protection were continually delayed or underfunded, and there appeared to be no strong voice to propose larger investments to prevent flooding in case of higher category hurricanes (see U.S. Government Accountability Office 2005).

The events that occurred with hurricane Katrina did not come as a surprise to researchers and emergency managers in the New Orleans area. In a 2004 article, after Hurricane Ivan had struck the U.S. coast just west of Gulf Port, Alabama, in September of 2004 as a category 3 hurricane, Shirley Laska from the Center for Hazards Assessment, Response, and Technology at the University of New Orleans discussed the question: "What if Hurricane Ivan Had Not Missed New Orleans?" Laska answered that hurricane Ivan would have "pushed a 17-foot storm surge into Lake Pontchatrain." It would have "caused the levees between the lake and the city to overtop and fill the city 'bowl' with water from lake levee to river levee, in some places as deep as 20 feet" and then "flooded the north shore suburbs of lake Pontchatrain with waters pushing as much as seven miles inland." Laska concluded, "Up to 80 percent of the structures in these flooded areas would have been severely damaged from wind and water" (Laska 2004).

Others made even more dire predictions. In 2002 Walter Maestri, then a public emergency manager in Jefferson Parish, imagined the following scenario for a category 4 hurricane or stronger:

The hurricane is spinning counter-clockwise, it's now got a wall of water in front of it some 30 to 40 feet high, . . . it tops the levees—and first the communities on the west side of the Mississippi river go underwater . . . now that water from the Lake Pontchartrain is pushed on the population that is fleeing from the western side and everyone is caught in the middle. The bowl now completely fills and we've got a community under water, some 20 to 30 feet under water. . . . We think 40,000 people could lose their lives in the Metropolitan area (Maestri 2002).

Jay Combe, then the Army Corps of Engineers chief researcher, considered the possibility of 100,000 deaths for a category 4 or 5 hurricane (Combe 2002).

The record clearly shows that 1) a deliberate decision was made in the 1970s and 1980s to build levees that could withstand a category 3 hurricane, but no stronger hurricanes; and 2) events involving hurricanes like Katrina were predicted, and, though rare, included consequences that were similar to or worse than those that occurred. There were many people, including those cited above, who could legitimately have said: "I told you so."

In this paper I will first examine the analyses underlying the decisions of the mid-seventies and eighties decision to fortify the then existing levees and flood walls to withstand a category 3 hurricane. Second, I will suggest an improved risk and decision analysis framework to re-address these decisions in designing a strategy for rebuilding New Orleans.[1] Third, I will address some of the methodological and implementation issues that policy and decision makers will face in the next few years in the process of analyzing and implementing these decisions.

Past Risk and Cost-Benefit Analyses

In 1974, the Army Corps of Engineers published a Final Environmental Impact Statement on the "Lake Pontchartrain, Louisiana, and Vicinity Hurricane Protection Project." The proposed plan involved the development of a series of barriers (levees and flood walls) in various areas surrounding New Orleans and the parishes in its vicinity. The plan intended to protect the area against a Standard Project Hurricane (SPH), which was then thought to be a category 3 hurricane that was estimated to occur approximately once every 200 years. Without the barriers, estimates concluded, a category 3 hurricane would "inundate a land area of approximately 700,000 acres to depths up to 16 feet in the study area" (U.S. Army Corps of Engineers 1974, p. I-2).

When this EIS was written, risk analysis was in its infancy. The first major risk analysis study, WASH-1400, which analyzed the risks of nuclear power plants, had not yet been published (Nuclear Regulatory Commission 1975). The authors of the EIS had the benefit of solid hydrological and meteorological data that allowed them to provide estimates of the likelihood and severity of hurricanes in the gulf region. The two environmental impacts statements listed seven historical hurricanes in New Orleans and its vicinity, including Camille, which resulted in 262 fatalities in 1969 (U.S. Army Corps of Engineers 1974, 1984).

The design base hurricane for the barrier project was a category 3 hurricane, although at least one of the previous hurricanes had risen above category 3. The 1974 EIS assigned this a chance of occurring once in 200 years in New Orleans. It is unclear how the EIS authors arrived at this estimate, but given several category 2 and 3 hurricanes striking New Orleans between 1900 and 1970 and at least two near misses (Betsy in 1965 and Camille in 1969) with category 3 or higher, it is difficult to understand this assessment. Based on this experience it appears that a category 3 hurricane would be occur much more often than once in 200 years.

The EIS authors expressed the benefits of the barrier plan in terms of the annual expected costs without the barriers and the annual expected costs with the barriers. This difference was estimated to be approximately $165 million in 1974 dollars, mostly due to protecting residential and industrial structures from flooding. They estimated the cost of the project to be $327 million in capital and $13 million in annual operation and maintenance costs. There was no question that the proposed system of levees and flood walls had a high benefit to cost ratio, and using appropriate procedures to annualize capital costs and discount the cost stream, the EIS concluded that the benefit to cost ratio was 12.6. There was some consideration of less protective alternatives, but no consideration of more protective alternatives, particularly building levees to withstand a category 4 hurricane.

After several project delays, design changes, and legal challenges to this decision, a federal court issued an injunction that halted all work on the barrier system (U.S. Government Accountability Office 2005). As a result of this injunction, the Army Corps of Engineers conducted and published a new environmental impact analysis in the early 1980s (US Army Corps of Engineers 1984). This analysis considered the no-barrier alternative, the original 1974 alternative to build a levee and flood wall system against the SPH hurricane (the "barrier plan"), and a third alternative involving higher levees ("high level plan"). The high level plan would build the levees to about 16 feet rather than 14 feet as planned in the barrier plan.

The risk analyses of the 1984 EIS were much improved, reflecting advances in hydrological, meteorological, and consequence analysis in the ten years following the 1974 analysis. Detailed flood elevation-frequency curves were developed for the different parishes. These curves are similar to modern complementary cumulative density functions (ccdfs), which are routinely used today to plot the exceedance frequency of possible consequences of disasters. For example, the elevation-frequency curve for the Orleans Parish showed that without to the project it was estimated that there would be a 1 in 100 chance per year of a flood elevation 13 feet above ground and a 1 in 500 chance of exceeding 16 feet. With the SPH level protection, estimates suggested that there was virtually no chance of exceeding a flood level above a couple of feet.

It is clear from this data that the EIS authors assumed that the levees would withstand the design hurricane. There appeared to be no consideration of levee breaches. Hurricane Katrina had a flood surge that exceeded the SPH design of 14 feet and caused several levee breaches, which were the ultimate cause of the disastrous flood. I therefore conclude that the probabilities of exceeding flood levels were underestimated.

A similar conclusion can be drawn for the consequence estimates, given a high-end hurricane event. As in the 1974 report, the 1984 EIS calculated annual benefits as the difference between the expected costs due to hurricanes without the proposed projects and the expected costs with the projects. The EIS estimates this difference to be between $66 and $80 million per year, about half of the estimate of the 1974 EIS. The costs, on the other hand, doubled to $600–800 million capital costs and $25–33 million annual operations and maintenance costs. As a result the benefit-cost ratio decreased from about 16 to about 4. The high level plan had a slightly higher benefit to cost ratio than the original barrier plan.

The benefit side of this equation is complex. Unfortunately, the EIS reports only net annual benefits and it is not easy to trace back the components of the calculations. Assuming that the expected costs with the barrier system are low (the elevation-frequency curves in the EIS suggest that at least for alternatives that protect against the SPH, they should be minimal), one can infer that the expected net benefits are close to the expected costs of not improving the levee and barrier system. If this is the case, the expected costs of not building these systems are, according to the EIS, somewhere between $50 million and $80 million per year. Using a 100 year horizon and without discounting, the total consequences of the SPH would then be $5 to $8 billion, much lower than the $200 billion that are estimated for hurricane Katrina.

It is also disturbing to note that in all consequence calculations of the EIS, there is no mention of lives lost. Considering the 1,000 fatalities in

Katrina and a value of life between $5 and $10 million, just the value of lives lost in Katrina is between $5 and $10 billion. This is comparable to the implicit economic value that the EIS attached to all other consequences. Other assumptions in the EIS are also noteworthy. The EIS authors, for instance, assume that flooded homes could be reoccupied within a couple of weeks as opposed to months and they did not consider the possibility that many flooded homes may have to be destroyed due to their contamination by toxic materials and mold. As a result, I conclude that the costs of an SPH event were underestimated.

Since both the probabilities and consequences of the hurricane events were underestimated, the benefits of the proposed levee systems and barriers were also underestimated. The degree of underestimation cannot easily be calculated, since it is impossible to reconstruct all the pieces of the risk and cost-benefit analysis represented in the 1974 and the 1984 EIS documents. Yet it is conceivable that the combination of underestimating the risks and the consequences resulted in a ten- or twenty-fold underestimation of the benefits of mitigation. Even at a ten-fold increase of the benefits of mitigation, other alternatives, including protection against a category 4 hurricane, may start to look attractive.

Following the 1984 EIS, the Corps of Engineers decided to select the "high level" alternative—increasing the height of several levees to about 16 feet. This was consistent with the risk and cost-benefit analysis and probably was reasonable in terms of the relative advantages over the 1974 plan or the no action alternative. Unfortunately, funding for this project evolved slowly and with many delays. According to the Government Accountability Office

As of 2006, the project was not expected to be completed until 2015—nearly 50 years after it was first authorized—and cost about $738 million, much of the cost increase due to inflation over the years and changes to the scope and design of the project. In recent years, questions have been raised about the ability of the project to protect the New Orleans area from hurricanes greater than Category 3. This issue was only beginning to be studied by the Corps when hurricane Katrina hit the area in August 2005 (U.S. Government Accountability Office 2005).

While it is difficult to ascertain how much of the project was completed when Katrina struck New Orleans, it seem clear that the levee and flood wall protection system could not provide the protection promised in the EIS of 1984.

In summary, there were several problems with the analyses and decisions regarding the development of levees and flood walls in the New Orleans area: (1) the probabilities and consequences of extreme hurricane events were underestimated; (2) alternatives that provided higher levels of protection were not explored; and (3) the preferred alternative was implemented slowly and with many funding delays. In the following section I describe how better risk and decision analysis processes can avoid these mistakes and lead to better decisions to protect New Orleans in the future.

A Framework for Risk and Decision Analysis

Beginning with a high-level decision analysis, the United States can now consider two potential alternatives. It can, for instance, rebuild and fortify the levees to pre-Katrina levels, or build levees to protect New Orleans against a more rare hurricane, for example, one that occurs only once in 1,000 years. To put the 1,000 year hurricane into perspective, note that the Dutch government decided after the catastrophic flood in 1953 to build a system of dykes and flood barriers that would withstand a 10,000 year flood at a cost of $8 billion (Groot 2005). This high-level analysis is to illustrate the power of thinking about the major issues prior to engaging in detailed risk and cost-benefit analysis at the level represented by the two EIS documents discussed previously.

The analysis assumes that another Katrina event is likely in the next 100 years. In particular, it assumes that the number of Katrina-like events (0,1,2, . . .) in 100 years has a Poisson distribution with an expectation parameter of 1 (this means that one would expect one Katrina-like event in 100 years, but there is a good chance of having 0 or 2 events and also a smaller chance of having more than 2 events. One alternative is to rebuild and fortify the levees to pre-Katrina levels at a cost of no more than $5 billion—this cost is probably at the high end and chosen for illustrative purposes only. If another Katrina event should occur with this alternative, there would be a chance (about 25%) of another levee breach with social costs of about $200 billion. Another alternative is to increase the level of protection to prevent flooding in a 1,000 year hurricane. This is possible, but only at significant costs of $25 billion—the cost again being chosen for illustrative purposes.

The analysis has only six parameters (in brackets—base case values):

1. Number of Katrina-like hurricanes in the next 100 years (0,1,2,3, . . .) using a Poisson distributions with an expected value of one (l=1)
2. Probability of levee failure with a Katrina-like hurricane given rebuilding to pre-Katrina protection levels (q=0.25)
3. Probability of levee failure with a Katrina-like hurricane given 1,000 year protection levels (r=0.05)
4. The cost of another Katrina-like event ($200 billion)
5. The cost of re-building and fortifying the levees to pre-Katrina levels ($5 billion)
6. The cost of building to a 1,000 year protection level ($25 billion)

I used a standard decision tree analysis to analyze this problem, and the analysis provided some profound insights.[2] If one assumes, for instance, that the probabilities and consequences are at the base case level shown above, building for a 1,000 year level of protection has an expected cost of $35 billion ($25 billion due to the cost of building the levee system and $10 billion due to the residual risk of the hurricanes over 100 years). Rebuilding and fortifying the levees to pre-Katrina levels has an expected cost of $54 billion ($5 billion due to the cost of rebuilding and $49 billion due to residual risk of the hurricanes). Thus, with the base case estimates, building a 1,000 year protection system would be preferred by about $19 billion dollars over rebuilding to pre-Katrina levels.

Several sensitivity analyses also provide useful insights. When varying the social cost of a Katrina-like event, while keeping all other parameters at their base level, the 1,000 year protection level decision has lower expected costs than the decision to rebuild to pre-Katrina levels for social costs above 100 billion. Hence, if we expect a Katrina-like event to cost above $100 billion, the 1,000 year alternative should be preferred.

The probability of a levee failure after rebuilding and fortifying to pre-Katrina levels is also a key parameter. For very low probabilities of a levee failure (0.10 and below), rebuilding to pre-Katrina levels is a better option than the 1,000 year protection option, no matter what the costs of a Katrina-like event are. But if the probability of a levee failure with a pre-Katrina protection system is above 0.20 and the social costs of a Katrina-like event are at least $150 billion, the 1,000 year protection level is preferred.

Another sensitivity analysis examines the effects of varying the costs of rebuilding to pre-Katrina levels vs. building a protection level for 1,000 years, again holding all other parameters constant. The costs of rebuilding to pre-Katrina levels ranged from $0 to $10 billion and the costs of building to a 1,000 year protection level ranged from $0 to $100 billion. In this comparison the 1,000 year alternative was better, if it cost less that $40–$50 billion dollars, and this depended very little on the cost of rebuilding to pre-Katrina protection levels.

A fourth sensitivity analysis considered the conditional probabilities of levee failures given a Katrina-like event with both levels of protection. In the base case the probability was set at 0.25 for the alternative to rebuild to pre-Katrina levels and at 0.05 for the alternative to build levees to protect against a 1,000 year hurricane. These probabilities are quite conservative and can easily be disputed. However, it turns out that the preferred alternative is relatively insensitive to these numbers as long as one can agree to a reasonable ratio (such as that a levee failure is three or five times less likely for a 1,000 year protection than for the pre-Katrina protection). In fact, the sensitivity analysis shows that the 1,000 year protection level is preferred unless the two probabilities are close to equal or if the conditional probability of a levee failure with pre-Katrina protection levels is less than 10%.

This simple analysis suggests that it may be worthwhile to consider higher levels of protection for New Orleans. In the coming year there will be significant discussions about the level of protection and other issues related to rebuilding New Orleans. One of the most important steps in this type of analysis is framing the decision. Some experts have suggested that the real decision is *whether or not to rebuild* the areas of New Orleans that are below sea level. Some researchers have expressed very strong objections to a rebuilding strategy, based on geophysical, hydrological, and meteorological concerns (Foster and Giegenack 2006). At the other end, one may consider a simple upgrade of the existing levee and flood wall system to provide protection similar to or perhaps better than the protection against the SPH event. In the middle, it is possible to conceive of mixed alternatives that combine some redevelopment in higher altitude areas with the construction of safe havens (such as an interior area surrounded by concrete flood walls). Whatever the alternatives are, they should be investigated and discussed by a large range of stakeholders.

Another part of framing the decision has to do with the values and concerns that should be addressed to compare decision alternatives. The previous EIS reports are a good start to collect these values and concerns into a set of objectives. It would be useful to go one step further and organize these objectives along the lines that Keeney (1992) suggested:

1. *Fundamental objectives*—values and concerns that matter in and by themselves (for example, protecting health and safety of the residents)
2. *Means objectives*—values and concerns that matter, because they influence fundamental objectives (for example, reducing the risk of levee breaches)
3. *Process objectives*—values and concerns that matter because they relate to an improved decision making process (for example, fairness and openness of the decision process)

In the end, all objectives should be considered, but only fundamental objectives should be used to evaluate alternative plans. The result of this step should be a list of alternatives and objective that the decision makers and stakeholders can agree on to submit to further analysis and evaluation.

This step is likely to identify some objectives and alternatives that have not been identified in the previous EIS studies. Regarding objectives, the indirect economic costs due to business disruptions and the shutdowns of major infrastructure facilities should be considered. The social costs of anguish due to dislocation and other psychological costs should be considered as well (see also Kunreuther 2005). Regarding alternatives, local, state, and national government should consider the creation of safe havens that can shelter evacuees in or near the city in the case of a pending severe hurricane.

Another part of framing the problem has to do with identifying the key uncertainties and risks that are to be addressed by the analysis. When considering decisions about hurricane protection, the key uncertainties include: 1) the size and pathway of the hurricane; 2) the possibility of overtopping the levees; 3) the possibility of breaching the levees; 4) the amount of flooding in different geographic areas as a consequence of overtopping or levee breaches; and 5) the consequences of flooding.

Risk analysis has come a long way since the publication of the first two EIS documents in 1974 and 1984. In particular, modern risk analysis methods use parametric uncertainty analysis with Monte Carlo simulation to determine how the probability distributions over the model parameters (such as the parameter of a Poisson distribution characterizing the frequency of extreme hurricanes) affect the ultimate consequences (such as lives lost and economic damages). There have also been significant developments in the use of expert judgments, both in the initial part of risk analysis (identifying initiating events and pathways describing the progression of a disaster) and in the elicitation of specific parameters (such as parameters describing the frequency of hurricanes and the strength of hurricanes and the chances of levee failures).[3]

The main improvements over the risk assessments of 1974 and 1984 are: 1) Explicit consideration of extraordinary events (such as large storm surges or major levee breaches; 2) Explicit consideration of secular trends (such as warming trends and hurricane cycles); 3) Explicit consideration of the availability of pumps and the duration of flooding as a function of receding flood waters and pumping; 4) Use of expert judgments to quantify uncertainties about model parameters in 1)–3); and 5) Use of Bayesian updating methods to consider recent events in combination with long term historical data.

The output of the risk analysis—similar to the 1984 analysis—would be complementary cumulative density functions (ccdfs) over the flood levels in the parishes of New Orleans and its vicinity. Each decision alternative would have a different ccdf. These outputs would be represented with uncertainty bands, reflecting the uncertainty in expert judgments and data. These sensitivity analyses could be used to explore what difference they make to the preferred decision.

Given flood levels, areas and duration of flooding, consequences can be calculated in a fairly straightforward manner. The main improvements over the consequence assessments of 1974 and 1984 are: 1) Explicit consideration of fatalities; 2) Explicit consideration of indirect and induced economic losses, for example due to business interruptions and the port shutdown (Park et al. 2006); 3) Explicit consideration of the costs of relocation of hurricane victims and other social costs; and 4) Use of expert judgment to quantify uncertainties in consequence models. The outputs of the consequence assessment would be ccdfs over consequence measures with associated uncertainty bands.

In the previous risk and cost-benefit analyses consequences were calculated based on the direct losses of structures and businesses. A more complete analysis would consider a wider spectrum of consequences, including loss of lives, dislocation costs, and cultural and social impacts. It is useful to involve stakeholders and public groups in the determination of the consequences that are to be considered (see von Winterfeldt 2001)

As in the risk analysis, many parameters of a consequences assessment are uncertain. For example, the percentage of homes that experience significant flooding and have to be destroyed and rebuilt is uncertain. Another example is the time it takes for residents to move back into their homes. It is important to quantify these uncertainties using state-of-the-art expert judgment methods (see, for example, Keeney and von Winterfeldt 1989) and to present decision makers, stakeholders, and the public with an appropriate representation of these uncertainties.

To complete an evaluation of the decision alternatives, one must evaluate the consequences at the end of the decision tree. Multi-attribute utility analysis and cost-benefit analyses are useful tools for this purpose (Keeney and Raiffa 1976; von Winterfeldt and Edwards 1986). To evaluate alternatives like the SPH or 1,000 year designs for levees and flood walls one compares the expected costs or utilities across the alternatives. Given the significant uncertainties and disagreements among stakeholders in many parts of the analysis, the evaluations should be supported by extensive sensitivity analyses.

None of the above recommendations will work, however, if the analysis is not embedded in a decision making process that involves key stakeholders and decision makers. Several years ago, the National Academy of Sciences recommended the use of an "analytic-deliberative process" for decision making, especially in cases involving risks (National Academy of Sciences 1996). This process has both a strong analysis component and a strong participative component. The participants in this process are involved throughout all stages of the analysis, including the framing of the problem, identifying experts and reviewing intermediate and final analysis results. Such an analytic-deliberative process will enhance the likelihood that the decision will ultimately be accepted and implemented.

Complexities and Conclusions

The analytical capabilities and tools to conduct a sound risk and decision analysis for hurricane prediction are in place. In fact, the hurricane risk analysis capabilities are better than in other disaster areas like earthquakes and terrorist attacks, since there exists a large data set on the meteorology and hydrology of hurricanes as well as significant experience with past hurricanes and their consequences. In addition, cost-benefit and multi-attribute methods are readily available to evaluate alternative proposals for protecting New Orleans against hurricanes. Thus the problem with implementing the analysis approach described in the previous section does not lie in the availability of models and tools, but with more fundamental complexities related to the political aspects of the problem.

Past expenses for the flood barrier system around New Orleans were paid primarily by federal funds (about 87% according to the U.S. Government Accountability Office 2005). It is likely that most future expenses will also come from federal funds. Should all U.S. taxpayers pay to reduce a local risk or should the cost of risk reduction be shifted to those who benefit from this investment (Kunreuther 2006)? This may be a moot point, since the one million residents and the businesses in New Orleans area would not be able to pay for the multi-billion dollar costs that it will take to rebuild and fortify the flood protection system. It is quite obvious, though, that the problems with implementing the 1984 projects had a lot to do with the reluctance of both the federal and the local funding agencies to pay their share. This problem is unlikely to go away.

Moreover, there will always be competing needs to fund other projects with more tangible near-term benefits than the fairly abstract benefit of reducing a small risk over a period of decades. Shortly after a disaster like Katrina there usually is a political momentum to aid in response and recovery. However, this willingness to relieve the immediate hardship often fades, when it comes to expensive long-term mitigation measures. It is hard for politicians, government officials and the general public to appreciate the value of an investment that only pays off in decades (see also Kunreuther 2005).

The decision to rebuild the flood protection system in the New Orleans area is not unique in that respect. Instead the reluctance to invest *ex ante* in risk reduction measures seems to be common across the disaster spectrum, and it is especially prevalent when it comes to low probability, high-consequence events. As a result the tendencies for delays and inadequate funding are reinforced.

Katrina demonstrated very vividly that a disproportionate share of the consequences of catastrophes often falls on poor and disadvantaged communities. Furthermore, a large proportion of those most affected by the disaster were African American, hence adding a racial dimension to the inequities. Past analyses to support decisions on protecting New Orleans from hurricanes were silent about these inequities.

Cost benefit analyses usually emphasize efficiency over equity. It is possible to track consequences by socioeconomic and racial categories and describe the distributional impacts of disasters. At a minimum, these distributional impacts should be made explicit in the analyses. In addition, measures to mitigate these inequities should be considered.

Disadvantaged minorities also have less impact on the decision making process than the more affluent groups of society. This is largely due to the fact that they have less access to the decision making processes, less time to participate, and little or no resources to obtain legal or expert representation on their behalf. To facilitate more participation of disadvantaged minorities in the decision making process, resources should be made available to these communities to inform themselves about the issues and to obtain legal and expert advice.

In the past, both the probabilities and the consequences of a Katrina-like hurricane were underestimated and, as a result, the benefits of flood protection were underestimated. In years following Katrina, major decisions about rebuilding New Orleans and its flood protection system will be made. Risk and decision analysis can play an important role in supporting these decisions. These tools have great potential for improving decisions, but they also face fundamental political complexities. One way to address these political complexities is to embed the analyses in a carefully designed decision making process that involves key stakeholders to assure that all concerns are incorporated in the analyses, that opposing points of view are considered, that experts with different perspectives of the issues are included, and that the results are presented in an impartial way to inform the stakeholders and decision makers.

Notes

This research was supported by the National Science Foundation's Multidisciplinary Center for Earthquake Engineering Research (MCEER) under contract number R315752 and by the United States Department of Homeland Security through the Center for Risk and Economic Analysis of Terrorism Events (CREATE) under grant number EMW-2004-GR-0112. However, any opinions, findings, and conclusions or recommendations in this document are those of the author and do not necessarily reflect views of the United States Department of Homeland Security or any other agency. I would like to thank Mayank Mohan for his assistance in reviewing the literature and developing the decision analysis models.

1. In this paper I take it for granted that at least parts of New Orleans will be rebuilt in the areas below sea level. Thus the key decisions are how to develop an improved flood protection system and possibly how to provide safe havens and better evacuation capabilities.

2. In the original draft of this chapter, the decision tree analysis was illustrated with several figures. Unfortunately, the production process of this book did not allow the reproduction of figures. I apologize to the readers for having to explain

some very powerful graphical material with words and numbers. An expanded version of this chapter that includes the figures was published as a working paper (von Winterfeldt 2005) and can be obtained from the author.

3. For summaries and examples of both innovations, see Bedford and Cooke (2001) and Keeney and von Winterfeldt (1989).

Planning for a City on the Brink

KENNETH R. FOSTER AND ROBERT GIEGENGACK

The landfall of Katrina against the coast of Louisiana, Mississippi, and Alabama on August 29, 2005 resulted in an unprecedented human catastrophe. Hurricane Katrina itself was not unprecedented, either in magnitude or trajectory. However, the catastrophe was immense because that stretch of the coastline of the Gulf of Mexico, including the city of New Orleans, was both unprepared for Katrina and rendered acutely vulnerable to storm damage by 200 years of well intentioned but ultimately counterproductive efforts to manage the Mississippi River and its delta. We believe that the city will ultimately be doomed by the progressive deterioration of the complex environmental system of the Mississippi River and its delta. The magnitude and immediacy of this risk raises urgent ethical and practical issues in planning for the future of the city.

Modern New Orleans lies between a broad loop of the Mississippi River and the south shore of Lake Pontchartrain, and Lake Borgne lies nearby. Both of these lakes are connected directly to the Gulf of Mexico, and their water levels vary with the tidal cycle and rise when water is blown into the lakes by storms.

About seventy percent of New Orleans now lies below sea level, and even farther below the level of water in the Mississippi and Lake Pontchartrain that border the city. The average high-water level of the Mississippi is 14 feet above sea level: when ocean-going ships tie up in the port of New Orleans at River elevations, their keels are *higher* than the Astroturf on the floor of the Superdome. The normal water level in Lake Pontchartrain is one foot above sea level, but this level rises during a storm surge (a temporary rise in the level of the Gulf when water is blown into the area by tropical storms). The city is protected by extensive systems of levees (reinforced earthen banks) and floodwalls (cement walls erected on top of the levees) and, in normal times, the city is kept dry by full-time active dewatering by many municipal pumping stations.

Because of its low elevation and exposed location, New Orleans has always faced grave risks of floods. These risks are constantly growing, due to a complex set of interrelated geologic factors. First, the land beneath the city is subsiding at a present rate of at least 5mm a year (Burkett et al., in press). There are several reasons for this subsidence. A major factor is the compaction of near-surface sediment beneath the city when water is removed by the pumps that work full time to keep New Orleans dry. Other causes are the depression of the Earth's crust under the load of sediment deposited in the northern Gulf of Mexico by the Mississippi River and its predecessors over at least the last 100 million years, and (although it is disputed by some spokespeople from the energy industry) the extraction of vast volumes of petroleum, natural gas, and associated fluids from a thickness of about 5,000 meters of Gulf Coast sediments.

Second, sea level is rising by at least 1.8 mm a year. This is a consequence both of return of water to the ocean from melting glacier ice around the world, and of the thermal expansion of the surface layer of the ocean in the post-glacial warming phase.

Finally, flood management projects that have been undertaken on the Mississippi over the past two hundred years have created an environmental instability that increases the threat of flooding. To summarize:

The Mississippi River and its tributaries form the largest river system on the North American continent, and the third largest watershed in the world. The lower Mississippi flows across a thick sequence of alluvial sediment deposited by the river in the deep gorge that it had previously excavated when the level of the Gulf of Mexico was lower. Like other alluvial rivers, the Mississippi responds quickly to changes in its flow regime by redistributing the sediment in its bed and its banks, primarily during periods of flood, and has often changed course in the past. Well-intentioned efforts by the U.S. Army Corps of Engineers (USACE) and others to control the Mississippi have interfered with this natural process.

Many attempts have been made over the years to control the Mississippi and make it more suitable for human use. To prevent floods and to maintain a clear channel for sea-going commerce from the Gulf of Mexico to the ports of New Orleans and Baton Rouge, the USACE has undertaken, at least since 1812, to erect artificial levees to contain the river. These include, in 1876, the construction of a system of jetties between New Orleans and the mouth of the river that concentrated the flow of the river across a series of sedimentary bars that had previously blocked the upstream passage of deep-draft ships. Thus channeled by the jetties, the river flushed out the sandbars, enabling New Orleans to be developed as a major international port.

Many other modifications to the Mississippi system have been undertaken to reduce the risks of floods to communities near the river. After a flood, and there have been at least 50 major floods on the Mississippi since the 1700s (Trotter et al. 1998), the typical response has been to engage in additional rounds of levee building. Also to prevent floods, the USACE has blocked outlets to many flood-plain basins and distributaries that formerly would have absorbed excess water from the main channel in times of flood. These projects prevented the frequent inundation of lands near the river during floods and allowed economic development to proceed, but they also prevented the Mississippi from diverting excess water onto its flood plain in times of flood.

As a result, the Mississippi has been gradually transformed from "a freely meandering alluvial river to a highly trained and confined meandering channel" (Smith and Winkley 1996). An unintended result was a growing instability that has enhanced the risk of flooding and increased the extent of disruption that flooding can cause—what one authority calls "flood magnification" (Pinter 2005). As Charles Ellet, the eminent American engineer, put it in his report to Congress in 1852, "[F]uture floods throughout the length and breadth of the delta, and along the great streams tributary to the Mississippi, are destined to rise higher and higher, as society spreads over the upper States, as population adjacent to the river increases, and the inundated low lands appreciate in value" (Ellet 1852).

Attempts to manage and contain the river have had other consequences, some of potentially catastrophic importance to New Orleans. Big Muddy carries immense amounts of sediment—230 million metric tons per year. Before modern attempts to control the river, much of this sediment had been deposited in the flood plain of the river, compensating for subsidence of the land and replenishing land lost to the sea along the margin of the delta.

Now confined to a narrow distributary in its path to the sea, the river discharges much of its suspended sediment to deep water in the Gulf of Mexico. This creates a growing delta near the mouth of the river. However, much of the sediment is now deposited beyond the edge of the continental shelf and beyond the reach of the waves and currents that formerly distributed that sediment along the face of the Delta.

As a result of the diversion of that sediment from coastal wetlands and erosional loss of less-well-protected wetland in times of storms, "Louisiana is experiencing the highest rates of shoreline erosion in the United States" (Penland et al. 2005a). The average rate of shoreline loss in the state was nearly 20 ft. per year between 1955 and 2002; it has increased to 31 ft per year after 1988 (Penland et al. 2005a). As a result, large areas of wetlands along the coast, which are natural buffers to flooding, have been lost, making New Orleans and other coastal communities acutely more vulnerable to damage from storm surges driven by tropical storms. In the words of one expert, "the largest river ecosystem in the United States is collapsing right in front of us" (Penland 2005a). As a result, in a few decades, New Orleans will find the Gulf shoreline at its door—unless effective steps are taken to halt and reverse this process.

Containing the Mississippi has other consequences as well. As the river deposits sediment and builds out its delta, its level must rise far upstream to maintain the gradient needed to carry its discharge to the sea. As a result the Corps of Engineers must constantly work to improve the artificial levees far upstream to protect property adjacent to the river. This guarantees continued employment for the USACE, and systematically increases the instabilities now engineered into the system.

But there is more bad news for New Orleans, Baton Rouge, and other communities in Louisiana: Old Man River is long overdue for a sudden change in course. In the process of normal growth of a delta, the gradual lengthening of the river and the consequent increase in its level will eventually cause the river to escape from its channel to follow a shorter, and hence steeper, pathway to the Gulf. These sudden shifts in the course of the river have occurred regularly in the history of the River (Fischetti 2001).

This is about to happen once again. One of several potential sites for diversion is near Simmesport, 145 miles northwest of New Orleans, where the Atchafalaya (a major distributary of the Mississippi) is connected to the Mississippi through a segment of the old channel of the Red River, now called the Old River.

Changes in the course of the Red River over the past century set the stage for the imminent changes in the course of the Mississippi and illustrate the geologic processes that are at work. Until the late nineteenth century, the Red River was the southernmost tributary to enter the Mississippi from the west. This major stream rises in western Texas, flows across Oklahoma and the southwest corner of Arkansas, and, for the last 75 miles of its course, flows across the flood plain of the Mississippi.

Historically, the Red River flowed into the Mississippi at Simmesport. In times of flood, the waters from the Mississippi have backed up the Red River all the way across the Mississippi flood plain, causing the Red River to spill out of its banks and flood farmland adjacent to the river. Those flood waters then flowed to the Gulf of Mexico down the Atchafalaya River, which drains much of the lower delta west of the present course of the Mississippi. When these flood waters overflowed into the Atchafalaya, they fell down a steeper gradient than that of the "normal" course of the Red River, causing the Red-Atchafalaya system to erode its bed lower even as the Mississippi was elevating its bed. By 1880, the Red had been fully captured by the Atchafalaya, and the short segment of the lower Red River between the head of the Atchafalaya and the Mississippi, called the "Old River," then came to serve as an overflow channel of the Mississippi.

These changes have set the stage for the inevitable capture of the entire

Mississippi by the Red-Atchafalaya system. To block, or perhaps only delay, this process, the USACE built the Old River Control Structure (ORCS) at the Mississippi head of the Old River from 1950 to 1962, and has since operated the ORCS as a relief valve in times of high water on the Mississippi. Over the last 50 years, the USACE has apportioned up to 30% of the flow of the Mississippi to the Atchafalaya.

The course of the Atchafalaya from Simmesport to the Gulf of Mexico is 150 miles *shorter* than that of the Mississippi, and as a result it is also steeper. The excess Mississippi flow down the Red-Atchafalaya contributes to erode its bed, even as the bed of the Mississippi rises by a few mm each year. As a result, the vertical disparity between the Mississippi and the Atchafalaya near Simmesport, and hence the instability of the present course of the Mississippi, increases each year. The ORCS was acutely threatened in the floods of 1973 and 1993; at present only die-hard USACE regulars would still insist that the ORCS can prevent the escape of the entire Mississippi to the Atchafalaya.

Should that happen—should the entire flow of the Mississippi be diverted into the Atchafalaya—the cities of Baton Rouge and New Orleans would find themselves on the banks of a still-water bayou with no access to the Gulf of Mexico for sea-going ships. Salt water would back up into the old channel of the Mississippi, and the municipal water-intake facilities of Baton Rouge, New Orleans, and other river towns would be contaminated by salt water and, soon thereafter, would become choked with sediment. Refineries, petrochemical plants, fertilizer factories, and other industries along the Mississippi below the ORCS will also lose their water supplies from the river. The event would leave New Orleans bereft of a navigable passage to the Gulf, destroying it as a port city. Kazmann and Johnson (1980) suggest that massive dredging of the historic channel might enable limited ocean-going shipping to use the old ports of New Orleans and Baton Rouge, but they offer no estimate of the cost of such maintenance.

Capture of the Mississippi by the Atchafalaya would have far-reaching consequences elsewhere in the state, including the almost certain destruction of Morgan City, a town of 12,000 located on the east bank of the Atchafalaya River at the intersection of the Gulf Intracoastal Waterway. Diversion of the Mississippi into the Atchafalaya would cause extensive damage to roads, railroads, pipelines, and other infrastructure along the Atchafalaya (Kazmann and Johnson 1980).

The Floods as an Engineering Failure

The catastrophic flooding of the city during Katrina occurred when water flowed over the floodwalls or through breaches in the floodwalls or levees, a consequence of rising water level in Lakes Ponchartrain and Borgne due to the storm surge produced by the hurricane. The levees on the Mississippi failed as well, but most of these breaches occurred downstream near its entry into the Gulf.

Shortly after the Katrina disaster, the American Society of Civil Engineers (ASCE) commissioned a study to provide an early assessment by a panel of eminent engineers of the factors that led to the unanticipated severity of damage from the Katrina event (Seed et al. 2005). The hurricane produced a storm surge estimated to be 18 to 25 feet, which "rolled by about 5 to 10 feet over the levee protection system along the northeastern edge of the protected basin" containing the Ninth Ward and adjacent St. Bernard Parish (Seed et al. 2005). In addition, the investigators found "dozens of breaches" due to structural failures of the floodwalls in the levees in the area in response to Katrina-driven flooding. Many of these failures occurred when water overtopped the floodwalls and eroded their foundations; other failures occurred without overtopping, which the investigators attributed to inadequate foundations or other construction problems.

Thus, the failures of the flood-control system arose in part from the intensity of the storm, which produced a storm surge that exceeded the design capacity of the floodwalls, and in part from structural failures in floodwalls that might, conceivably, have withstood the surge. "While levee failures may be expected when overtopping occurs," Nicholson concluded in his testimony before the U.S. Senate (Nicholson, 2005), "the performance of many of the levees and floodwalls may have been significantly improved, and some of the failures likely prevented, with relatively inexpensive modifications of the levee and floodwall system."

Apart from any construction deficiencies in the system, gradual environmental changes over the years would have eroded the safety factors originally designed into the system. The Corps established the heights of most of the levees in the 1960s, with a design goal of withstanding an imaginary storm called the Standard Project Hurricane, which is roughly equivalent to a fast-moving Category 3 storm. In the 45 years that have passed since those levee standards were established, the river has grown longer and the bed of the river has risen, so that designs that might have offered adequate protection in 1960 are of uncertain adequacy to withstand a present Category 3 storm.

The ASCE report, and Nicholson in his Senate testimony, made a number of important recommendations. Some of these recommendations concerned technical improvements in the levees and floodwalls. Others concerned larger issues: the committee recommended that the USACE use an Independent Board of Consultants to review the adequacy of the design ad construction of the flood-control system, pointing out that the USACE uses similar Boards to oversee the adequacy of dams, and that the flood-control system in New Orleans "protects more life and property than almost any major dam in the United States" (Seed et al. 2005). Such a program surely needs to be implemented.

Can a Technological Fix Save New Orleans?

The press coverage of the ASCE report focused on the engineering problems with the levees and floodwalls. The media also paid great attention to comments by one of the members of the ASCE panel about "malfeasance" of contractors in their construction of the floodwalls (Ichniowski 2005). The public, and many policymakers, are likely to gain the mistaken impression that better engineering (less politely, a technological fix) will ensure the future safety of New Orleans.

Certainly, remedying the construction deficiencies in the floodwalls would have reduced the flooding (although water overtopping the floodwalls, not failure of the walls, was the principal cause of the flooding). Closer inspection of the floodwalls, and reexamination of the original designs using modern methods and taking into account the changes in the environment in the nearly half century since the system was originally designed, might have led to changes that could have averted catastrophe. While some outspoken critics called attention to the weaknesses in the flood-control system of the city, government at all levels was inactive (if not asleep) on the issue. "No clear bureaucratic mandate exists for reassessing the blueprints once levees are built," journalists McQuaid and Schleifstein wrote in a prescient 5-part story in 2002 about the flood dangers to New Orleans in the (New Orleans) *Times-Picayune* (McQuaid and Schleifstein 2002). "Congress appropriates money for levee construction based on Corps studies that take years to complete. Dramatic changes or reassessments typically occur after major disasters, when political momentum generates for preventing a repeat."

But New Orleans faces much deeper problems than the need to "fix" construction defects in the levees. The city faces risks that are immense compared to those for which policymakers routinely plan.

To give an example: USACE designed the lakeside floodwalls to withstand a "standard project hurricane," which is equivalent to a fast-moving Category 3 hurricane (with a storm surge assumed to be 11.5 ft above sea level). The floodwalls on the river side were designed to handle water levels 18 ft above sea level (4 ft above the average annual high-water level in the river).

This is hardly the level of protection that most citizens would want, given the frequent occurrence of severe hurricanes in the region. The National Oceanographic and Atmospheric Administration (NOAA) estimates that Category 3 hurricanes have a 30-year "return period" (the average time between passage of a storm of a given strength within 75 miles of a given location) for New Orleans (the return periods are 73 and 230 years for Category 4 and 5 hurricanes).[1] (http://www.nhc.noaa.gov/HAW2/english/basics/return.shtml). According to the standard Saffir-Simpson scale for hurricanes, the storm surges associated with Category 3 storms are "generally 9–12 feet above normal," while those for Category 4 and 5 storms are "generally 13 to 18" and "generally greater than 18 feet above normal," respectively (http://www.nhc.noaa.gov/aboutsshs.shtml).

The shockingly low level of protection (given the high statistical risk of severe storms) is clear by comparison with the flood-control systems in The Netherlands. In that country, the flood-control systems are designed to limit the occurrence of floods to 1 in 10,000 years for provinces with high economic value, and 1 in 4000 years for provinces with lower economic value (Jonkman et al. 2005). We are not aware of any cost-benefit analysis that was reported by the USACE in designing the capacity of the flood-control system. We conjecture that the USACE design goals may have reflected USACE practices for flood-control structures in areas of lower economic value (undeveloped land, for example). They may also have been influenced by the anticipated level of funding that would be available for the project, tempered by the dramatically increasing costs of protecting against more intense storms. Whatever the reason, the flood-control system in New Orleans was capable of protecting only against storms that would be infrequent but not particularly rare.

For three reasons, future improvements in the flood-control system of New Orleans can reduce the risks of future flooding but cannot prevent Katrina-like incidents in the future:

First, the engineering that is needed to protect the city from future Katrina-like floods pushes the limits of conventional engineering practices and, indeed, borders on the heroic. Thus, for example, the 2000 edition of the USACE manual "Design and Construction of Levees" says that the height of flood walls built on levees, like those used in New Orleans, "rarely exceed" seven feet (USACE 2000). But in numerous places the floodwalls that protect New Orleans from the deluge are far higher than this, for example rising to 11 feet above the dirt berms along the 17th Street and London Avenue canals—and these were designed to protect against a Category 3 hurricane.

The efforts that would be needed to design and construct systems to prevent flooding in more severe storms are truly heroic. There are presently calls to improve the flood-control system to withstand a Category 5 hurricane. (This is not, strictly speaking, a well-defined goal because a Category 5 hurricane has no defined upper limit to its wind speed and storm surge.) For example, one proposal is to construct a gate across the Rigolets strait,[2] which connects Lake Pontchartrain to Lake Borgne (which is actually a lagoon to the Gulf of Mexico), to prevent a storm surge from entering Lake Pontchartrain. The gate would have to span a long distance of water (nearly 2/3 of a mile) and would be a very expensive undertaking (Schwarz 2005). The costs presently being discussed in the news media for upgrading the flood-control system of the city to withstand a Category 5 storm exceed $30B. And even then, the statistical likelihood of failure (by being overwhelmed by a large storm) is far higher than in similar projects in The Netherlands.

Second, the environmental conditions in and around the city are deteriorating, and will continue to deteriorate unless immense investments are made in wetlands restoration and other measures to reverse the process of "flood magnification" described above. In short, we might design a flood-control system that would withstand a 100-year flood (defined as the maximum flood that is expected to occur within 100 years), but maintaining that level of protection in the future would require constant and increasingly expensive engineering efforts as the river continues to rise while the city sinks and the shoreline of the Gulf approaches ever closer to the city.

The problem is the gradual deterioration of the environment in the lower Mississippi delta, largely a result of two centuries of well-intentioned but ultimately self-defeating attempts by the USACE and other agencies to manage the river, which have led to loss of large areas of Gulf coast wetlands and other changes described earlier in this chapter. Reversing this process would require wetlands restoration and, indeed, a rethinking of long-established policies for management of the Mississippi river and coastal lands. And even then, the geologic processes described above (rising sea level, subsidence of the land beneath New Orleans, the periodic diversion of the Mississippi into other distributaries, and so forth) are irreversible. As a result, the margin of safety provided by even well designed flood-control systems will continue to diminish with time, and increasingly heroic efforts will have to be made to continue to provide a given level of protection.

Third, given the complex system of levees and floodwalls extending over some 350 miles in the New Orleans District alone, there is simply no way to anticipate all possible failures that will occur in future Katrina-like scenarios. The ASCE study identified numerous construction problems that led to massive failures of the floodwalls during Katrina, but there is no reliable way to identify all possible failure modes in the levee system; the system is too complex for that. As the ACSE report pointed out, levees and floodwalls are "series" systems with "less redundancy than many other engineered systems." (Seed et al. 2005). In short, the failure of any component of the flood-control system is tantamount to the failure of the whole system. The piecemeal approach to building the system that has been taken in the past makes it extraordinarily difficult to identify all weak links in the system.

The overarching problem is the essential fallibility of engineering in projects that push the limits of standard design. Engineering is supposed to work: when an engineer builds a structure, it is supposed to stay up, and there are consequences if it fails. Most engineering projects fall well within the current state of the engineering art (or may even be technically mundane), and consequently they rarely fail. That is clearly not the case with New Orleans, where the flood-control system pushes the limits of engineering design, there is little margin of safety, and the environment itself is deteriorating.

One might ask what justifies our pessimism for the long-term prospects for New Orleans, given the success with which the Dutch have managed their system of levees over the years, and the ability of engineers to design and operate complex systems, nuclear power plants or nuclear submarines for example, that can operate for decades without major incident. But even the ongoing, so far successful, efforts to protect that portion of the Netherlands that lies below sea level is far simpler than the task we contemplate here. Amsterdam does not lie on a coast subject to the kinds of storm surges routinely associated with tropical storms, and Amsterdam faces a potential enemy at only one front: it does not have one of the world's largest rivers carrying 550 billion cubic meters of water every year through the heart of the city on an elevated trackway. And nuclear power plants and submarines are designed with far higher margins of safety than the floodwalls in New Orleans ever can be, and they are designed for an operating life that is far shorter than one would choose for the city of New Orleans. Imagine a nuclear power plant that was designed with little redundancy (so that a failure of one component would lead to catastrophic failure of the whole system), and was only designed to withstand a hundred-year storm! That said, nuclear power plants and submarines are operated with a great deal more care than the flood-control system ever was in New Orleans, and there are surely lessons to be learned about how to maintain the flood-control system in New Orleans more safely.

Americans like to think that a technological solution can be found to any problem. But in reality practical considerations limit what can be done. For example, it is at least theoretically possible to engineer a system that would capture that sediment carried by the Mississippi and redistribute it over the subsiding delta and rebuild the land that has been lost to the sea. But consider the scale of that undertaking: If we distribute that sediment via conventional 10-ton dump trucks, we must plan to distribute 23 million such loads each year—equivalent to 60,000 truckloads per day, or 2,500 per hour. A plan has, in fact, been proposed to restore the Louisiana wetlands using a more sophisticated approach than out-lined above, at an estimated cost of about $15 billion. But some experts have questioned whether such efforts would have prevented the Katrina disaster, pointing out that the storm waters in Katrina approached the coast from the east and that additional wetland would have done little to mitigate the impact of that storm to New Orleans (Pilkey and Young 2005).

Compounding these problems has been the overoptimism of the USACE about the level of safety provided by its flood-control projects. The 2002 *Times-Picayune* articles noted that the USACE designed the levees protecting the Lower Ninth Ward to hold against a 200-year flood. An assessment of the flood danger by an independent consultant concluded that the risks were much higher than the Corps asserted. Moreover the Corps, long focused on flood-control projects in the Mississippi, designed the levees against the River to a higher standard than those against the Lake—providing more protection for the city against a river-caused flood than against the far more damaging flood that actually occurred from the failure of the lakeside levees. Also compounding the problem is the human characteristic of complacency: if a system fails rarely, people can easily come to forget that it can fail at all.

So we predict with confidence: the city can look forward to additional Katrina-like tragedies, with a greater or lesser frequency depending on the level of investment that is made in the flood-control systems. But the idea that the city can be made "safe" by repairing construction defects in the levees is an illusion based on a very short-term vision and on a lack of understanding of the geologic processes at work. "In our model," con-cluded a recent analytical study of New Orleans after Katrina "'natural dis-asters' are the inevitable outcome of the mismatch between policy based on short-time-scale economic calculations and stochastic forcing by infre-quent, high-magnitude flooding events" (McNamara 2005). The city can surely be made "safer" than it was before Katrina, but the residual risks to the city will inevitably be very high.

Apart from the risks of flooding to New Orleans, the region faces another catastrophic risk: the impending capture of the Mississippi by the Atchafalaya, which will eventually send the entire flow of the Mississippi down a river that ordinarily carries only a small fraction of that flow. When the Mississippi takes this course (and it will inevitably do so), a major tragedy will result for communities along the Atchafalaya.

The Army Corps of Engineers, of course, is well aware of this possibility, and has taken extensive measures to prevent it by manipulating the flood-control structures in the elaborate installation at ORCS on which it spends many millions of dollars each year in maintenance. But surely the failure modes of the ORCS and other infrastructure that keep the Mississippi in its present channel are unknown. Journalist and nature writer John McPhee, in his excellent book *The Control of Nature* (1989), gave a harrowing description of the near-failure of Old River Control Structure near Simmesport in the flood of 1973, when the water scoured out a hole 75 ft beneath the structure. (These disastrous floods were caused by a series of exceptional rains in the South and exceptionally large snowfalls in the upper Mississippi valley, not by a tropical storm in the Gulf.) John M. Barry, in his popular history of the 1927 flood, *Rising Tide* (1997), says that "keeping the Mississippi in its old channel is by far the most serious engineering problem the Corps of Engineers faces."

In summary, we are faced with the certainty of multiple catastrophic events in the region: the flooding of New Orleans during another Katrina-like storm, and the diverse catastrophic events that would follow the capture of the Mississippi by the Atchafalaya. The risks (that is, the probabilities of such events happening in any particular year) are difficult to estimate. We are not talking about geologic time scales, however, but about events that will most likely occur within the span of a human lifetime. The last catastrophic flood in New Orleans was in 1927 (many lesser floods have occurred since then), and the near-disaster at the Old River Control Structure occurred in 1973. Assuming that the mean time between such catastrophic failures is 100 years (which seems very optimistic), this corresponds to a yearly risk of 0.01, which far exceeds the risks of other catastrophic events for which governments prepare.

None of this information is new. The acute vulnerability of New Orleans to flooding, whether from tropical storms in the Gulf or from upstream precipitation, has been documented persuasively and repeatedly for at least 150 years. For several generations, the history of river management in the Mississippi watershed has served as the basis of at least one lecture in most introductory geology courses in the United States as an iconic example of the exercise of human hubris in undertaking to manage powerful natural processes for economic gain.

Mark Twain, in *Life on the Mississippi* (1983), described the situation nicely:

Ten thousand River Commissions, with the mines of the world at their back, cannot tame that lawless stream, cannot curb it or confine it, cannot say to it, Go here, or Go there, and make it obey; cannot save a shore which it has sentenced; cannot bar its path with an obstruction which it will not tear down, dance over, and laugh at. But a discreet man will not put these things into spoken words; for the West Point engineers have not their superiors anywhere; they know all there is to know of their abstruse science; and so, since they conceive that they can fetter and handcuff that river and boss him, it is but wisdom for the unscientific man to keep still, lie low, and wait until they do it. Captain Eads, with his jetties, has done a work at the mouth of the Mississippi which seemed clearly impossible; so we do not feel full confidence now to prophesy against like impossibilities. Otherwise one would pipe out and say the Commission might as well bully the comets in their courses and undertake to make them behave, as try to bully the Mississippi into right and reasonable conduct.

The same can be said for the Gulf and New Orleans.

Rebuilding the City

Walter Maestri, Director of Emergency Services for Jefferson Parish, was quoted in the 2002 series in the *Times-Picayune* as wondering: "A legitimate question to ask is: Given this kind of catastrophe, given the city is on its knees, many of its historic structures have been destroyed, considering the massive influx of federal dollars that will be required, do you rebuild it. . . . I don't know the answer to that. Especially since we're below sea level and it can happen again the next week." Now, in the wake of Katrina, that is no longer a hypothetical question.

It remains to be seen how many Federal dollars will materialize, or the plans for reconstruction that will finally be implemented. It is politically unthinkable simply to abandon the city—although that may be the decision of many former residents of the city in the absence of a strong plan by the Bush Administration for reconstruction. Calls for complete and immediate rebuilding of the city by state and city officials (as well as by many citizens) are also unrealistic. Some middle-way solution is needed.

An important study by the Urban Land Institute (ULI), which was commissioned by a New Orleans committee under sponsorship of Mayor Nagin, was uncovered in mid-November 2005 (Urban Land Institute, 2005). Among numerous other recommendations, the ULI study recommended the selective rebuilding of the city to create "new open spaces . . . to mitigate future flood damage," immediate rebuilding of the flood-control system to pre-Katrina levels and, ultimately, "a complete rethinking of the [flood-control] system for an urban setting with links to development." Our comments below focus on the physical security of the city.

We agree with the need for a "complete rethinking" of the flood-control system of the city. More than simply rebuilding the levees, there is a need for a fundamental debate about the level of flood protection that is to be provided to the city, how much it will cost, who will pay for the improvements, and how the effectiveness of the system will be evaluated in the future. This is not a matter that can be left to the technocrats alone. However, the debate needs to be informed by realistic estimates of the probability of flooding and the economic and human costs of such events. A stronger and more visible participation by scientists and engineers in public forums is needed. But public participation, in view of the extraordinarily high risks that the city faces, is absolutely necessary as well.

But government also needs to plan for the inevitable occurrence of future Katrina-like tragedies in the city as well as the inevitable shift in course of the Mississippi. In his recent book *Laws of Fear* (2005), noted legal scholar Cass Sunstein proposed a strategy for dealing with "catastrophic risks to which probabilities cannot be assigned."

This approach, which Sunstein called the Anti-Catastrophe Principle, provides useful guidance for the government for the future of New Orleans. When faced with the prospect of catastrophic risks, Sunstein argues, regulators and government officials should identify the worst-case scenarios and choose the approach that eliminates the worst of them. As applied to New Orleans, elements of this approach would include:

1. Move as many people as possible out of harm's way. No technical fix will ensure the safety of residents in the Lower Ninth Ward. These and other low-lying areas should not be repopulated, despite the obvious wishes of the city's residents. This conclusion clearly imposes significant economic and political burdens on the process of relocating former residents, but that would minimize the loss of life in a future flood after a Katrina-like event. An alternative, which has been suggested by some commentators, would be to reconstruct houses with their living spaces above the likely high-water line in future floods.
2. Provide safe exits in the face of a future tragedy like Katrina. Providing a "safe exit," in the context of engineering ethics, refers to designing elements into a system to protect people in case the system fails (Martin and Schinzinger 2005).

It is unsafe and shortsighted to allow people to live in the city without a well-conceived and tested evacuation plan—safe exits in a literal sense. Given the reluctance or inability of many residents of the city to leave in the face of Katrina, however, this will not be sufficient.

Other safe exits should be engineered as well, including infrastructure to minimize loss of life during the next major flood. One promising approach is the "Community Havens" project, developed by Joseph Suhayda, formerly Director of the Louisiana Water Resources Research Institute at Louisiana State University (2000). The plan would involve erecting massive concrete walls down the middle of New Orleans, to prevent flooding of large parts of the city in the event of another Katrina, safeguard vital infrastructure such as hospitals, and provide a haven for tourists and residents trapped by the storm. This concept was proposed before Katrina and attracted interest among disaster-preparedness experts, but was not implemented. Given the near-certainty of future Katrina-like floods in the city, the concept warrants re-examination.

Another "safe exit" is needed for residents along the margins of the Atchafalaya River from Simmesport to its mouth at the Gulf. Presently, the Atchafalaya carries a designed share of the Mississippi discharge, up to

30% of the river's flow in times of flood. Plans need to be developed and made public for managing the consequences of failure of the Old River Flood Control Structure resulting in the capture of the Mississippi by the Atchafalaya. Few students of river hydrology share the optimism frequently expressed by the Corps of Engineers that they can engineer a permanent deterrent to the natural course of events represented by the diversion of the Mississippi into the Atchafalaya.

Should We Relocate New Orleans?

Slowly, New Orleans is returning to life, and it seems perverse to discuss moving the city. But planners must look beyond the short-term needs to repair the flood-control systems and plan for a sustainable city that does not face a fully predictable repetition of Katrina, or the certain fate of being separated from its river by the fully predictable diversion of the Mississippi into the Atchafalaya Distributary. The only rational long-term solution to the future of New Orleans would be to relocate the city and its many vital functions to a safer location—or in the alternative to provide conditions to encourage a new city to grow in a safer place and provide economic opportunities at that site to many of the present residents of New Orleans and their children and grandchildren.

This is clearly not a message that citizens, who are caught up in the day to day issues related to putting their lives back in order after the catastrophe, would like to hear. Long-time residents of New Orleans, as well as many visitors who value the cultural traditions of our most exotic major city, often insist that New Orleans must be rebuilt in its present location, and that it would be unthinkable to abandon the rich cultural tradition that the city represents. Many residents naturally want to return to their homes and would resist any attempt to move the city to another location. Many residents might sensibly choose to remain in the city in its present location, and their autonomy should be respected—but they should be adequately informed of the risks.

This present chapter contemplates events in the Mississippi system that will, most likely, occur over a period of years or decades, and perhaps beyond the expected lifetimes of many present residents of the city. Provided that the floodwalls are repaired (and the USACE is presently installing deeper pilings in the floodwalls), New Orleans can be made habitable until the next Category 3 storm, which may strike the city as early as the 2006 hurricane season, or may be delayed for decades.

Thus there may be no inconsistency between a carefully planned rebuilding of the present city and its flood-control systems to preserve the city in the short term, and planning for the development of another city in Louisiana that would eventually replace New Orleans as a major commercial and shipping center. Both of these planning processes can offer humane and just treatment to residents of New Orleans—or not, depending on how government and the private sector go about their work. The social and economic incentives that might be used to induce people to take up residence at a new locality deserve careful study, but, whatever the cost of preparing the groundwork for the new city and inducing economic activity to develop there, it will surely be vastly less expensive than the eventual cost of maintaining New Orleans at its pre-Katrina size in its historic location for the indefinite future. (Maintaining a smaller New Orleans, focusing on higher-lying regions of the city including the historical district, would be much less costly.)

If this new city were to be allowed to develop close to the Gulf of Mexico, a mound would have to be constructed to elevate the base of the city high enough above sea level to be protected from predictable future subsidence and sea-level rise. Preferably, to provide the new city with the longest lease on life, development should occur upstream of the point where the Mississippi would enter the Atchafalaya, north of Simmesport. That configuration would require the Corps of Engineers to maintain a much longer channel open to the Gulf, but that responsibility would be much more tractable than the growing challenge of protecting New Orleans from the consequences of more than a century of well-intended but ultimately self-defeating attempts to manage the River.

And what are the alternatives? It seems to us, from the limited attention that New Orleans is presently receiving from the Bush Administration, that a much worse outcome may be in store: that the flood-control system will be patched up in an ad-hoc manner, insufficient funds will be made available to bring the entire system up to the design goal of withstanding a Category 3 hurricane—much less the vastly greater funds needed to provide reliable protection against more intense storms—and former residents will be invited to return to the city. "I want you all to come back, and we can work this out," city mayor C. Ray Nagin was quoted recently (2005) while addressing an audience of evacuees. A short-term political solution, enticing residents to return to the city without the high levels of commitment needed to provide adequate levels of protection, would set the stage for another Katrina-like tragedy in the future. The possibility that the city by itself could "work this out," absent a strong commitment by the federal government, seems remote to nonexistent.

The United States has not been accustomed to planning for events that would result in the physical or economic loss of a city. But cities have been lost repeatedly in the past. We need only consider the history of such ancient cities as Pompeii, Tikal, Knossos, Machu Picchu, Leptis Magna, or Santorini—the list goes on—to realize that major cities have been destroyed by natural processes in the past, and the societies that made those cities the cultural beacons they became moved their cities else-where. Indeed, archeologists now speculate at great length about the specific event that led to the abandonment of each of those cities. We will not have to engage in such speculation in the case of New Orleans: future generations will know the city was abandoned because it grew too large for its vulnerable location on the banks of a major river flowing at high elevation across a growing delta.

As an introspective society, we are fond of insisting that one of the characteristics that elevates humans above the stature of the animals with whom we share this planet is our ability to analyze the world around us and make plans for our secure future. But one need not review many such plans to reach the conclusion that humans do not plan for the future any better than the groups of animals we choose to disparage as responding only to instinctual cues. Major changes in human behavior do not result from carefully considered plans, but, like changes in behavior in animal societies, from human response to crises. We need only examine the current response of society to the well documented decline in petroleum production to realize that a constructive response to that trend will only be forced on the global economy when the shortfall in energy resources reaches crisis proportions.

The Katrina event, while a great human tragedy, also represents an opportunity for an enlightened national community to dedicate the imagination and resources that will be required to get New Orleans right this time. The recent destruction of New Orleans represents a human crisis of the first magnitude. But, in the words of Paul Romer, professor of Economics at the Stanford Business School: "A crisis is a terrible thing to waste" (Romer 2005). We must not waste the opportunity that the current crisis in New Orleans represents.

Notes

1. The "return period" is a measure of the likelihood of a storm coming within 75 miles of a given point; it does not predict when a storm will actually hit. Thus, a return period of 30 years indicates a probability of about 3% that the storm will hit during any given year—not that the storms will hit like clockwork every 30 years. The probability is proportional to the distance to the point of interest: a 30 year return period (based on 75 miles to the point of interest) corresponds to about a 0.3% probability of a storm hitting within 7.5 miles of the point in any given year. Thus the likelihood of a major storm hitting New Orleans is lower than might be inferred on the basis of a 30-year return period. On the other hand, a storm need not approach New Orleans very closely to produce a damaging storm surge. These probabilities are based on historical data from the twentieth century, and are highly uncertain in any event. <http://www.nhc.noaa.gov/HAW2/english/basics/return.shtml>

2. A video image of the strait can be found at http://www.washingtonpost.com/wp-dyn/content/panorama/2005/10/03/PA2005100301590.html

JARring Actions That Fuel the Floods

CAROLYN KOUSKY AND RICHARD ZECKHAUSER

The ability of ecosystems to reduce the risks and scales of natural disasters, for example, by attenuating floodwaters and storm surges, has largely been neglected in natural disaster planning and policymaking. Both the 1993 flood on the Mississippi and Hurricane Katrina point to a loss of such "ecosystem services" in the Mississippi watershed, from the northern states down to the Gulf. The actions that cause the loss of these services are often remote from the impacts—whether in time, space, or due to the probabilistic nature of natural disasters. We employ the acronym JAR—Jeopardize Assets that are Remote—to refer to these actions. JARring actions can be taken by private entities or by governments. Policies to prevent such actions are difficult due to the near impossibility of assigning responsibility and to collective action problems since there are so many injured parties, and often many injuring parties as well. JARring actions is a generic concept, and applies whenever remote risks are imposed. They need have no relation to ecosystems or natural disasters, though that is the application in this paper. While the damage (or expected damage) JARring actions cause is often to property, human lives can also be lost and are frequently disrupted from the increased vulnerability to adverse outcomes that JARring actions bring.

This paper assesses two prominent disasters—the 1993 flood and Hurricane Katrina—that were exacerbated by JARring actions. Those actions exemplify our failure to give sufficient attention to ecosystem services that reduce risks. After reviewing these two disasters on the Mississippi and the role of ecosystem services in reducing the risks of such disasters, we turn to the concept of JARring actions, discussing both private and public examples. We then outline a variety of possible policy responses for addressing the external costs associated with the JARring actions undertaken by private entities and by government.

The pictures of a submerged and ruined New Orleans will not soon be forgotten. With over a thousand lost lives and up to a million displaced, Hurricane Katrina left its mark on the nation's psyche. On August 31,

2005, about 80% of the city was underwater largely because levees around Lake Pontchartrain failed. This could have been due to the fact that the levees were only built to withstand a Category 3 hurricane, or due to design flaws or shoddy construction. In any case, what physically caused the failure were high winds, heavy rainfall, and a massive storm surge, that is, water pushed to shore by strong winds. Katrina's storm surge—the difference between the maximum sea level during the storm and the normal seal level—ranged from about 4 to 13 feet along the Gulf Coast. It reached its maximum between Bay St. Louis, Mississippi and Mobile Bay, Alabama where it was near the highest recorded storm surge for that area (National Weather Service Forecast Office Mobile-Pensacola 2005).

The vulnerability of coastal Louisiana, including New Orleans, to Katrina's storm surge was heightened by the loss of coastal wetlands, which naturally buffer storm surges (NOAA 2005). While it is impossible to confidently quantify the extra damage from Katrina attributable to wetland loss, experts agree that wetlands do provide substantial protection. Some indication of this ability comes from Hurricane Andrew. As noted in the Coast 2050 report, a coastal restoration plan for Louisiana, a decrease in storm surge was measured as Hurricane Andrew made its way through Louisiana's coastal marshes. The reduction amounted to a decrease of 3.1 inches in storm surge per linear mile of marsh (and open water) in one site and 2.8 inches per linear mile of marsh in another location, giving total reductions in storm surge of 6 feet and 4.4 feet respectively (Louisiana Coastal Wetlands Conservation and Restoration Task Force and The Wetlands Conservation and Restoration Authority 1998).

While the exact quantitative relation between marshes and storm surges may be imprecise, it is clear that a significant storm buffer has disappeared. Louisiana contains about 40% of the country's wetlands but is also home to 80% of the country's wetland loss; since 1900 over 1 million acres have vanished (Louisiana Coastal Wetlands Conservation and Restoration Task Force and The Wetlands Conservation and Restoration Authority 1998; Stone and McBride 1998; Environmental Protection Agency 2005; van Heerden 2005). Even accounting for several small restoration projects underway, it is estimated that another 513 square miles (a little over 328,000 acres) of land will be lost by 2050 (Barras, Beville et al. 2003). The rate of wetland loss has dropped from a high of about 40 square miles per year in the 1960s to 24 square miles per year today (Britsch and Dunbar 1993; National Research Council 2005). Thus, an area of wetlands close to the size of Manhattan is lost annually off the Louisiana coast, or as the Louisiana Department of Natural Resources puts it, about one football field of wetlands is lost every 38 minutes. This is largely due to the mistreatment of the Mississippi River through private and governmental failure to address the external costs associated primarily with the construction of levees, jetties, and canals.

Inland wetlands also reduce an area's vulnerability to floods. One of the worst floods in U.S. history was the 1993 flood of the Upper Mississippi River, which the National Oceanic and Atmospheric Association estimated flooded 20 million acres in nine states. Damage estimates range from $12 to $16 billion (U.S. General Accounting Office 1995). The flood was triggered by above-average precipitation that saturated the ground, but years of mistreatment of the Mississippi system also played a role. In the nine affected states, 57% of original wetlands had been converted to other land uses or development (Faber 1996). In the Upper Mississippi River basin, flood damage has also been found to be higher in areas with fewer wetlands (National Research Council 2005). While there is not full consensus on whether wetland restoration in the Upper Mississippi could completely handle a flood of the magnitude of 1993, the benefits are quite clear for subbasins and more frequent flood levels (Hunt 1997).

These cases, and many more like them, exemplify the idea of "ecosystem services," a term that has emerged in ecology and spread to the social sciences and to policy discussions. Ecosystem services are the benefits people derive from ecosystems. These benefits can include commodities, like timber and food, or services, such as carbon sequestration, water purification, or recreation. The concept that ecosystems provide benefits to people, and equally importantly, that human actions can deplete these services, dates back to at least Plato. He wrote: "Hills that were once covered with forests and produced abundant pasture now produce only food for bees. Once the land was enriched by yearly rains, which were not lost, as they are now, by flowing from the bare land into the sea. The soil was deep, it absorbed and kept the water" (quoted in Daily 1997). What is new is the growing focus on the economic benefits ecosystems can provide. In this paper, we highlight a particular ecosystem service—the reduction in risk from natural disasters, or an amelioration of the consequences of such events.

Attention to risk-reducing ecosystem services can improve policies to mitigate natural disasters. Previous policy experiments in using ecosystems in this way show that it can be cost effective. For example, the 1970s decision to use wetlands to reduce flood risks along the Charles River in Massachusetts, which flows past the authors' offices, was one-tenth the estimated cost of the dam and levee project that would have stored an equivalent amount of flood water (National Research Council 2004). In addition, the protection of ecosystems can provide additional benefits, such as the protection of habitat for fish, waterfowl, or other species; water purification; and increased recreational opportunities. Finally, ecosystems are not subject to human or technical error. For example, levees around New Orleans have been widely alleged to have had design flaws, or worse yet, contractor malfeasance (Warrick 2005). Commissioned projects that protect against low probability risks are particularly prone to misdesign because we have little experience with the extreme situation creating the risk. Such projects are prone to malfeasance, since the crime is unlikely to be detected. For example, an inadequate levee may not be tested for decades, possibly long after the contractor has left the scene. Mother Nature does not make such mistakes. Of course, the capacity of wetlands to hold water can be overwhelmed, just as levees can be overtopped, but ecosystems continuously function at capacity without human or technical design or maintenance that may go awry, mistakenly or purposefully. To capture the benefits an ecosystem provides they do, however, need to be understood and protected.

JARring Actions

Society continually allows ecosystem services to be lost. One major reason is that the continued provision of risk-reducing ecosystem services is challenged by JARring actions—actions that jeopardize assets that are remote. A JARring action is defined by the fact that it inflicts damage on one or more persons that are distant from the individual undertaking the action; it is a particular type of negative externality. JARring actions are undertaken for the private benefits they bring, as the entity taking the action has no incentive to consider the harm it brings to others, particularly since those others are remote. There is a gulf between the recipients of benefits and the recipients of costs. This gulf is most often due to one of three reasons, spatial or temporal separation, or the probabilistic nature of the imposed costs. These three cases are the focus of this paper.

There are, however, at least two other ways in which costs can be remote from the entity taking the action: First, the impacts of an action can be remote from the political decision to take that action. Most commonly, this occurs when concentrated interests push for privately beneficial but socially wasteful actions that impose modest costs on each of a large number of people (Olson 1990). Second, the impacts can be remote because we do not understand causal relationships; that is, in the case that there are unforeseen consequences, a subject we address below.

Policies to reduce JARring actions are challenged by the very remoteness of the actions from the damage. One reason is that individuals tend to look for proximate causes to events and often fail to investigate remote explanations. A second is that when the externality is imposed on an actor who is far away, or when the damages would occur well into the future, or when the externality is only a hard-to-assess increase in the probability of damages, it is exceptionally difficult to assign responsibility. Thus, there remains plausible deniability to the charge that any particular action caused or even contributed to the damage. Furthermore, JARring actions are often undertaken by many individuals and the costs are imposed on many individuals, creating collective action problems, severely handicapping the common methods to address negative externalities—contracting, liability, and regulation. This section examines JARring actions taken by individuals or private organizations, notably corporations, and those taken by government, that particularly increase the risks and magnitudes of floods.

As with other negative externalities, private landowners undertake JARring actions because they fail to value the costs of their actions that are borne by others. Self interest dictates such behavior, particularly given that the chances of being penalized are slim. When a private landowner fills a wetland on her property, she decreases the natural water storage capabilities of the entire watershed. This increases the potential flood damage to other residents in the watershed, even if they are in different towns or even states far from her property. Since there is only a probability of a flood in any given year, it is expected damages that have increased. This increase in risk may not be noticed until the next major flood, further removing the affected parties from the individual or corporation who filled the wetlands. In addition, if there is no major flood for many years, those who will suffer damages will be future residents in the watershed who cannot affect current decisions. Finally, with the exception of private entities with extremely large landholdings, the effects of any party's JARring actions will likely be marginal and undetectable by any standard that would hold up in court, even if the cumulative effect of many landowners undertaking such actions is substantial.

There are a variety of inland, JARring land-use decisions that reduce the natural environment's ability to slow and absorb floodwaters. Urban and suburban developments expand the amount of impervious surface cover in a region, increasing the speed of run-off and preventing beneficial infiltration. As just suggested, many small actions, when aggregated, can become significant. John McPhee wrote regarding the Mississippi watershed: "Every shopping center, every drainage improvement, every square foot of new pavement in nearly half the United States was accelerating runoff toward Louisiana. . . . The valley's natural storage capacities were everywhere reduced. As contributing factors grew, the river delivered more flood for less rain" (McPhee 1989).

When development fills wetlands, the natural storage capacity of the watershed is even more drastically reduced. Freshwater wetlands act like a sponge, absorbing floodwaters and then slowly releasing them over time, thereby reducing flood heights. Since 1780, almost 26 million acres of wetlands have been lost in the Upper Mississippi and Missouri River basins. It has been estimated that had they been in place, these wetlands could have stored the 40 million acre-feet of water—enough water to more than cover the state of Georgia with a foot of water—that passed St. Louis during the 1993 flood. Given that a marsh could be around three feet deep in water during a flood, a back of the envelope calculation made by Hey and Philippi (1995) suggested that the wetlands would have been able to accommodate the 1993 floodwaters. Yet, regaining this capacity would not just entail the restoration of an equivalent acreage of wetlands in the basin, but would need to be more strategic. Flood attenuation is determined not just by the total area of wetlands, but by their distribution within the entire watershed (National Research Council 2000), such that flood values are not the same for every acre of wetland (De Laney 1995).

Conversion of natural lands to agriculture also alters the hydrology of a watershed. In the Missouri-Mississippi watershed, agriculture accounts for over 65% of land-use (Hey and Philippi 1995). The grasses of the prairie that once covered much of the Upper Mississippi basin slowed floodwaters, and the rich soil held water and promoted infiltration to aquifers (Hunt 1997). Agricultural lands, however, often are lined with outlet ditches and tile drains to wash water off the land quickly, thereby exacerbating flood risks. Beyond this, the erosion of topsoil has reduced the land's capacity to hold water. (Certain farming techniques, such as conservation tillage, increase water retention. For more on the link between water and soil conservation techniques and flooding, see Hunt 1997.) In addition, an estimated 3 million acres of agricultural lands in the Upper Mississippi are on drained wetlands within the 100-year flood plain (Hey, Montgomery et al. 2004). Finally, farmers along the Mississippi and other rivers often personally invest in agricultural levees to protect their fields from floods; this increases flood heights at the levee and upstream, as the restricted waters back up (although levees are clearly only one of the factors that determine flood heights) (U.S. General Accounting Office 1995).

Coastal ecosystems, including marshes, mangroves, seagrass beds, coral reefs, and sand dunes, protect inland areas from storm surges and erosion. These services can be critical: 43% of the U.S. population lives within 100 kilometers of the coast (WRI 2005). Mangroves reduce erosion by stabilizing the coast and protect inland areas by absorbing storm energy; seagrass beds slow water velocity and thus limit erosion; and coral reefs are a natural breakwater, protecting the shore from erosion by lessening the force of currents and waves (Moberg and Ronnback 2003). Coastal wetlands absorb storm energy and attenuate storm surges, reducing damage to coastal areas, as mentioned earlier. Barrier islands also attenuate storm surges and act as a protective barrier for the wetlands themselves. Coastal landowners may be tempted to build on sand dunes, destroying the first line of defense against storms, or erect seawalls and riprap (rock used to stabilize shorelines or riverbanks) to protect their own property from the erosive energy of waves, but which can increase erosion for their neighbors (Reddy 2000). In the lower basin of the Mississippi, less than 20% of the original bottomland forest (forested wetlands) still stood in the 1980s, the cutting largely due to conversion for agriculture (Environmental Protection Agency 2005). (Although governmental actions are discussed next, it is important to note that the economic incentive for conversion to agriculture was increased by federal flood-control and drainage projects (Stavins and Jaffe 1990).)

JARring actions on the Mississippi have also resulted from attempts to use a river for commerce. For example, oil companies operating in the Gulf have dredged canals through marshes off the coast of Louisiana, directly destroying wetlands, and also accelerating further damage from erosion and saltwater intrusion into freshwater areas.

The federal government has often been involved. The U.S. Army Corps of Engineers has been improving transportation on rivers since the early 1800s, and the Mississippi is one of the country's major river transportation routes. Canals have been created to facilitate the entry of ships from the Gulf up the river, largely for the benefit of the nation's shipping and grain industries. We thus now turn to public actions more generally.

Just as private entities fail to take account of the remote consequences of their actions, the government can also fail to do so, whether because of a failure to analyze external impacts or due to a neglect of such impacts in response to the pressure of interest groups. The incredible loss of marshland off the coast of Louisiana reflects the convergence of several factors (Britsch and Dunbar 1993). Wetlands require the continual nourishment of sediment. Dam and channel control works constructed in the 1950s halved the total amount of sediment reaching the Louisiana coast (Louisiana Coastal Wetlands Conservation and Restoration Task Force and The Wetlands Conservation and Restoration Authority 1998). The Missouri River had historically been the principal supplier of sediment to the Mississippi, but the construction of five dams for hydropower and irrigation, undertaken between 1953 and 1963 under a joint Corps of Engineers and Bureau of Reclamation plan, all but eliminated sediment from the Upper Missouri River Basin (Meade 1995). The "Big Muddy" no longer delivers as much mud to the Mississippi. In addition, sediment that does reach the mouth of the river is prevented from feeding the marshes by levees that channel the sediment deep into the Gulf. In McPhee's colorful language, the sediment is "shot over the shelf like peas through a peashooter, and lost to the abyssal plain" (McPhee 1989).

This lack of nourishment is exacerbated by the subsidence of New Orleans and the surrounding areas, which creates a high relative rate of sea-level rise that inundates the marshes and speeds wetland loss. The alluvial soils of the delta naturally sink over time unless new sediment restores them. The withdrawal of enormous amounts of oil, natural gas, and saline formation water by oil companies operating in the Gulf have intensified subsidence (Bourne 2004). Finally, the creation of nine major shipping lanes and an 8,000 mile network of canals to facilitate oil exploration (Bourne 2000; Bourne 2004) has degraded the marshlands, increasing erosion and the infiltration of deadly levels of saltwater to those areas of the marsh not directly dredged. The largest shipping canal, the Mississippi River Gulf Outlet (MRGO), was built by the Corps of Engineers to reduce travel time into New Orleans from the Gulf. It bears little traffic, yet has imposed heavy environmental costs—the destructions of 20,000 acres of wetlands, saltwater intrusion in the marshes, and the acceleration of land loss (National Research Council and Committee on the Restoration and Protection of Coastal Louisiana 2005). Before this hurricane season, Hassan Mashriqui, at Louisiana State University's Hurricane Center, predicted that MRGO could funnel and intensify storm surges. It appears that this indeed happened during Hurricane Katrina (Grunwald 2005; Warrick 2005).

The effects of structural flood control projects—the construction of levees, floodwalls, and dams—on the loss of wetlands, and thus their ability to buffer storm surges, are made clear in Louisiana. Structural projects can also alter inland risks. First, such projects often provide a false sense of security, encouraging development behind levees and floodwalls and downstream of dams. When a flood overwhelms these structures, the damage can be quite substantial (for example, see an assessment of the 1979 Jackson flood: Platt 1982). Second, structural approaches seek to move floodwaters off the land quickly. This concentration of water increases pressure on the flood control system, and when a breach occurs a large amount of water rapidly inundates an area, causing more devastation than had the waters been slower and less concentrated (Hunt 1997). Levee construction, which forces water through a narrow area, increases flood heights at the levee and upstream, as mentioned above (U.S. General Accounting Office 1995; Faber 1996; Pinter 2005). This increase in flood heights from levees was observed as early as 1930 (Hunt 1997), if not before. As John McPhee puts it, "Nature was not the only enemy. Anywhere along the river, people were safer if the levee failed across the way" (McPhee 1989), so that floodwaters would spread on someone else's land. The system of flood control levees on the Lower Mississippi River (from Cairo, Illinois to the Gulf) is longer than the Great Wall of China (Meade 1995).

Thus, structural approaches to flood control impose negative externalities on communities upstream and downstream from the project. In Hirsch's metaphor about mass externalities, when everyone stands on tiptoe, all are uncomfortable but no one gets a better view (1976). So too, "structural flood control quickly became its own justification as governments began building one flood-control structure to compensate for the side-effects of another" (Faber 1996).

Of course, some levees, dams, and floodwalls are beneficial investments, particularly those that protect unusually valuable assets. The floodwall at St. Louis, for example, has saved the city and its residents from much damage over the years. Yet, the external costs of altering rivers and coastal lands must enter decision-making. Historically there has been a strong tilt in federal projects toward structural approaches, with little attention paid to the externalities and the long-term or environmental impacts they impose. Happily, this approach is changing (Crosson and Frederick 1999). While the Corps of Engineers originally only undertook navigation and structural flood control projects, in the 1990s, Congress expanded the Corps' mission to include environmental protection and restoration projects as well.

Policy Responses

Individuals do not take account of the external effects of JARring actions when making decisions that fuel floods and often governments fail to do so as well. Vast resources are thereby exposed to destruction. To avoid such waste, policies must be implemented to internalize the external costs that JARring actions impose. Since liability systems and private contracting cannot address the often small and hard-to-detect increment of risk imposed by numerous actors, government intervention is likely required. If transaction costs were zero, the Coase Theorem might assure efficient compensation to keep those who JAR from doing so. However, with myriad affecting and affected parties, and the remote relationship between actions and costs, transactions costs will render private contracting impotent.

Our paper is focused primarily on flooding, but while a focus on flooding and JARring actions—from both the private and public sectors—is quite pertinent following Katrina's devastation of New Orleans, JARring actions have numerous other applications. If global warming proves to be a significant problem in the decades to come, as scientists suggest it will, many greenhouse gas emitting actions we take today, as individuals, corporations, or the government, will come to viewed as the ultimate JARring actions, jeopardizing assets that are quite remote, albeit extraordinarily valuable. While the policies that follow are related to disasters of the Mississippi, this is not meant to suggest that far greater policy challenges for other types of JARring actions do not deserve equal or greater attention.

The most straightforward approach to reduce JARring actions would be direct regulation. Land-use regulation is usually the purview of local governments, some of which already regulate activities such as wetland filling or levee construction. However, localities have no incentive to effectively control JARring actions that have physically distant effects. Moreover, a state may prevent localities from regulating activities the state deems important to its economy, such as transportation or mining, and localities cannot regulate federal and state property (U.S. General Accounting Office 1995). In larger watersheds, such as the Mississippi watershed, local governments will also encounter their own collective action problems. For example, if one local government restricts the filling of wetlands, this will benefit all other localities within the watershed, but if it allows its wetlands to be drained for development, the local community gets all the economic development and taxes. Economic theory therefore predicts that local governments would free-ride on the regulations of neighboring jurisdictions, leading to less regulation and more filled wetlands than would be desirable.

Thus, regulations would need to be undertaken at the state or more likely the federal level, that is, at a level that its jurisdiction embraces both the JARring actor and the parties put at risk. There is precedent for both types of regulation. Five of the nine states affected by the 1993 flood do regulate the construction of agricultural levees (U.S. General Accounting Office 1995). Although not used for this purpose, these regulations could be designed to directly address the externality that levee construction imposes on others in the watershed. The federal government has several programs addressing wetland loss, although none is well targeted for local flood concerns. The programs are either reactive, as with 404 permitting under the Clean Water Act, which regulates the dredging and filling of wetlands by responding to permit applications to allow filling, or opportunistic, as is the Wetland Reserve Program, in which only those landowners that stand to receive private gains enroll; "neither process ensures that the benefits of wetland functions and values are optimized throughout the landscape" (McAllister, Peniston et al. 2000). Another approach would be the creation of a regional entity to coordinate land-use regulations in a watershed. This echoes growing discussion of using the watershed as a unit for policymaking.

A larger barrier to a regulatory approach at any scale of government is likely to be the political opposition it might engender. For example, the Supreme Court has recently agreed to hear cases regarding federal wetland policies (most notably *John Rapanos v. United States*), and in November 2004, opponents of state regulation of private property helped pass Measure 37 in Oregon, which requires compensation to property owners for zoning and environmental regulations.

When direct regulation is politically infeasible, the government could provide appropriate incentives. For example, JARring actions such as the construction of a levee or filling of a wetland could be taxed or actors could receive subsidies for refraining from taking such actions on their property. Such taxes or subsidies could be administered through property taxes, but other incentives could also be used. For example, development credits granted to private parties could be used strategically to decrease development in floodplains by allowing denser development off the floodplain in exchange (Sheaffer, Mullan et al. 2002). Credits could also potentially be used to encourage development that minimizes increases in impervious surface area and other disruptions to natural drainage. However, for an incentive approach—especially one based on taxes—to provide an efficient level of ecosystem services, or fully internalize the external costs of JARring actions, the government would need fairly accurate estimates of the social costs of each JARring action. That is a hefty information requirement, though once a system was in place information would accrete rapidly. In addition, taxes inevitably meet political resistance. Subsidies for favorable actions would likely be more acceptable, particularly since strongly affected parties dominate most political decisions, and deficit control is not a current political priority.

Fee simple purchase of all the land needed to provide an ecosystem service is another policy option, and one that can prevent JARring actions in perpetuity. This was the instrument used by the Corps of Engineers in the 1970s to preserve wetlands along the Charles River in Massachusetts, as mentioned earlier. If local governments were to attempt to purchase wetlands on their own, in a large watershed such as the Mississippi, coordination problems among various local and state governments in acquiring the necessary land would inevitably make such a policy difficult to implement. The principal argument against acquisition as a primary tool to secure ecosystem services, however, is that it is overkill in most circumstances, hence extremely expensive and inefficient. Since many other land-uses are compatible with ecosystem service provision, the government need not acquire all property rights to the land. Conservation easements are one such alternative to full fee simple purchase that is commonly employed. In acquiring easements, governments could also work in cooperation with local land trusts or groups like the Nature Conservancy, which raise or receive money to acquire land or permanent conservation easements. However, much smaller payments for less severe restrictions might also address the problem.

One potentially attractive policy option is voluntary contracts between the government and landowners, whereby landowners refrain from JARring actions in exchange for payments. Such contracts would need to be for actions that are easily monitored and enforceable. Fortunately, most land-use contracts, such as maintaining a certain amount of one's property as wetlands, would be easy to enforce. Contracts could also be for "contingent services," in which landowners agree to undertake or not undertake particular actions under specified contingencies. For example, they might agree to allow floodwaters to inundate their land in the event of a major flood, thereby saving much more vulnerable or valuable resources elsewhere (on such contracts, see Manale 2000; Hey 2001). The contract could specify the compensation to be paid after a flood, there could be an option payment upfront, or some upfront payment with additional payment later if flooding occurs. One thing is clear: once the waters are rising, it is too late to make the arrangements.

When JARring actions are undertaken by multiple landowners, there would be high transaction costs associated with negotiating the contracts, but having a unified party on the buying side—rather than myriad individuals or localities—reduces the complexities many fold. Institutional arrangements could also likely be arranged to reduce contracting costs. The federal government, could, for instance, announce a price for refraining from a particular JARring action for a period of time. Presumably, the landowners with the lowest costs of provision would be sellers.

The duration of these contracts would reflect a tradeoff between the savings in transaction costs from not having to contract frequently and the benefit of making the future more predictable, against the loss from not being able to respond if conditions change significantly. One possible remedy would be to have permanent contracts, with provisions for buyout. That is, the government might have a per-acre price for permanent preservation of wetlands in an area, which would change every year as better scientific knowledge emerges regarding the risk and as the amount of land under conservation changes. A landowner could buy back her right to develop by paying say a 25% premium on that price. This option protects against the situation in which land becomes very valuable, so that retaining it under conservation for the services it provides is no longer economically rational. (The premium for repurchase also prevents landowners from merely joining the program while waiting to develop their land.)

Contracts of this nature would allow the government to protect the interests of future citizens who would bear costs from the JARring actions of yesteryear. The federal Wetland Reserve Program is based on a similar contracting philosophy—it pays farmers to leave wetlands on their property—but it is not designed to maximize floodwater retention. The use of contracts to address JARring actions falls under the category of "payments for ecosystem services" that have been put in place for other services, such as water quality improvements.

As we have seen, the government often perpetrates its own JARring actions. Policies must be developed to help ensure that the government addresses the externalities from its own projects. One important step in this direction would be to eliminate the bias toward large structural projects within the U.S. Army Corps of Engineers. The continuous existence of the Corps of Engineers dates back to 1802. The Corps, from the start, undertook both military and civil works projects, although for most of its history it focused on navigation and structural flood control projects. As mentioned above, in the 1990s, Congress expanded the Corps' mission to include environmental protection and restoration projects. For example, the Corps must now consider non-structural solutions to flood control and environmental improvement.

This institutional shift is encouraging the current attempts to improve and include environmental impacts in Corps project assessments. In the past, these analyses were notoriously biased in favor of the large engineering projects the Corps prefers. At times, attention has been drawn to the Corps' shady methods to make such projects look more economically attractive, such as the February 2000 scandal when the Corps was found to have misrepresented numbers in an analysis of a lock expansion project on the Mississippi. As a columnist for Slate noted, the Corps of Engineers "gets away with it because members of Congress and powerful interest groups love water projects, and because few others care about water projects, and because water project studies can be somewhat complex" (Grunwald 2003). To the Corps' credit, it is making a concerted effort to improve its environmental benefits analyses. The incorporation of environmental values into decision-making should be supported and encouraged, as well as should a more holistic approach to project evaluation: "Part of the failure to recognize flood magnification owing to levees is because incremental levee expansion projects are evaluated individually, even when many projects are proposed for a given river reach" (Pinter 2005). This prevents a consideration of cumulative effects leading to "'death by a thousand blows' through the incremental loss of floodplain land to development" (Pinter 2005).

The JARring actions that are most difficult to address politically are those whose impacts are distant in time and also unforeseen. An early example is the 1850 Swamp and Overflow Land Act, which deeded swamps to the states. As McPhee summarizes, "these river swamps had been the natural reservoirs where floodwaters were taken in and held, and gradually released as the flood went down. . . . The new owners drained much of the swampland, turned it into farmland, and demanded the protection of new and larger levees. At this point, Congress might have asked itself which was the act and which was the swamp" (McPhee 1989). While the value of these swamps as natural flood control reservoirs is clear now, at the time filling them for agriculture appeared the most productive policy. Similarly, when extensive canal building by oil companies in the Gulf began many decades ago, the long-term consequences were not fully understood. When time-distant consequences were unforeseen, it is usually not possible retroactively to secure compensation or remediation. Correcting for the damages of past actions will thus remain a needed policy at times.

Though preservation has vast cost advantages over restoration—a dime of prevention is worth a dollar of cure—some situations are so dire that highly expensive and politically challenging restoration must be considered. The coastal marshes of Louisiana represent such a situation. Several restoration projects are currently underway, including projects under the Federal Coastal Wetlands Planning, Protection and Restoration Act (The Breaux Act); two large diversion projects to bring Mississippi sediment back to marsh areas—the Caernarvon and Davis Pond Freshwater Diversions; and the Coast 2050 effort. Coast 2050 is a multi-stakeholder endeavor to develop a comprehensive restoration plan for Louisiana's coastal wetlands (see Louisiana Coastal Wetlands Conservation and Restoration Task Force and The Wetlands Conservation and Restoration Authority 1998). Construction of the Coast 2050 plan would cost about $14 billion.

Before Hurricane Katrina, full funding for the Coast 2050 effort did not receive political support, but disasters focus the mind, or at least the political process. Compared to the costs of Katrina, the $14 billion required may now seem a more attractive investment. Quite apart from the monies involved, rebuilding the coastal marshes of Louisiana is politically difficult since the various interests in the Gulf—shipping interests, oil companies, fishermen, farmers, and coastal communities—can often be at odds. Coast 2050 makes an effort to develop a consensus among as many stakeholders as possible to get full support for its projects along with other recovery efforts.

Restoration efforts also occur on a smaller scale. Both Napa, California, and Reno, Nevada are undertaking flood projects that involve wetlands restoration. The local governments, in partnership with federal agencies, have acquired land and have let their rivers return to their natural floodplain. When land along a river is not already highly developed, this can be an attractive option for smaller scale flood control that also provides additional benefits to the communities, such as a more attractive riverfront, recreational opportunities, less polluted rivers, and habitat for fish and birds.

Conclusion

JARring actions have reduced the ecosystem services that protect communities from such natural hazards as floods and storm surges. Individuals, companies, and even governments fail to account for the costs their actions impose on those who are remote from them, leading to outcomes that are suboptimal for society as a whole. Addressing the externalities of JARring actions is challenging due to the remoteness of those undertaking actions from those affected, the large number of affected parties, and often the large number of entities taking JARring actions. Yet the challenge must be met or we will continue to put assets including, most importantly, human lives and livelihoods, at risk. While we can never contract with the future or accurately predict all of the consequences of our actions and policies, policymakers must extend their thinking about their impacts beyond the local, the near term, and the likely. They must recognize that watersheds are interconnected systems, and that actions in any part of them, for example on any part of a river, may have consequences elsewhere in the system. As John Muir wrote, "When we try to pick out anything by itself, we find it hitched to everything else in the Universe" (Muir 1911).

Part Two
Thinking About Risk

Behaviorally Realistic Risk Management

BARUCH FISCHHOFF

Managing risks is a human enterprise. Its success depends on risk managers' ability (a) to anticipate behavior before, during, and after potentially disastrous circumstances; (b) to assemble and integrate the expert knowledge relevant to that understanding; and (c) to provide that knowledge to those who must act on it, in a relevant, comprehensible way. These processes have been studied extensively by social scientists. However, their research receives little attention in most risk analyses. In its place, one finds risk managers' folk wisdom, with occasional allusions to research summaries in secondary sources. Ignoring relevant research has both direct costs—misleading those who rely on faulty plans—and opportunity costs—taking the place of better methods.

Social science has three critical roles in risk management (Fischhoff 1977, 1980, 1989, 1994, 2000, 2005): (1) When a risk depends on human behavior, the analysis of it should be grounded in the relevant social science. (2) The cognitive and emotional biases of those who analyze risks should be considered in light of social science research into expert judgment, when deciding much trust to place in risk analyses. (3) Risk managers should reflect research regarding how to create and communicate information that meets the needs of those who must deal with risks. These three roles for social science are considered next, followed by discussion of how to incorporate them in risk management and the institutional barriers to achieving this goal.

Risk Analyses Should Be Grounded in Scientific Study of Human Behavior

Risk analysis studies the threats arising when people interact with their material surroundings. At times, people create the risk; at times, they just bear its burdens. At times, they play both roles. For example, people who chose to live in New Orleans exposed themselves to risks of flooding which were shaped by how its levees were designed, built, inspected, monitored, and repaired. These residents' risks depended further on how they responded to hurricane warnings, which depended on their own resources (such as transportation), as well as those provided by officials, public service organizations, firms, and others. Assessing these risks requires understanding the behavior of those who create and manage them. That understanding should be based on the best available social science. Most analytical teams, however, are dominated by natural scientists and engineers, who just guess at what social science might tell them.

When social scientists are consulted, their status may shift rapidly from being irrelevant to being late. If they can't produce the desired numbers quickly enough, then risk analysts might make something up, in order to keep social variables in their analyses. Unfortunately, social scientists are often unaccustomed to translating their knowledge into analysis-friendly terms. They may have difficulty interpreting the implications of their general theories in a risk analysis's specific context. Their science may focus on statistical significance, showing which social variables might appear in an analysis, rather than effect size, showing which social variables really matter.

Three recent examples, from my personal experiences, suggest the opportunities and obstacles to creating behaviorally realistic risk analyses. Each was unsatisfying, yet potentially a small step in the right direction.

A couple of years ago, I got a call from a consulting firm, saying, "We've got the contract for modeling [biohazard X]. We know it depends on things like whether people notice symptoms, get vaccinations, sue for side effects, obey quarantines, believe that their loved ones are being cared for. . . . Can you come here, for a day, to give us the numbers for behavior, so that we can estimate those parameters in our model?"

It was nice to be asked. However, how could any one person know all the relevant research, represent its results, uncertainties, and controversies, in a single day, while ensuring that the model has been properly formulated, and then monitor the use of those behavior estimates as the model evolves over time? I didn't think that I could and declined. This may have been a mistake. The firm had at least asked, yet I had refused to say anything at all, rather than saying something that would not be used as well as I would have liked.

Subsequently, I was asked about the soundness of a device for detecting the presence of a toxin that terrorists might disperse. One of my first questions was, "How can you ensure its usability, in terms of both how well operators can use it and how risk managers will respond to its stream of true and false signals? Will users know when there might be trouble? Will they feel empowered to sound the alarm? Will they be believed?" The answer was, "We have a couple of veteran first responders coming in one day a week, telling us how well they think that people like them could use it."

That was certainly better than just imagining its use and, arguably, better than asking me to shoot from hip with an opinion, without the discipline of evidence testing my judgment. Nonetheless, those two users could hardly know the relevant human factors science, devise valid performance standards, monitor adherence to their advice, anticipate the range of possible uses, and represent alternative approaches. Although initially dismissive, I came to realize that the analysis could benefit from having two users raise potentially awkward questions. However, realizing this potential required someone on the analytical team having the authority and expertise needed to translate the two users' concerns into analytical terms, and supplemental empirical research. Unless the users had high social status (like that of military pilots), vendor push might carry more weight than their needs in shaping the technology.

One Friday in July 2005, a colleague wrote an email saying, "[X] is writing [a federal government white paper] and needs to know the ratio of 'worried well' to actual injured to expect, in the event of a terror attack." If the ratio is small, then hospitals only need to plan for the surge of those actually injured. If the ratio is large, then hospitals must plan for many more people, who are unsure about whether they have been exposed to harm. It was nice that [X] didn't just make up a number or ignore the problem altogether, yet this task seemed as problematic as the previous ones. How could one number do it all, given the variety of possible attacks and possible definitions of "worried well"? How could one number capture the uncertainties in the research literature? How could any response avoid feeding the disrespect inherent in the question, with its implication of "needlessly worried well"?

Over the weekend, we assembled a small team electronically and produced a short memo with two numbers. It said that the research suggests a ratio between 1.02 and 100,000. At one extreme lie situations where the only unexposed individuals showing up at hospitals are the (fortunately few) people who somaticize stress, perhaps 2% of the population (for a ratio of 1.02). At the other extreme lie situations where communication is so hard, or so badly bungled, that many people are left legitimately wondering whether they have been exposed to a toxin or pathogen that is treatable if they get help soon—as happened in the 2001 anthrax crisis (Thomas 2003). The worst-case communication failure might have 100,000 people concerned about being exposed for each person who actually was. Our little team hoped to provide some crude guidance, while noting that we could do better, drawing just on existing social science research, if we had a more precise specification of the terrorist attack and response (Fischhoff and Wessely 2003; Mawson 2005; Tierney 2006). We could do even better with additional research focused on policy makers' specific concerns.

Although researchers always feel aggrieved when their work is ignored, the path forward, for social scientists hoping to affect risk analysis, may require such small steps, swallowing hard and saying something consistent with existing research, hoping that the next request will allow saying and doing more. We might also reflect on cases where the tables are turned, and social scientists treat natural science and engineering issues too lightly, for example, studying risk perceptions, without analyzing which facts are really worth knowing (Fischhoff 2005).

Risk Analysts Are People, Too

About 25 years ago, I had the opportunity to spend an afternoon at the University of Bath (UK), with Stephen Cotgrove, an early student of conflict over environmental protection. One of his comments that particularly struck me was, "The hardest thing for me to do is convince engineers that they have emotions."

In Cotgrove's view, as I understood it, the engineers' denial had two important consequences. One made him less sympathetic to engineers, the other more. The former was that seeing themselves as relying entirely on reason made it too easy for engineers to dismiss their critics as being driven by emotion. We all have our favored *ad hominem* arguments. "Hysterical public" is a convenient, ego-enhancing one, when citizens object to an engineered system. However, it is not a helpful diagnosis unless supported by evidence.

A while ago, I was invited to address a largely technical group about risk communication regarding terrorism. The ensuing discussion was lively and constructive, until someone began a question with, "As I understand it, the accepted wisdom is that if an attack occurs, the public will panic."

I had devoted one slide to that exact topic and it had said exactly the opposite. I realized that the questioner was not disputing my claim, but simply had not heard it, because it so contradicted his expectations. (Psychologists use "selective perception" to describe such processes.) I replied undiplomatically, saying that although psychologists have made a living documenting the foibles of lay judgments, few compared to this fable about lay people, which was widely held in the expert community (Tierney 2006). This derision of the public seemed particularly common among those, like nuclear engineers, whose technologies had been subject to public censure, leading their judgment to be clouded by their emotions.

Looking at natural disasters, wartime experiences and other collectively stressful events, scientists have found that panic is rare, while pro-social, even brave behavior is the norm (Glass and Spoch-Spana 2002; Janis 1951; Tierney, Lindell and Perry 2001). For example, British authorities quickly closed the mental health clinics that they had opened at the beginning of the Blitz, because of a dearth of business. Ordinary citizens ordinarily provide most of the first response to disasters, helping those around them to leave wrecked buildings and make it to hospitals or shelters. As a result, underestimating citizens' capabilities has relatively small practical consequences for the management of actual disasters. Citizens have done their work before the professionals arrive to do theirs. Although reports of mass looting and violence saturated the media following Hurricane Katrina's devastation of New Orleans, it seemed that most of those who stayed behind were calm, treated one another with respect, and tried to help one another (Pierre and Gerhart 2005).

Underestimating the public's competence may be very costly, however, if our society is put on a permanent wartime footing due to anxiety over potential disasters. In that case, the false image of an incompetent public, supported by the myth of panic, could foster militarization of the home front, undermining civic society and misdirecting protective resources. Over time, repetition of the myth might even create a self-fulfilling prophecy. In late 2002, despite believing that citizens behaved well on September 11th, Americans feared that panic would follow a future attack (Fischhoff et al. 2003). It is irresponsible for experts to feed that insecurity, based on their intuitive theories of behavior in disasters, while being too arrogant or lazy to consult the relevant social science research. We will all pay the price, if "experts" induce social disorganization, by undermining people's confidence in their fellow citizens' resilience and humanity.

The persistence of the panic myth follows from Cotgrove's second conclusion regarding the impact of engineers' denial of emotion, the one that increased his sympathy toward them. Engineers often bear enormous responsibility for solving intellectually challenging problems, where others' life, limb, and economic wellbeing are at risk. Those employing engineers may leave them without clear guidance on how to make these difficult tradeoffs. Or they may make a socially unacceptable decision, then leave the engineers as its frontline defenders or holding the bag when things go wrong and people suffer. Small wonder, if engineers feel some emotion regarding their work. One source (and amplifier) of that emotion is a public that seems not to appreciate or even trust them. For those without training in the social sciences, citizens' skepticism (or hostility) can be hard to understand, increasing the attendant emotions.

Over the past twenty years, researchers have learned a lot about the effects of specific emotions on specific judgments (Lerner and Keltne 2001; Loewenstein and Lerner 2003). For example, anger, unlike other negative emotions, makes people more optimistic. It also encourages attributing problems to other people rather than to general circumstances. In contrast, sadness reduces optimism and encourages attributing problems to circumstances, which seem harder to address than troublesome people (Small et al., in press). The mobilizing properties of anger can help people to get things done, if it does not cloud their judgment and keep them from acting effectively. Sadness, on the other hand, can evoke the compassion needed to remember just how complicated circumstances can be, while evoking sympathy (or at least empathy) for those caught in them. Thus, when facing a conflict, angry people should be more likely to lash out at a perceived enemy, while sad people should be more likely to undertake sustained negotiations (Thompson 2005).

In this light, emotion is neither good nor bad, just a fact of life that needs to be recognized, if people are to make the best use of their knowledge and judgment. Balanced emotions may be as important as balanced judgments, when attempting to understand complex, uncertain problems (Morgan and Henrion 1990; Moore et al. 2005).

Risk Analyses Should Focus on the Information Needs of Those Whose Fate Depends on Them

The tragedy of Hurricane Katrina should give pause to anyone in the risk business. The "blame game" has been widely played and, one can assume, will continue to be played for several years. What might fade, though, is the "shame game," in which we wonder whether we have somehow contributed to this risk management failure. Risk analyses (and risk analysts) serve the public to the extent that they create the facts that it needs for effective decision making and, then, deliver those facts in a comprehensible, credible form (Cabinet Office 2001; Canadian Standards Association 1997; Presidential/Congressional Commission on Risk 1997). These goals clearly were not achieved for many people along the Gulf Coast. An investigation worthy of those who perished or had their lives disrupted, as well as those who labored to save them, would examine the roles played by the following factors.

To what extent did people fail to act "sensibly," despite receiving good information in a timely fashion? Where this happened, an emergency system that relies on communication has failed the test of behavioral realism. Evaluating this possibility requires empirically establishing citizens' goals and beliefs. Did they know the risks, but stay behind for loved ones? Did they hear conflicting messages (stay/go, we'll help/you're on your own) and not know which to trust? As discussed earlier, risk managers may naturally tend to discount their public's competence. That can create a vicious circle, whereby systematic communication hardly seems worth the effort, leading to citizens making suboptimal choices that reinforce disrespect for them.

To what extent did citizens not understand what they were told? Where they did not, either the emergency system should be abandoned or better communications are needed. Evaluating this possibility requires evidence regarding how actual messages were interpreted and how far the envelope of understanding could be expanded with properly designed messages. Although that design process can be informed by the relevant scientific literature (Fischhoff et al. 2002; Morgan et al. 2001), it is incomplete without empirical testing of the messages. Sadly, although officials would not release a drug without premarket testing, they are often comfortable disseminating risk communications that "look OK" to them. During Hurricane Rita, many people evacuated who should have stayed at home, but apparently misunderstood official advice (Horswell and Hegstrom 2005). A spokesperson was quoted as saying that the Texas Department of Transportation had no psychologists among its 15,000 employees (Blumenthal and Barstow 2005). That excuse for not dealing with "irrational" citizens also explains what TDOT's messages had been evaluated to ensure that they would be interpreted as intended (Fischhoff 1994).

To what extent did messages contain the information that citizens needed most? Where they did not, the emergency system should be redesigned to identify the facts that are most critical to citizens' needs (and that do not go without saying). One threat to the relevance of risk communications is having their content driven by public affairs concerns (focused on the welfare of the source) rather than public health concerns (focused on the welfare of the audience). An organization might need a public affairs staff to tell its story. However, in time of need, citizens want the unvarnished truth, regarding the situations that they must manage (Fischhoff et al. 2003). Public affairs specialists rarely have the substantive and analytical skills needed to identify that information. Their predisposition to spin the facts may make their organization look more capable than it actually is, setting the stage for it to disappoint those who rely on it.

To what extent did citizens not find the messenger a credible source? (Löfstedt 2005; Powell and Leiss 1997) Where that happened, the messenger needs to be improved or replaced. Evaluating that possibility requires determining the perceived honesty and competence of both the communicators and the institutions that they represent, in specific context. The person who is right for one crisis might be wrong for another. It is my impression, that Mayor Giuliani was much more effective providing inspiration after September 11th than providing technical information during the anthrax crisis and Ground Zero cleanup (Thomas 2003).

To what extent did communicators not know what to say, because the risks had not been analyzed properly? Where that happened, officials should have admitted their ignorance and remained silent about risk esti-mates until they had done their homework. Evaluating this possibility requires looking at staffing and work practices. Unfortunately, the prob-lems described above increase the chances of organizations not realizing their own inadequacies. It would require unusual self-awareness and self-disclosure to realize and admit that plans are based on hunches about cit-izens' behavior and information needs.

To what extent did communicators have nothing useful to say, because they had no help to offer citizens? Where that is the case, the honest thing to say is, "You're on your own. We'll try to be more useful the next time." Once the scientific reconstruction of responses to Katrina and Rita is com-pleted, it may show that this should have been the harsh content of mes-sages aimed at many low-income residents who had disabilities or were caring for others who did. Without such awareness and candor, officials not only fail to provide needed services, but reduce the response capacity of citizens, left waiting for help that will not come (Glen 2005; Jordan 2005).

These are intellectually challenging evaluations, requiring systematic research, not just speculation. Like other forensic work, it is best pursued in a non-partisan manner, with the needed natural, engineering, and social science expertise. Lawyers have a valuable role in such inquiries, as experts in the legal constraints on official actions and as cross-examiners of witnesses who might be playing with the truth. However, lawyers can undermine an inquiry if they become arbiters of politically acceptable truth, or mix inquiry and adjudication (Wecht and Weed 2005). Having local residents on the forensic team should increase its relevance to their concerns, realism about their circumstances, and comprehensibility to others like them. Residents' presence should also help to sustain the pas-sion for getting it right next time (Institute of Medicine 1998).

Principle and Practice of Recognizing Behavior in Risk Management

The challenges of addressing behavioral aspects of disaster risk manage-ment are variants of general issues common to risk management, whether it be for food handling, hazardous technologies, medical procedures, infectious disease, or whatever. Addressing social concerns has been advo-cated by many expert panels considering risk management practices (Cabinet Office 2001; Presidential-Congressional Commission on Risk 1998). One such statement is the Canadian Standard Association's (1997), *Risk Management Guidelines for Decision Makers*, which is slowly being imple-mented in government agencies and those working with them. It proposes a fairly standard process of risk management, with stages of Initiation, Preliminary Analysis, Risk Estimation, Risk Evaluation, Risk Control, and Action/Monitoring. Its conceptualization of this process is noteworthy in requiring an explicit evaluation of each transition. That is, its model recognizes the need to repeat the work until it has been performed adequately—and the possibility that this goal might not be achieved. Even more distinctively, the model requires *two-way* risk communication at each step. That is, citizens have a right to hear *and* to be heard from the very beginning, when risk analyses are initially formulated, to the very end, when risk management plans are set into action and monitored for their success. In so doing, the model assumes that citizens have (or can be afforded) the expertise needed to inform all stages of risk management, in addition to having a right to know about its content. This is a striking departure from the one-way communication strategy, sometimes called "decide-announce-defend." The British government's ongoing risk initiative offers similar guidance (HM Treasury 2005), including elements drawn from behavioral decision research into value elicitation (Fischhoff 2006).

The evolving conceptual foundations for this commitment to behaviorally realistic risk management can be traced in a series of U.S. National Academy of Sciences reports that are milestones in risk management. The "red book," *Risk Management in the Federal Government* (National Research Council 1983), recognized that risk analysis inevitably reflects both science and politics. Even if scientists could scrupulously avoid conflicts of interests, the choice of focal outcomes reflects what matters to those who commission and use an analysis. So do the decisions to invest in obtaining data and creating assessments relevant to particular concerns. For example, environmental or social justice (or economic) consequences will be neglected, if they are not officially recognized and scientifically documented. The red book advocated acknowledging these issues explicitly. Although the red book presaged two-way communication, the immediate response to it was actually a quest for fuller separation between science and politics: Scientists would assess the risks and benefits of proposed policies, while politicians decided what to do about the analytical results. That separation was designed to keep scientists from spinning their results and politicians from claiming unwarranted expertise. It was naturally appealing to scientists hoping to perform purely "objective" research (and ignore how political power shapes their research agendas).

Improving Risk Communication (1989) asserted the public's right to know the results of risk analyses, making communication integral to risk management. That commitment envisioned an active public, doing more than just waiting for scientists and officials to manage its risks. It reflected the growing body of research finding that citizens' can understand enough about most risks to make reasonable choices, if the relevant facts are competently communicated. One element of this research has been finding that disagreements between citizens and experts can reflect more than just citizens' lack of understanding. It shows that the account of any disagreement must consider whether laypeople and expert (a) use terms differently (for instance, which outcomes they treat as "risks"; how they weight catastrophic potential); (b) fall prey to self-serving biases, when evaluating others' motivation and competence; and (c) are insufficiently critical of their own beliefs. A common finding is that citizens tend to be most skeptical of claims for which experts' evidence is weakest, such as those regarding low-probability, high-consequence events (Fischhoff et al. 1981, 1983, 2002).

Science and Judgment in Risk Assessment (National Research Council 1994) explicitly recognized the central role of judgment in risk analysis—given the great uncertainty surrounding many issues, often involving complex interactions among environmental, industrial, social, psychological, and physiological processes. As a result, expert-lay disagreements were not just discrepancies between "real" and "perceived" risks, but between two sets of perceptions, one held by experts and the other by lay people. The report offered standards for disclosing the role of expert judgment, as well as for eliciting it in a disciplined way (Morgan and Henrion 1990). Other critiques have warned about social risks of risk analysis itself. One is that it can stifle creativity, by focusing on the justification of existing proposals. A second is that it can emphasize readily quantified factors (such as monetary costs) relative to more qualitative ones (such as impacts on public morale or minority group feelings). A third is that risk analysis can disenfranchise those unfamiliar with its formalisms, even if they have substantive knowledge of risk topics (O'Brien 2000).

Understanding Risk (National Research Council 1996) revived the red book's intertwining of science and values. It challenged the assumption that scientists can simply do their work, and leave the politics to others. Rather, it showed how a risk analysis's framing inevitably expresses some values. They are seen in its choice of topics (why some outcomes are studied and not others) and its definition of terms. For example, "risk" could mean just mortality or also include morbidity. It must assign weights to whichever consequences it considers. Even weighting all deaths equally expresses values: giving equal weight to deaths of young and old people and to people exposed to a risk voluntarily and involuntarily (Fischhoff et al. 1981, 1984). The report argued that these definitional choices should be made by those whose fate depends on them, in what it called an "analytical-deliberative process"—a term intended to capture the need for scientifically informed discussion of which risks matter most.

Citizen involvement in risk management was further endorsed by the congressionally mandated Committee on Setting Priorities for the National Institutes of Health (Institute of Medicine 1998a). It led to creation of a Citizens Advisory Panel, chaired by the head of the Institutes. *Toward Environmental Justice* (Institute of Medicine 1998b) called for "participatory science," involving citizens in the design and conduct of studies affecting their community. Doing so takes advantage of their expertise (such as in exposure processes), while ensuring that they learn as much about their conditions as the outsiders examining them. It should improve citizens' scientific and policy-making sophistication, while increasing the chances of their accepting the results of risk analyses (which they would see as collaboratively produced).

In Practice, There Are Institutional Barriers to Behaviorally Realistic Risk Management

Given this recognition of social processes and social sciences, the lack of behavioral realism in much risk management is a persistent puzzle. I believe that there are problems on both the supply and the demand sides.

On the demand side, much risk management has changed little from its early days, when it was conceptualized in purely technical terms. This inertia reflects the natural tendency for organizations to perpetuate their existing functions. Current staff tend to hire people like themselves and to create procedures that they are comfortable applying. Political and legal processes tend to focus on concerns that have already been recognized (for example, litigation is more likely to focus on an existing analysis than on a missing one). When a new competency appears to be needed, there is a tendency to try to get it cheaply (for instance, through consultants who promise to do a lot for a little money; through junior hires). As a result, there is little opportunity for serious social science or social scientists, sustaining the incumbent risk managers' feeling that "there is not much [social science] out there." When investments are made in social science research, they may favor variants that resemble traditional ways of thinking. Thus, engineers might be most comfortable with accounting-like approaches to evaluation, like cost-benefit analyses, rather than, say, consultative ones (Gregory et al. 2005).

On the supply side, the academic social sciences have been relatively uninterested in the bridging research needed to serve risk management. Despite sustained lip service, interdisciplinary research is spottily rewarded. Academic accolades tend to go to sweeping statements about the human condition and to ascetic models, rather than to the muted statements that are possible with complex problems. It is time-consuming for researchers to understand risks well enough to estimate the relative importance of different behavioral processes in them. After investing that time, researchers may discover that their own work is not that relevant in that context. They may not receive much credit in promotion-and-tenure decisions, if they do the socially responsible thing and focus on getting other researchers' work incorporated in risk management plans. Over the long run, that experience may strengthen their science, by revealing boundary conditions and new phenomena. Over the short run, though, it will not lead to publications.

As the hurricanes of 2005 have shown, behaviorally realistic risk management is essential as we face a future whose potential disasters include hurricanes, pandemics, earthquakes, environmental collapses, and terrorist attacks. It would be a shame, and even shameful, if the indifference of risk managers or social scientists kept the relevant social science from being created and used. Optimistically, one could hope that the urgency of the problems will make this a turning point in the demand and supply sectors, with both parties rolling up their sleeves to work together, in order to overcome this inertia and reduce the risks of disaster. As a social scientist, though, I have to assume that past behavior is the best predictor of future behavior. In the absence of unusual leadership, institutional inertia will prevail.

Note

Three sections of the paper are based on President's Columns in the Society for Risk Analysis's *RISKNewsletter*, volume 25, numbers 2–4, 2005 <www.sra.org>.

Rationales and Instruments for Government Intervention in Natural Disasters

MICHAEL J. TREBILCOCK AND RONALD J. DANIELS

The world, over the course even of its relatively recent history, has known many natural disasters, including earthquakes, volcanic eruptions, tsunami, hurricanes, floods, droughts, and pandemics. The 1918–1919 Spanish flu pandemic killed more than 20 million people (some estimates run as high as 50 million). The current AIDS pandemic has already killed more than 20 million people (most in sub-Saharan Africa), and there are serious concerns that a new avian flu pandemic could kill hundreds of millions of people around the world. The recent earthquake in Pakistan is estimated to have killed over 70,000 people. The tsunami in the Indian Ocean in December 2004 killed 300,000 people (Winchester 2003; Winchester 2005; Barry 1997). Richard Posner, in his recent provocative book, *Catastrophe* (2004), worries about much more remote but more devastating natural disasters such as asteroid collisions with the earth or extreme forms of global warming followed by an ice age.

Although hurricanes and floods may not be as catastrophic as some natural disasters, such as asteroid collisions or medical epidemics, we focus on them and on the role of government in natural disasters with which there is first-hand and recent experience. In examining the role of government in responding to natural disasters we seek to understand the normative rationales for government intervention and the instruments, both *ex ante* and *ex post* a disaster, that governments can actually use to intervene. In doing so, we evaluate how effective a given instrument is likely to be in vindicating a particular rationale for intervention and at what cost (public and private). We then ask how well actual government policy-making in the recent past in natural disaster contexts comports with this analysis. To the extent that there are major divergences, we explore whether these simply reflect policy misjudgments or errors—to give a public choice or political economy perspective its due—or whether they reflect systemic infirmities or vulnerabilities in the political and policy-making process. Policies that did not substantially correct problems can be altered in the future through superior information or ideas. Systemic infirmities or vulnerabilities in the political process pose a more daunting challenge and require us to investigate whether there are strategies or mechanisms whereby governments can credibly commit themselves *ex ante* to pursuing more normatively coherent or defensible policies (Iacobucci, Trebilcock and Haider 2001; Daniels and Trebilcock 2005).

Rationales for Government Intervention

In considering the various rationales for government intervention, we acknowledge the complex interplay between our positive and normative analysis. On the one hand, natural disasters engage certain normative concerns that justify government intervention, even though state action was not the source of the risk in question (although government failure to address these risks may contribute to the public injury sustained) because of the highly concentrated (and often recurrent) losses they inflict on certain segments of the population. On the other hand, there are a host of other foreseeable shocks that inflict concentrated losses on certain communities but which nevertheless do not command the same political salience.

A libertarian perspective in responding to natural disasters would emphasize the importance of individual autonomy and view individuals as possessing the ability to determine for themselves a view of the good life, subject to avoiding actions that deprive other individuals of similar scope for the exercise of individual autonomy. This perspective would imply a minimal role for government and in particular would resist coercive government policies such as constraints on locational decisions or housing preferences through zoning laws or building code requirements or mandatory insurance, but conversely would view government as having no responsibility to individuals for the consequences of their choices in this respect and would oppose policies that permit individuals to externalize all or some of the costs of their decisions onto others through, such as subsidized insurance or disaster relief. However, where choices do not reflect underlying preferences, because they are predicated on false information about relevant costs and benefits of alternative choices, there may be a role for a soft form of paternalism in regulating the accuracy or provision of such information (Sunstein and Thaler 2003; Camerer, Issacharoff, Lowenstein, O Donaghue, and Rabin 2003).

This is not to say that governments, particularly lower level governments, would be precluded from offering citizens a matrix of policies aimed at addressing the risk of natural disasters under a libertarian model. It is possible that different governments could develop different policy bundles to respond to the threat of natural disasters, and then footloose citizens could migrate to the government offering the most congenial mix of policies. Different governments could decide, for instance, to make differential investments in public infrastructure designed to reduce the risk of community injury, could impose different levels of regulation on private development in the jurisdiction, or could commit to provide different levels of social insurance in the event that a natural disaster occurred and inflicted damage. Of course, for such a Tiebout selection process to work, citizens would require accurate information respecting the content of different policies offered by different governments, competing governments would need to have the scope to differentiate their policies regarding the risks of natural disasters without the prospect of policy negation by, or risk externalization to, higher levels of government, and finally competing governments would be precluded from changing their policy mix opportunistically after migrating citizens made sunk investments in the jurisdiction.

A corrective justice approach would attach particular normative salience to providing legal redress for victims harmed by either private or public wrongdoing such as negligence. For example, if the consequences of a natural disaster were exacerbated by the negligence of government officials (or their agents) in the design and maintenance of public infrastructure, such as levees or flood works, or negligent provision of public information on underlying risks or imminent storms, corrective justice theorists would think it is appropriate that relevant government agencies and their officials should bear responsibility for the consequences of their wrongdoing to persons harmed thereby (although causal attribution of losses to particular acts of negligence may be problematic). More controversially, the dictates of corrective justice might suggest special claims for relief from the effects of natural disasters where these bear disproportionately on low-income blacks concentrated in urban ghettos (such as some of the most vulnerable wards in New Orleans) if these are the legacy of a prior history of racial discrimination (see Fiss 2003 and commentaries thereon). However, to the extent that interventions predicated on corrective justice require a demonstration of government fault that must be determined in contested and complex judicial proceedings, the provision of assistance to citizens in need may face endemic and wrenching delays. This is obviously a salient issue in the context of Hurricane Katrina given allegations of government negligence in the design and operation of various infrastructure assets in New Orleans.

From an economic efficiency perspective, which is closely congruent in important respects with some strands of utilitarianism, one would ask whether in natural disaster-prone areas of the kind that we are contemplating, there is some form of market failure that government intervention might plausibly remedy. In the case of hurricanes, a number of important potential precautionary strategies that are designed to mini-mize the expected costs or consequences associated with a natural disas-ter (but not the risk of its occurrence, which we are assuming to be exogenous) have many of the characteristics of public goods and if left purely to private markets are likely to be under-demanded and under-sup-plied as a result of collective action problems. The case for intervention is heightened when government-sponsored infrastructure projects enjoy sig-nificant economies of scale, require the exercise of powers of eminent domain to develop the projects, and/or exhibit natural monopoly char-acteristics. As with many other forms of public infrastructure, this appears to be true of precautions such as construction of dams, levees, dikes, and other forms of flood works where public involvement would seem likely to yield more socially optimal levels of investment than purely private deci-sion making. This may also be the case with respect to various forms of information that exhibit public goods characteristics—for example, the generation and provision of information relating to the underlying risks and expected costs of locating in vulnerable areas, weather forecasts of impending storms and their likely severity, and so forth. However, in each instance, the case for the superiority of government as opposed to private delivery (or, at least, subsidization) of the goods and services in question requires careful analysis. Governments, for instance, may not be the most efficient supplier of a structural mitigation project, and private sector development, albeit with public sector subsidization, may be optimal (Daniels and Trebilcock 1996). In a similar vein, reductions in the cost of information gathering and analysis as a result of technological innovation, coupled with the existence of endemic agency costs within government bureaucracies, may negate the desirability of vesting government with an exclusive role in this area. Finally, irrespective of whether government directly supplies or subsidizes a structural mitigation project, we have yet to discuss the nature or scale of investment by government that might be socially optimal with respect to these kinds of precautions, which is an issue we return to below.

Beyond public investments in *ex ante* precautions or information, there is a more debatable case for government provision or subsidization of insurance for the risks associated with these natural disasters on the grounds that private insurance markets are unlikely to work well or at all in these contexts. Kunreuther and Roth argue that market failures in the insurance industry are a result of ambiguity, correlated risk, adverse selec-tion, and moral hazard (1998). The problem of correlated risk is particu-larly acute in the contexts of concern to us. A crucial feature of insurance markets is risk aggregation, also known as the law of large numbers, which specifies that for a series of independent and identically distributed ran-dom variables, the variance of the average amount of the claim payment decreases as the number of claims increases. However, catastrophic risks of the kind we are considering are not independent variables; rather the risks are highly correlated, meaning that numerous losses occur simultaneously from a single event. Private insurers who write hurricane, flood, or earthquake insurance in disaster-prone areas are carrying an extremely risky portfolio of policies, which risk can only be partly mitigated through laying off the risk through re-insurance. Thus, there is the threat of insurer bankruptcy when losses eclipse the assets that insurers have on hand. Compounding the problems with private insurance is the existence of endemic cycles in insurance markets that periodically cause the withdrawal of insurance coverage from the market, and which make it difficult for consumers to secure comprehensive insurance against certain risks at any price. Thus, purely private, unsubsidized hurricane, flood and earthquake insurance is either not available at all in disaster-prone areas of the U.S. or is extremely expensive, pricing many consumers, especially low-income consumers, out of the market.

Whether government can mitigate these failures or limitations of private insurance markets is controversial. Kaplow (1986) and Priest (1996) both take the view that government-provided insurance does not reduce the risk faced by government, relative to private insurers, but simply spreads it over the body of citizens at large, at least if rates do not reflect the actuarially fair rates for different risk classes of the population, and is in effect a form of income redistribution from them either as taxpayers or as mandatory rate-payers to individuals who choose to locate in disaster prone areas, but who do not now face the full costs of their decisions. On this view, problems of adverse selection and moral hazard that private insurance markets have to manage (through deductibles and co-insurance, for instance) are exacerbated, not mitigated. To the extent that government abandons any attempt to price this insurance or to require its purchase, and instead relies on *ex post* disaster relief, these adverse selection and moral hazard problems will be even further exacerbated.

A distributive justice perspective, at least in its Rawlsian form (which focuses on the welfare of the least advantaged members of society), would assign overriding weight to public policies that benefit these citizens. Because individuals who settle in disaster prone areas are often disproportionately (but by no means exclusively) representative of least advantaged groups (as in the case of Hurricane Katrina), in part because property values and rentals in disaster-prone areas tend to be lower than in other areas, their plight will engage the special concern of distributive justice theorists and are likely to elicit support from them for investments in *ex ante* precautions and for generous forms of *ex post* disaster relief—in sharp contrast to the previous normative perspectives.

A communitarian perspective, like a distributive justice perspective, tends to focus on the effects of a natural disaster and not its causes. Communitarians see individuals as incomplete and unintelligible outside their social relationships and social context and are likely to favor generous government investments in *ex ante* precautions to protect vulnerable communities and generous *ex post* disaster relief assistance to help rebuild existing community and social organizations and the social networks surrounding them. Conversely, in contrast to a distributive justice perspective, they are likely to disfavor policies that would entail relocation of individuals and families to less disaster prone areas, such as may be entailed in some forms of voucher proposals (see Glaeser 2002), or proposals to adopt stringent zoning and building code laws that would compel relocation of many existing residents to other communities. Equally, they are likely to be opposed to mass public housing projects such as the 300,000 unit trailer parks that FEMA has proposed (*The Economist* 2005b, 29, 30) on the grounds that by concentrating members of least advantaged groups in these artificial "communities," all the social and economic pathologies that low-income housing analysts have identified with mass public housing projects in the past would be exacerbated, creating the antitheses of vibrant, well-functioning communities (see Daniels and Trebilcock 2005). Of course, this still begs the question on where (and how) citizens displaced by a disaster should be located.

The lack of congruence among these major normative perspectives on both the rationales for government intervention in natural disasters and the choice of instruments that might be deployed by government to vindicate these rationales is, of course, disconcerting and significant. As we have already acknowledged, we have no meta-theory that enables us to resolve these fundamental incongruencies or to rank these normative perspectives in order of normative salience in a particular context. Moreover, this incongruence carries with it a political risk that politicians motivated to act only by virtue of a political support maximization imperative will be able to find normative cover for these self-serving policies in one or another of the above perspectives, enabling them to appeal not only to the self-interest of beneficiaries of policies espoused for this reason, but also to the values of other citizens who do not share these interests. Thus, almost any politically self-serving policy can be given a veneer of an apparently plausible normative justification. This problem of political dissembling or opportunism is particularly acute in the case of the natural shocks of the kind that we are considering, where the costs entailed are typically geographically concentrated, while many of the potential policy responses entail spreading the costs of intervention diffusely over a much broader base of citizens and tax payers, rendering the beneficiaries of these policies much more politically salient than the cost-bearers.

How can this daunting dilemma be addressed? Here we believe that

Lindblom provides useful advice (1959). When disagreement over the most important value to be pursued in a particular policy context is insurmountable—and such disagreements are legion in practice—government decision makers and their critics should focus on particular policies, rather than on values in the abstract. When trade-offs of incommensurable values are involved, the response in the specific case may require identifying particular policy options in order to evaluate the normative objectives in a meaningful way. That is to say, a given policy instrument may have enormous long-run negative efficiency consequences, while only modestly, or at all, advancing other normative objectives relative to other policy options. Again, certain policy options motivated by distributive justice or communitarian concerns may have less deleterious long-run efficiency consequences than other policies motivated by these concerns. None of these trade-offs can be brought sharply into focus in the abstract, but require evaluating one policy instrument against another in a particular context in terms of their relative impacts on this range of normative values or objectives. In this spirit, we turn briefly to a review of two case studies that we have developed in our previous work that we think usefully illuminate this approach, the 1993 U.S. Midwest flood and the 1997 Red River flood (both of which we acknowledge, while serious disasters in their own right, entail dramatically more limited economic and social consequences than Hurricane Katrina),[1] and extend the policy implications of these two case studies to Hurricane Katrina.

The 1993 U.S. Midwest Flood, the 1997 Red River Flood, and Hurricane Katrina

In 1993, unusually heavy snowmelt, excessive and prolonged rainfall in the upper Mississippi River Valley and the Great Plains, and subsequent soil saturation combined to produce one of the most damaging disaster events in U.S. history. At their peak, the floodwaters covered approximately 20 million acres of land in nine states. The flood was estimated to have caused 52 deaths and property damage in the amount of $12.7 billion to 70,000 homes and buildings, and to have left more than 74,000 people homeless. Total economic losses were approximately $18 billion. Although the flood-affected area contains only 10 percent of the population, it supports nearly 20 percent of all farm employment. The flood destroyed 5.1 million acres of corn and 3.1 million acres of soybeans. The closure of the upper Mississippi River rendered more than 2,000 barges idle for nearly two months and produced losses to barge companies in the amount of $600 million. Rail traffic was also brought to a standstill. Physical damage to railroads and revenue losses ran in the amount of $240 million and $169 million respectively. A history of flooding in these areas has driven down property values, with housing in low-lying regions available at the time at prices below $25,000, meaning that lower-income households, elderly couples, young families, people on assistance, and mobile-home dwellers often inhabit flood plains.

Four years later in 1997, a combination of extreme natural circumstances, including high soil moisture, heavy winter snow fall, and a major late spring blizzard, produced what was dubbed the flood of the century in the Red River Valley, first hitting North Dakota in mid-April and then spilling northward into Manitoba. North Dakota was severely affected: 40 percent of the state's economy directly depends on agricultural production, and close to two million acres of farmland were left submerged. Floodwaters were estimated to have immersed 90 percent of the town of Grand Forks and damaged 11,000 houses and buildings. The National Weather Service drastically underestimated the depth of the approaching torrent by four feet (arguably negligently), enough to drown the whole town, and discouraging feasible emergency mitigation measures. Down river, Manitoba had more time to adjust forecasts of the impacts of flooding and to prepare accordingly but the damage was still considerable. In all, 28,000 Manitobans were evacuated from flood risk areas, and 5,200 residences and businesses were damaged. The flood inundated 5 percent of Manitoba's farmland—some 200,000 hectares. The damage would have been worse, especially in Winnipeg, the provincial capital, were it not for the Red River Floodway, a forty-seven-kilometer channel completed in 1968, which directs a portion of the Red River to flow around Winnipeg during floods. Unfortunately, two nearby towns, Saint Agathe and Grand Pointe were severely damaged in the flooding, in part as a result of the diversion of water away from Winnipeg through the Floodway and related ring dikes.

In both the Midwest and Red River floods, structural flood control projects continue to play an important role in the management of the flood plains. As of 1996, Myers reports that the U.S. federal government had spent over $11 billion to protect the country's flood plains through levees, dams, and reservoir projects (Myers 1996). However, Grand Forks did not have much permanent flood protection in place at the time of the Red River flood, relying instead largely on hastily constructed, temporary dikes to keep the flood waters out, a situation in stark contrast to that in Manitoba, which had a good deal of permanent flood protection. The Manitoba Water Commission reports that in the absence of the Floodway, which cost a total of $63 million to build, losses within the city of Winnipeg could have reached 5 billion to 7 billion Canadian dollars (as opposed to about $37 million actually incurred). The U.S. Army Corps of Engineers estimates that the levees and dams prevented more than $19 million in potential damages in large cities such as Kansas City and St. Louis in the

Midwest floods (Iacobucci et al. 2001). In the U.S. Midwest, the few cities that were flooded were those protected only by privately built levees that were not well constructed. The suburbs and agricultural lands did not fare well either; several suburbs suffered severe damage and hundreds of thousands of acres of farmland and countless homes and businesses in nine Midwestern states were swamped. The waters that flooded agricultural land mostly broke through or swept over levees not as tall as those guarding the cities.

At first blush this evidence suggests that investments in structural flood control projects have large social pay-offs that more than justify the expenditures involved. However, some caution here is required. For example, the comparison above of the costs of the projects relative to losses avoided are misleading in that these losses need to be, first, discounted by the probability of their occurrence, and second, discounted to present value terms so that up-front expenditures on structural flood control projects can be accurately compared with their expected benefits (in present value terms) (Posner 2004). Thus, to take the case of Hurricane Katrina and New Orleans, some estimates of potential federal assistance to New Orleans run, in an extreme case, as high as $200 billion, which of course does not include the 1,000 deaths entailed or costs incurred by other levels of government or private costs incurred by homeowners, businesses, local residents and insurers (Glaeser 2005). Generally, these kinds of damage figures are often compared with the much smaller costs of maintaining or improving the levee system around New Orleans. Whether this expenditure is socially justified or not can only be determined by comparing it with the expected benefits of the expenditure which is presumably the cost of another major hurricane discounted by the probability of its occurrence over the useful life of these levees and discounted again to present value terms. Thus, it cannot be the case that spending, for instance, up to $200 billion on structural flood control projects, or anything like this, could be socially justified. Richard Posner gives the following example ("Lessons of Katrina" forthcoming):

A study in 1998 had estimated that New Orleans could be made safer—but not completely safe—against flooding caused by powerful hurricanes, at a cost of $14 billion, by restoring and sustaining Louisiana's coastal ecosystem. The Army Corps of Engineers had estimated a close to 1/300 annual probability of a disastrous flood, and that equates to a probability of almost 9 percent over a 30-year period. That is a high probability, but a $14 billion expenditure that would not make New Orleans safe, but only safer, may not have been cost-justified after all. Suppose the damage inflicted by such a flood were estimated at $200 billion; then, as a first approximation, preventive measures that reduced the probability of the flood from, say 9 percent to 3 percent would not be cost justified if they cost more that $12 billion (6 percent of $200 billion).

For smaller communities and agricultural land, with low density populations, erecting effective levees the length of the Gulf Coast is unlikely to make any economic sense. Moreover, costs and benefits need to be compared at the margin. As Posner notes, even a substantial additional expenditure on levees and the like is unlikely to reduce to zero the expected costs of a future hurricane of Hurricane Katrina's intensity or worse (and, even if it would, there are still substantial time lags in constructing these changes that would entail risks for residents). That is to say, one could, for example, raise levees by two feet (or increase their thickness) and reduce expected costs of a hurricane somewhat, raise them four feet and reduce expected costs somewhat more, and so forth, but any sensible assessment of socially justified investments in structural flood control will surely mean that there is some residual risk for residents of these areas that require control or insurance by individual citizens. Given this residual risk, levees may give people a false sense of security, but in any event will have the effect of encouraging more intensive habitation and development of the flood plains, and discourage what may be a socially less costly mitigation strategy, such as securing crop insurance for flooding of agricultural land, or relocation. In other words, the socially optimal level of investment in structural flood control projects can only be determined relative to costs and benefits at the margin of alternative *ex ante* and *ex post* mitigation strategies. *Ex ante* a major natural disaster, there may be a tendency to ignore or under-estimate low-probability risks and under-invest in precautions (Kunreuther 1996). Politicians will rationally neglect the need to invest in low-probability events if they believe that the occurrence of such an event is likely to occur outside their expected tenure in government and they will therefore will not suffer any personal consequence from having under-invested in socially desirable projects. Their failure to invest is further assured by the lack of sustained attention that media gives to the prospect of low-probability events (at least as against other more concrete "here and now" issues) and the coordination problems that interested citizens face in advocating for such investment. *Ex post* a disaster, influenced by the availability heuristic, there may be the opposing danger of over-investment in *ex ante* precautions Sunstein 2002). This is particularly problematic when reliance on these precautions limit use of more efficient solutions such as subsidized citizen re-location to safer and perhaps more economically dynamic communities.

Even if politicians were minded to make socially optimal investments in structural mitigation in relation to low probability events, there is still the challenge of who can be entrusted with the task of undertaking robust cost-benefit analyses of alternative projects. Quite apart from the difficulties that inhere in making accurate assessments of the likelihood of different stochastic events, cost-benefit analysis is notoriously vulnerable to manipulation as a result of the scope for choice in selecting different values for the costs of injury, the benefits of prevention and discount rates.

Nevertheless, structural flood control measures are congenial to many of the normative perspectives reviewed above. First, they are likely, up to some level, to be efficient social investments. Second, they reduce the expected costs of flooding to least advantaged citizens. And thirdly, they protect and preserve existing communities. And quite apart from the normative perspectives we have identified, use of structural flood control measures has desirable political properties because of the symbolic value to politicians of demonstrating progress on an issue. For libertarians, however, such expenditures are likely to be less congenial, particularly if they are not financed either privately or collectively by the residents of these disaster-prone areas themselves, but by taxpayers in other communities who are, in effect, being coerced into underwriting the locational choices of others.

Before the 1993 U.S. Midwest flood, no North American jurisdiction had employed buy-out and relocation strategies to reduce the consequences of natural disasters, but they emerged at the forefront of U.S. federal flood reforms as an instrument warranting attention along with that of structural control works. Under the Hazard Mitigation and Assistance Act of 1993, Congress legislated that funds be made available for projects to acquire and demolish homes that should not be rebuilt, to elevate at-risk buildings or relocate them to higher ground, and flood proof at-risk structures (Quinn, 1996). Several communities accepted the federal government's proposal and removed homes and businesses from flood plains. Within three years of the 1993 Midwest flood, the federal government, with the aid of state and local governments, had removed or relocated more than 8,000 families from flood hazard areas in the Mississippi and Missouri water basins and, in the process, converted more than 100,000 acres of partially flooded farmlands into wetlands, which serve as a sponge for rising waters, and offer an attractive alternative for meeting future flood control needs. Commentators estimated that when the program was implemented it would save some $200 million over twenty years, even without another near record flood, and that while the initial cost of relocating communities would be substantial, the price would be a one-time only payment and people in these communities, once moved, would never be returned to the flood plain and taxpayers would never again have to pay literally to bail them out of a problem that had been anticipated. Government could simply make it illegal for individuals and communities to return, credibly committing itself not to compensate future flood victims and therefore alleviating the moral hazard that may explain many people's decision to stay on the flood plains. The difficulty of making a credible political commitment not to help flooded communities may be a major reason why subsidized relocation is economically desirable; it helps government to commit itself not to help those who do not relocate. However, the U.S. buy-out program has not been without its controversies. Economists at the University of Missouri estimated that their state would lose $200 million U.S. a year in economic activity and 3,200 jobs if farmers cease planting in the flood plain. As a result, the federal government and the landowners sought a compromise that would move many homeowners out of the flood plain while leaving farmers and businesses there if they insure themselves against the flood risk. The insurance requirement would help solve the problem of farmers not internalizing the risks associated with agriculture on flood plains. Of course, another difficulty with buyouts emanates from the adverse impact on the welfare of government officials (both elected and unelected) in the jurisdiction having experienced a natural disaster. Outward migration necessarily entails a loss in the number of residents and the size of the tax base, and may trigger a contraction in the size and influence of local government that invites a backlash from residents remaining in future elections.

A variant on this strategy has been proposed by Harvard economist Edward Glaeser (2005). Glaeser notes that New Orleans reached its peak of economic importance to the U.S. in 1840. New Orleans began to decline, in absolute terms, in 1960. Its population declined from 627,000 residents in 1960 to about 445,000 in 2004. The 2000 Census reported that more than 27% of New Orleans' residents were in poverty (relative to 12% for the U.S. as a whole). The New Orleans median family income was only 64% of the median family income in the U.S., and in 2004 the unemployment rate for the city was over 11%. Glaeser argues that there is a big difference between rebuilding lives and rebuilding communities. He invites us to imagine that on one scenario we will spend $100 billion on infrastructure for the residents of the city, but on an alternative scenario, we would give each one of the city of New Orleans residents a check for more than $200,000—enough to send several children to college, to buy a modest home, and/or to relocate and start a dreamed-of business. If this money were spread over the 1.33 million residents in the larger New Orleans metropolitan area, each resident would still receive $75,000, still enough to pay for a home in many areas of the country. This proposal, while provocative, needs further amplification and refinement.

First, although Hurricane Katrina did inflict significant concentrated losses on the residents of New Orleans, it is not clear that the *actual harm* suffered by many citizens (in terms of the loss of physical assets) is qualitatively different from losses that citizens routinely suffer in their housing and other investments as a result of different exogenous shocks that may, indeed, implicate deliberate government policy (such as trade liberalization, macro-economic adjustment policies). Further, as we point out in

Rethinking the Welfare State: The Prospects for Government by Voucher, voucher proposals such as Glaeser's raise some difficult design issues. Is the $200,000 check that he imagines for each resident of the city of New Orleans an untied cash transfer that they are free to spend on anything they like, rather akin to the proposal by Bruce Ackerman and Anne Alstott in *The Stakeholder Society* (1999), where they propose that every American citizen who has graduated from high school and avoided significant criminal activity would receive an untied flat grant of $80,000, to be spent as he or she sees fit—a proposal that has attracted a range of legitimate criticisms, including excessive expenditures on consumption or risky investments, predicated on the ability to externalize costs onto the social welfare system in the event of exhaustion of these resources (Daniels and Trebilcock 2005)? If these vouchers are tied, instead, to particular classes of goods or services, how are these conditions to be defined (in terms of eligibility for receipt of vouchers and on required forms of expenditure)? Moreover, in order to avoid severe moral hazard problems of people relocating in disaster-prone areas, would payment for housing amenities be conditional on relocating to non-disaster-prone areas—perhaps other cities in Texas or in neighboring states? (Daniels and Trebilcock 2005; Fiss 2003)[2] If the vouchers are so conditioned, this may attract objections from communitarians who will see such a scheme as undermining the pre-established social fabric of communities in New Orleans (see Steven Gregory in Fiss 2003). On the other hand, it seems preferable, perhaps even on communitarian criteria, to FEMA proposals to build massive trailer parks of up to 300,000 units in New Orleans, which seems scarcely designed to promote vibrant and well-functioning communities. Libertarians may also be concerned that personal choices are being coerced through conditions attaching to receipt of these vouchers. One option may be, as in the 1993 U.S. Midwest floods, to allow people to remain in flood-prone areas, but only on the condition that they obtain and maintain a specified minimum level of coverage of flood and hurricane insurance, and that this condition is more effectively enforced with respect to all residents than it has been in the past. However, such a decision should not qualify for eligibility for a voucher designed to induce individuals to relocate to safer communities. Again, here a critical issue is the credibility of government pre-commitments and not the bailing out, through recurrent disaster relief, of people who choose to make risky locational decisions. Finally, what is the argument for a universal voucher for all citizens of New Orleans, irrespective of means or losses incurred? At the present time, there is discussion that FEMA intends to make housing vouchers available to all residents whose homes were located in areas (as determined by aerial surveys) that suffered the greatest damage even without a demonstration that the prospective recipient did not hold insurance or did in fact suffer damage. From a distributive justice perspective, there would be much more to be said for targeting these vouchers on a means-tested basis on low-income citizens of New Orleans and other affected communities (see Daniels and Trebilcock 2005).

Some jurisdictions have used zoning regulations to prevent habitation or development of the highest risk areas of flood plains. However, higher levels of government have difficulty in promoting such regulations, because of the need to garner cooperation from local governments with jurisdiction over zoning issues and who often have been unwilling to impose or enforce such regulations because of the desire for unconstrained development and the larger property tax base that this entails, given the ability to externalize the costs of disaster relief to higher levels of government. It is indeed noteworthy that despite the frequency of natural disasters suffered by Louisiana, the state is viewed as having chronically lax building code and zoning requirements. Just as one is properly concerned about individuals externalizing onto others some or all of the costs of their locational decisions through the provision of disaster relief assistance, there is also legitimate concern over inter-jurisdictional externalities where one level of government externalizes all or part of the costs of its decisions onto other levels of government. One option that the U.S. federal government has pursued in the past is to address the problem of misaligned local government incentives by linking the provision of federally subsidized insurance to communities to the development and enforcement of zoning legislation and building standards designed to mitigate the consequences of natural disasters. One concern with this set of policies is that they may impose an overwhelming economic burden on those who have to replace or repair their property or also elevate or relocate their homes or businesses—a burden that is likely to be most severe for low- or fixed-income individuals and families and may engage the concerns of distributive justice proponents. Thus, it is likely that policies relying on zoning regulations and building standards would have to be linked to buy-out and relocation policies. Moreover, there are inherent limits to the application of zoning regulations and building standards, rendering them applicable only to the highest-risk areas of natural disaster-prone regions. For example, zoning all of New Orleans as non-residential is unrealistic, so that (or with structural mitigation measures) residual risks will remain. Thus, in a second-best world where the credibility of government pre-commitments is a serious issue, they might be persuaded to accept as unavoidable, a combination of buy-out/relocation and zoning regulation and building standard policies that constrain individual choices if adverse selection and moral hazard problems are to be contained in individual locational decisions that are predicated on externalizing a are sensitive to the difficulties of quantifying a number of criti[...] and are also sensitive to the noneconomic values that nat[...] legitimately engage. However, at least a cost-benefit fra[...] Richard Posner argues in his recent book), sensibly deployed[...] to identify a zone of potential policies that fall within what h[...] erable windows approach," and which set of policies fall out[...] erable windows (Posner, 2004). It seems clear to us that[...] policies relating to natural disasters fall outside the tolerabl[e...] socially optimal policies or normatively defensible trade-offs a[...] and instruments. Moreover, making up these policies on[...] atmosphere of crisis after a disaster has occurred not only r[...] of inappropriate policies for the current crisis, but perhap[s...] seriously exacerbates the risk of future policy errors by furth[...] ing a political precedent or path dependency effect that c[...] mous shadow over the U.S. government's already pre[...] imbalance.

future residents who choose to remain in numerous means-tested inducements to relo- would be available to current (but not ing restrictions or building code require- costs of new policies.

t in any such combination of policies is ally constructed links between helpless vic- ibed by Landis, and strengthening politi- locational decisions can legitimately be responsibility and the exercise of moral at citizens that are especially constrained e burdens of race, class and poverty have to them beyond high-risk, low-priced dis- ppropriately designed means-tested relo- , would assume a special importance. For main in these areas, confronting the full ecisions with respect to the residual risks ced by structural mitigation measures, lly subsidized disaster insurance seems a them to bear, given that they have chosen y available, less disaster-prone locational

Notes

We gratefully acknowledge helpful comments on earlier drafts of t[...] Richard Posner, Edward Iacobucci, Peter Schuck, Owen Fiss, G[...] Anita Anand, Howard Kunreuther, Donald Kettl, Richard Brooks, [...] and Henry Hansmann, while absolving them from any responsibili[ty...] expressed herein.

1. For fuller development of these case studies, see Iacobucci et al[...] ter 5.

2. See Daniels and Trebilcock (2005), chapter 4, for proposals fo[r...] for low income citizens that attempt to respond to these kinds of[...] see Fiss (2003), for similar proposals for facilitating exit by low-inco[me...] urban ghettos.

3. Kunreuther (1996) largely discounts this explanation, base[d...] dence, and instead suggests that individuals routinely disregard ve[ry...] ity risks.

for a non-interventionist strategy on the g the risk or reality of natural disasters. fication from several normative perspec- itically completely unrealistic, given past rventions in such disasters. Thus, a strict on unconstrained individual freedom of Similarly, a strict communitarian perspec- preserving or reconstituting preexisting sters at the cumulative expense of mem- quite unrealistic. Rather, the focus must rious forms of intervention in the light of ative values of economic efficiency—util- distributive justice—canvassed earlier in critical challenge is ultimately a political ent credibly commit to a set of policies and politically sustainable (Elster 1984; r 2005)?

naire proponents of cost-benefit analysis,

large faction of the costs of those decisions onto other members of the community through disaster relief.

As noted earlier, private flood and hurricane insurance markets are almost non-existent in many parts of the U.S. In 1968, the U.S. Congress, in recognition of the limits of private disaster insurance markets, created the National Flood Insurance Program (NFIP) to provide relief from the impacts of flood damages in the form of federally subsidized flood insurance to participating communities, contingent on flood loss reduction measures embodied in local flood plain management regulations. However, despite the availability of subsidized insurance at rates that averaged only one-third of actuarial rates for such insurance, as at the time of the Midwest flood apparently only about one in four people on flood plains had bought it. This outcome seems attributable in part to the existence of extensive relief payments (but see Kunreuther 1996).[3] FEMA provides disaster relief that is generous enough to dissuade many people from purchasing insurance protection. For example, in total, insurance claims for the Midwest flood amounted to $250 million, in contrast to the $6.4 billion paid out in federal assistance (to repair public infrastructure as well as compensate individuals for losses). Apparently many property owners who were harmed by the 1993 flood and did not hold federal flood insurance nevertheless received federal disaster assistance in amounts nearly equal to benefits provided to property owners who were insured. The U.S. federal government has attempted to address some of these concerns. In September 1994, Congress passed the National Flood Insurance Reform Act which imposed penalties on lenders who do not ensure that mortgage holders obtain flood insurance; it also closed a loophole that allowed borrowers to drop the insurance after obtaining a mortgage. Further, after the Midwest flood, the NFIP was amended to provide coverage not simply for repairing flood damaged homes but also mitigation coverage that would enable an owner to pay for additional measures to prevent or reduce future flood damage, including relocating the structure or elevating the foundations or flood proofing. However, despite all these attempts to increase flood insurance coverage, the *Economist* magazine recently reported that in Mississippi's coastal areas, less than one in five households have flood insurance and in New Orleans under half (2005b, 30). Renters and those who own homes outright without mortgages are the most likely to be uncovered (*The Economist* 2005a).

In the wake of the 1993 Midwest flood, the U.S. Small Business Administration (SBA), which provides loans to businesses *inter alia* that suffer property and other economic losses stemming from a natural disaster, approved more than 20,000 subsidized loans. These loans, because in theory they must be repaid, involve (depending on the extent of the subsidy) greater internalization of costs of individual locational decisions than disaster relief. However, in practice businesses that have the most success in obtaining SBA disaster loans were those that would have qualified for commercial loans relatively easily and conversely the businesses that had least success in acquiring SBA loans were firms which would have found it difficult to qualify for and obtain private commercial loans, suggesting that the beneficiaries of loan subsidy and guarantee programs generally come from middle- and lower-middle-income strata and that the least advantaged are not much helped, offending some notions of distributive justice.

Federal disaster relief has a long history in the U.S., dating back to the last years of the eighteenth century and arguably provided much of the political genesis for the New Deal social welfare programs (Landis 1999; Landis 1998; Moss 1999). As Michele Landis argues, social and political construction of claimants for relief as helpless victims of external forces beyond their control ("Acts of God") have exerted an enduring influence on American political discourse, which has manifested itself in heavy reliance on prior political precedents and analogies in constructing responses to current disasters ("natural," social or economic) (see also Bumiller 1998). Some political constituencies have invoked the precedents and analogies to argue for a broader social safety net, while other constituencies have invoked the helpless victims of uncontrollable forces to argue for a minimalist U.S. social welfare system.

After both the 1993 Midwest flood and the 1997 Red River flood, the U.S. Congress authorized large amounts of funding in emergency aid. In the context of Hurricane Katrina, President Bush has promised to do "whatever it takes" to rebuild New Orleans and other affected Gulf Coast communities, with enormous figures for federal assistance being frequently quoted—up to the $200 billion range. However, *ex post* disaster relief, as already noted, has all kinds of perverse incentive effects, severely exacerbating problems of adverse selection and moral hazard in locational decisions by enabling residents of disaster-prone areas to externalize a large fraction of the cost of their locational decisions onto other members of the community. Hurricanes are an annual occurrence on the Gulf Coast (albeit not of the severity of Katrina). As Priest notes, studies of the 1993 Midwest flood demonstrate sustained and repeated losses from disasters, year after year, in the same counties or states (Priest 1996). Tom Szilaszi, a building commissioner in St. Charles County, Missouri, was quoted in *Newsweek* (August 2, 1993) as saying, "Taxpayers have bought some of these people refrigerators and chainsaws ten times over." These relief programs not only create perverse incentives at the individual level, but provide disincentives for states and communities to develop effective flood prevention strategies because they fail to internalize the costs of natural disasters, given the knowledge that federal disaster relief is available.

Social Inequality, Hazards, and Disasters

KATHLEEN TIERNEY

Social science research on disasters began in the early twentieth century with the publication of Samuel Henry Prince's sociology doctoral dissertation on the 1917 Halifax explosion (Prince 1920). However, disaster research did not begin to coalesce as a field until pioneering research was carried out by the National Academy of Sciences and the National Opinion Research Center in the early 1950s, as research teams were sent into the field to collect data on individual, group, and organizational responses to disasters (see Fritz and Marks 1954). The Disaster Research Center, established in 1963 at the Ohio State University and now located at the University of Delaware, continued the practice of conducting "quick-response" studies following major disasters, with an emphasis on organizational and community response. Over subsequent decades, other research centers were established both nationally and internationally. The terrorist attacks of September 11, 2001 generated additional interest in disaster research, as questions were raised concerning a range of topics, including behavioral, psychological, and social-psychological responses to terrorism.

Classic sociological research on disasters emphasized the pro-social and adaptive dimensions of disaster-related behavior. Studies consistently documented such patterns as widespread helping behavior among community residents, the emergence of new groups focusing on victim and community needs, increases in social cohesion, the convergence of volunteers and material resources into disaster areas, and the suspension of community conflicts as community residents and public and private-sector organizations put aside their pre-disaster agendas in the interest of overcoming disaster-induced challenges. Disasters were framed in the literature as "consensus" crises and contrasted with "conflict" crises such as riots. Outcomes following disasters include the emergence of "therapeutic communities" that support victims and maintain high community morale. Therapeutic communities help to cushion the negative psychological consequences of disasters, and as a result, negative psycho-social reactions tend to be short-lived following disasters (see Fritz 1961; Barton 1969; Dynes 1970; Stallings and Quarantelli 1985; Drabek 1986).

Ongoing research on disasters provides additional support for these earlier empirical findings. At the same time, it has become increasingly evident that earlier consensus-oriented perspectives paid insufficient attention to the diverse ways in which individuals, groups, and communities experience disasters. In contrast with classic studies, newer research has emphasized those diverse experiences. Research has also shown how disaster-related experiences are shaped in important ways by the same dimensions of stratification and inequality that influence people's lives during non-disaster times. Disaster scholarship now recognizes that factors such as wealth and poverty, race and ethnicity, gender and age influence vulnerability to hazards, disaster victimization, and disaster recovery outcomes (Blaikie et al. 1994; Peacock, Morrow, and Gladwin 1997; Bolin and Stanford 1998; Fothergill 1998).

As a consequence of these developments, disasters are no longer seen as producing common or typical challenges for at-risk populations. While morale and cohesiveness may undoubtedly be high within some groups within a disaster-stricken community, other groups may be excluded. Post-disaster experiences that are therapeutic for some may be corrosive for others. Some groups may be able to return to their pre-disaster status with relatively difficulty, while others may never fully recover. And to a greater degree than has been recognized before, disasters may become arenas not only for consensus-based social action but also for contentious intergroup interactions. Measures taken to deal with disasters may be welcomed by some groups but denounced by others. Relief programs may benefit some within the population while disadvantaging others

Research also shows that groups are differentially vulnerable and also differentially resilient in the face of disasters, depending upon their position in the stratification system. The sections that follow discuss recent advances in the study of the social factors that affect disaster vulnerability and that contribute to resilience in the face of disasters. Using examples from both Hurricane Katrina and other U.S. disasters, these discussions illustrate how large-scale social trends, structural forces, and group characteristics influence preparedness for, responses to, and recovery from disasters. A key point made in these discussions is that while Hurricane Katrina revealed the devastating consequences of social inequality more vividly than any recent U.S. disaster, Katrina has a great deal in common with other disasters the nation has experienced. One implication of these findings is that diverse patterns of vulnerability and resilience must be taken into consideration both in programs that provide disaster aid and in overall planning frameworks for disaster loss reduction.

Inequality, Vulnerability, and Resilience

Disasters have long been recognized as arising from the juxtaposition of physical events or disaster agents, vulnerable natural and built environments, and vulnerable populations. This way of conceptualizing disasters was originally articulated by geographer Gilbert White and his collaborators. Their work emphasized the importance of understanding how those three systems—physical, infrastructural, and social—produce the potential for harm and damage within specific geographic and social contexts. It also sought to elucidate factors affecting human "adjustments" to hazards, which consist of protective actions and decisions that are carried out (or, quite often, not carried out) to protect societies and communities from disaster losses. Adjustments include a range of activities, including outright avoidance of hazardous places, land-use measures, protective public works such as levees, hazard-resistant building codes, disaster planning and preparedness, and evacuation under threat conditions (Burton, Kates, and White 1978, 1993). This line of research also recognized that both knowledge about potential adjustments and the ability to carry out such measures are socially structured.

More recently, a new multidisciplinary approach to hazards and disasters, known as vulnerability science, has begun to systematically explore disaster vulnerability as a function of both physical place and social conditions that expose some social groups to the potential for greater harm and that limit their ability to cope when disasters strike. Vulnerability science seeks to explore the various dimensions of physical and social vulnerability as well as the societal, political, and economic forces that expose people and places to potential loss. The vulnerability science perspective is equally concerned with analyzing factors that help make different social units (such as households, businesses, communities) more resilient—that is, able to avoid and withstand disaster impacts and capable of rapidly recovering from whatever events they experience.

The influential book *At Risk: Natural Hazards, People's Vulnerability, and Disasters* (Blaikie et al. 1994), which looked at disasters and their impacts in a global context, laid out a framework for conceptualizing vulnerability as rooted in unsustainable development practices, social conditions and trends that diminish the coping capacity of at-risk populations, and extreme events that act as catalysts, producing casualties, physical damage, and other types of losses. Within this perspective, geologic, atmospheric, and other types of physical events are seen only as "triggers" that must be distinguished from the root causes of disasters, which are social, political, and economic. The key to understanding disaster impacts and outcomes thus lies in the ability to recognize how long-term, macro-level trends and everyday life conditions set the stage for disaster events.

Recent contributions to vulnerability science include the work of geographer Susan Cutter and her collaborators. Using the techniques of spatial social science, database development, and quantitative data analysis, Cutter and others have developed a variety of methods for assessing and modeling social vulnerability and disaster-related losses. Their social vulnerability indices make it possible to compare place-based and group vulnerabilities across U.S. communities and over time. Additionally, new methodologies that integrate population characteristics, hazard vulnerability, and locational data enable both researchers and practitioners to identify factors that contribute most to vulnerability within specific community contexts (Cutter, 2001).

Employing the vulnerability science framework, Cutter (2005) recently linked the Hurricane Katrina catastrophe to several factors. With respect to physical vulnerability, New Orleans was a large urban area, located below sea level and surrounded by water. Faith in the ability of technology to conquer nature led to the development of a complex system of levees and other public works, while an extensive pumping system was also developed to keep the city dry. Both the levees and the pumps failed during Hurricane Katrina.

With respect to social trends, the movement of African Americans from rural areas to the city during the twentieth century was followed by the flight of white and middle class residents from the city to the suburbs. Demographically, New Orleans became a majority black, poor city with few employment and educational opportunities. Both the infrastructure and the housing stock in the city were substandard. The city's population came increasingly to be made up of what social scientists and emergency management professionals refer to as "special populations," including residents who were very poor, elderly, disabled, and otherwise unable to function well on their own. Such groups typically lack the ability to evacuate cities without substantial assistance—assistance they did not receive during Hurricane Katrina, with tragic results. They also require specially tailored forms of support during disasters, such as emergency and temporary shelter arrangements capable of addressing their medical needs. Again, no such provisions were made during Katrina for those types of supportive services. Nor was assistance available for ill and disabled hospitalized and institutionalized disaster victims.

Cutter observes that the roots of social vulnerability and resilience are complex, encompassing (2005) "the basic provision of health care, the livability of places, overall indicators of quality of life, and accessibility to lifelines (goods, services, and emergency response personnel), capital, and political representation." By these standards, large segments of the population of New Orleans were indeed highly vulnerable, both on an everyday basis and with respect to extreme events. The magnitude of the hurricane, the city's precarious geographical location, and social conditions that rendered many residents incapable of helping themselves, and the unbelievably incompetent governmental response combined to produce the worst natural disaster in U.S. history.[1]

Knowing that social inequities are correlated with disaster vulnerability is not the same as being able to explain causal linkages and processes that shape vulnerability. The section that follows will focus on how and why social inequality translates into vulnerability for subpopulations within the U.S., as well as how broader social circumstances either enhance or undermine social resilience. Discussions will incorporate examples from the Katrina disaster, but will also focus on other recent U.S. disasters, again making the point that the same patterns of vulnerability and victimization that have been documented following Katrina were also found in other disaster events. Three dimensions of social inequality—social class, race and ethnicity, and gender—will be discussed separately. However, discussions will also stress that these axes of stratification intersect and interact with one another, and in turn produce a variety of impacts on life-safety, economic well-being, and other disaster-related experiences.

Axes of Inequality and Their Effects on At-Risk Populations

Social class position is perhaps the most obvious contributor to disaster vulnerability and resilience. Just as higher socioeconomic status confers benefits during non-disaster times, dimensions of social class, including education and income, affect the ability to engage in self-protective activities across all phases in the hazard cycle. Educational achievements and literacy competence influence access to information on disaster risks and risk-reduction measures. Social class influences media use, which in turn helps structure what people learn about both the scientific and social dimensions of hazards. Home ownership, which is positively associated with socio-economic status, is also associated with the willingness and ability to undertake actions oriented toward property protection, but the poor cannot afford to own their own homes. In contrast with homeowners, renters are dependent on their landlords to carry out activities that can reduce disaster vulnerability, such as making routine repairs and improvements, complying with building and safety codes, and carrying out specific disaster loss-reduction measures. Since undertaking such actions costs money, landlords will generally not do so voluntarily. For example, many of the units that are available to low-income renters in Los Angeles are located in older unreinforced masonry buildings that present a life-safety hazard in earthquakes. To ensure the passage of legislation to structurally retrofit these highly hazardous buildings, seismic safety advocates had to fight for many years to overcome organized opposition by landlords who wanted to avoid the costs associated with building retrofits (Alesch and Petak 1986)

After disasters strike, renters are also dependent on the willingness and ability of landlords to rebuild and repair their rental properties. Following the 1994 Northridge earthquake, for example, many apartment complexes became vacant and blighted "ghost towns" because owners lacked the wherewithal to repair their buildings (Stallings 1996). Renters were given temporary rental assistance but were left to fend for themselves when that assistance ran out. Fortunately, vacancy rates in Los Angeles were relatively high in 1994, so rental units were available. That may not be the case when the next disaster strikes another large U.S. city.

Social class factors influence disaster vulnerability in a variety of other ways. The lack of affordable housing in U.S. metropolitan areas forces the poor to live in substandard housing that is often located in physically vulnerable areas and also to live in overcrowded housing conditions. Manufactured housing may be the only viable housing option for people with limited resources, but mobile homes can become death traps during hurricanes and tornadoes. The vulnerability of manufactured housing has become even more evident during the last two hurricane seasons in Florida. At a more general level, the risk of death, injury, and homelessness that low-income Americans face is connected to U.S. housing policies affecting the poor (Comerio 1998).

Many people with disabilities have difficulty carrying out self-protective actions during and following disasters. Rates of disability are higher for the poor than for their better-off counterparts. A study conducted during the 1980s in Los Angeles showed that disabled persons lived disproportionately in older unreinforced housing units (mainly apartment buildings) that lacked earthquake resistance (Tierney, Petak, and Hahn 1986). Many of those who are least able to care for themselves are doubly vulnerable when they live in unsafe structures.

Those who lack disposable income cannot upgrade vulnerable housing and undertake other recommended loss-reduction measures, such as stockpiling food and supplies for use during disasters Inability to afford the expenses associated with car ownership causes low-income community residents to rely on public transportation. However, community evacuation plans generally assume that residents have access to private automobiles. In New Orleans, for example, it was recognized that approximately 300,000 residents would not be able to evacuate on their own in a timely manner under the threat of a hurricane. Instead, they were dependent upon governmental capacity to bring in vehicles (and drivers) to assist with evacuation—capacity that was nonexistent in Hurricane Katrina.

Disaster evacuation scenarios are also based on other assumptions, such as the idea that in addition to having their own transportation, households also have the financial resources to leave endangered communities when ordered to do so. This is definitely not the case for the poor. Hourly workers risk losing income if they fail to show up for their jobs, whereas middle- and upper-middle-class employees can typically expect to continue to be paid if they are forced to evacuate. While the public may have an abstract understanding of what it means to earn little money and to live from paycheck to paycheck, there seems to be a lack of awareness of what that means in the context of disasters—for example, that many poor households across the country are not in a position to afford to evacuate under disaster conditions. Striking the Gulf Region on August, 29, Hurricane Katrina occurred at a time when many households living from paycheck to paycheck may well have had absolutely no resources that they could expend on bus fares—even if buses had been available—or hotel rooms. Higher-income residents of areas threatened by Katrina could afford enough high-priced gas to travel drive hundreds of miles to escape the storm if necessary, but the poor could not.

Affluence offers other levels of protection from disaster impacts that are not available to the poor. Home ownership makes it possible to purchase hazard insurance and also to access a wider range of disaster assistance programs. Salaried employees are typically able to take time off work to focus on coping with and recovering from disasters without losing their incomes. Social and cultural capital constitute resources that facilitate disaster coping and recovery. Well-off disaster victims typically have skills that the poor lack, such as knowing how to access resources and navigate bureaucratic requirements successfully. Better-off disaster victims are also more likely to have direct access to governmental and disaster assistance programs and more likely to have their concerns addressed. This greater ability to access diverse sources of aid and official program guidance following disasters is merely an extension of the privileges members of the middle and upper-middles classes enjoy during non-disaster times.

Judgments concerning who constitutes a "deserving" disaster victim are also shaped by social class factors. The poor are often characterized in media and official discourses as taking advantage of programs and entitlements following disasters and as responsible for the conditions under which they are forced to live. This victim-blaming pattern was shockingly evident during the Katrina disaster. Both the mass media and public officials characterized the poor and desperate disaster victims who were trapped in New Orleans as taking advantage of the disruption Katrina caused to engage in wanton and indiscriminate looting as well as violent attacks on fellow victims, businesses, shelter sites, and disaster response personnel. Poor and mostly African-American victims were simplistically framed either as looters and dangerous thugs or as "deserving" victims— mainly women and children—who were helpless and unable to care for themselves in the aftermath of the disaster. Missing from these accounts was any attempt to understand how poor African Americans aided and supported one another during the disaster through extended family arrangements and community-based organizations. Equating poverty and race with violence and dysfunctionality, news reports helped provide justification for the repressive measures that were applied to control disaster victims in New Orleans.

Poverty also causes families to have to "double up" in order to be able to make rent and house payments. Since the housing stock available to the poor tends to be substandard and often located in unsafe areas, the poor are at greater risk of becoming homeless when disasters strike. However, disaster assistance programs tend to be based on a "one housing unit, one household, one head of household" policy. The consequences of this policy were made evident following the 1989 Loma Prieta earthquake, which left many low-income Hispanic residents homeless. Because of economic need, these victims had been living in multi-family households, yet FEMA made disaster assistance funds available only to one household per living unit. The agency was later criticized for its failure to recognize that its policies unfairly discriminated against not only low-income households, but also the homeless and people in transient living situations (U.S. General Accounting Office 1991).

Like social class, *race and ethnicity* are also associated with differential vulnerability to disasters. In many cases this is because in the U.S. race and ethnicity are strongly correlated with social class. However, other factors that are specifically associated with these dimensions of stratification also have an independent influence on hazard-related behavior, disaster experiences, and disaster outcomes. For example, research indicates that members of ethnic subcultures differ from the mainstream white majority, and also from one another, in their perceptions regarding different risks, the extent to which they are embedded in social networks that can serve as a source of information on hazards and disaster assistance programs, where they turn to seek information during normal times and in disasters, and which hazard-related information sources they most trust (Turner, Nigg, and Heller Paz 1986; Perry and Lindell 1992; Flynn, Slovic, and Mertz 1994; Lindell and Perry 2005). African Americans typically lack trust in official information sources—a pattern that has undoubtedly been strengthened in the aftermath of Hurricane Katrina.

Members of racial and ethnic minorities are more likely than whites to live in large households, and often to live in extended family arrangements. These living patterns have implications for evacuation behavior. Decisions regarding evacuation are household decisions, not individual ones, and families prefer to evacuate as units. The larger the household, the more difficult such decisions become, especially in light of the costs associated with evacuating. There may be concerns about elderly and disabled family members, about whether evacuation will result in lost income, and about living conditions in public evacuation shelters, since often such shelters are the only places poor and minority group members can stay if they decide to leave their homes (Tierney, Lindell, and Perry 2001; Lindell and Perry 2005).

Non-English speaking minorities experience a range of problems with respect to hazards and disasters. Although some improvements have been made in making hazard-related information available in Spanish and some Asian languages, a large proportion of detailed guidance is available only in English. For example, despite being touted as an information source for the entire nation, the Department of Homeland Security's ready.gov website only contains information in English and Spanish. This is particularly ironic with respect to the terrorist threat, since residents of large urban centers, many of whom speak languages other than English and Spanish, are commonly thought to be most vulnerable to attack. Because multi-lingual and minority outreach programs are unavailable in all but a few communities nationwide, immigrants lacking experience with disasters in the U.S. may have very little understanding of the risks they face, what to do when disasters strike, or what types of emergency and longer-term assistance may be available to them. At the same time, officials seem not to recognize that providing information on web sites and in English isolates those who cannot afford computers, are not experienced in their use, and are not literate in English.

Warnings cannot be issued for all types of disasters, but even when they can, non-English speakers are again at a disadvantage with respect to receiving timely warning information. Warnings are issued in English and are disseminated most rapidly and clearly through mainstream English-speaking media. Warnings provided in languages other than English may be delayed or may lack sufficient detail to enable recipients to undertake necessary self-protective actions. For example, in May of 1987, a tornado struck Saragosa, Texas, a town with a population of 400, most of whom were Spanish-speaking. The local Spanish-language cable station that most people in the town watched did not broadcast the warnings that had been disseminated by the National Weather Service. The warnings that did get disseminated in Spanish were translated on the spot and, unlike the English-language warnings, they did not effectively communicate the severity and urgency of the tornado threat. They were also disseminated later than the warnings issued in English. The tornado killed thirty Saragosa residents and injured 120. A National Academy of Sciences report on the Saragosa disaster concluded that "warnings, to be effective, require either a common shared culture or an adaptation of the warning system to multicultural social contexts. In Saragosa neither requirement was satisfied" (Aguirre 1991).

It would be overly optimistic to think that the situation has improved since the 1980s. In fact the opposite may be the case. Population diversity is continuing to increase, as is the diversity of media sources to which people turn for information. Warning a diverse public is even more challenging in an era of increasingly specialized media use, "narrowcasting," and "pod-casting." While new technologies make communications media ubiquitous for many segments of the U.S. population, the implications of continuous information flows for disaster-related behavior have not been explored. Despite the plethora of new communications devices, vulnerable populations who need accurate and timely information most during crises may be the least likely to get it.

Members of immigrant and minority groups often respond differently to disasters than their white counterparts. Occasionally they also express group-specific grievances during disasters. In earthquakes in California, immigrants from Mexico and Central America, following practices in their native countries, have showed a distinct preference for sheltering outdoors, as opposed to going to indoor public shelters (Tierney 1988). Following the 1989 Loma Prieta earthquake, many Latino victims in Santa Cruz County refused to utilize official shelters. Instead, they set up improvised outdoor living arrangements in a city park. They did so not only out of concerns about sheltering indoors but also as a protest against the government's lack of responsiveness to the needs of the Latino community. They were concerned that their special circumstances would be ignored if they allowed themselves to be dispersed into Red Cross shelters (Simile 1995). There were grounds for those beliefs; official service providers had done little to address the needs of culturally diverse groups and had also failed to include the Latino community in pre-disaster planning (Phillips 1993).

Unlike members of the white majority, minority group members and immigrants must often deal with questions related to their citizenship status, even during disasters. Victims may lose citizenship and immigration documents in a disaster and may fear deportation if they attempt to use official shelters or apply for disaster aid (Phillips, Garza, and Neal 1994; Bolin and Stanford 1998). Again, those fears are not unfounded. A number of Hispanic and Haitian immigrants in South Florida were deported after Hurricane Andrew (Phillips, Garza, and Neal 1994). Eligibility for many disaster services is now predicated on proof of citizenship. Undocumented persons are typically eligible only for immediate emergency assistance (such as shelter services) and not for the full range of programs that are available to citizens.

Immigrants and minority group members also share a general mistrust of police and the military. Tensions have long existed between African Americans and the police in the U.S. Immigrants may have unpleasant and even traumatic memories of encounters with police, the military, and paramilitary groups in their native countries. Since 9-11, and especially since the creation of the Department of Homeland Security and the U.S. Northern Command (NORTHCOM), homeland security has been conflated with law enforcement and military operations, and under these conditions all immigrants are being subjected to increased scrutiny. The presence of so many uniformed personnel in disaster settings—whether law enforcement, National Guard, or members of the U.S. military—may be reassuring to members of the white majority, but fear-inducing for immigrants and people of color. During Hurricane Katrina, the responses of desperate New Orleans residents were characterized in the media alternately as rioting and as urban guerrilla warfare (Tierney, Bevc, and Kuligowski forthcoming).

Since the hurricane, many officials, including the President, have called for greater military involvement in disaster management functions. Others have argued that disaster management should remain the domain of civil society institutions. If current trends continue, disaster victims will increasingly be seen as "problem populations" requiring strict social control, and immigrants and minority group members will feel even more marginalized and fearful.

Especially in large urban areas in the U.S., poor and minority neighborhoods also suffer from blighted conditions, a lack of community-based services, high crime rates, and high fear of crime. At the same time, as our population ages, more and more people are living alone—and also dying alone. While the implications of these trends for disaster victimization are not immediately apparent, urban blight, crime, fear of crime, and the social isolation that results from living alone actually affect victims' life chances during disasters. Eric Klinenberg (2002) studied the 1995 Chicago heat wave, an extreme event that killed nearly 800 people but that was not defined as a disaster when it occurred. Focusing on two adjacent inner-city neighborhoods, one majority African American and one majority Hispanic, he found significant differences in death rates even though both neighborhoods experienced the same weather conditions. Deaths were higher in the majority black community, in part because of general social disorganization and in part because elderly people living alone tended to stay indoors because of fear of crime. In contrast, the Hispanic neighborhood, which experienced fewer deaths, was a bustling urban community with a high degree of social cohesiveness. The Catholic churches, which provided many services to residents during non-disaster times, became hubs for heat relief services during the heat wave.

Gender is yet another dimension of inequality that affects vulnerability to

disasters, just as it influences many other factors associated with socioeconomic well-being. Gender is linked to power, privilege, social expectations
concerning behavior, and everyday social roles. Although gender has not
been as well-studied as race and class in the context of disasters, it is clear
that gender also strongly influences the behaviors and experiences of
men and women at all phases of the hazards cycle (Enarson and Morrow
1998). Large numbers of women in the U.S. and around the world live in
poverty, which is in turn related to disaster vulnerability. Conditions are
worse in the U.S. for women of color. The fact that most single-parent
households are headed by women means that care giving and other
demands on women-heads-of-households are great, both on an everyday
basis and during disasters. At the same time, these women are most likely
to lack financial resources with which to cope (Fothergill 1998).

Women also tend to be more risk-averse than men, particularly with
respect to technological hazards such as toxic pollution. They are more
willing to believe disaster warnings and more willing to evacuate in the
face of impending disasters, but since evacuation decisions are typically
made by males in the family, women are often overruled (Drabek 1969).

The risk of death and injury in disasters is also associated with gender,
although in complex ways. Research suggests that these risks are linked to
gender-specific social roles, including the manner in which women are
socialized in different societies. Particularly in developing countries, it is
clear that mortality and morbidity are also related to the differential value
placed on men and women, girls and boys. Men are thought to be more
vulnerable to hazards encountered by working outdoors, such as lightning, thunderstorms, and winter storms. In other cases, death and injury
rates for women are higher, often because women put themselves at
greater risk in order to protect children and elderly household members
(Fothergill 1998).

Male-female differences in deaths and injuries are significantly higher
in the developing world than in more-developed societies. Such disparities are related to power relations between males and females—relations
that often severely constrain women's behavior and decision-making
authority. For example, higher rates of female mortality in the December
2004 Indian Ocean tsunami are attributable in part to the heavy garments
women were required to wear to maintain modesty, which limited their
movements, and to the fact that fewer women than men knew how to
swim.

In many earthquake-prone areas of the world, women are confined in
their homes and prevented from going out without being accompanied by
a man. Their duties are restricted to the domestic sphere: caring for children and elderly family members and doing all the work associated with
housekeeping. Since many household dwellings in the developing world

are not constructed to resist earthquake forces, those who are required to routinely remain indoors are at greater risk. At the same time, women's devotion to their children and other family members in the same household may cause women to put others' safety before their own (Glass et al. 1977; Chowdhury et al. 1993).

Although not as starkly evident in the U.S. as in many other societies, the disadvantaged position of women is also evident here. For example, in male-headed households, women typically have less decision-making power with respect to how disaster aid is used. Women's care giving responsibilities and tasks associated with "emotion work" increase during disasters, particularly when schools close and when dependent elderly family members need additional care. Women typically also face the responsibility of comforting partners who have lost jobs, while seeking aid and trying to figure out how the family will survive on the meager resources available through official sources (see, for example, Fothergill 2004 on women and their families following the 1997 Grand Forks flood).

In the U.S., women's greater life expectancy may also be associated with disaster vulnerability. As women age, they are more likely to end up living alone, often on fixed incomes, and often with various disabilities. They may thus be less able to engage in self-protective actions during disasters. If they have become socially isolated, they may be cut off from informal and formal sources of assistance. The same can be said of elderly males, of course, but the point is that women live longer than men and are thus more exposed to vulnerabilities associated with age.

After Disaster: Coping and Resilience

The foregoing discussions have focused primarily on how social class, race and ethnicity, and gender structure vulnerability to disasters. However, these same factors are also associated with varying degrees of resilience. The concept of resilience refers to the capacity to endure disaster impacts, and also to cope with those impacts and recover as rapidly as possible. Following Rose (2004) resilience can be thought of as composed of two components. The first, *inherent resilience*, refers to the ability to withstand disasters without suffering extensive loss and disruption of everyday life activities. The second, *adaptive resilience*, refers to the ability to adapt, improvise, and access resources following disasters. To clarify the distinction, being able to afford to live in a home that was designed and built to resist disaster forces, to stockpile emergency supplies, and to save money for use during emergencies are indicators of inherent resilience for households. The ability to pursue a wide range of options and to access multiple sources of aid following disasters are indictors of adaptive resilience. Both forms of resilience are related to such factors as wealth, social and cultural capital, and political influence. These factors are associated in turn with social inequality. Thus not only are different groups within society differentially vulnerable to disasters, but they also differ with respect to inherent and adaptive resilience.

Having financial resources enables individuals and households to have access to a variety of protections against hazards. Wealth is associated with access to high-quality housing options, the ability to afford upkeep on a home, and access to good insurance coverage. After disasters, more affluent people typically have a wider range of sheltering and housing options, as noted above. More generally, affluence also translates into the ability to choose how to deal with disaster-related problems, rather than to experience powerlessness in the face of disasters. At the same time, wealth is closely interwoven with race. Research indicates that with respect to financial resources, the gulf in opportunity and achievement that exists between whites and blacks in U.S. society is directly related to longstanding intergroup disparities in wealth (Oliver and Shapiro 1995). Just as they act as a cushion against other crises, greater wealth and the privileges that enable different groups to amass wealth are associated with higher levels of post-disaster resilience.

Hurricane Katrina vividly illustrated patterns of differential vulnerability and also highlighted the vast differences that exist between better-off community residents who have wider options and poor disaster victims who lack such choices. During Katrina differences in the coping options available to affluent and poor, and to majority and minority residents, strongly influenced the risk of surviving or dying once the levees breached and flooded the city.

If a major earthquake were to strike affluent majority communities on the west side of Los Angeles—communities such as Beverly Hills, Santa Monica, Brentwood, Bel Air, Westwood, and Pacific Palisades—and left tens of thousands homeless, it is inconceivable that the experiences of west Los Angeles residents would in any way resemble those of the poor African American residents of New Orleans. Not only would well-off Los Angeles residents have many more choices regarding how to find temporary shelter (such as second or third homes), and how to recover following the earthquake (for instance, by using savings, selling stocks, and drawing on generous insurance policies), but, owing to their political power, government agencies would be more responsive to their needs. In contrast, many victims of Katrina lost everything and had few options available for getting back on their feet. Worse yet, instead of having their needs addressed in a timely manner, those stranded in New Orleans after Katrina were not so much assisted as they were policed. Literally treated like criminals, they were confined to shelters under strict control. Later, they were transported, again under the control of law enforcement agencies and the military, to over forty states around the country, without even having the opportunity to choose where they would be sent. Family units were broken up and sent in different directions. As of this writing, three months after the hurricane, many of those who were displaced are still searching for loved ones. Traumatized and exhausted disaster victims who had been sent to the Houston Astrodome were referred to as "underprivileged" people who were quite satisfied with their new living arrangements.

As of the end of 2005, essentially nothing is being done to plan for the return of an estimated 350,000 people displaced by Katrina, as debates proceed on whether it is even worthwhile to rebuild New Orleans. The inescapable truth is that assisting poor people of color in recovering from this disaster is simply not a priority. Deprived even of the solidarity and social support that comes from living among neighbors, the scattered victims of Katrina are in a particularly poor position to press their claims.

Resilient responses are limited for many because the assistance that is provided following disasters typically reinforces social inequities, rather than compensating for them. This tendency to reinforce the status quo can be seen in differential patterns of aid provision to white versus minority communities. For example, of the two largest communities that were heavily damaged by Hurricane Andrew in 1992, one community, Homestead, had a white majority and was more affluent, while the other, Florida City, had a black majority and was significantly less well off. Disaster losses were proportionately greater in Florida City, but that community received less aid than Homestead and experienced greater problems recovering from Andrew. Besides having access to fewer resources, like many poor communities, the city lacked an effective administrative structure, further complicating the recovery process (Dash, Peacock, and Morrow 1997).

A study of business losses and recovery in four communities following the 1987 Whittier earthquake—communities with majority white, Hispanic, African-American, and Asian populations—found significant variations in Small Business Administration loan decision making across the four communities. Fifty-two percent of all loan applications from the four communities were accepted, but acceptance rates varied across communities. Businesses in the predominantly African-American community had an acceptance rate of only 23%, while approvals in the majority Hispanic, white, and Asian communities hovered at or above the 50% rate. Businesses in the majority white community were significantly more likely to receive the SBA's favorable 4% loan repayment rate—which is reserved for applicants who are in great need and who are unlikely to be able to receive loans on the commercial market—even though that community was more affluent than the others (Dahlhamer 1992).

With respect to gender differences in vulnerability and resilience,

Amartya Sen's pioneering work on the gendered nature of famine in the less developed world also provides insights into how gender influences the distribution of resources in the context of disasters. When food is scarce, women and female children typically receive a smaller share of available food than men and boys, and consequently they are more likely to suffer from malnutrition (Sen 1982, 1988). Households headed by women are at an extreme disadvantage following disasters, in part because their status is so precarious during normal times. One researcher who focuses on disasters in poor societies observes that even for intact family units, "the moral economy binding the family together is severely challenged by poverty, powerlessness, and recurrent disaster. Usually by the time a family breaks down, the personal assets of a women have already been exhausted" (Wiest 1998).

Woman- and minority-owned businesses may find it especially difficult to recover following disasters, in part because of their vulnerability to failure during normal times, but also because they may experience more difficulty accessing needed resources. These types of businesses tend to be undercapitalized and only marginally profitable during non-disaster times, and they tend to be located in highly competitive sectors of the economy, such as retail trade and service businesses. The intersection of race and ethnicity with gender results in further inequities. In the Whittier earthquake discussed above, African-American and Hispanic women were the least likely of all the applicants to receive SBA loans. Small businesses tend to experience poorer recovery outcomes than larger ones, and minority- and woman-owned businesses tend to be concentrated in the small business sector. Even within the minority business sector, African-American businesses are more vulnerable to failure during normal times than businesses owned by other minority group members—a pattern that may also carry over into disasters (for more information on business vulnerability to disasters see Tierney, forthcoming).

Other forms of post-disaster assistance also serve to reinforce existing inequalities. Homeowner insurance is a case in point; race and class factors affect both the types of coverage homeowners can obtain and the manner in which insurance applications are handled. Among those who filed claims following Hurricane Andrew, black and Hispanic households had significantly fewer of their losses covered; differences were particularly glaring in South Dade County, where 45% of African Americans indicated that that their insurance reimbursements has fallen short of what they required in order to recover. Some of these disparities were associated with the types of companies from which different class and racial groups had purchased insurance, with well-off whites more likely to be covered by leading large companies. Researchers also found evidence of "red-lining," in which those same large and more solvent companies had avoided writing insurance in majority black neighborhoods (Peacock and Girard 1997).

One caveat warrants emphasis here. Even with the abundant evidence that exists with respect to social inequality and disaster risk, it would be a mistake to characterize the poor, people of color, and women as wholly unable to cope with hazards and disasters. Although socially and politically marginalized both during normal times and during disasters, non-mainstream groups also possess significant inherent and adaptive resilience. While lacking access to the broad range of support services that majority whites take for granted, these at-risk subpopulations have their own internal networks of social support and their own community-based institutions on which they can rely when disasters strike. Following disasters, self-help efforts coalesce rapidly, often out of pre-disaster collective efforts that were originally developed to cope with other community problems. Even in the devastation wrought by Katrina, hurricane-stricken neighborhoods are bonding even more closely in their efforts to help one another, obtain equitable treatment, and actively engage in the recovery process (Davis and Fontenot 2005). After the Loma Prieta earthquake, Latino protests centering on post-disaster needs developed out of networks that had mobilized earlier to demand fair treatment for Latino farm workers in Santa Cruz County (Simile 1995). After Hurricane Andrew, women formed their own organization, "Women Will Rebuild," in response to their exclusion from the well-funded but white male dominated "We Will Rebuild" coalition that had emerged in the aftermath of the disaster (Morrow and Peacock 1997).

Although vulnerable, marginalized communities are also resilient. The policy and programmatic challenge is to engage social networks and the indigenous coping capacity of communities at risk at all stages of the hazards cycle—before, during, and after disasters. Put another way, the nation must provide appropriate forms of support that can transform at-risk groups from potential disaster victims to active agents in the disaster loss reduction process.

One such effort was already underway in Louisiana before Katrina struck. Following the participatory action research model, researchers from universities within and outside Louisiana had been working with the low-income Native American community of Grand Bayou, a subsistence community that made its living primarily from fishing. This university-community collaboration focused on reducing the disaster vulnerability of Grand Bayou, but did so in the context of broader efforts to help the community overcome a long history of political marginalization and to enable the community press for governmental responses to its many non-disaster-related needs. Katrina obliterated the physical place that was Grand Bayou, but the residents and their sense of community survived. Grand

Bayou now struggles with new and even larger challenges, and the participatory action research project continues (Laska 2005).

Conclusions

Systems of social stratification constitute the means through which power, privilege, rights, and access to resources are distributed within societies, often resulting in widely diverse life chances and life experiences. Social class, race and ethnicity, and gender are key components of stratification systems. The effects of these and other axes of stratification are reflected in virtually every aspect of social life in societies around the globe. Findings from classic U.S. studies that emphasized the power of disasters to unify stricken communities and level social distinctions are now complemented by equally compelling findings that stress the manner in which societal inequities are made manifest during disasters. Inequality and its effects are as important for understanding the social dimensions and impacts of disasters as they are for understanding health and illness, crime, the manner in which attitudes, beliefs, and behaviors vary within and across societies, and other social phenomena. Just as they permeate all aspects of social life, the effects of class, race, and gender manifest themselves before, during, and after disasters.

In the U.S., the populations of virtually all large urban centers are already very diverse and are becoming more so. At the same time, many large metropolitan areas are also highly vulnerable to future disasters. Greater Los Angeles and the San Francisco Bay Area will likely experience major earthquakes within the next twenty to thirty years. As more hurricanes develop in the Atlantic and make landfall, Miami is a sitting target for future major hurricanes, for which Andrew was only a precursor. The Gulf Coast may once again be overwhelmed by a massive hurricane; that possibility is only as far away as the next hurricane season. New York City and Long Island could experience catastrophic impacts in even moderate-sized hurricanes. New York, the National Capital Region, and Los Angeles are perhaps the most likely targets in the U.S. for future terrorist attacks.

In Hurricane Katrina, the nation witnessed for the first time what it means to experience a modern catastrophic disaster. Katrina revealed to a national and worldwide audience the reality and consequences of the stark inequities that exist in contemporary U.S. society. No one should be lulled into thinking that Katrina was unique in this respect. Instead, in laying bare the destructive potential not only of nature but also of a viciously inequitable social structure, Katrina foreshadows catastrophes to come.

Katrina has shown that without sustained programs focusing on the transportation needs of the poor, U.S. urban centers cannot be evacuated in a timely manner for any type of extreme event. Katrina has revealed that intergovernmental institutions are wholly incapable to responding to the needs of diverse publics during disasters. It has also shown that in the eyes of governmental response agencies, poor inner city residents are objects of fear and hostility, "problem populations" to be policed, rather than allies in the struggle to respond and recover. The disaster has also demonstrated in an alarming manner that U.S. governmental institutions are unable to address the relief and recovery challenges associated with massive regional catastrophes.

Finally, if recent polls are any indication, Katrina has further reinforced the gaping racial divide that exists between white and African American populations—differences that are evident not only in contrasting judgments about the handling of this particular disaster, but also in divergent views on government leadership and trustworthiness (Pew Center 2005). Equally worrisome, Katrina has acted as a catalyst for new trends that do not bode well for poor and powerless populations, such as the growing move toward the militarization of disasters.

These lessons from Katrina have very serious implications for how communities and the nation as a whole will manage extreme events in the future, not only disasters but also crises associated with epidemics and willful attacks on our society. How will poor and minority communities respond to public health efforts to contain avian flu, or to governmental responses to future terrorist attacks, particularly if those efforts have a strong law enforcement component? Will they receive warnings and advisories early enough? To whom will they look to for guidance? It is more likely that they will seek information from trusted local community-based institutions, such as churches and the minority media, than from what the administration calls "official sources," whose credibility was damaged, perhaps irreversibly, in Katrina.

In future extreme events, will we witness minority communities robbed of their dignity and "managed" by command-and-control institutions, as they were in Katrina, while members of the white majority are accorded respect and rapid assistance? Will the media once again cast poor males of color as villainous thugs, as it did in Katrina? And after Katrina demonstrated before all the world the pernicious, deadly effects of institutional racism, how many at-risk inner city residents will have faith in the government's willingness to treat them fairly and equitably in future crises? Among the most tragic consequences of Katrina is the damage done by the catastrophe to the nation's social fabric and to trust in its institutions.

Note

1. For more extensive discussions on vulnerability science and its applications,

see Cutter, Mitchell, and Scott (2000), Cutter (2001), and Cutter, Boruff, and Shirley (2003).

Equity Analysis and Natural Hazards Policy

MATTHEW D. ADLER

A standard claim in the natural hazards literature is that natural hazards policy should be sensitive to equity concerns (Mileti 1999; Berke et al. 1993; Cochrane 1975; Heinz Center 2000; Kunreuther and Rose 2004). But is equity really a normative consideration that is distinct from efficiency or overall well-being? Assuming it is, what does equity mean? Is equity group-based or individualistic? If the latter, what is equity's "currency?" Does equity concern the distribution of income, of fatality risk, of well-being generally, or perhaps of some other item? Further, is individualistic equity comparative or noncomparative? Is the idea to equalize the distribution of income/risk/well-being across the population, or rather to give priority to those who have lower levels of income/risk/well-being?

These questions are crucial to the design of natural hazards policy. For example, if equity is not a distinct consideration, then cost-benefit analysis should probably be the exclusive policymaking tool here. If it is, then cost-benefit analysis will need to be supplemented by an additional tool— an "equity analysis"—which will rank possible policies in terms of equity. And the appropriate structure of equity analysis will depend on deep and difficult questions about the nature of equity.

This paper will consider these questions in a preliminary way, suggesting that equity *is* a distinct consideration additional to efficiency/overall well-being and that it is individualistic; that its focus is *ex post*, not *ex ante*; that the "currency" for equity should be well-being; and that, at a minimum, equity analysis should focus on avoiding "poverty" (meaning a serious deprivation with respect to *any* component of well-being, not merely income poverty). Concretely, this means that equity analysis for natural hazards policy should be focused on reducing death, serious physical injury, psychological trauma, homelessness, hunger, social exclusion, and other grave harms to human welfare.

My account of equity may surprise natural hazards scholars—at least if they look to scholarship on "human hazards" (toxins, radiation, dangerous technology, and other hazards that result from human activities and do not involve extreme natural events). Human hazards scholarship often adopts a very different conceptualization of equity than that proposed here—using fatality risks rather than well-being generally as its currency, and adopting an *ex ante* rather than *ex post* view. The account I propose is much closer to the conception of distributive justice adopted by a body of scholarship that has recently emerged in development economics. This literature, inspired by the work of the economist Amartya Sen, attempts to measure poverty using a plurality of "functionings"—in effect, aspects of well-being or readily measurable proxies for these aspects.

In principle, equity analysis as I propose it should inform all aspects of natural hazards policy: not only mitigation policy but also choices about how to structure preparedness, response and recovery. Of course, decision-cost considerations may limit the scope for full-blown equity analysis (as they do for cost-benefit analysis itself) (Adler and Posner 1999). Still, it is important to get a sense of what a full-blown equity analysis for natural hazards policy would involve.

Efficiency/Overall Well-Being and Equity

Economists tend to think that governmental policy should be sensitive both to efficiency concerns and to equity concerns. By "efficiency" economists mean "Kaldor-Hicks efficiency." A policy is Kaldor-Hicks efficient if, in principle, those whom it benefits could fully compensate those whom it harms. The technique of cost-benefit analysis is seen, by economists, as a tool for identifying Kaldor-Hicks efficient policies (Just et al. 2004, 1–13).

In my own work, I have taken issue with the economists' normative picture, arguing that the relevant standard is not Kaldor-Hicks efficiency but rather overall well-being. For practical purposes, however, the difference between Kaldor-Hicks efficiency and *overall well-being* is not huge. The two criteria significantly overlap, and *both* are best implemented through cost-benefit analysis (Adler and Posner 2006; Adler and Posner 2001; Adler 2000; Adler and Posner 1999).

In other words, whether the underlying normative framework is efficiency plus equity (the framework of many economists) or overall well-being plus equity (the replacement framework I would defend), cost-benefit analysis should be *part* of the decisionmaking apparatus for administrative policymaking—including natural hazards policy. Cost-benefit analysis implements the *first* term in the framework—be it efficiency or overall well-being.

Cost-benefit analysis is now routinely used outside the area of natural hazards, for example by the EPA in regulating pollutants (Adler and Posner 1999, 169–76; Morgenstern 1997). And it has long been employed for certain aspects of natural hazards policy, for example by the Army Corps of Engineers in designing flood-control structures. FEMA, the chief federal natural hazards agency, has been relatively slow to adopt cost-benefit analysis—perhaps because the Presidential cost-benefit orders, in place since the Reagan administration, have required an agency to prepare a full analysis only when it acts by regulation and issues a sufficiently major rule (Exec. Order 12,866; Exec. Order 12,291). It seems that FEMA, unlike the EPA, rarely (if ever) meets this standard.

To be sure, cost-benefit analysis of natural hazards policy raises many difficult problems (Kunreuther and Rose 2004; Benson and Clay 2004; Committee on Assessing the Costs of Natural Disasters 1999; Ewing et al. 2005; Heinz Center 2000; Mechler 2003; Yezer 2002).

How should nonmarket goods be valued? What about indirect rather than direct costs—for example, the ripple effects on the general economy that occur when a flood, hurricane, or earthquake hits one location? Should the cost-benefit analysis simply aggregate willingness-to-pay amounts: the traditional technique? Or should these be adjusted to reflect the variable marginal utility of money? Much more work on these matters needs to be undertaken. But there is no reason to think that they are insoluble, or even particularly murky. The questions are the same as, or at least similar to, those that arise in other policy areas—for example, environmental law—where cost-benefit analysis has proceeded apace. Further, the overall structure of cost-benefit analysis is clear: summing (adjusted or unadjusted) willingness-to-pay amounts as a way to test whether policies are Kaldor-Hicks efficient or increase overall well-being.

By contrast, the second term in the efficiency/overall well-being plus equity framework remains *extremely* murky. There is little consensus within economics about the meaning of equity. Often the concept is seen as being irreducibly subjective, by contrast with efficiency—a matter for political choice rather than normative argument (Just 2004, 10). The current Presidential cost-benefit order tells agencies to take account of "equity" and "distributive impacts" in choosing policies, rather than relying exclusively on cost-benefit analysis, but neither the order nor OMB's guidance documents takes a position about the meaning of equity (Executive Order 12,866; Office of Management and Budget 2003).

There is no reason to think that equity is necessarily subjective and political. Just as normative argument might persuade us that efficiency/overall well-being has normative significance, so it might persuade us that equity also does, and that equity has a particular content. To be sure, in a democratic system, any policy choice or policy-analytic tool (such as cost-benefit analysis or equity analysis) is subject to being overridden by a legislative mandate—but normative analysis can help shape legislative mandates, and can help structure administrative policy in default of a legislative mandate.

132   Matthew D. Adler

Does Equity Matter?

Which view of equity for natural hazards policy is most supportable, as a matter of normative argument? To begin, is the most attractive normative framework one that contains equity as a separate consideration, additional to efficiency/overall well-being?

To see the force of this question, consider the following point—a familiar point in the literature on tax policy. Maximizing overall *well-being* might require equalizing the distribution of *income*. Assume that money has declining marginal utility—by which I mean an interpersonally comparable measure of well-being (Adler and Posner 2006). The increment of well-being that a given individual reaps from his first dollar of income is larger than the increment he reaps from the second, which in turn is larger than the increment he reaps from the third, and so on. Further, assume that two individuals P and Q have the same utility function, and that P is richer than Q. Then (bracketing incentive effects) transferring income from P to Q increases well-being. In this sort of case we can justify income redistribution without positing an equity factor in our normative framework additional to the factor of overall well-being.

A similar point is suggested by the literature on the special "vulnerability" of the poor and other groups to natural hazards (Fothergill and Peek 2004; Fothergill et al. 1999; Heinz Center 2000, 114–19; Mileti 1999, 122–25; Morrow 1999; Peacock et al. 1997; Wisner et al. 2004). As one review article summarizes this literature with respect to socioeconomic status:

[S]ocioeconomic status is a significant predictor in the pre- and post-disaster stages, as well as for the physical and psychological impacts [of disasters]. The poor are more likely to perceive hazards as risky; less likely to prepare for hazards or buy insurance; less likely to respond to warnings; more likely to die, suffer injuries, and have proportionately higher material losses; have more psychological trauma; and face more obstacles during the phases of response, recovery, and reconstruction (Fothergill and Peek 2004).

These findings are extremely plausible. For example, because the poor tend to live in lower cost, less sturdy housing, poor individuals who fail to evacuate are likelier to incur fatal or nonfatal injuries in building collapses than wealthier individuals. But this sort of asymmetry between the effects of disasters on the rich and the poor does not demonstrate that natural hazards policy needs to be sensitive to equity. Rather it suggests that, *even if* policymakers care only about maximizing welfare, some degree of special attention to the poor may well be justified. For example, if the policy choice presented is whether to spend limited mitigation funds in subsidizing building upgrades in poor or rich neighborhoods, the welfare-maximizing choice might well be the former. The risk of building collapse is larger in the former case and therefore the expected welfare benefit, in the form of avoided injuries and fatalities, that would result from upgrading buildings to the point where the risk of collapse is zero or *de minimis*, is also larger.

The point generalizes beyond poverty. Another recent review of the "vulnerability" literature points to a variety of groups that are particularly likely to be harmed by natural disasters: residents of group living facilities; the elderly; the physically or mentally disabled; renters; poor households; women-headed households; ethnic minorities; recent immigrants; large households; large concentrations of children; the homeless; and transients (Morrow 1999).

The author suggests that disaster planners in each community should maintain a "community vulnerability inventory" showing where these vulnerable groups are concentrated, and that preparedness, response, recovery and/or mitigation activities should, to some extent, be targeted at them. If indeed members of some such group *are* particularly vulnerable to a given natural hazard—in other words, the expected welfare harm to them if that hazard occurs is especially high—then preparedness, response, recovery and/or mitigation dollars have a greater impact when expended to reduce their exposure to the hazard than when expended to achieve an equivalent reduction in the exposure of the average community member.

In short, just as a welfare-maximization criterion plus the declining marginal utility of money can justify income redistribution to the poor, so a welfare-maximization criterion plus the heightened vulnerability of group G to natural hazards can justify "redistribution" of governmental efforts to protect citizens from natural hazards to the members of G. Equity isn't *necessary* to justify hazards policymakers in making special efforts to protect vulnerable groups; indeed, if our intuitions that the group members deserve extra concern can be borne out without invoking the fuzzy concept of equity, why invoke it?

Ironically, then, the "vulnerability" literature might move us away from an equity-inclusive framework for regulating hazards, and towards utilitarianism. But such a move should probably be resisted. It is fair to say that most modern scholarship in moral philosophy rejects utilitarianism—in other words, rejects the view that makes overall welfare the sole morally relevant consideration (Kagan 1998). Why listen to the moral philosophers? Unlike many economists, philosophers have embraced the notion—the notion I want to entertain here—that problems of equity *are* problems for serious analysis and argument (Rawls 1971; Dworkin 2000; Nagel 1991; Sen 1992; Temkin 1993; Arneson 2000; Clayton and Williams 2000; Pojman and Westmoreland 1997). And the upshot of modern philosophical work has generally been to recognize some role for equity.

Why? At the risk of wildly oversimplifying, let me suggest that two themes emerge in the philosophical literature. One is the theme of *fairness*—a central theme, for example, in John Rawls' work. Imagine that we work together in some common enterprise—a kitchen garden for the neighborhood, digging a common well, or, more grandly, sailing from the old world to the new and setting up a new society. Then if we make equal efforts we should share equally in the gains from the enterprise, or proportionately if our contributions are unequal. If you and I have made equal contributions then we're entitled to the same share of the social product even if our utility functions are shaped and positioned such that giving you more would increase overall well-being.

The second theme is *urgency* and need. Change the hypothetical and assume that neither you nor I have made any contributions to the project. Perhaps we've arrived too late on the scene. The garden has already been planted, the well already dug, the new world settled. But we could each benefit from the project, and the contributors are prepared to share some of it with us if they are morally obliged to do so. You're in a state of deprivation; I'm not. You're famished, or dehydrated, or about to be killed by pirates. I have my own supplies, or my own protection, although things would be easier for me if I could share in the common food, water, or protection. In this sort of case many have the intuition that the contributors have a distinctive moral obligation or reason to help you, not me. Note that overall welfare can't explain that intuition, since both of us would benefit from the common stuff. As a matter of overall welfare or efficiency, the distinction between us can only be quantitative, not qualitative.

So intuitions about fairness and urgency provide a strong tug towards equity. And normative analysis, in turn, is (in part) a matter of intuitions—of constructing a theory that is both reasonably coherent and systematic *and* fits reasonably well with our intuitions (Daniels 1996). Utilitarianism is highly systematic but, for many, quite counterintuitive. A pluralistic view that incorporates both overall welfare and equity as separate factors is a bit messier than utilitarianism, but better coheres with intuitions that demand redistribution of resources to those who are entitled to them as a matter of fairness, or desperately need them, even in the teeth of welfare maximization. And a pluralistic view of this sort need not be super messy. For example, the view might be unified through the currency of well-being. Overall welfare demands the maximization of well-being. And equity could demand an appropriate distribution of well-being, or of the constituents or preconditions of well-being, such as food, shelter, health, and income.

Is Equity Group-Based or Individualistic?

I shall henceforth assume that equity is a separate normative consideration, distinct from overall well-being/efficiency. What, then, is equity's content? To begin, is equity group-based or individualistic? An individual-istic equity view focuses on the distribution of some currency (income, other aspects of well-being, risks to well-being, and so forth) among indi-viduals; a group-based view focuses on the distribution of some currency among groups.

Group-based views may seem thoroughly wacky. But in fact some of the views of equity proposed by the natural hazards literature, or the related body of scholarship that studies human hazards, turn out to be group-based views. One important example consists of views that seek *geographic equity*. Here, the idea is that different geographic areas should have equal impacts (in some sense) from human or natural hazards. Concretely, this might mean locating hazardous waste dumps so that each geographic jurisdiction has the same number of dumps, or the same total chemical exposure (Been 1993). A parallel geographic-equity account for natural hazards policy can readily be constructed: for example, mitigating some category of hazard so that the number of hazard events, or deaths, or total economic costs, or percentage of the population affected by hazards, for each geographic jurisdiction, is equalized (Cross 2001; Cutter 2001).

A different kind of group-based view, pressed by the so-called "environ-mental justice" literature, focuses on the allocation of chemical and tech-nological risks among *racial groups* (Rechtschaffen and Gauna 2002). Parenthetically, let me note that this literature also expresses concern with the allocation of risks among socioeconomic groups, but because that concern is clearly quite close to a plausible individualistic equity view, I will ignore it here and train my attention on the race-based variant of "envi-ronmental justice." Placing a hazardous waste site or some other polluting activity in a location where it will have a disparate impact on racial minori-ties is seen to be especially problematic—a view that is endorsed by the President's Environmental Justice Order and by EPA's guidance state-ments regarding Title VI (Executive Order 12,898; Mank 2000). One can readily imagine a race-based analogue for natural hazards policy. Natural hazards that disparately impact racial minorities (for example, hurricanes or earthquakes in cities with especially large minority populations) should receive higher priority; mitigation policies that fail to attend to such haz-ards, but instead disproportionately benefit whites (for example, tornado-mitigation policies or other policies that would benefit rural areas outside the South, which are disproportionately white) should be viewed more skeptically.

What to make of these group-based views? Consider first geographic views. Certain variants of geographic equity turn out to be equivalent to plausible individualistic views. In particular, if we normalize by each juris-diction's population, then equalizing total fatalities per jurisdiction is effectively the same as equalizing individual fatality risks across the entire population. But other variants of geographic equity—for example, equalizing the total number of hazard events or the total hazard damage per state (without normalization), or equalizing the percentage of each state's population affected by natural hazards—are genuinely group-based. Why, as a normative matter, should equity in one of these senses be a concern? If the equitable distribution of natural hazard impacts across individuals is preserved, why should it matter that the impacts on certain states (or other geographic units) is much higher than the impacts on other states (or units)?

Political feasibility may require the policymaker to spread her mitigation resources equally across different geographic units—but that simply shows that politics may constrain the pursuit of normative goals like overall welfare or equity, not that equity means geographic equity. On a more normative note: jurisdictions with smaller populations may be less well positioned to prepare for/respond to/recover from/mitigate hazards than jurisdictions with larger populations. For example, it has been argued that:

The immense power and resources of large settlements confer considerable resilience. Most major cities are able to harness massive financial resources and expertise . . . to combat disaster and to aid recovery—in many cases as part of the normal functioning of the city. To varying degrees, this counters the potential increased vulnerability of megacities to certain types of hazards (Handmer 1995; quoted in Cross 2001, 77).

Thus, expending governmental resources on small communities out of proportion to their populations may sometimes be cost-benefit justified. The private and public goods normally supplied in cities—big hospitals, extensive fire and police departments—may in some cases mean that additional expenditures for hazard mitigation/preparedness/response/recovery are less cost-effective than in non-urban areas. But that effect should, in principle, be captured by a sophisticated cost-benefit analysis; there's no need for a separate geographic-equity analysis.

A similar response addresses the point that hazards which hit smaller communities are likelier to entirely disrupt community life—with special costs—than hazards which hit cities. If there are extra costs to the wholesale rather than partial disruption of a community, then cost-benefit analysis should capture those costs and—without more—would warrant special attention for smaller communities.

What about the equity accounts that focus on the distribution of natural hazards across racial groups? To begin, a disparate impact test may be used to smoke out conscious or unconscious racial discrimination. The fact that a particular state government agency regularly pursues mitigation policies that disproportionately benefit whites should raise a red flag for federal overseers. Are the state decisionmakers consciously or unconsciously discounting the interests of nonwhites? Further, racial minorities may be especially vulnerable to natural hazards—either because minority groups are disproportionately poor, or independent of that. For example, if "redlining" practices mean that racial minorities in certain communities tend to be underinsured, and therefore tend to take fewer individual mitigation measures, mitigation dollars spent in these communities would tend to have a greater benefit (Fothergill et al. 1999; Peacock et al. 1997). Finally, the visible existence of policies that disparately affect minorities— for example, the clustering of hazardous waste dumps in inner-city neighborhoods, or a failure of rescuers to do much for hurricane refugees in such neighborhoods—may have substantial costs in terms of racial divisiveness, or in enhancing the "social exclusion" of certain minority-group members (Sunstein 1994).

This analysis suggests that race-based equity should not be a concern for a genuinely impartial and sophisticated social planner. Divisiveness costs and social exclusion costs are effects on individuals, and will be incorporated in a sophisticated cost-benefit analysis or sophisticated individualistic equity analysis, as will the enhanced vulnerability of members of certain racial groups. Race-based tests will also evidence the motivations of other actors; but the well-meaning social planner won't need to police her own motivations.

In our present circumstances, where techniques for quantifying costs such as racial division and social exclusion are still undeveloped, race-based tests plausibly function as practicable decision procedures that supplement cost-benefit analysis and individualistic equity analysis. The same may even be true of geographic equity tests. Still, it is hard to see why the normative criterion of equity should itself be group-based, any more than the criterion of overall welfare. Groups don't have interests apart from the interests of the individuals who comprise them. Avoiding disruption to groups, or disparate effects on groups, may be important in preventing harms to the groups' members—to the extent that members' goals and plans are bound up with the groups, or that others in society see them as group members. But the notion of protecting groups per se, let alone defining a basic moral construct such as equity in group-based rather than individualistic terms, is extremely puzzling.

Individualistic Equity: *Ex Post* or *Ex Ante*?

For the remainder of the paper I will focus on individualistic construals of equity: views that constrain the distribution of some item across individuals. Within this broad family of views, we might distinguish, first, between *ex ante* and *ex post* approaches to equity. The distinction is subtle but very important. Imagine that the item for distribution is income, and that the view is noncomparative. In particular, it seeks to ensure that everyone is above some threshold. The *ex post* variant of this approach would seek to ensure that everyone's actual income is above some threshold; the *ex ante* variant would instead define a threshold of expected income (Morduch 1994).

The distinction persists if we shift to a comparative, income-based view. Comparativists want to equalize rather than raise everyone above a threshold. But what's being equalized: actual income or expected income?

Shift, now, to a different currency: life. Consider first the threshold view using this currency. The *ex ante* version of that view seeks to ensure that no one's risk of death is too high. Indeed, this view is reflected in much toxics regulation; agencies such as EPA, OSHA, or the FDA often determine whether the exposure of the population to a given toxin is "safe" by asking whether maximally or highly exposed individuals would incur an incremental fatality risk above some numerical threshold (such as a 1 in 1 million, 1 in 100,000, 1 in 10,000, or 1 in 1000 incremental fatality risk) (Adler 2005). By contrast, the *ex post* version of the view that uses life as its currency, and that cares about thresholds, would try to avoid deaths that occur before a certain age—be it a fairly young age (18), or an intermediate age (40), or an substantial age (70), or a very advanced age (100).[1] The first choice would be the *ex post* analogue of an *ex ante* view that sets a fairly high fatality risk threshold; the last choice would be the analogue of setting a very low risk threshold (1 in 1 million) and would be virtually equivalent to a policy of minimizing all deaths.

Clearly, the *ex ante* approach of minimizing the number of individuals whose risk of death exceeds some threshold, and the *ex post* approach of minimizing the number of deaths, can diverge. This divergence, indeed, is a recurrent theme within the literature on equity in the regulation of human hazards, and connects to discussions of geographic equity (Adler 2005; Adler 2003; Finkel 1996). A central question in this literature is whether policymakers should aim to reduce "individual risk" (an *ex ante* approach) or "population risk," that is, the total number of deaths (an *ex post* approach). Imagine that EPA can choose to remedy a rural waste dump with a high concentration of dangerous chemicals, which exposes 10,000 individuals to a 1 in 10,000 incremental fatality risk; or instead to clean up an urban waste dump with a lower concentration of dangerous chemicals, which exposes 8 million individuals to a 1 in 2 million incremental fatality risk. The first policy mitigates many high risks but saves fewer lives; the second mitigates no risks above even a low threshold, but saves more lives.

If we kept the "currency" fixed, but focused on equalizing rather than raising the above thresholds, a similar divergence would arise. The *ex ante* planner focuses on equalizing the distribution of fatality risks from some source; the *ex post* planner focuses on regulating the source so that the resultant distribution of longevity is more equal.

A final example of the divergence between *ex ante* and *ex post* approaches—now using the currency of welfare itself, rather than income or life. A simple case will show how the two can diverge here. The policy-maker for a society of N individuals is choosing between the status quo, where everyone's welfare is at utility level 100, and a policy which will moderately improve the welfare of 90% of the society (raising them to level 110) and dramatically decrease the welfare of 10% (lowering them to level 20). The identity of the 10% is unknown. The *ex ante* policy maker definitely approves this choice: Everyone's *ex ante* utility increases from 100 to 101 and equality of *ex ante* utilities is preserved. But the *ex post* policy maker may decline the policy, because in each state of the world it would produce a highly skewed outcome, with 10% of the society dramatically worse off than the remainder.

It might be thought that equity analysis inevitably adopts an *ex ante* approach, given uncertainty on the part of the policymaker. This is incorrect. *Both approaches are consistent with policymaker uncertainty.* The difference concerns the stage at which uncertainty enters the equity analysis. The *ex post* approach views equity as a feature of the possible outcomes of policy choice. Assume that $C_j(O_i)$ is individual j's holding of the relevant currency for equity in outcome O_i and that there are N individuals in the population. For a given policy, the *ex post* analyst: (1) identifies the possible outcomes $\{O_1 \ldots O_M\}$ of the policy; (2) performs an equity analysis for each outcome O_i, examining the distribution of the relevant currency (for instance, income, life, well-being) in that outcome; (3) ideally, summarizes the equity status of each outcome O_i with a number $E(O_i) = E(C_1(O_i), C_2(O_i), \ldots C_j(O_i), \ldots C_N(O_i))$, which represents how equitable the distribution of the currency in that outcome is; and (4) determines the expected equity of the policy as $\sum p_i E(O_i)$, where p_i is the probability of outcome O_i. By contrast, the *ex ante* analyst: (1) identifies the possible outcomes $\{O_1 \ldots O_M\}$ of the policy; (2) determines, for each individual j, her expected value of the relevant currency, that is, $\sum p_i\, C_j(O_i)$; and (3) performs an equity analysis on these N individual expected values. In short, the *ex post* approach to equity estimates the degree of inequity in each policy outcome, and then (discounting each outcome by its probability) estimates the expected degree of inequity; the *ex ante* approach determines each individual's expectation from the policy (expected income, expected utility, risk of death) and then determines the degree of inequity of these expectations.

The choice between *ex ante* and *ex post* approaches to equity has been largely overlooked by philosophers of distributive justice; but it has been examined by a body of scholarly work in welfare economics, with no clear resolution (Broome 1984; Diamond 1967; Hammond 1982; Mongin and d'Aspremont 1998). The best argument for the *ex post* approach, one that seems (to this author) pretty compelling, is that morality is ultimately a matter of producing good outcomes. Poverty means being poor—not having an expectation of a low income or utility. Psychological trauma means experiencing mental illness or suffering—not having the expectation of mental illness or suffering. Normative criteria, such as equity, are applicable to the consequences or outcomes of our choices—to what might actually occur as a result of the policies society chooses or refrains from choosing. In other words, the *ex post* approach to equity sits naturally with a "consequentialist" approach to policy choice (Scheffler 1988). To put the point more technically: the so-called "sure thing" principle, an intuitively appealing principle of rationality, leads to the *ex post* approach.

These are difficult matters, and the reader not already familiar with the social choice literature on *ex ante* versus *ex post* approaches to policy choice may be more puzzled than enlightened. Suffice it to say that the *ex post* approach views inequity as a property of the outcomes or consequences of policy choice, not of individual expectations; and that there are strong arguments in favor of this approach. More concretely: if equity cares about raising individuals above some threshold (as I will argue it minimally does), then the threshold should be defined in terms of individuals' actual holdings of some "currency," not individuals' risks or expectations. Consider the exemplary case where the policymaker has to choose between mitigating a high probability natural hazard that imposes a high risk of fatality, serious injury, psychological trauma, and other sorts of serious deprivation on each member of a small population; or a lower probability natural hazard that imposes a low risk of fatality, injury, trauma, and other such serious deprivation on each member of a large population, but with a higher expected number of fatalities, serious injuries, psychological trauma cases, and other instances of serious deprivation. Then the *ex ante* approach will argue for mitigating the first hazard, while the *ex post* approach will argue for mitigating the second.

What Is the Currency for Individualistic Equity?

I have argued that equity is "individualistic" and *ex post* in its structure. Equity analysis should determine the possible outcomes of a policy choice and, for each outcome O_i, should evaluate the distribution across individuals—not groups—of the relevant items. But which items are those? What is the "currency" of equity? (Arneson 2000).

One policy area where issues of equity and distributive justice have been salient concerns the alleviation of poverty. Economists have traditionally conceptualized poverty as a low level of income or expenditure (Laderchi et al. 2003). The problem with these "currencies" is that they track well-being quite imperfectly. As Amartya Sen argues:

Our physical and social characteristics make us immensely diverse creatures. We differ in age, sex, physical and mental health, bodily prowess, intellectual abilities, climactic circumstances, epidemiological vulnerability, social surroundings, and in many other respects. Such diversities . . . can be hard to accommodate adequately in the usual . . . framework of inequality assessment (Sen 1992, 28).

Consider the "currency" of expenditure. The fact that P's expenditure level is greater than Q's doesn't mean that P is better off than Q, all things considered. P may be physically disabled; he may need a high level of expenditure to facilitate activities that Q can perform effortlessly, such as locomotion. Or, P and Q may both be physically able but Q may benefit from various public goods (she lives in a cleaner or sunnier climate), or a sunnier disposition, or a bigger circle of friends, that compensate for her lower level of expenditure. Similar points can be made about the inadequacy of income as a "currency" for measuring deprivation and, more generally, equity—at least if income is defined in the standard, readily measurable way as cash income (wage, investment, and transfer income) (Bojer 2003, 65–77).

In the literature on environmental and technological risk, a different "currency" tends to be used for discussions of equity: the risk of death (Adler 2005; Adler 2003, 1414–36). A policy that leaves some individuals with an above-threshold risk of dying as a result of some hazard (a 1 in 1 million, 1 in 100,000, 1 in 10,000, or 1 in 1000 risk, say), or that produces a skewed distribution in the risk of death from the hazard, is seen as inequitable. This approach is doubly problematic. First, as already discussed, it takes an *ex ante* approach to equity, focusing on each individual's expectation of premature death rather than on the actual occurrence of premature death. Second, and additionally, the "currency" of death or the risk of death is too narrow. Hazards—natural as well as human—produce a range of bad outcomes: not just death, but also non-fatal injury and disease, the loss of income and expenditure, unemployment, psychological trauma, and the disruption of family and community life. Policy analysis of preparedness/response/recovery/mitigation measures—both equity analysis and cost-benefit analysis—should, in principle, capture all of these dimensions, not just the life/death dimension.

Clearly this is true for cost-benefit analysis (whether understood as a tool for implementing the criterion of Kaldor-Hicks efficiency, or a tool for implementing the criterion of overall welfare). Cost-benefit analysis aims to aggregate willingness-to-pay for all the welfare-relevant aspects of a policy, not just its effect on premature death. But it is no less true for equity analysis. Consider a natural hazards policy that focuses on warning and evacuation, with little effort given to strengthening structures or to recovery. This policy might be very effective in preventing fatalities, but would fail to prevent the host of serious non-fatality setbacks that occur when individual homes and a community's infrastructure are destroyed. In general, to its credit, the existing literature on natural hazards policy recognizes that good analysis should be inclusive in characterizing the impacts of hazards (Cochrane 1975; Ewing et al. 2005; Heinz Center 2000; Mileti 1999).

So what *should* the "currency" for natural hazards equity analysis be? The answer is well-being itself—not merely particular components of well-being, or particular preconditions for well-being, or particular resources that facilitate well-being, such as income or life. One objection to this approach is that well-being is subjective. Different individuals have different conceptions of well-being. Although this is surely true, well-being is objective to the extent that conceptions overlap (Smith 1994, 173). If there were no overlap, how could there be *any* "currency" for equity analysis? But, in truth, virtually all of us have conceptions of well-being that view life and income as intrinsically or instrumentally valuable. Similarly, virtually all of us have conceptions of well-being that view physical and psychological health, social interaction rather than isolation, meaningful employment, and other such items (not captured by the income and life "currencies") as intrinsically or instrumentally valuable.

A different critique of the welfare "currency," advanced by some philosophers, is that equity requires an equitable distribution of *opportunities* for well-being—not well-being itself (Arneson 2000). After all, some individuals will end up with a low level of well-being because of their own choices; others, because of bad luck. Surely these two sorts of individuals should be treated differently by equity analysis. The answer to this point is twofold. First, equity analysis *should* in principle integrate considerations of choice and responsibility—but we don't yet have the practicable tools to do that (Laderchi 2003, 255). Second, and more to the point, the choice/responsibility criticism hardly argues for a narrow rather than more inclusive currency. If we try to ensure that no one has a low income, or dies prematurely, then we will be aiding some individuals who are responsible for their deprivation (those who have squandered their resources, or knowingly engaged in risky activities), no less so than if we aim to ensure that no one is psychologically traumatized, socially isolated, or unemployed.

What, then, is human welfare? What are the components of an individual's life that, most of us will agree, contribute to the well-being of that individual? This sort of question can be answered more or less systematically, through reflection, or discussion, or surveys. The World Health Organization has recently undertaken an impressively systematic effort to answer the question, organizing focus groups and surveys in many different countries to arrive at a list of the components of "quality of life" and a matching survey instrument that can be used to inform governmental policymaking, both in the health care field and perhaps in other fields too, as well as decisions by medical professionals and other private actors (Szabo 1996; The WHOQOL Group 1998; Bonomi et al. 2000). This so-called "WHOQOL" list consists of 24 "facets" or dimensions, organized into 6 domains. These facets are: (1) pain and discomfort, (2) energy and fatigue, (3) sleep and rest, all falling in the "physical" domain; (4) positive feelings, (5) thinking, learning, memory, and concentration, (6) self-esteem, (7) body image and appearance, and (8) negative feelings, all falling in the "psychological" domain; (9) mobility, (10) activities of daily living, (11) dependence on medication or treatments, and (12) working capacity, all in the "independence" domain; (13) personal relationships, (14) social support, and (15) sexual activity, all in the "social" domain; (16) physical safety and security, (17) home environment, (18) financial resources, (19) health and social care, (20) opportunities for acquiring new information and skills, (21) recreation/leisure, (22) physical environment, and (23) transport, all falling in the "environment" domain; and finally (24) spirituality, constituting its own domain.

The philosopher Martha Nussbaum has for some time been intensively engaged in a broadly similar effort to define a list of the constituents of the quality of life that could guide governmental decisions—in particular, the definition of a "social minimum" that every citizen is entitled to. Her list of the central human capabilities is: (1) life; (2) bodily health; (3) bodily integrity; (4) the senses, imagination and thought; (5) emotions; (6) practical reason; (7) affiliation; (8) other species; and (9) play (Nussbaum 2000, 78–80). Nussbaum's list and the WHOQOL list are presented here, not as the definitive lists of the constituents of well-being, but rather as particularly comprehensive and carefully constructed examples of this sort of list. Numerous other examples can be found in the philosophical and economic literatures (Alkire 2002, 78–84). A meta-analysis of this literature would be one plausible way to generate a consensus list of the dimensions of well-being that a governmental agency could employ in policymaking, including equity analysis.

There are two apparent difficulties with the proposal that equity analysis should employ the currency of well-being, as identified by the sort of multi-dimensional list of the different constituents of welfare that the WHOQOL framework and Nussbaum's list exemplify. One difficulty is commensurability—integrating the different dimensions into a single measure of well-being. Let me bracket this problem for the moment, to return to it in the next section.

The other problem is the sheer multiplicity of the dimensions. Consider the WHOQOL list. None of the dimensions is inherently immeasurable, but many are difficult to measure, and the decision costs of evaluating policies with respect to all 24 of the WHOQOL dimensions would be overwhelming.

The answer is that equity analysis should be sensitive to ease of measurement and to the related problem of decision costs. Equity analysts may need to make rough and ready, threshold assessments about which dimensions are worth quantifying—depending both on expected measurement costs, and the likelihood that measurement will provide choice-relevant information (that is, lead the policy maker to adopt a different policy than she would have absent the measurement). Analysts will also sometimes find it cost-effective to use proxy variables for certain dimensions or sets of dimensions: items that are not themselves an intrinsic component of well-being but are readily measurable and correlate with certain aspects of well-being.

In many instances this sort of threshold assessment will suggest that a variety of dimensions should be quantified and, in particular, that focusing on the traditional equity currencies of income and life/risk-to-life is too limited. Consider, by way of analogy, cost-benefit analysis of environmental policies, where a variety of welfare effects are now routinely included in analyses, in particular health, visibility, water quality, and recreational values, along with changes in consumption and fatality risks (Cropper 2000).

An even closer analogy is the scholarly literature in development economics, inspired by Amartya Sen's work, which seeks to use a plurality of "functionings"[2] (in effect, particular aspects of well-being or proxy variables for such aspects) rather than income as the scales of poverty and development (Alkire 2002; Balestrino 1996; Fukuda-Parr 2003; Kuklys 2005; Klasen 2000; Laderchi 2003; Qizilbash 2002). To give one illustrative example, Stephan Klasen measured the extent of poverty in a sample of South African households in two ways: first, by determining each household's expenditures; second, by measuring each household's achievement with respect to 14 different functionings: education, income, wealth, housing, water, sanitation, energy, employment, transport, access to financial services, nutrition, health care, safety, and perceived well-being. A household was judged seriously impoverished with respect to expenditures if its expenditures were below the 20th percentile, and seriously impoverished with respect to functionings if its overall functioning (an average of the 14 individual functionings) was below the 20th percentile. Klasen found that the expenditure- and functioning-based analyses gave quite different pictures of the extent and distribution of poverty in South Africa.

Individualistic Equity: Comparative or Noncomparative?

A very important distinction evident within the philosophical literature on equality is the distinction between comparative and noncomparative accounts (Clayton and Williams 2000; Crisp 2003; Frankfurt 1987; Symposium 2003). Assume welfare is the "currency" for equity—as I've argued it should be. The comparativist, then, cares about the overall pattern of welfare levels. Her concern is how individual P fares, as compared to Q and R and S and so on. The noncomparativist does not have this concern: rather, her view is that improvements in someone's welfare become more important, morally speaking, the lower that person's overall level of welfare. In effect, the comparativist has a fairness-based view of equity, while the noncomparativist has an urgency-based view. More formally, the noncomparativist's ranking of outcomes is "separable" in individual welfares, while the comparativist's is not.

Intuitions pull in both directions. Further, existing practices of measuring equity are sometimes comparativist, sometimes noncomparativist in spirit. For example, the popular "Gini coefficient," often used to evaluate the distribution of income, is a comparativist measure. By contrast, evaluating an income distribution by counting the number of individuals below a poverty line trades on the noncomparativist idea that it is particularly morally urgent to benefit individuals who are very badly off (Bojer 2003, 92–106, 118–22).

Are we at an impasse? Maybe not. Some progress can be made by seeing that a transfer of a fixed amount of well-being from an individual who is well off to one who is below some threshold of well-being will be counted as an equity improvement both by comparativists and by noncomparativists. To begin, comparativists should agree that such a "Robin Hood" transfer improves the equity pattern. (If it doesn't—if reverse-Robin Hood transfers are seen as possibly improving the overall pattern— then the theorist can hardly be said to care about equity.) Further, noncomparativists may disagree about whether effects on well-being have variable weight above a threshold of poverty, but at a minimum they will surely agree that increments to the well-being of someone below such a threshold are more urgent than decrements to the well-being of someone above it.

In short, a noncomparative, threshold approach that quantifies the extent to which individuals lie below some "poverty line" of well-being should be the core of any equity analysis. Specific views of equity may require further analysis, but every equity theorist would presumably agree that, holding overall welfare constant, measures that benefit some (and harm none) below the poverty line are good policies. To be clear, I use the term "poverty" as a term of art, to mean the deprivation of *well-being*. "Poverty" in the vernacular, meaning income poverty, is only one aspect of well-being poverty, for reasons already discussed. *Equity analysis should, at a minimum, quantify the effect of natural hazards policies on well-being poverty.* That is the essence of my recommendation.

Many complexities remain, to be resolved through further discussion, surveys, and technical work. One important question is whether to set a single all-dimensions-considered well-being poverty line, or rather poverty lines for each of the measured welfare dimensions. The first approach is more theoretically compelling, but more demanding in terms of measurement. The notion of an interpersonally comparable utility scale is, I believe, a coherent one, but we as yet lack a practicable set of tools for readily operationalizing this scale in policymaking.

Assuming the disaggregated approach is pursued, the problem of setting dimension-specific poverty lines arises. Since poverty lines, as described here, are meant to represent a kind of "overlapping consensus" across equity theories, the relevant line should be calibrated so as to capture the point of substantial deprivation—that point such that moving someone above the line, at the expense of someone who is well off, would be seen as an equity improvement by virtually all equity theorists. In principle, the poverty line should be absolute rather than relative—because it is meant to appeal to noncomparativists who are concerned with absolute deprivation, and not merely comparativists who focus on relative welfare. But some goods, most clearly social status, are intrinsically relational. The income poverty line understood as a proxy variable for social status will be relative, not absolute; if your income is only a small fraction of your society's median income, you are likely to be ostracized and feel shame, even if that income is sufficient to nourish, clothe and shelter you. More generally, percentile, fraction-of-median, or other relative measures for many welfare dimensions will be a practicable way to set the poverty line in default of an implementable absolute threshold (Qizilbash 2002, 758–59; Bojer 2003, 118–20).

A third and related problem is that of specifying the time period for measuring achievement with respect to a given dimension of well-being (McKerlie 1989; Temkin 1993, 232–44). The literature on income distribution is relevant. Should we evaluate the distribution of lifetime income or of periodic (for example, annual) income (Bojer 2003, 74–76, 90–91)? Generally scholarship takes the latter approach, because lifetime values are hard to measure. The same would be true for measuring non-income welfare dimensions. For many dimensions, the simplest approach would be momentary rather than lifetime or periodic. Being in a state of seriously bad health at any time counts as a momentary deprivation of health; being homeless at any time counts as a momentary deprivation of shelter; being unemployed at any time counts as a momentary deprivation of meaningful work; being seriously psychologically traumatized at any time counts as a momentary deprivation of mental health; being hungry at any time counts as a momentary deprivation of nourishment; living without any social support at a time counts as a momentary deprivation of social support. Total bad health, homelessness, unemployment, and so forth, is then (most straightforwardly) a matter of the total time in which individuals are in the deprived state. Life can be handled in a related manner: not being alive counts as a momentary deprivation of life, and the change in total longevity resulting from a policy is a measure of its equity effect on the life dimension.[3]

A fourth issue is how to handle uncertainty. For a simple illustration of the issues, assume that we have two welfare dimensions, f and g. We are choosing between a status quo S and a policy with two possible outcomes O and O*. $f(\_)$ is the extent of deprivation with respect to f in the given outcome; similarly for $g(\_)$. Probabilities p and $(1 - p)$ are the probabilities of O and O*, respectively, if the policy is chosen. The *ex post* approach to equity says that we should measure overall poverty in each outcome as a function of f-deprivation and g-deprivation, and then discount by outcome probabilities to determine expected equity. Formally, $E(f(\_), g(\_))$ measures overall poverty in the outcome. The status quo has equity measure $E(f(S), g(S))$; the policy has an equity measure equaling its expected equity $pE(f(O), g(O)) + (1 - p)E(f(O^*), g(O^*))$.

If the function E is assumed to be roughly linear, then we can separate out the two dimensions. Imagine that $E(f(\_), g(\_)) = k_f\, f(\_) + k_g g(\_)$. Then the expected equity of the policy is $p\ [k_f\, f(O) + k_g\, g(O)] + (1 - p)$ $[k_f\, f(O^*) + k_g\, g(O^*)] = k_f\ [p\, f(O) + (1 - p)\, f(O^*)] + k_g\ [p\, g(O) + (1 - p)$ $g\ (O^*)]$. In other words, the expected equity of the policy is the weighted sum of the expected measures with respect to the two welfare dimensions. More generally, if overall poverty in an outcome is approximately a linear function of poverty with respect to the underlying dimensions, equity analysis of a given policy can proceed by determining the change in expected poverty produced by the policy for each dimension, and then aggregating these values using weighting factors to produce an overall equity score for the policy. Concretely: if the equity analyst measures deprivations with respect to the six dimensions of (say) longevity, hunger, homelessness, serious disease or injury, unemployment, and psychological trauma, then she will ideally establish weighting factors for these dimensions. Through reflection, discussion, or surveys, she will need to establish the equity importance of a day spent hungry, as compared to a day spent homeless, in a serious disease or injury state, unemployed, in a state of psychological trauma or (at the extreme) a day in which the subject is not alive at all. Equity analysis of a natural hazards policy will then consist in: (1) estimating the change in the expected amount of longevity, hunger, homelessness, serious disease or injury, unemployment, and psychological trauma, as produced by the policy relative to the status quo; and (2) applying the weighting factors to these quantities and aggregating.

Conclusion

Through normative argument, we can make progress in understanding what equity analysis for natural hazards policy should involve. There is no reason to think that equity analysis is wholly subjective or political, any more than cost-benefit analysis—although of course in both cases any governmental decision is ultimately subject to political control through the legislative process. The focus of equity analysis, I have argued, should be *well-being poverty*: serious deprivations with respect to any dimension of well-being. Well-being should be the basic "currency" for equity analysis—not fatality risk, income, or other such traditional currencies. Analysts should start with a basic list of well-being dimensions. The WHOQOL's list and Nussbaum's list are reasonable places to start, but there are other plausible lists in the literature as well, and one possibility is to meta-analyze this literature to produce a consensus list. Once a list of well-being dimensions is in place, a rough-and-ready "value of information" approach should be used to decide whether to include a given dimension in the analysis: the dimension should be included if doing so seems likely to make a difference to the analysis, and if the dimension can be measured (directly or with proxy variables) sufficiently easily given the stakes of the policy decision at hand. A "poverty line" needs to be set for each included dimension. This should in principle involve absolute, not relative poverty—for it is meant to represent the point of "overlapping consensus" among virtually all equity theorists, noncomparativist as well as comparativist—and, relatedly, should involve a serious deprivation (not just the absence of full flourishing). It should be the point at which individual claims become sufficiently urgent that overall-well-being-preserving transfers to individuals below the line, from those above, is—fairly uncontroversially—good policy.

The equity analyst will also need to develop some sense of how the amounts of poverty along each well-being dimension, in a given outcome, interact to produce the overall degree of poverty in that outcome. Assuming the interaction is roughly linear, then equity analysis will have the following, simple structure: first assess the policy's expected impact with respect to each dimension, then weight and aggregate to determine an overall equity score for the policy. Concretely, this would mean predicting the extent to which the policy can be expected to increase longevity, reduce serious injury, stop serious psychological trauma, prevent hunger or homelessness, lessen unemployment, prevent family breakdown, and reduce other such instances of serious well-being deprivation that typically accompany natural hazards—and then weighting and aggregating these poverty-reduction benefits. More generally, whatever specific dimensions are included, and whatever assumptions are made about the interaction of those dimensions, the basic thrust of equity analysis should be to quantify the change in expected well-being poverty produced by each policy under consideration.

Because this proposal departs from the accounts of equity common in the human hazards literature—in adopting an *ex post* rather than *ex ante* focus, and using well-being not fatalities as the currency—it may strike some readers as very odd. Suffice it to say that the proposal draws on a growing body of scholarship in development economics, inspired by Amartya Sen's work, and that the implementation of equity analysis would also benefit from that scholarship—for example, in identifying dimensions and drawing poverty lines.

Clearly, even if this general approach is adopted, there is much room for debate and argument, in three areas: (1) further specifying the approach (identifying dimensions, poverty lines, methodologies for measuring dimension-specific poverties, and weights for the dimensions); (2) determining whether other sorts of equity analyses should also be performed (such as, a Gini-type analysis, which comparativists might approve but noncomparativists will not); and (3) determining how to "balance" the results of cost-benefit analysis and equity analysis. But structured argument is different from an undisciplined "value choice." Whether because of global warming, meteorological or seismic cycles, or burgeoning populations in hurricane- and earthquake-prone areas, we seem to be entering a period when natural hazards will command national attention and resources as never before. It should be possible to bring some intellectual rigor and structure to the expenditure of those resources—not just at the stage of maximizing overall well-being/efficiency, but also at the stage of determining what an "equitable" expenditure would be.

Notes

Many thanks to Paul Dolan and Eric Posner for their comments.

1. More precisely, these age thresholds would emerge from a combination of (1) using life as the "currency" for equity; (2) adopting an *ex post* rather than *ex ante* approach; and (3) using whole lifetimes rather than periods or moments as the temporal framework for measuring individual "holdings" of the "currency." This

last issue is discussed below, in the section on comparative and noncomparative views.

2. Sen argues that the currency for equality should be "capabilities," which are opportunities to achieve "functionings." (Sen 1992) In practice, much of the Sen-inspired work in development economics has used "functionings" not "capabilities," given the difficulty of measuring opportunities (Laderchi 2003, 255). I therefore generally use the term "functioning" in discussing the Sen-inspired approach.

3. Using lifetimes as the relevant time period for measuring well-being achievements with respect to the "life" dimension means measuring the equity impact of a policy as the change in the number of deaths that occur before some age threshold. By contrast, using moments as the equity period means measuring the change in longevity (the total years that individuals are alive). On this approach, each increment to longevity relieves a momentary deprivation.

Part Three
Private Sector Strategies for Managing Risk

Why We Under-Prepare for Hazards

Robert J. Meyer

Upon many witnessing the immense destruction caused by Hurricane Katrina in August 2005, feelings of sympathy were coupled with those of puzzlement: how could so much carnage be caused by a hazard that was so predictable? In 2004 the region had the benefit of a full dress rehearsal for Katrina when Hurricane Ivan—another category 5 storm while in the Gulf—triggered full-scale evacuations of the same areas, revealing many of the same weaknesses of preparedness procedures that were observed during Katrina. In addition, just weeks before the storm planners in New Orleans engaged in a training exercise that simulated the impact of a hypothetical hurricane—Pam—that breached the levees of New Orleans, submerging 87% of the city. Finally, the warnings of impending catastrophe could not have been stronger or more accurate in the days and hours leading up the storm's landfall. Substantial numbers of residents nevertheless failed to heed urgent warnings to leave, few organized efforts were made to assist those who lacked the means to do so, and governments failed to have sufficient resources in place to deal with the disaster when it was realized.

What went wrong? Lost in the debate over affixing blame is the fact that the human errors that amplified the tragedy were, in many cases, no less predictable than the storm itself. Over the past four decades a sizable academic literature has emerged warning of the inherent weakness that exist when individuals—both planners and residents—are faced with making decisions about protection from low-probability, high-consequence events. In many ways, Hurricane Katrina was a case study of these weaknesses: opportunities to learn from experience went unexploited, mitigation measures with long-run benefits were under-funded, and the principals emerged as both overconfident before the event and over-matched afterward. Indeed, one might argue that as Hurricane Katrina bore down on Louisiana on the evening of August 28th, the residents of Louisiana and Mississippi faced what was, in fact, a greater risk than they

knew—one born in the failure of advance planning to anticipate the frailties of likely limitations of human responses to the storm.

The purpose of this essay is to review some of what we know about biases
that arise when individuals and planners try to make decisions about
investing in mitigation against low-probability, high-consequence events,
and steps that can be taken to mollify them. I argue that the quality of
investment decisions is often degraded by three deep-rooted biases in how
we learn and process information:

1. A tendency to learn by focusing on short-term feedback
2. A tendency to see the future as a simple extrapolation of the present
3. A tendency to overly discount the value of ambiguous future rewards
   compared to short-term costs.

Taken together, these biases not only produced many of the decision
errors that were made in the days (and years) leading up to Katrina, but
also carry a warning: unless we become better students of our own psy-
chologies, we have little long-term hope of insuring that tragedies like Katrina do not occur again.

Learning Biases: Why Experience Is Not Always the Best Teacher

On Tuesday, September 14, 2004, the *USA Today* ran the following article
that described the problems the Mayor of New Orleans was facing complying with a mandatory evacuation order in advance of Hurricane Ivan—
at the time a category-5 hurricane near the western tip of Cuba:

> Mayor Nagin said he would "aggressively recommend" people evacuate, but that it
> would be difficult to order them to, because at least 100,000 in the city rely on pub-
> lic transportation and have no way to leave. "They say evacuate, but they don't say
> how I'm supposed to do that," said Latonya Hill, 57, who lives on a disability check
> and money she picks up cleaning houses or baby sitting. Despite the potential
> need for emergency housing, no shelters had been opened in the city as of Tues-
> day night. Nagin said the city was working on setting up a shelter of "last resort"
> and added that the Superdome might be used, but a spokesman for the stadium
> said earlier Tuesday that it was not equipped as a shelter (USA Today On Line,
> September 14, 2004, 5:28PM).

Less than a year later as an even stronger Hurricane Katrina approached
the dilemma faced by emergency planners in New Orleans was essentially
unchanged. Again 100,000 of the city's poorest had little means of complying with evacuation calls, and the Superdome was no better equipped
to serve as a long-run shelter.

The city seemed to learn so little from the false alarm of Ivan, in part,
because of an all-too-familiar bias in how we naturally learn: by and large,
we are much better at learning from the mistakes we actually make than

those we *almost* make. History is replete with apparent examples; In the domain of natural hazards, Brown and Hoyt (2000) offer evidence that a significant predictor of individuals' decisions to purchase federal flood insurance is simply whether flood losses are incurred in the previous year—an effect observed after controlling for such factors as price, income, and whether the homeowner had engages in other kinds of mitigation.

Human cognitive evolution is one reason for why we are prone to learn this way. Through time we have developed strong instincts to learn things by trial and error, avoiding actions (or inactions) that yield bad outcomes and repeating those that yield good ones. It is, after all, how we learn to walk, acquire food preferences, and develop video-game skills. The problem comes when this—otherwise efficient—approach to learning is applied to settings where replications are few and the feedback we receive is noisy—the very features that define low-probability, high-consequence events. In such environments, learning by trial and error can be frustratingly slow, marked by tendencies to draw the wrong associations between actions and outcomes, and a cyclical recurrence of under-investment errors.

The Paradox of Feedback

In late October of 2005 hurricane warnings were issued for South Florida in advance of Hurricane Wilma. A general evacuation was ordered for the Keys, and residents throughout the region were urged to begin taking preparations such as securing supplies of bottled water and batteries and filling the cars with gas. To South Floridians these actions would have been all-too familiar; it was the fourth time that year that hurricane warnings had been issued for the region, and the seventh time in the past two years. Yet, after Wilma had departed there was widespread evidence of under-preparation, particularly in highly-populated cities of Miami and Ft. Lauderdale: people stood in hours-long lines awaiting supplies of bottled water after a boil-water order was issued, and gas lines stretched, in some cases, for miles. Florida Governor Jeb Bush expressed the frustration felt by many planners when seeing the lines: "People had ample time to prepare. It isn't that hard to get 72 hours worth of food and water" (October 26, 2005).

One explanation for this outcome is that while residents had extensive experience in *preparing* for storms, far fewer had direct experience *recovering* from them: almost all of the previous hurricane warnings had proven to be false alarms. As trial-and-error learners, what people in southeast Florida were instinctively learning was *not* that preparation actions were essential, but rather that hurricane hazards can be survived without them.

Kahn and Luce (2005) discuss this same effect in the context of false-secu-
rity effects in decisions about personal safety, such as failures to wear bike
helmets). Although all knew, abstractly, the damage and chaos that hurricanes can cause (from Andrew in 1992 and Katrina earlier in the year),
this knowledge did little to motivate personal action; direct experience
trumped abstract notions of what *might* have happened.

An example of problems caused by sparse feedback is the often-heard
critique of warning systems: while they are essential in the prevention of
losses of lives and property, they may also act to discourage marginal
propensities to comply when warnings are issued. The problem is that
because warning zones are invariably much larger than impact zones, for
most people warnings prove to be false alarms. The effect of such
repeated exposure to false alarms is that it both diminishes overt beliefs in
reliability of warnings, as well as the perceived relationship between mitigation acts and safety. While emergency management planners might try
to offset this by repeatedly reminding residents of what would have happened had the hazard struck and they were not prepared, such calls are
often lost in the sea of more tangible real evidence that protective actions
were taken that were unneeded.

When Correct Outcomes Teach Us the Wrong Thing

A perhaps even more disturbing feature of trial-and-error learning is that
even the absence of false alarms is no guarantee that it will lead to optimal
mitigation decisions. In fact, in some cases successful learning will be self-
defeating: the more one invests in mitigation against hazards, the less one
is likely to receive feedback that encourages additional investments; that
is, the experience of losses. This censoring bias is difficult to overcome:
because the decision maker cannot observe the counter-factual of what
would have happened had a mitigation investment *not* been made, he or
she will be unsure whether to attribute the lack of damage to the mitigation investment or the docility of the hazard itself. That is, it is quite possible that no losses would have been incurred even if no investment had
been made in mitigation. Given such a feedback structure, a trial-and-
error learner would have a tough time making progress; the more he or
she invested in protection, the more ambiguous the feedback that would
be received about its benefits. One might thus see evolutionary convergence to a world of limited remedies; damage caused by hazards induces
an initial round of investments in protection, but the very success of these
investments then limits the motivation to make further investments
(Meyer and Kunreuther 2005).

A case example of such a truncated learning process might be found in
the repeated decisions by state and federal governments to under-fund

flood control projects in greater New Orleans prior to Hurricane Katrina. After the floods of Hurricane Betsy in 1965 the federal government authorized funding to bolster the levee system around the city—the Lake Ponchartrain and Vicinity Hurricane Protection Project. Although the project was not expected to be completed until 1978, by 1969 the early stages of investment had already paid off: the city was spared flooding when Hurricane Camille—a much stronger storm than Betsy—passed just to the east. But, ironically, this success—combined with the lack of storms in the years that followed—seemed to deflate rather than spur interest in completing the project. Reduced funding (combined with cost overruns) forced planned dates of completion to be postponed—first to 1991, then 2008. In addition, recommendations made in 1982 to upgrade the original plan for the height of the levees around New Orleans was never funded (U.S. General Accounting Office, 1982). The longer New Orleans went without a flood, the harder it was to make a politically expedient case for a multi-billion-dollar investment in additional protection.

The presence of ambiguous feedback can also produce an opposite— and more perverse—consequence: the perpetuation of superstitious beliefs about protection. The flip side of the tendency for ambiguous feedback to preclude people from fully investing in mitigation when it is truly effective is that it can also fail to extinguish tendencies to invest in mitigation measures that are, in fact, *in*effective. As an example, for years it had been a time-honored belief throughout the Midwest that the best way of insuring that one's house did not blow apart during a tornado was to open its windows in advance of the storm. The logic was that open windows would act to equalize the pressure between the inside and outside of the house as the funnel passed, reducing the tendency for houses to "explode." It was not until the early 1980s that it was conclusively shown that this is not why houses fell apart during tornados—open windows and doors were, in fact, the *cause* of collapse, not the remedy. Winds coming in through open windows and doors tended to destabilize roofs which, in turn, tended to destabilize walls.

The myth of open windows proves so persistent, in part, because of spurious reinforcement. If people lost their houses in a twister, they would be motivated to seek remedies that would prevent the calamity from recurring in the future—in this case adopting the wisdom of opening windows in advance of the storm. The next time the home is threatened by a tornado the homeowner will thus open the windows—and likely find positive results. The reason, however, would not be because the measure was effective, but because the odds that a house will survive a brush with a tornado are far greater than being demolished by it (windows open or not). Moreover, even if the owner had the misfortune of having the house destroyed again, the outcome would more likely be attributed to the overwhelming force of the twister rather the possibility that the homeowner's own actions contributed to the calamity.

Learning about mitigation investments is likely to be a frustratingly slow process, one that may never achieve individually (or socially) optimal levels. The advent of a disaster at one point in time triggers a rash of reactive protective actions designed to preclude a recurrence. But the most likely subsequent feedback decision makers will receive after that works to suppress, rather than enhance, subsequent investments. The fact that most encounters are false alarms provides an overtly negative association between investments and outcomes. Likewise, the very effectiveness of mitigation works to make the cues that are needed to trigger additional investments—losses—less likely to be encountered in the future. Hence, what likely emerges is a slow proves where societies learn the wisdom of mitigation only in fits and starts.

A Different Take on Decision Errors: Imperfect Calculations of Risk

While the mistakes we see in mitigation decisions might well resemble a trial-and-error learning process, few would suggest that this is the actual mechanism that produces errors. Rather, in most cases mitigation decisions involve at least an attempt to engage in a reasoned process that trades off costs with benefits (Kunreuther 2006). In this view, if a coastal resident elects not to evacuate in the face of a hurricane, it is not simply because she has been conditioned to do so, but because she consciously perceives that the benefits of leaving (such as eliminating the risk of drowning) are overshadowed by the perceived costs (such as securing lodging and making the home vulnerable to looting). The errors in mitigation decisions described above could also have origins in mistaken beliefs about either the likelihood of hazards or errors in forecasts of likely consequences.

Seeing Is Believing: Biases in Inferences About Likelihood

Another way of explaining the tendency for people to be overly swayed by the outcome of recent events when making risky decisions is that they form beliefs about the likelihood of hazards by looking at just the most recent data; that is, we underweight long-term base rates of hazards. Supportive of this, there is ample evidence that subjective perceptions of the probability of hazards often dramatically departs from actuarial values in a way that is suggestive of an excessive focus on recent (or more memorable) instances (Kahneman and Tversky 1973; Lerrner et al. 2003).

For example, Lerner, Gonzalez, Small, and Fischhoff (2003) report data showing that when a sample of 973 Americans were asked to provide an estimate of the probability that they will be harmed by violent crime in the course of the coming year, the mean estimate was 43%—an exaggerated estimate just slightly less than the perceived likelihood of getting the flu (47%). Likewise, Burger and Palmer (1992) report evidence showing how California Bay residents' beliefs about the likelihood they would suffer personal harm from a natural disaster rose immediately after their encounter with the 1989 Loma Prieta earthquake—only to fall again a few weeks later.

All of these findings are suggestive of an availability bias—the tendency for people to construct perceptions of likelihood based on the mental availability of instances (Folkes 1988; Kahneman and Tversky 1973). People likely overestimate the likelihood of death by violent crime or gunshot accidents because examples of these things are easily brought to mind, perhaps fostered by their pervasive depiction in media. Deaths from accidental falls, on the other hand, suffer from the opposite bias: while it is easy to retrieve instances of friends and family members who survived falls from chairs and ladders, few can recall instances where such falls produced deaths. The changeable perceptions of natural-hazard risk reported by Burger and Palmer (1992) follows suit; in the days immediately following the earthquake it was likely far easier for residents to imagine future calamities than weeks later, when memories of the quake faded compared to more recent memories of life without hazards.[1]

It is important to note that too much should not be made of the fact that in these studies of subjective probability people's stated likelihoods of rare events tend to exceed their actuarial values—a finding that would seem counter to the evidence that people under-mitigate. Remember that subjective estimates of probability are simply ratings of how certain people are that some event will occur as measured on a 0-to-1 scale. Because these judgments are not mathematical probabilities, raw comparisons to actuarial likelihoods may not be particularly meaningful. What is important about these findings is that subjective estimates of risk are influenced by factors that have no normative stature—such as how easy it is to imagine harmful events—something that, in turn, could cause harmful distortions of subjective *orderings* of risk to be distorted.

Beliefs that small samples tell all. Another reason why assessments of risk may be overly influenced by the recent past—even in the absence of availability effects—is a tendency for people to believe that the statistical properties of large samples should be evident in small samples—a bias Kahneman and Tversky (1973) term the *representativeness heuristic*. To illustrate the effect, consider a person who tosses a fair coin four times. The common intuition is that the most likely outcome of this experiment will be two heads and two tails—that is, the large-sample properties of the coin toss should be evident in the small sample. While this indeed the most likely outcome, people tend to think this outcome is far more likely than it really is (3/8ths). By reciprocal logic, the percentage mix observed in a small sample is taken to be a good estimate of the mix in the whole population. Hence, if the four coin tosses yield four heads, the instinct will be to conclude that the coin is biased—not that one is seeing a chance event consistent with a fair coin (on average such an outcome would occur once in every sixteen experiments).

In the context of hazard perception, the representative heuristic has two implications. One is that it validates the intuition that recent history is a fair guide to long-term likelihoods. If a region goes without a hurricane hit for a few years, it must be because the odds of getting hit have gone down (or were previously overestimated), not that such a run should be expected under a constant base probability.

The second is that it makes people see deeper meaning in runs of events than would normatively be justified and *fail* to see trends that are evident in long-run data. To illustrate this, between 1887 and 1969 387 hurricanes were recorded in the Atlantic basin, of which 27 directly impacted the extreme southern tip of Florida from Miami southward through the Keys—about 7 percent of all storms. But between 1970 and 1991—the year before Andrew—the same area was hit only twice (both minimal storms), including a run of 15 years when there was no hit at all. Had the region become a safer place? In a long-term sense, no. As early as the 1960s climatologists recognized that hurricane activity in the Atlantic Basin tended to run through multi-decade cycles of higher and lower activity, and that the lull in the 1970s and 80s was likely to be temporary (see, for example, Dunn, 1964). Developers and residents, however, acted as if the lull was a permanent regime. This increased sense of safety, in turn, contributed to diminished interest in the development and enforcement of building codes (heightening the damage caused by Andrew in 1992) and spurring coastal development along the Atlantic and Gulf Coasts (the source of much of the damage caused by the hurricanes of 2004 and 2005).

Optimistic biases: I'm at risk, but you're more so. A final source of bias that arises in subjective judgments of likelihood is the tendency for people to believe that hazardous events are more likely to strike others than themselves—an effect termed the *optimistic bias* (Chandler, et al. 1999; Sjoberg 2003; Weinstein 1980; 2000). The standard take on the effect is that while people might well hold a general appreciation of the risks of hazards in their environment—be they hurricanes, earthquakes, or terrorist attacks—they are more likely to impact others than ourselves. Part of this effect may be explained in terms of the availability bias noted above: for the vast majority of us what we know about the damaging effects of hazards comes from witnessing their impacts on other people in other places—such as tsunamis in Asia, avalanches in the Alps, and floods in a distant part of the country. As a result, there is a tendency to uniformly see disasters as other people's problems: a very real risk from which we are likely to be spared (Weinstein 1980). As an illustration, after the 9-11 terrorist attacks Lermer et al. (2003) asked people to judge the probability that they would be hurt in a terrorist attack over the next 12 months. The data revealed a strong self-versus-others bias: people judged their own probability as being 20.5% (median 10%), while that for the "average American" as being 47.8% (median 50%).

In other cases optimistic biases come from a tendency to believe that personal risk is lower because of an ability to control it. In these cases the mechanism appears to be a tendency for people to be more prone toward image scenarios that would *not* lead to a negative outcome (for instance, braking in the nick of time) than would (Weinstein 1980).

Seeing the Future as an Extension of the Present: Biases in Forecasts of Impacts

When things go wrong after a natural hazard the first line of defense one often hears from emergency management officials is that things happened that were beyond the scope of predictability. After Hurricane Katrina, for example, FEMA officials were quick to cite the extreme nature of the storm surges experienced along the Mississippi coast (which exceeded actuarial predictions for a storm of its strength), and how the storm revealed flaws in the New Orleans levee system that were unknown prior to the event.

Even President Bush joined the fray when he told ABC news on September first, "I don't think anybody anticipated a breach in the levees." While few seemed to buy the defense in the case of Katrina, in a more general sense the logic has merit: the instant one makes a decision not to protect against all possible risks, one accepts the possibility that errors will occasionally arise—cases where one would have invested more had one the benefit of hindsight.

But the legitimacy of this analysis rests on a critical assumption that the beliefs about the likely consequences of hazards that are the basis of decisions are unbiased. That is, if it were somehow possible to reproduce the hazard a large number of times, in half of these instances we would see damage that is less severe than these expectations and half the time more severe. How can planners (or individuals) be sure that their beliefs have this property? They cannot, of course, and therein lies the problem: by definition almost all forecasts of the outcome of rare hazards are subjective conjectures about what *might* happen, conjectures that are known to be subject to a number of systematic—and potentially quite damaging—biases.

Consider the Rachlieu Apartment tragedy that occurred during Hurricane Camille in 1969. The Rachlieu Apartments were a 2-story complex that enjoyed a prime location facing the Gulf Coast in Pass Christian, Mississippi. The complex was well-built, indeed so much so that the complex was designated as a civil defense shelter. As Hurricane Camille approached the coast with 190-mph winds a general evacuation was ordered, and most complied; 23 residents of Pass Christian, however, elected to ride out the storm in the Rachlieu complex. The reason was simple: it was hard to imagine forces of nature that could seriously damage—much less destroy—such a formidable structure. But shortly after midnight on August 17th the category-5 storm did just that: a 25-foot storm surge took the complex down to its foundation. Twenty-one people died (Pielke et al. 1999.[2]

The inability of the Rachlieu residents to imagine their complex in a vastly different state is an example of what Lowenstein, O Donoghue, and Rabin (2003) term a *projection bias*—a tendency for subjective forecasts about the future to be biased toward what is being experienced and felt in the present. At some level we all know this intuitively, such as in the age-old adage that one shouldn't go grocery shopping when hungry. The rationale is that one will end up buying a quantity and mix of goods that appeal to one in a hungry state (for example, junk food) rather than later when one is more satiated. Read and van Leewuen (1998) offer laboratory evidence showing this very effect: in an experiment where hungry and satiated subjects to choose a snack that they would consume in a week when they were in a different hunger state. Consistent with a projection bias, their choices much more closely corresponded to their current states than their future ones: hungry subjects tended to choose unhealthy snacks to eat later (when they would be satiated) while satiated subjects did the reverse.

In the context of hazard planning, the projection bias offers a natural mechanism for explaining the reluctance of many decision makers to engage in costly acts of mitigation—such as the reluctance of many in New Orleans who had the means to evacuate before Katrina to do so. The projection bias implies that a contributing factor here may have been the mere difficulty people likely had imaging an environment vastly different from the one that they were currently facing, or how they would feel when faced with such an altered environment—in this case a residential neighborhood under twenty feet of water. The more difficult this future became to imagine, the more short-term decisions would tend to be anchored toward those that make the most sense in the present—here a preference for home versus the unfamiliar confines of distant shelter.

But the projection bias also has a more positive flip side: a tendency for individuals who suffer damage from hazards to underestimate the time it will take to recover, both physically and mentally. In press briefing on September 5th after Hurricane Katrina, for example, the US Corps of Engineers estimated that ir might take "months" for floodwaters to be fully drained from city—an estimate that reflected the discouraged feelings of many that the timetable for the city's recovery might best be measured in years rather than weeks. But the reality was not quite as bad as first feared: some parts of city became accessible by natural drainage within a week of the storm, and drainage operations were completed by the beginning of October. Likewise, by early October commerce had also begun to return, with most clubs and restaurants in the French Quarter re-opening for business—albeit to few customers.

Underestimation of recovery times has other examples. Gilbert and colleagues (Gilbert et al. 1998; Wilson and Gilbert 2003) offer several lines of evidence showing that people underestimate their ability to bounce back from negative life events—such as being denied tenure or incurring a disease. By comparing forecasts that people make about how they will feel after a negative event with the expressed feelings of those who have already incurred them, the general evidence is that people tend to be too pessimistic about their ability to mentally recover—they presume that the immediate negative reactions they would have to negative events would persist in the future. In all these cases the excessive pessimism that immediately follows a negative event is the mirror image of the optimistic bias that arises before it: we simply find it difficult to imagine a negative set of circumstances (such as city under water) being made right again.

Implementation Errors: Procrastination and Preferences for the Status Quo

Not all decisions to under-invest in mitigation arise from biased beliefs about probabilities or outcomes. In some cases such errors arise from the mere fact that people are unsure what acts of mitigation to undertake, or when. There is an extensive body of research showing that when people are faced with choosing among a set of options whose merits are uncertain versus a default of doing nothing, people will often prefer the latter—an effect known as the *status-quo bias* (Samuelson and Zeckhauser 1988).

It is just such a bias, for example, that Schwitzer and Hershey (1997) argue contributes to the tendency for employees to under-contribute to flexible medical spending accounts. While many may recognize the need for a larger allocation in a coming year, uncertainty about just what amount this should be leads many to retain the previous year's default. Likewise, preferences for inaction have been found to increase with the number of available choice options (Dhar 1997; Tversky and Shafir 1992)—in essence, the more confusing the menu, the more one is likely to order nothing from it.

It should be emphasized, of course, that initial decisions to defer actions are rarely seen as being permanent; one imagines one is merely postponing the decision to a point in the near future when, hopefully, the correct course of action will become clearer, or one has more resources to pursue action. It only becomes permanent when this cycle of procrastination becomes repetitive, or when people perpetually see a more favorable set of choices lying just around the bend.

A good example of this is the decades-long under-funding of the Lake Pomchartrain Hurricane Protection Project mentioned earlier. The policy makers who supported funding legislation that contributed to successive postponements were under no illusions about the risk the region faced from a catastrophic flood. Hurricane strikes in the region were known to be frequent, and the impacts of Hurricanes Betsy, Camille, and another flood-inducing storm in 1947 provided clear case studies for predicting impacts. Yet, due a series of cost overruns and funding cuts, the original project was never completed. Earlier we suggested that a contributing factor may have been the very success of the early stages of the project: the absence of flood events in the years that elapsed after 1965 likely diminished perceptions of the need for—or at least the urgency of—additional funding. But another explanation lies in the psychology of deferral and procrastination. Few policy makers likely saw their votes to restrict funding as expression of a desire to *withhold* protection; rather, they were merely expressions of a desire to momentarily delay protection to a time in the near future when its costs could be more reasonably affordable.

Decisions to invest in protection against low-probability events are particularly susceptible to procrastination for a straightforward reason: because the actuarial odds that a hazard will occur within any one short period of time are exceedingly small (odds heavily favor your yard *not* being stuck by lightning this afternoon), small differences in the timing of mitigation investments have little impact on overall risk exposure (one is not incurring a lot of additional risk by choosing to wait until tomorrow to buy a lightning rod). On the other hand, small differences in the timing of out-of-pocket expenditures can have a large impact—at least psychically. The psychic benefits of putting off an investing in mitigation for a day will almost always seem large relative to the psychic costs of incurring an added day of exposure to a hazard. Legislative decisions to defer funding for mitigation projects have this flavor. In 2005, given that New Orleans had gone 40 years without a major flood, odds would seem to favor that it could make it through one more—hence freeing up money that could be used for other investments that seem more urgent (for instance, a war in Iraq).

O Donoghue and Rabin (1999; 2001) explain this effect in terms of the tendency for people to engage in *hyperbolic discounting* when considering the relative merits of current versus future events (Lowenstein and Prelec 1992). Hyperbolic discounting is a tendency we have to disproportionately value immediate versus delayed actions. The effect is intuitively illustrated by common feelings about the prospect of delays in payments: one is much more likely to be perturbed hearing that a check one expected to get in the mail today will not come until tomorrow than hearing that a check one expected to get next week will be delayed a day.

When making a choice between a current or delayed mitigation investment this contrast is particularly acute. In the context of mitigation decisions, the benefit one is receiving is, by definition, uncertain and distant. One buys storm shutters not because they will used tomorrow but because they will be useful at an uncertain future date—perhaps later that year, perhaps ten years from now. In contrast, expenditures for mitigation are tangible and immediate. Hyperbolic discounting predicts that people will see a huge—and recurring—psychic benefit to delaying the investment relative to a more ambiguous—and unchanging—psychic cost. In this way, deeply held beliefs that investments in mitigation are worthwhile can (paradoxically) co-exist with failures to invest in mitigation. Failures to invest come not from a conscious sense that such investments are not cost-effective, but rather from a recurrent series of decisions to postpone the investment one more day—with the end result being that no investment is ever made until it is too late.

This explanation for procrastination is somewhat less compelling, however, in cases where procrastination is observed in the face of an imminent hazard whose arrival time and severity is reasonably certain—such as when a coastal town has been put under a hurricane warning. In such cases all outcomes lie in the immediate future, and one might imagine that the psychic benefits of putting off the costs of mitigation for a few hours would be negligible, and offset by the psychic penalty of delaying receipt of its certain benefits—feelings of safety. Nevertheless, procrastination is often observed in such cases: people wait to the last second to evacuate (only to find they can't), and wait until a storm is upon them to secure supplies (only to find that none are available).

A somewhat different mechanism by which people may evaluate options in time that could explain explanation procrastination in such cases is Trope and Liberman's (2002) *Temporal Construal Theory*. Construal Theory is a hypothesis that people focus more on costs (or downsides) of options when considering immediate actions and benefits (or upsides) when considering delayed options. As an illustration, consider the tendency we noted earlier of Floridians to under-stock supplies in advance of Hurricane Wilma in October of 2005. Residents faced the dilemma of whether to buy supplies early in advance of the storm or wait and buy them on an as-needed basis afterward. Each of these options had a clear downside: buying now presents one with the unpleasant prospect of spending money for supplies that turn out to be needed. Delaying has the downside that the supplies might not be available to buy after the storm. Construal theory would predict a preference for the latter—more risky—act. The reason is a difference in valuations: when considering the option to buy in advance there would be a tendency to focus more on the costs of the action (the chance of buying unneeded supplies) than on the benefits (reassurance), but when considering the option to delay the focus would be more on the benefits (avoiding buying unneeded supplies) than the costs (the possibility of unavailability). The consequence is a preference for procrastination: future, risky options seem more attractive than current, conservative ones (see Sangristano, Trope, and Liberman 2002).

Planning Fallacies

Few accounts of the losses of human lives during natural disasters are more tragic than that of the 260 World War I veterans who lost their lives in the Florida Keys during the great Labor Day Hurricane of 1935. The story has been often told (Drye 2002): the veterans had come to the Keys as part of a depression-era works program to build an overseas highway through the Keys, and were being housed in a camp of lightly-constructed shelters. Early on the Sunday before Labor Day of 1935 the Weather Bureau warned that a developing hurricane was moving toward the Florida Straits, and would begin affecting the Keys with gales that evening. Aware of the precariousness of the veterans' location, Federal Relief Agency officials ordered that a train be sent to the Keys to evacuate them to the mainland. But something went wrong: the agency underestimated the amount of time that would be required to assemble a train (for instance, the engine was pointed in the wrong direction), and by the time it was poised to rescue the workers the storm was already upon them. The train never made it (it was washed off the tracks), making the large loss of life inevitable.

The tragedy of the Labor Day Hurricane illustrates what is popularly known as the planning fallacy: the tendency to underestimate the amount of time (and just as often costs) it takes to complete tasks (Buehler, Griffin, and Ross 1994; Kahneman and Lovallo 1993; Roy, Christenfield, and McKenzie 2005). The bias is thought to come from a confluence of two cognitive tendencies: that of being overly optimistic when imagining future sequences of events, and having overly optimistic recollections of *past* durations (Roy et al. 2005). The fallacy has several clear implications for hazard response. The most transparent is that it will cause people (and organizations) to be unable to complete planned acts of mitigation before the arrival of a hazard, such as the above example of underestimating evacuation times.

It is also an error that seems to arise even in the most well-practiced of settings. A good case in point was the massive traffic jams that arose when 1.5 million residents of Galveston and Houston, Texas were ordered to evacuate in advance of Hurricane Rita in 2005. Although emergency traffic-control plans for hurricane evacuations had long been on the books in Texas, the plans proved inadequate. Unforeseen, for example, was the fact that that many more residents would attempt to evacuate than were required to do so (2.7 million; *Austin American Statesman*, October 27, 2005) which produced traffic jams of a Herculean scale. Anecdotes included motorists taking up to 15 hours to travel 13 miles (*Houston Chronicle*, September 22), with delays being exacerbated by the fact that few motorists, for their part, had planned enough fuel, food, or water for such long waits. Tragically, the greatest loss of life during the storm occurred in the course of attempts to flee it, when 23 nursing home residents died in a bus fire during the evacuation.

The second implication is that it may contribute to underestimation of the damaging impact of hazards when they arrive—hence, in turn, underestimation in protection. The prime example is underestimation of interdependencies that exist in the production of physical damage (Kunreuther and Heal 2003). During hurricanes, for example, it is quite likely that if one's home is damaged by a flying object, that object likely came from a neighbor's yard (or house), not one's own. Such interdependencies are another source of future contingency that may overlooked when considering a hazard's likely impact. After Hurricane Wilma struck South Florida in October 2005, for example, structural engineers were "dumbfounded" by the extensive damage done to windows in high-rise structures in the downtown areas of Miami and Ft. Lauderdale—in many cases in buildings built to conform to stronger codes set for the region after Hurricane Andrew in 1992 (*Miami Herald*, October 26). The explanation for the unforeseen damage was that it was a compounding effect of flying debris from damage elsewhere—such as broken glass and pebbles—effects that were, apparently, under-predicted in the course of structural design.

Errors in Planning for Others

A final class of errors that we consider are those that arise when mitigation decisions are not made by an individual directly, but are rather overseen by a central planning agent. Most real-world mitigation scenarios, of course, involve at least some of this element; county emergency planning officials are charged with the responsibility of ordering evacuations, central governments oversee decisions about the overall level of investment in mitigation as well as where these investments will be targeted. In such cases errors made by policy-makers are subject to many of the same sources of bias discussed above, and also two more: an inability to accurately anticipate the preferences and actions of those who will be directly affected by the hazard, and a tendency to underestimate the time and costs associated with implementing plans.

Why we can't make decisions for others: Empathy Gaps. People have a hard time putting themselves in the shoes of others. This effect, which has been referred to as both the empathy gap (Van Boven, Dunning, and Loewenstein 2000) and the false-consensus effect (Hoch 1988; Marks and Muller 1987; Ross, Greene, and House 1977) is an extension of the projection bias in personal forecasting discussed earlier; in the same way that people have a hard time decoupling current emotions and preferences from forecasts of future preferences, people also have a hard time imagining the preferences they would have were they in someone else's shoes. In such cases, forecasts tend to be biased toward their own (Hoch 1988; Holmes 1968). This limitation in perspective-taking has been used, for example, to explain why buyers and sellers often have a difficult time reaching agreements: buyers have a hard time fully appreciating the aversion for loss that causes sellers to (often) overvalue their possessions (the endowment effect), while sellers have an equally hard time viewing their possessions from the perspective of a buyer who is spared this bias (Van Boven, Dunning, and Loewenstein 2000).

In the context of policy-making for hazard mitigation such biases are, of course, potentially lethal in their consequences. Policies for mitigation, by definition, are formulated in environments that are physically and emotionally remote from those that will exist at the time of the hazard, and rarely by the same people who will be the targets of the hazard. As such, planners face the prospect of succumbing to errors in both faulty projection—such as underestimating the likelihood of panic—and temporal construal—such as implementing plans that presume a willingness to adopt formidable levels of risk (Sangristano, Trope, and Liberman 2002).

Conclusions: Can Anything Be Done?

While there may be many flaws in how we go about making decisions, second-guessing does not appear to be one of them. After disasters we are astute judges of what *should* have been done to better prepare for them.

Yet, this skill does not seem to translate to increased abilities to take effective preventive action beforehand. The key lesson of this essay is that in many cases these failings simply accrue to our own psychological make-up; as human decision makers we are not well equipped to make effective decisions in settings where feedback is rare, ambiguous in its meaning, and where optimal decisions require astute skills in foresight. In particular, we are overly prone to succumb to three classes of decision bias: an excessive tendency to learn by focusing on recent outcomes, a tendency to see the future as a simple extrapolation of the present, and an inability to see the value of long-term benefits when compared to short-term costs.

I argue, however, that these limitations need not have been fatal. If a criticism is to be leveled at past governmental policies (both local and national) on mitigation it is that they have tended to look far more to economics for guidance than psychology. Yet, it is the latter that will ultimately determine the effectiveness of policies. Developing programs that offer individuals economic incentives to engage in mitigation is but a first step. Policies are also needed to assist people in overcoming the psychological barriers to adopting those measures.

In this same spirit, policy makers need to be made aware that they are no less subject to decision biases than their constituents. In fact, a case can be made that most tragedies are not the result of an aggregation of a large number of errors made by individuals, but rather by a single error made by a policy maker that impacts a whole population. While it is hoped, for example, that the individual victims of Hurricane Katrina will learn from the experience, it is clearly more critical that governments learn.

Enhancing What We Learn from Experience

To illustrate this point, the natural urge that governments have to learn as much as possible from a disaster to insure that it does not happen again often competes with a conflicting need to return to a normal way of life, that is, make the event a thing of the past. For example, consider Pielke et al.'s (1999) description of the reconstruction that took place along the Mississsppi Gulf coast after hurricane Camille in 1969:

A massive rebuilding effort took place in the months and years following the hurricane. Ironically, hurricane mitigation was not a key thought to those rebuilding immediately after Camille. A need for structures to live and work out of led to a rapid rebuilding effort. The same characteristics which led to absolute destruction of homes and businesses were repeated in the months immediately following the hurricane (Pielke et al. 1999).

While new building codes were indeed developed and suggestions for systematic redevelopment were proposed, the former were spottily enforced and the latter set aside in the understandable urge for people to get their lives back on course. But as we discovered in the summer of 2005, this haste has a real cost; most of what was rebuilt during Camille was destroyed again during Katrina.

A major challenge to both policy makers and individuals is thus to design recovery efforts that manage to achieve two seemingly conflicting goals: righting communities as quickly as possible while rebuilding in a way that maximally learns from past mistakes. The only way it can effectively happen, of course, is if such recovery planning is done *ex ante* in the form of long-term contingent reconstruction and recovery plans. One of the major critiques of hurricane planning in New Orleans was that policies in place dealt only with the earliest stages of a flood disaster—how to get people to survive the initial impact of the event. Shockingly absent was careful foresight into the longer-term problems of recovery that would obviously follow, such as transportation and housing of those in temporary shelters and the treatment of displaced businesses. Likewise, the Mississippi Gulf coast now faces the same set of challenges it did after Camille: there is a widespread appreciation for the need for rebuilding to be done carefully and safely, but such time-consuming planning processes are fighting a losing battle of time against the greater need to provide homes and places of employment for residents.

While the virtue of advance recovery planning might seem transparent, the greatest obstacle in many cases may be a psychic one. It requires individuals and communities to think the unthinkable—the real possibility that they may be confronted with a disaster that destroys their way of life. But as painful as such a planning exercise may be, the costs of engaging in it as a hypothetical event are small relative to those of engaging in the process after a disaster has impacted.

Aiding Foresight: Tools to Increase Compliance with Mitigation Advice

The reluctance of both individuals and communities to engage in advance contingent planning accrues, at its core, to one of the fundamental classes of biases that we discussed earlier: the inability of people to have clear insights into how they would respond to future life events. Not only does limited foresight impair abilities to set long-term plans, but also manifested in highly short-term aversions of mitigation, such as failing to see the values of mitigation.

In recent years a large body of work has developed seeking to find the best means of overcoming short-term thinking biases in a number of domains of personal safety. For example, consider the problem of how one might overcome misperceptions of the likelihood that one will be harmed by a hazard. Two closely related correction mechanisms have explored such cases, both with some success. One involves facilitating the mental generation of risk-consistent instances—such as helping people imagine the different ways that an area protected by levees might find itself inundated (Raghubir and Menon 1998). Earlier we noted that overly optimistic beliefs about hazards sometimes arise from proportional availability biases—the harder it is to think of ways that a hazard could occur relative to *not* occur, the less likely the hazard is perceived to be (Schwartz et al. 1991). In a series of studies designed to explore the effectiveness of advertisements aimed at increasing protective behavior with respect to the spread of the hepatitis C and AIDS viruses, Menon, Block, and Ramanathan (2002) and Raghubir and Menon (1998) find that personal-optimism biases can be over come by designing messages that either facilitate visualization of the mechanics by which the virus can be transmitted (such as through unprotected sex; Raghubir and Menon 1998) or by including examples of transmission methods that people recognize as occurring comparatively often (for example, contracting hepatitis C by from a shared toothbrush).

Closely related is the approach of tailoring persuasions to unique circumstances of the decision maker. When governments offer advice to residents about how to protect against hazards it usually takes the form of generic catch-all lists where only a subset of precautions would be seen as relevant to any one decision maker. For example, a recent preparedness guide for hurricanes prepared by the NOAA and the Red Cross (U.S. Department of Commerce 2001) included a lengthy list of preparations designed to encompass most possible circumstances—such as reminders to be sure to bring baby food and diapers if one is going to a shelter with small children, the need to identify a safe room within every home, and make conditional plans to insure the safety of pets.

The downside of such communications is as above; the more personally relevant cues are lost among a myriad of less relevant ones, the less persuasive becomes the overall message. Consistent with this idea, Kreuter and Strecher (1995) report evidence that personal estimates of risk are improved in programs that customize communications to conform to the lifestyle characteristics of decision makers. An extension of this idea to hazard settings would seem natural; in many cases what people look for is advice about how, for example, someone living in an inland condominium should prepare—not a generic list from which they must make their own judgments about personal relevance.

In contrast to this work, research that has attempted to enhance compliance with mitigation by encouraging people to anticipate their future *emotional* responses to hazards—such as fear or dread—has proven less successful (Weinstein 1995). There are a couple of impeding factors. The first is that emotions are difficult to vicariously reproduce. In the same way that it is impossible for people to accurately recall past sensations of pain or pleasure (Read and Loewenstein 2001), the emotions triggered by communications that encourage people to *imagine* future floods will likely pale relative to those likely to felt given its actual realization

The second is that when communications *are* effective in triggering strong emotional responses—such by showing people vivid depictions of corpses—these emotions have the unintended by-product of suppressing processing of the message itself. This explains, for example, why extreme fear appeals have repeatedly been found to be ineffective in inducing behavioral change (Block and Williams 2002; Krisher, Darley, and Darley 1973). The reason is simple: our natural response to a threatening stimulus is to flee from it. Hence, when we are exposed to a communication that triggers feelings of fear a common response is *not* to pay closer attention to the content of the message (for example, wear seat belts) but rather to turn away from it. Hence, intuitions that the best way to encourage compliance is to show vivid depictions of the consequences of *non*compliance is often misplaced; the greater effect is decreased message comprehension rather than increased hazard avoidance.

On the other hand, there is some developing evidence that appeals that tap into other emotional responses to hazards—most notably regret—*can* be effective in creasing compliance. In a recent paper Passyn, Luce, and Kahn (2005) offer showing that undergraduates were more likely to adopt proactive condoms after viewing communications designed to trigger regret emotions compared to communications that carried a fear appeal and one that carried factual risk information. The regret appeal seemed to work in this context because it heightened senses of personal responsibility for preventive action while at the same time being unthreatening—hence allowing the content of the message to be processed.

Overcoming Temporal Planning Biases

The final courses of remedy are those aimed at aiding errors that accrue to poor inter-temporal judgments about the optimal timing of mitigation. A couple of solutions come to mind. One is a familiar timing aid used in retailing: create perceptions of rigid time limits. In some hazards settings this is done already; NOAA, for example, annually has a "hurricane preparedness week" at the start of each hurricane season designed to both heighten awareness and consolidate decision making. Likewise, governments could publicize mitigation calendars that organize "to do" lists around fixed completion dates.

Biases due to a reluctance to incur out-of-pocket expenses are, clearly, far harder to remedy by persuasion alone. In such cases government intervention would seem required—such as Florida's pilot program to provide no pay-back loans for the purchase of storm shutters. Unfortunately, even those remedies may be limited in their effectiveness, as the loans themselves might be seen as costly to secure (in time and hassle), and they do little, of course, to compensate the non-monetary costs of the mitigation.

Postscript: The Role of Governments Versus Individuals

The fact that human decision makers are limited by cognitive biases is sometimes taken to imply that the best remedy lies in placing restrictions on the freedom of decisions; that is, improved benevolent central planning that either legislates action by individuals (for instance, imposes more rigid rules on evacuation behavior), or channels public funds to provide financial incentives for specific actions. The central limitation of such an argument, however, is that it has legitimacy only to the degree that benevolent central planning is free of the decision biases that it is meant to cure. Such an assertion could not be further than the truth; in most cases the most far-reaching decision errors we illustrated were those being made by policy makers charged with responsibility of building safer societies. In our view, if a resource emphasis should be placed, it is to develop policies that encourage individuals to improve the quality of decisions they make for themselves, not cede these choices to agents.

Notes

The author thanks Edward J. Blum, Baruch Fischhoff, and Don Kettle for comments on an earlier draft of this manuscript.

1. The mere passage of time. however, does not always induce a decrease in beliefs about the likelihood of certain hazards. In a follow-up to the Lerner, et al. (2003) study of public concerns about terrorism measured immediately after the 9-11 attacks, Fischhoff, et al. (2005) found that personal estimates of the likelihood of harm from terrorism among the same participants in the 2001 survey were only slightly lower measured 3 years later. The immense and unrelenting media attention given to terrorism as well as attacks elsewhere likely contributed to the persistence.

2. In 1995 the lot where the Rachlieu apartments once stood was redeveloped as a shopping center. When Hurricane Katrina hit in 2005, the new structure was again demolished to its foundation.

Has the Time Come for Comprehensive Natural Disaster Insurance?

HOWARD KUNREUTHER

Hurricane Katrina has raised a number of questions regarding the role that insurance can or should play in providing protection against natural disasters. Preliminary estimates suggest that it will be the most costly disaster in the history of the insurance industry with total claims ranging between $40 and $55 billion (Towers Perrin 2005). The previous year's Hurricanes Charley, Frances, Ivan and Jeanne that hit Florida in the fall of 2004 produced a combined total loss of $24 billion. Each of these disasters was among the top 10 most costly insurance losses in the world from 1970–2004 (Wharton Risk Center 2005). As a result of these losses, some insurers are reexamining the role they can and should play in providing financial protection against losses from mega catastrophes from natural disasters.

Victims from Katrina have been complaining about receiving substantially less than the actual cost of repairing or rebuilding their damaged or destroyed residence. A standard homeowner's policy, normally required as a condition for a mortgage, provides protection against damage from fire, hail, winter storms, tornadoes and wind damage, but not from rising water due to floods and hurricanes.[1] Many homeowners suffering rising water damage did not have flood insurance even though they were eligible to purchase such a policy through the National Flood Insurance Program (NFIP), a public program administrated by the Federal Emergency Management Agency (FEMA) that was established in 1968.[2] In the Louisiana parishes affected by Katrina the percentage of homeowners with flood insurance ranged from 57.7 percent in St. Bernard's to 7.3 percent in Tangipahoa. Only 40 percent of the residents in Orleans parish had flood insurance (Insurance Information Institute 2005).

The federal government is committed to providing liberal disaster assistance to aid the victims of Katrina and rebuild the Gulf Coast. A few days after Katrina hit landfall, the US Senate voted nearly $60 billion in federal aid. Under the Federal Emergency Management Agency (FEMA) Individual and Households Program, an eligible household may receive up to $26,200 in grants for disaster-damaged property.[3] In addition, the Small Business Administration (SBA) offers loans of up to $200,000 to eligible homeowners for repairs to damaged primary residences and loans of up to $1.5 million for damage to business property, machinery and inventory.[5]

Following a cataclysmic disaster such as Katrina, there is considerable interest by the media and key interested parties in taking steps to reduce the consequences of another such event and to examine alternative ways of spreading the losses should such a disaster occur. However, unless one takes action in the near future to address these problems, it is likely that the next crisis will push this issue off the legislative agenda.

This paper examines the role that insurance can play in combination with other strategies for encouraging loss reduction and for aiding the recovery process following natural disasters. In a book on the topic written eight years ago, as part of a National Science Foundation–funded grant spearheaded by Dennis Mileti on assessing the damage from natural disasters, we noted the following:

> Our position is that the economic costs of natural disasters to the nation are too high and are likely to soar in the future unless some steps are taken to change recent trends. Insurers can address these problems in a constructive manner *only* through joint efforts with other stakeholders, and through the use of strategies that combine insurance with monetary incentives, fines, tax credits, well enforced building codes, and land-use regulations. For example, one way to reduce future losses is to utilize insurance with well-enforced building codes and land-use regulations to successfully reduce losses (Kunreuther and Roth, Sr. 1998).

The time appears ripe for formulating a comprehensive disaster insurance program whereby all natural hazards are required to be part of a standard homeowner policy. Under such a program rates should be based on risk and residents in hazard-prone areas should be provided with economic incentives or required to undertake cost-effective mitigation measures.

The next section examines the decision processes of three interested parties who would be at the centerpiece of such a hazard management program: residents in hazard-prone areas, insurers and reinsurers who sell financial protection prior to a disaster and the federal government who often provides victims with financial assistance following a catastrophic event such as Katrina. Section 3 suggests a rationale for comprehensive disaster insurance as an integral part of a hazard management program and discusses how it could be utilized in combination with other initiatives to achieve a set of desired objectives. After discussing the set of challenges in implementing such a program in Section 4, I outline the elements of a possible public-private partnership in the following section. Section 6 provides a summary and conclusions.

Decision Processes of Key Interested Parties

When a person at risk makes a decision on whether to buy insurance and an insurer determines whether to sell it, there are two basic components that economic theory suggests should be taken into account: the likelihood of a disaster and the resulting damage from such an event. These concepts can be illustrated with the following simplified example with respect to actions taken by a hypothetical homeowner and insurer concerned with the hurricane risk:

> *Homeowner:* The Lowe family has a house in New Orleans that it owns outright and wants to determine whether to purchase insurance to cover wind damage from a future hurricane. Utilizing historical records and the best available information from experts, it estimates the likelihood of such a disaster damaging its house next year to be 1 in 100.[5] Should a hurricane occur the wind damage will be $55,000. A homeowners insurance policy has a $5,000 deductible so that the Lowes will be responsible for covering the first $5,000 in damage and the insurer would pay for the remaining amount.[6] *How much is the Lowe family willing to pay for such coverage?*
>
> *Insurer:* The ABC insurance company wants to determine how much it should charge the Lowe family to cover damage to its house from wind damage, knowing that it will also be insuring a number of other homes in the New Orleans area. It uses the same data as the Lowe family collected and thus estimates the likelihood of such a disaster damaging its house next year to be 1 in 100 and the resulting wind damage to be $55,000. *How much should ABC charge for an insurance policy with a $5,000 deductible?*

To answer this question, the ABC company first determines that the expected annual claims payment to the Lowe family given the $5,000 deductible would be $500 (that is, $1/100$ ($55,000–$5,000)). To cover its cost of capital, marketing and other administrative expenditures and still make a normal profit, ABC sets the premium at $750. The Lowe family makes a decision on whether to buy insurance from ABC by comparing the premium of $750 with the 1 in 100 chance of losing $50,000. If the Lowe family is sufficiently risk averse, being concerned with the impact of a loss of $55,000 on their ability to meet other normal expenditures, they should be willing to pay $750 to protect themselves against the possibility of a catastrophic loss. By parting with a relatively small amount of money, they avoid a low-probability high-consequence event.

Residents' Decisions Regarding Insurance[7]

Variations on this hypothetical example are often used in textbooks to explain why it is rational for well-informed individuals and businesses to purchase insurance even though they are charged rates above their expected losses. In reality, most residents in hazard-prone areas have limited knowledge of the hazard. There is considerable evidence from field studies and controlled experiments that prior to a disaster individuals underestimate the chances of a catastrophic disaster occurring. In fact, many potential victims of disaster perceive the costs of getting information about the hazard and costs of protection to be so high relative to the expected benefits that they do not consider investing in loss reduction measures or purchasing insurance (Kunreuther and Pauly 2004).

This reluctance to invest in protection voluntarily is compounded by *budget constraints*. For some homeowners with relatively low incomes, disaster insurance is considered a discretionary expense that should only be incurred if there are residual funds after taking care of what they consider the necessities of life. In focus groups on the topic, a typical reaction of such a homeowner living in a hazard-prone area to the question "Why don't you have flood or earthquake insurance?" is "I live from pay day to pay day."

Another factor that has been purported to limit homeowners from wanting to purchase insurance is the expectation of liberal disaster assistance following a catastrophic event. As discussed below, earlier studies on this issue suggest that individuals did *not* anticipate receiving any federal aid following a disaster. Given the media coverage of the disaster assistance promised to uninsured victims after Hurricane Katrina, the general public may revise their views as to whether the government will come to the rescue if they are unprotected.

The decision process for many residents in hazard prone areas appears to follow a sequential model of choice. As a first stage in such a process individuals relate their perceived probability of a disaster (p) to a threshold level of concern (p^*), which they may unconsciously set. If $p<p^*$ they do not even think about the consequences of such a disaster by assuming that the event "will not happen to me". In this case they do not take protective actions. Only if $p>p^*$ will the individual or family consider ways that they can reduce the risk of future financial losses.

The contingent weighting model proposed by Tversky, Sattath and Slovic (1988) provides a useful framework for characterizing individual choice processes with respect to this lack of interest in purchasing insurance voluntarily. In this descriptive model, individuals make tradeoffs between the dimensions associated with alternatives, such as probability and outcomes. The weights they put on these dimensions are contingent, because they may vary depending on the problem context and the way information is presented.

The decision to ignore events where $p<p^*$ may be justified if a person

claims that there is limited time available to worry about the vicissitudes of life. Hence s/he needs some way of determining whether to pay attention to some risks. For these individuals only after the occurrence of a disaster does this event assume sufficient salience that it is on their radar screen.

Data supporting such a sequential model of choice has been provided through homeowners surveys of insurance purchase decisions in flood, hurricane and earthquake-prone areas undertaken over 25 years ago (Kunreuther et al. 1978). Data from more recent surveys of homeowners in California undertaken by Risa Palm and her colleagues lend further confirming evidence to such a process. Four mail surveys undertaken since 1989 examine the spatial and demographic characteristics of those homeowners who had purchased earthquake insurance. The findings indicate that insurance purchase is *unrelated* to any measure of seismic risk that is likely to be familiar to homeowners. Rather past experience plays a key role in insurance purchase decisions (Palm 1990; Palm 1995).

To illustrate, consider the Loma Prieta earthquake of 1989, which caused substantial damage to property in Santa Clara County, and to a lesser extent, Contra Costa County, California. In these counties, there were major differences in responses to the 1989 and 1990 survey. In 1989 prior to the earthquake, about 34 percent of the uninsured respondents in both counties felt that earthquake insurance was unnecessary. By 1990, only about 5 percent gave this response. This finding suggests that a disaster causes individuals to think about ways they can protect themselves from the next event and that insurance now becomes an attractive option.

There is also empirical evidence that many homeowners who purchase insurance are likely to cancel policies if they have not made a claim over the course of the next few years (Kunreuther, Vetschera and Sanderson 1989). In the case of flood insurance this finding is particularly striking since the NFIP requires that homes located in Special Flood Hazard Areas purchase insurance as a condition for federally-backed mortgages. To determine the extent FEMA examined applications for disaster assistance from 1549 victims of a flood in August 1998 in Northern Vermont and found that 84 percent in special flood hazard areas did not have insurance, 45 percent of whom were required to have it. A study by Geotrac revealed that more than one-third of the properties damaged in a 1999 flood in Grand Forks, North Dakota were non-compliant with the mandatory insurance purchase requirement (Tobin and Calfee 2005).[8] With respect to earthquake insurance, eight years after the creation of the California Earthquake Authority (CEA) in 1996 by the state of California, the take-up rate for coverage is down from 30 percent to 15 percent (Risk Management Solutions 2004).

Insurance is thus likely to be treated by many individuals as an investment rather than a protective measure, so that those who purchased insurance and did not collect on their policies over the next few years feel that their premium payments have been wasted. In the case of flood insurance, this finding also indicates that some banks, who were expected to enforce the requirement that individuals in high-hazard areas purchase flood coverage, looked the other way.

Insurers' Decisions Regarding Coverage[9]

Based on economic theory insurers who supply coverage to those at risk are assumed to maximize expected profits. If the insurer is concerned about the variability of profits, the ideal risk is one where the potential loss from each insured individual is relatively small and independent of the losses from other policyholders. As the insurer increases the number of policies it issues in a year, the variance in its annual losses decreases. In other words, the *law of large numbers* makes it highly unlikely that the insurer will suffer an extremely large loss relative to the premiums collected.

Fire is an example of a risk that satisfies the law of large numbers since losses are normally independent of one another.[10] To illustrate its application, suppose that an insurer wants to determine the accuracy of the estimated fire loss for a group of identical homes valued at $100,000, each of which has a 1/1,000 annual chance of being completely destroyed by fire. If one assumes that only one fire can occur in any structure during the year, the expected annual loss for each home would be $100 (that is 1/1000 x $100,000). As the number of fire insurance policies n increases, then the variance of the expected annual loss or mean decreases in proportion to n. As a general rule, it is not necessary to issue a large number of insurance policies to reduce the variability of expected annual losses to a small number if the risks are independent of each other.

Insurers are also concerned with providing coverage against events, such as earthquakes and hurricanes, where they can suffer severe losses should they write a large number of policies in the affected region due to high correlation between policies. Actuaries and underwriters both utilize heuristics that reflect these concerns.

Consider the case of estimating the premium for wind damage to homes in New Orleans from future hurricanes. Actuaries first use their best estimates of the likelihood of hurricanes of different intensities to determine an expected annual loss to the property and contents of a particular residence such as the Lowe home. They then increase this figure to reflect the amount of perceived ambiguity in the probability and/or the uncertainty in the loss. Underwriters utilize the actuary's recommended premium as a reference point and then focus first on the impact of a major disaster on the probability of insolvency or some prespecified loss of surplus to determine an appropriate premium to charge. In some states there is a premium on file with the state insurance department that guides their actions.[11] Underwriters then consider the impact that marketing coverage at different feasible premium levels will have on the number of policies sold and the firm's expected profits (Kunreuther 1989).

Roy (1952) first proposed a safety-first model to characterize this type of firm behavior. In the context of insurance, such a model explicitly concerns itself with insolvency when determining the maximum amount of coverage the insurer should offer and the premiums to charge. Stone (1973) formalized these concepts by suggesting that an underwriter who wants to determine the conditions for a specific risk to be insurable will first focus on keeping the probability of insolvency below some threshold level (q^*).

The focus of insurers on insolvency will vary depending on the character of share ownership and managerial agency costs. Mayers and Smith (1990) suggest that the transaction costs associated with insolvency explains the demand for reinsurance by property/liability companies. Greenwald and Stiglitz (1990) contend that managers suffer damage to their personal career prospects if their companies become insolvent and that they cannot diversify their risk as owners of the firm can. By this logic, underwriters would focus on the insolvency constraint where the owners of the firm would be less likely to do so.

To illustrate the nature of a safety-first model for underwriters, suppose that the insurer expects to sell m policies, each of which can produce a loss L if a natural disaster occurs. Then the underwriter would like to set the premium z^* at a level so that the probability of insolvency is no greater than q^*. Risks with more uncertain losses or greater ambiguity will cause underwriters to want to charge higher premiums. The situation will be most pronounced where the losses are likely to highly correlated as in the case of hurricanes and earthquakes.

The underwriter may realize that for some risks the desired premium z^* will be higher than the rate the State Insurance Department will allow the firm to charge. Even if the desired premium z^* is allowed, it may not yield a positive expected profit given the resulting low demand and the cost of capital, marketing and administrative expenses. In either case the risk will then be viewed as uninsurable by the underwriter.

The empirical evidence based on surveys of actuaries and underwriters supports the hypothesis that higher premiums will be recommended for risks with ambiguous probabilities and/or uncertain losses.[12] In a mail survey of professional actuaries conducted by the Casualty Actuarial Society, 463 respondents indicated how much they would charge to cover losses against a defective product where the probabilities of a loss was well specified at $p=.001$ and where they experienced considerable uncertainty about the likelihood of a loss. When losses are independent the median premium values were five times higher for the uncertain risk than for the well-specified probability. This ratio increased to ten times when the losses were perfectly correlated (Hogarth and Kunreuther 1989).

For underwriters a questionnaire was mailed to 190 randomly chosen insurance companies of different sizes asking them to specify the prices which they would like to charge to insure a factory against property damage from a severe earthquake, to insure an underground storage tank and to provide coverage for a neutral situation (that is a risk without any context). Probabilities and losses were varied. The probability of loss and the size of the claim were either well-specified or there was ambiguity regarding the likelihood of the loss and/or the claim size. The underwriters wanted to charge more for the same amount of coverage when either the probability was ambiguous and/or the claim size was uncertain (Kunreuther et al. 1993).

Hurricanes, where there is significant damage from the wind, could have a noticeable impact on the surplus of insurers who have provided standard homeowners and business coverage to a large number of residents and businesses in the impacted areas. Eleven smaller property-casualty insurance companies with a large book of business in Florida became insolvent as a result of losses from Hurricane Andrew, in 1992, the largest number of hurricane-related insolvencies in U.S. history On the other hand, there was only one insolvency, a small insurer, following the four hurricanes in Florida in 2004 (King 2005). To date there have been no reported insolvencies after Hurricanes Katrina, Rita and Wilma in the fall of 2005.

Following Hurricane Andrew property insurance became more difficult to obtain as many insurers limited their concentrations of insured property in coastal areas to reduce the likelihood of future catastrophic losses from hurricanes. To increase the supply of coverage by insurers the state established the Florida Hurricane Catastrophe Fund (FHCF) in 1993 as a mandatory reinsurance program.[13] The Cat Fund has been activated three times—twice in 1995 when it paid $13.1 million for Hurricane Opal and $47.2 million for Hurricane Erin and again in 2004 when the Fund paid out $2.3 billion due to the four hurricanes that hit Florida out of total insured losses of $21 billion (King 2005).

At a theoretical level, Winter (1988, 1991), Gron (1994), and Doherty and Posey (1997) postulate that a particular severe flood, earthquake or hurricane could have a very negative impact on the availability of insurance. They develop a *capacity constraint model* that predicts insurers will cut back on their supply of coverage after a catastrophe if their surplus is significantly reduced and they cannot obtain reinsurance or the post-disaster reinsurance prices have risen so it is unprofitable for them to purchase coverage. Doherty, Kleffner and Posey (1993) suggest that a principal reason why insurers restricted their coverage against wind damage immediately following Hurricane Andrew was because some insurers' surplus were significantly reduced. Premiums were increased to reflect the shortage in supply, which created opportunities for new investment. The establishment of a number of start-up insurers, notably the new Bermuda companies, following Hurricane Andrew, can be explained in this way. Eventually the insurance market settled down and prices and capacity returned to normal levels (Wharton Risk Center 2005). In fact, during in the past few years there has been a considerable influx of new capital in the insurance/reinsurance, market as will be discussed below.

Harrington and Niehaus (2003) show that tax costs could be substantial for catastrophic coverage due to the large amount of capital that must be held in relation to the expected claim costs. Under U.S. tax policy, insurers cannot establish tax deductible reserves for losses until they have occurred. Harrington (2006) concludes that the current tax on private sector investment of capital to back catastrophe insurance is counterproductive and proposes a system of tax-deferred reserves to help correct the problem.

Government Decisions Regarding Disaster Assistance

If individuals are unprotected against financial losses from a large-scale disaster the government is likely to respond with disaster assistance.[14] Federal disaster assistance is purported to create a type of Samaritan's dilemma: providing assistance after a catastrophe reduces the economic incentives of potential victims to invest in protective measures prior to a disaster. If the expectation of disaster assistance reduces the demand for insurance, the political pressure on the government to provide assistance after a disaster is reinforced or amplified.

The empirical evidence on the role of disaster relief suggests that individuals or communities have *not* based their decisions on whether or not to invest in mitigation measures by focusing on the expectation of future disaster relief. Kunreuther et al. (1978) found that most homeowners in earthquake and hurricane prone areas did not expect to receive aid from the federal government following a disaster. Burby et al. (1991) found that local governments that received disaster relief undertook more efforts to reduce losses from future disasters than those that did not. This behavior seems counter-intuitive and the reasons for it are not fully understood.

Whether or not individuals incorporate an expectation of disaster assistance in their pre-disaster planning process, a driving force with respect to the actual provision of government relief are large-scale losses from disasters (Moss 2002). The Alaska earthquake in 1964 and the spate of disas-

ters that followed over the next eight years led the Small Business Administration (SBA) to provide low interest loans, and in some cases forgiveness grants, to aid uninsured victims of earthquakes, floods and
hurricanes. The most extreme example of liberal disaster relief was after
Tropical Storm Agnes in June 1972 that caused severe flooding in Pennsylvania and New York, five months before a Presidential election. Few
homes had flood insurance so that the SBA provided $5000 forgiveness
grants and 1% loans to rebuild the house and in some cases to retire existing mortgages. Of the $675 million in homeowners loans following Agnes,
67% were in the form of forgiveness grants (Kunreuther 1973).

Disaster Insurance as an Integral Part of a Hazard Management Program

Insurance can encourage risk mitigation prior to a disaster through premium reductions and/or lower deductibles while providing financial
assistance after a disaster through claim payments. If insurance is to play
a central role in a hazard management program then rates need to be
based on risk so that those in disaster-prone areas are responsible for the
losses after a disaster occurs. A limitation of any government insurance
program is that premiums are not likely to be risk-based given political
pressure to make coverage affordable to those residing in high-hazard
areas.

Current Insurance Programs for Natural Hazards

Current insurance programs for residents in hazard prone areas are seg-
mented across perils. Standard homeowners and commercial insurance
policies, normally required as a condition for a mortgage, cover damage
from fire, wind, hail, lightning, winter storms and volcanic eruption.
Earthquake insurance can be purchased for an additional premium in all
states except California where today one normally buys an earthquake policy for residential damage through the California Earthquake Authority, a
state-run privately-founded earthquake insurance program. Earthquake
coverage for businesses in California is often included in a commercial
policy or can be purchased from private insurers as a separate rider. As
noted in the introduction, flood insurance for residents and businesses is
offered through the National Flood Insurance program, a public-private
partnership created by Congress in 1968.[15]

Insurers provided coverage against earthquakes, floods and hurricanes
without any public sector involvement until after suffering severe losses
from a major disaster. In the case of earthquakes, the Northridge, CA
earthquake of January 1994 caused $12.5 billion in private insured losses

while stimulating considerable demand for coverage by residents in earth-quake-prone areas of California. Insurers in the state stopped selling new homeowners policies because they were required to offer earthquake coverage to those who demanded it. This led to the formation of the California Earthquake Authority (CEA) in 1996 which raised the deductible from 10% to 15% and limited the losses that insurers can suffer from a future earthquake (Roth, Jr. 1998).

Flood insurance was first offered by private companies in the late 1890s and then again in the mid 1920s. The losses experienced by insurers following the 1927 Mississippi floods and severe flooding in the following year led all companies to discontinue coverage by the end of 1928 (Manes 1938). Few private companies offered flood insurance in the next forty years. Following Hurricane Betsy in 1965, which caused considerable damage to New Orleans, Congress passed the Southeast Hurricane Disaster Relief Act, which provided up to $1,800 in forgiveness grants for those who suffered damage not covered by insurance. A study on the feasibility of flood insurance authorized by the Act reached the conclusion that some type of federal subsidy was required. Building on this study Congress passed the National Flood Insurance Program (NFIP) in 1968. Today the federal government is the primary provider of flood insurance for homeowners and small businesses. Private insurers market coverage and service policies under their own names, retaining a percentage of premiums to cover administrative and marketing costs. Communities that are part of the program are required to adopt land use regulations and building codes to reduce future flood losses (Pasterick 1998). Private insurers provide coverage for larger commercial establishments. The private insured losses for commercial property damage and business interruption losses from Hurricane Katrina have been estimated to be as high as $15–$25 billion (Hartwig 2005).

As pointed out above, coverage from wind damage is provided under standard homeowners and commercial insurance policies. Following Hurricane Andrew, which caused $21.5 billion in insured losses (in 2002 prices) to property in the southern coast of Florida, some insurers felt that they could not continue to provide coverage against wind damage in hurricane-prone areas within the State, especially in view of the risk that insurance rate regulation might prevent them from charging the high rates that would be required to continue writing coverage. This led to the formation of the Florida Hurricane Catastrophe Fund that reimburses a portion of insurers' losses following major hurricanes (Lecomte and Gahagan 1998).

A Case for Comprehensive Disaster Insurance

The idea of a comprehensive disaster insurance program where all natural disasters are covered by a single policy is not a new one. In 1954 Spain formed a public corporation, the Consorcio de Compensation de Seguros (CCS) that today provides mandatory insurance for so-called "extraordinary risks" that include natural disasters and political and social events such as terrorism, riots and civil commotion. Such coverage is an add-on to property insurance policies that are marketed by the private sector. CCS pays claims only if the loss is not covered by private insurance, if low-income families did not buy insurance and/or the insurance company fails to pay because it becomes insolvent. The government collects the premiums and private insurers market the policies and handle claims settlements (Freeman and Scott 2005).

In France, a homeowners policy also covers number of different natural disasters along with terrorism. The main difference comes at the reinsurance level which is partially provided by a publicly owned reinsurer, the Caisse Centrale de Reassurance, for flood, earthquakes, and droughts, and by an insurance pool with unlimited government guarantee for terrorism. There is no public reinsurance for storms (Michel-Kerjan and de Marecellus in press).

Prior to Hurricane Katrina some insurers discussed the need for a national disaster insurance program that covers all natural hazards. Katrina has brought this issue to the fore since there were a number of residents in the area who had homeowners insurance but not flood coverage and were told that their damage was caused by rising water not wind. Those who did have flood insurance and suffered large losses from the rising waters were only able to cover a portion of their losses with their claim payments because the maximum coverage limit of the flood insurance program is $250,000.[16]

Expanding the standard homeowners policy marketed by private insurers to include earthquake and flood has considerable appeal if the rates reflect the risks faced by those residing in hazard-prone areas. By setting risk-based premiums, one signals to those considering moving into hazard-prone areas what the expected losses are from natural disasters. If the resident decides to adopt mitigation measures against one or more hazards, then the insurer can reduce the premium to reflect the lower loss that would occur from future disasters.[17]

An all-hazards insurance program also reduces the variance associated with insurers' losses relative to their surplus in any given year. Consider an insurer marketing coverage nationwide. It will collect premiums that reflect the earthquake risk in California, hurricane risk on the Gulf Coast, tornado damage in the Great Plains states and a flood risk in the Mississippi Valley. Using the law of large numbers discussed above, this higher premium base and the diversification of risk across many hazards reduces the likelihood that such an insurer will suffer a loss that exceeds its surplus in any given year.

Of course, there is some chance that there will be a series of disasters leading to greater catastrophic losses than if one were covering fewer hazards. One only has to look at the damage from Hurricane Katrina to understand this point. If insurers were covering the water and wind damage from hurricanes, then their losses would have been considerably higher than they currently are estimated to be, but the premiums they collected would also have been greater to reflect the additional risk. If insurers wanted protect themselves against such large losses, they could purchase private reinsurance and/or utilizing risk-linked securities such as catastrophe bonds. An open question that we will discuss in the next section is whether there is a need for public sector involvement for covering a portion of insured losses from a mega-catastrophe.

An all-hazards program may also be attractive to both insurers and policyholders in hurricane-prone areas because it avoids the costly process of having an adjuster determine whether the damage was caused by wind or water. This problem of separating wind damage from water damage has been a particularly challenging one following Hurricane Katrina. Across large portions of the coast, the only remains of buildings are foundations and steps where it will be difficult to reach a settlement due to the difficulty in determining the cause of damage. In these cases insurers may decide to pay the coverage limits rather than litigating about whether the damage came from water or wind because of the high costs of taking the case to court. For a house still standing, this process is somewhat easier since one knows, for example, that roof destruction is likely to be caused by the wind and water marks in the living room are signs of flooding (Towers Perrin 2005).

Another reason for having an insurance policy that covers all hazards is that there will be no ambiguity by the homeowner as to whether or not she has coverage. Many residing in the Gulf Coast believed they were covered for water damage from hurricanes when purchasing their homeowners policies. In fact, lawsuits were filed in Mississippi and Louisiana following Katrina claiming that homeowners policies should provide protection against water damage even though there are explicit clauses in the contract that excludes these losses (Hood 2005).

The attractiveness of insurance that guarantees that the policyholder will have coverage against all losses from disasters independent of cause has also been demonstrated experimentally by Kahneman and Tversky (1979). They showed that 80 percent of their subjects preferred such coverage to what they termed probabilistic insurance where there was some chance that a loss was not covered. What matters to an individual is the knowledge that she will be covered if her property is damaged or destroyed, not the cause of the loss. Furthermore by combining all hazards in a single policy, it is more likely that a property owner will consider purchasing insurance against the financial loss from a disaster because it is above her threshold level of concern. Such a policy has added benefits to the extent that individuals are unaware that they are not covered against rising water or earthquake damage in their current homeowners policy and if uninsured victims do not demand or obtain disaster assistance to repair their property.

Naturally, an all-hazards insurance policy will be more expensive than the standard homeowners policy because it is more comprehensive. A resident in New Orleans would now have coverage against both wind and water damage and would be paying more for this added protection. If premiums are based on risk then policyholders would only be charged for hazards that they face. Thus a homeowner in the Gulf Coast would theoretically be covered for earthquake damage but would not be charged anything for this additional protection if the area in which they reside is not a seismically active area. In promoting this all-risk coverage one needs to highlight this point to the general public who may otherwise feel that they are paying for risks that they do not face.

Linking Insurance with Mitigation Measures

In theory insurance can encourage individuals to adopt loss reduction measures through by lowering premiums. In practice, it is hard to sell this idea because the premium reduction given to the homeowner is normally relatively small compared to the cost of a mitigation measure. To illustrate, suppose that the Lowe family can reduce its loss from wind damage caused by a hurricane by bracing their roof trusses and installing straps or clips where the roof decking and roof supports meet at a cost of $1,500. If the annual probability of a hurricane causing wind damage to their house is $1/100$ and reduction in loss due to strengthening the roof in this manner is $27,500, then the expected annual benefit from roof mitigation to the Lowes is $275 and a risk-based insurance premium should be reduced by that amount.

To evaluate the expected benefit to the Lowe family from investing in such a mitigation measure, one should take into account the expected life of the Lowes' home and then determine what the discounted savings would be over this period of time. If the house were expected to last for the next 15 years and the Lowes' annual discount rate were 8%, then the expected discounted benefits would be $2,092, which would exceed the cost of the roof mitigation measures by $592. In fact, such an investment would be justified on cost-benefit grounds for any house that would be expected to last more than 8 years.

If the insurer reduced the Lowes' homeowners premium by $275, would the family invest in the mitigation measure? Empirical evidence on individuals' decision processes with respect to adoption of protective measures suggests that they would not. Individuals tend to be myopic and often compare the expected benefits next year with the incurred costs. If the Lowes' used such a short time-horizon to determine whether they should invest in roof mitigation, they would consider it to be an unattractive use of funds since they would incur an upfront cost of $1,500 in return for a lower premium of $275. In addition, if the Lowe family had budget constraints they would consider this to be an additional reason not to invest in this loss reduction measure.

One way to encourage adoption of cost effective mitigation measures is to have banks provide long-term mitigation loans that could be tied to the property. The bank holding the mortgage on the property could offer a home improvement loan with a payback period identical to the life of the mortgage. For example, a 20-year loan for $1,500 at an annual interest rate of 10% would result in payments of $145 per year. If the annual premium reduction due to the adoption of the mitigation measure is greater than $145 per year, an insured homeowner would have lower total payments by investing in mitigation (Kleindorfer and Kunreuther 1999). In order for such a program to achieve its desired impact, insurance premiums need to be risk-based so that the premium reduction for undertaking the mitigation measure exceeds the annual home improvement loan payment.

Role of Building Codes

Building codes require property owners to meet standards on new structures but normally do not require them to retrofit existing structures. Often such codes are necessary, particularly when property owners are not inclined to adopt mitigation measures on their own due to their misperception of the expected benefits resulting from adopting the measure and/or their inclination to underestimate the probability of a disaster occurring.

Cohen and Noll (1981) provide an additional rationale for building codes. When a structure collapses, it may create externalities in the form of economic dislocations and other social costs that are beyond the financial loss suffered by the owners. For example, if a poorly designed structure collapses in a hurricane, it may cause damage to other buildings that are well designed and still standing from the storm. Knowing this an insurer may offer a smaller premium discount than it would otherwise have given to a homeowner investing in loss reduction measures.

Challenges in Developing a Comprehensive Insurance Program

To develop a comprehensive disaster insurance program where rates are based on risk one needs to obtain scientifically based estimates on the likelihood of each of the hazards occurring in different regions combined with estimates by engineers and other experts on the resulting damage to structures and to people in harms way. These risk assessments are essential ingredients for determining the actuarially fair rates for providing insurance coverage. After developing risk-based premiums, key interested parties from the private and public sector need to address several issues: whether special treatment should be given to low income residents who may be unable to afford coverage, how to promote cost-effective mitigation measures and the alternative options for providing financial protection against losses from mega-catastrophes.

Risk Assessment[18]

The science of assessing catastrophe risk has been improved in recent years through the development of computer-based models that have combined experts' estimates of the likelihood and consequences of future disasters with historical occurrences of these events. The resulting catastrophe models provide estimates of future losses to different regions of the country by overlaying the properties at risk with the potential risk from different natural hazards.

These data can be captured in an exceedance probability (EP) curve that specifies the probabilities that a certain level of losses will be exceeded for a given geographical area. The losses can be measured in terms of dollars of damage, fatalities, illness or some other unit of analysis. An EP curve is particularly valuable for insurers and reinsurers to determine the size and distribution of their portfolios' potential losses. Using an EP curve, they can determine the types and locations of buildings they would like to insure, what coverage to offer, and what price to charge. To keep the probability of insolvency at an acceptable level, insurers can also use an EP curve to determine what proportion of their risk needs to be transferred to reinsurers, the capital markets, and/or the government.

To illustrate with a specific example, suppose an insurer was interested in constructing an EP curve for a given portfolio of insurance policies covering wind damage from hurricanes in a southeastern U.S. coastal community. Using probabilistic risk assessment, the catastrophe model would combine the set of events that could produce a given dollar loss and then determine the resulting probabilities of exceeding losses of different magnitudes. Based on these estimates, the insurer can construct an EP curve that depicts the probability that losses will exceed a particular level.

An insurer utilizes its EP curve for determining how many structures it will want to include in its portfolio given that there is some chance that there will be hurricanes causing damage to a subset of its policies during a given year. More specifically, if the insurer wanted to reduce the probability of a loss from hurricanes that exceeds a critical level, it could reduce the number of policies in force for these hazards, decide not to offer this type of coverage at all (if permitted by law to do so), increase the capital available for dealing with future catastrophic events and/or transfer some of its risk to other parties in the private and/or public sector.

Given the uncertainties associated with risk estimates from an EP curve, insurers may want to limit their coverage against certain risks in order to reduce the chances of a large decrease in surplus through a catastrophic loss, such as some insurers experienced after Hurricane Andrew in 1992, the Northridge earthquake in 2004 and now Hurricane Katrina. This coupled with inadequate insurance premiums in high-hazard areas are why some insurers do not want to provide coverage today against earthquakes in California and wind damage from hurricanes in the Gulf Coast states.

Setting Risk-Based Premiums

If one believes that those residing in hazard-prone areas should be responsible for bearing their own financial burden after suffering losses from a natural disaster, then insurance rates should reflect the risk. Property owners residing along the Gulf Coast should pay considerably more for insurance against wind and water damage from hurricanes than in other parts of the country. Individuals residing in areas where floods, tornadoes and hurricanes are unknown should pay next to nothing for insurance that covers these hazards. However, if they face an earthquake hazard their premiums should reflect this risk. Such a system of risk-based premiums encourages individuals in low risk areas to buy coverage and avoids the problems of adverse selection.

The challenge in implementing such a program tomorrow is that the premiums charged to those residing in the highest risk areas are likely to be considerably greater than they currently are today. In fact, many states regulate rates so that premiums do not reflect the actual risks borne. As Harrington (2006) points out, programs in California, Florida, Hawaii and Louisiana as well as other states have put caps on market insurance rates and created state pools to provide catastrophic reinsurance coverage at subsidized rates. Such mechanisms are likely to expose policyholders to significant rate increases following large losses, as is now occurring in Florida and Louisiana following Hurricane Katrina (Hartwig and Wilkerson 2005).

Some homes in high-risk areas are owned by low income families who cannot afford the costs of insurance or the costs of reconstruction should their house suffer damage from a natural disaster. One issue that needs to be addressed is whether subsidies should be provided to this group in the form of low interest loans and grants for insurance by a federal, state or local government agency. Since uninsured low income victims are likely to receive federal assistance after a disaster, this type of subsidy would reduce the cost to taxpayers following a disaster. A risk-based insurance program with subsidies to low income individuals would enable insurers to set the appropriate rates over time unless they are prevented from doing so by state regulation.

Given the existing system of state rate regulation and the need for special treatment for low income residents in high hazard areas, there are political challenges in implementing the proposed program. The use of catastrophe models and exceedance probability curves can be extremely useful in this regard for legitimizing the types of rates that should be charged. An open question is whether regulators will use these models in determining the rates they are willing to approve.

Private Sector Protection against Catastrophic Losses

A study of the capacity of the U.S. property-casualty insurance industry to respond to catastrophic events during the late 1990s by Cummins, Doherty and Lo (2002) concluded that the industry could pay more than 90 percent of the losses from a $100 billion disaster. However, the authors indicate that such an event would cause the failure of approximately 140 insurance companies and would lead to significant premium increases and supply side shortages.

Given the large increase in insurance/reinsurance industry capital since that time, and some modest progress in the use of capital market instruments to spread risk further, insurers/reinsurers are much less vulnerable today than implied by the Cummins, Doherty, and Lo analysis. For example, Hurricane Katrina has spurred an influx of insurance and reinsurance capacity. As of Dec. 1, 2005, nineteen insurers announced plans to raise $9.95 billion in new capital and eleven new start-ups in Bermuda and one in the Caymans plan to raise an additional $8.65 billion. It is likely at least $20 billion will eventually be raised (Hartwig 2005). One needs a more detailed analysis over the coming months as to how much insurance and reinsurance will be available today to cover catastrophic losses from hurricanes and other natural disasters.

The capital markets have recently emerged as a complement to reinsurance for covering large losses from disasters. Through new financial instruments, known as catastrophe bonds, an insurer or reinsurer can access needed funds following a disaster. If the losses exceed a pre-specified amount, then the interest on the bond, the principal, or both, are forgiven. To justify the risks of losing their principal and/or interest, capital market investors demand a large enough risk-adjusted return to invest in these bonds. This comes in the form of a higher than normal interest rate when no disaster occurs. However, investors (such as hedge fund managers, pension fund managers) are concerned with the impact of the investment on the performance of their portfolio should they suffer a loss.[19] These factors partially explain why it has been necessary to issue cat bonds with relatively high interest rates.

The Wharton Risk Center working jointly with the three leading modeling companies (AIR Worldwide, EQECAT and Risk Management Solutions) recently completed an analysis of the performance of catastrophe bonds in reducing the risks relative to their costs for a hypothetical insurer providing protection to homeowners facing possible disaster losses in three U.S. cities: Oakland and Long Beach, CA (earthquake damage) and Miami/Dade County, FL (hurricane damage). The analysis revealed that while catastrophe bonds reduce catastrophic losses and hence the probability of insolvency, the relatively high interest rates reduce both an insurer's expected profits and return on assets (ROA). An analysis of multi-region cat bonds that provided protection against cat losses in Oakland, Long Beach and Miami revealed that it would lower the likelihood that an investor will lose a given amount of principal due to the diversification of the risk. Hence the interest rate on the cat bond could be reduced, thus making it more attractive to the insurer (Grossi and Kunreuther 2005, chapter 9).

To date catastrophe bonds have not been a major source of funding for catastrophic losses for the reasons described above. There have been only 120 cat bonds issued to date with approximately $10 billion raised by March 2005 (Cummins 2005). Regulatory, accounting and tax issues are also preventing the cat bonds from being used more widely. Another impediment to the widespread use of cat bonds is that it requires specialized knowledge and skills. Investors without these attributes are likely to allocate their funds elsewhere (Jaffee 2005).

Role of the States

In order for the private sector to be given the opportunity to provide insurance using risk-based premiums, state insurance departments have to support this effort. In theory there is no reason for regulators to have to approve rates and/or use models, but instead should rely on competition within the insurance industry. If some states decide to regulate, then they should consider all the evidence when determining what rates to approve. In particular, they should use the data from the modeling firms and other experts to allow rates in high hazard areas to reflect the likelihood and expected losses from future disasters. Furthermore there needs to be recognition that any insurance company established by the state cannot undercut private insurers with respect to the rates that are being charged.

Florida provides a graphic illustration of the challenges one faces in this regard. In recent years there has been considerable development in hurricane prone regions along the coast. Florida's coastal population rose from 7.7 million to 10.5 million between 1980 and 1993, an increase in 37% (Lecomte and Gahagan 1998). This trend is continuing, so it is not surprising that Florida has suffered more hurricane damage than any other state in the past 20 years.

Following Hurricane Andrew the Florida legislature established the Florida Windstorm Underwriting Association (FWUA) and the Florida Residential Property and Casualty Joint Underwriting Association (FRPCJUA), two residual market mechanisms providing insurance to individuals who are unable to obtain coverage in the voluntary market. In August 2002, Citizens Property Insurance Company, a state-run insurer, was established as a merger of these two entities. Following Hurricane Wilma in October 2005 the insurer's losses were estimated at $1.4 billion so that the Citizens Property Insurance Corporation Board approved a filing of a 16% increase for those homes in high risk areas. This follows a 7.8% assessment levied in the summer of 2005 for losses from the four hurricanes that occurred in 2004 (BestWire 2005).

Today there is recognition that the rates currently being charged are much too low relative to the risk. Unless the state insurer charges rates commensurate with the risk of loss it will be undercutting the private insurance market. Subsidized rates will also encourage further development in hurricane-prone areas of Florida and will not provide appropriate economic incentives for property owners to invest in mitigation measures.

Use of Multi-State Insurance Pools

In past years the National Conference of Insurance Legislators (NCOIL) has considered a multistate Natural Disaster Compact, modeled after the Florida Hurricane Catastrophe Fund, to increase available resources, and further spread geographic risks. A share of property premium collected in each state in the pool would be used to finance mega-catastrophes in these states. This concept has obvious appeal to the most disaster-prone states, and has an equal lack of appeal to states where disasters are rarer. These pools face a number of legal and political challenges which may make it difficult for them to be initiated (Kunreuther and Roth 1998).

A successful example of the use of an insurance pool is the one that provides coverage against catastrophic losses from nuclear power plant accidents in the United States. The Price-Anderson Act, originally enacted by Congress in 1957, limits the liability of the nuclear industry in the event of a nuclear accident in the United States. At the same time, it provides a ready source of funds to compensate potential accident victims that would not ordinarily be available in the absence of this legislation. Price-Anderson sets up two tiers of insurance. Each utility is required to maintain the maximum amount of coverage available from the private insurance industry - currently $300 million per site. If claims following an accident exceed that primary layer of insurance, all nuclear operators are obligated to pay up to $100.59 million for each reactor they operate payable at the rate of $10 million per reactor, per year. As of February 2005, the U.S. public currently has more than $10 billion of insurance protection in the event of a nuclear reactor incident (Wharton Risk Center 2005, chapter 2).

Federal Involvement

To deal with mega-disasters that cannot be covered by the private sector Lewis and Murdoch (1996) proposed that the federal government offer catastrophe reinsurance contracts, which would be auctioned annually. The Treasury would auction a limited number of excess of loss (XOL) contracts covering industry losses between $25 billion and $50 billion from a single natural disaster. Insurers, reinsurers, state and multi-state pools would be eligible purchasers.[20] XOL contracts would be sold to the highest bidder above a base reserve price which is risk based. Half of the proceeds above the reserve price would go into a mitigation fund, with the remainder retained to cover payouts. This federal reinsurance effort would be part of a broader program involving mitigation and other loss reduction efforts.

Another proposed option is for the federal government to provide reinsurance protection against catastrophic losses that cannot be covered by the private sector. Insurers would contribute to the fund by being assessed premium charges in the same manner that a private reinsurance company would levy a fee for excess-loss coverage or other protection. One advantage that the federal government has over private reinsurers is its financial ability through taxing and borrowing authority to cover a disaster that occurs in the next few years before sufficient funds are built up to cover these losses.[22]

A Private-Public Partnership for Mitigating Losses and Providing Financial Protection Following Disasters

The rationale for a comprehensive disaster insurance program seems sufficiently compelling in the light of past disaster experience that a concerted effort should be undertaken to develop such a program in the near future. In this section we sketch out the elements of such a program and suggest ways it can be combined with other public-private sector initiatives to reduce future disaster losses.

A Multi-Layered Insurance Program

In order to encourage those at risk to take protective measures while at the same time providing protection to private insurers against catastrophic losses there needs to be a multi-layered program that involves both the public and private sectors. The elements of such a program have been proposed by Doherty, Kleindorfer and Kunreuther (1990) for insuring against environmental pollution and by Litan (2005) for insuring against natural disasters.

The first level of disaster losses should be borne by the victims themselves in order to encourage them to adopt safer measures and to avoid moral hazard problems that might otherwise occur if individuals behaved more carelessly because they knew they were fully protected against the risk. This form of self-insurance is equivalent to having a deductible on an insurance policy. The magnitude of the deductible could vary depending on the amount of coverage in place (such as a percentage deductible), the needs of those at risk and their willingness to trade off a lower price for less first dollar protection.

Losses in Layer 2 would be covered by private insurers with the amounts of coverage based on their surplus, their current portfolio and their ability to diversify across risks. Firms with limited assets that insure policyholders in only one region of the country will want to take on a much smaller book of business than large insurers with policies written in many states and/or protect themselves through risk transfer mechanisms. Layer 3 would consist of private sector risk transfer mechanisms that include reinsurance and catastrophe bonds with the proportion of funds allocated by insurers to each of them depending on the prices and the available coverage. Layer 4 would cover large-scale losses. It could take the form of multi-state pools for providing coverage in certain regions of the country subject to particular hazards, such as hurricanes in the Gulf Coast states. The federal government could also offer catastrophe reinsurance contracts and/or provide pre-funded federal reinsurance for mega-catastrophes.

Linking Insurance with Other Initiatives

For a comprehensive disaster insurance program to reduce losses from future disasters it needs to be linked with other private-public sector initiatives. The importance of well-enforced building codes and land-use regulations to control development in hazard-prone areas becomes an important part of such a program. If some states and the federal government are providing protection against catastrophic losses, they can also require these risk-reducing measures as part of such a private-public partnership. As discussed in Section 3, banks and financial institutions can offer home improvement loans for mitigation measures tied to mortgages on existing structures. This option will be financially attractive to property owners if they obtain a yearly premium reduction on their insurance policy that exceeds the annual payments on the home improvement loan.

Communities can also offer tax incentives to encourage property owners to adopt mitigation measures. The city of Berkeley has encouraged home buyers to retrofit newly purchased homes by instituting a transfer tax rebate. The city has a 1.5% tax levied on property transfer transactions; up to one-third of this amount can be applied to seismic upgrades during the sale of property. Qualifying upgrades include foundation repairs or replacement, wall bracing in basements, shear wall installation, water heater anchoring, and securing of chimneys. Since 1993, these rebates have been applied to 6,300 houses, representing approximately $4.4 million in foregone revenues to the city (Earthquake Engineering Research Institute 1998).

Open Issues

In developing a comprehensive insurance program one of the open issues is whether all property owners should be required to have this insurance coverage. Since banks normally require homeowners coverage and commercial insurance as a condition for a mortgage, a sizable number of property owners would automatically have all-hazards protection.

There will be some individuals who either own their house outright or are not required by their bank to purchase insurance. They may decide to take their chances and not purchase coverage. If there are enough of these uninsured individuals and the past is a guide for the future, the federal government is likely to provide financial following the next large-scale disaster. In this case one would want to consider making insurance protection mandatory. A related option would be for the federal government to levy a tax on all property in the United States with the payment based on the actuarial risk. The government would then cover the catastrophic losses from natural disasters. If such a tax were imposed, then one would need to separate out the catastrophic portion of the loss from lesser damage that would continue to be covered by a homeowners or commercial insurance policy.

If insurance is to provide the appropriate signals to residents in hazard-prone areas, risk-based premiums must be charged. State insurance departments need to give insurers complete freedom to charge these rates subject to solvency concerns that regulators may have if unduly low premiums are proposed by some insurers. One of the advantages of a risk-based system is that it rewards individuals who undertake mitigation measures by providing them with lower premiums. If premium are subsidized in high-hazard areas then the insurer has limited economic incentives to provide coverage to these property owners and no reason to reward them with a lower premium that fully reflects the expected benefit of adopting a loss reduction measure.

If one wants to encourage the use of capital market instruments to cover catastrophic losses, it would be useful to reexamine the current regulations and accounting practices that restrict the use of these instruments today. Jaffee (2005) has indicated three issues that deserve consideration. Accounting standards currently do not allow insurance firms to reflect the risk transfer achieved by non-indemnity catastrophe funds on their financial reports filed with state insurance regulators. A new Financial Accounting Standards Board proposal as it relates to Special Purpose Vehicles (SPVs) used in issuing cat bonds may also have detrimental effects on the cat bond market. A third area is whether one can gain more favorable treatment for the SPVs issuing a catastrophe bond.

There are likely to be a number of low income residents who reside in high hazard areas. These individuals may not be able to afford the relatively high premiums that they would be charged on their disaster insurance policy. They also may not have funds available to invest in mitigation measures even if offered a home improvement loan. Serious consideration should be given to special treatment to this group by public sector agencies at either the local, state and/or federal levels on both equity and efficiency grounds. There needs to be a more detailed analysis as to what proportion of the homes in high-hazard areas are occupied by low income residents and the types of subsidies that should be offered them so they can afford insurance and invest in cost-effective mitigation measures.

Summary and Conclusions

This paper suggests the possible advantages of some type of comprehensive disaster insurance program as an alternative to current insurance arrangements where water and earthquake damage require separate policies. To encourage cost-effective mitigation and increase private sector involvement such a program would require *risk-based rates*. Policyholders would assume the first layer of losses, the private sector would cover the middle layers of losses and state, multi-state pools and/or the federal government would provide protection against truly catastrophic losses through some type of pre-funding arrangement. To reduce future losses there is a need for creative private-public partnerships through economic incentives and well-enforced regulations and standards (such as building codes). It is unclear whether coverage should be voluntary or mandatory and what types of special arrangements should be given to low income families in high hazard areas.

Future research should focus on ways of obtaining better data to reduce the uncertainties surrounding the risk assessment process, how one can provide better information on the risk, alternative ways of reducing the risk faced by different interested parties ranging from the potential victims to government agencies. There is also an opportunity to undertake studies as to how different stakeholders incorporate the concept of probability into their decisions. A 250-year flood has a very specific meaning to an actuary determining insurance rates, but is likely to be interpreted in a very different way by residents in hazard-prone areas subject to this type of disaster.

By reducing uncertainty of the risk and more fully understanding the decision making process of the key interested parties, there is a better chance of developing a sustainable comprehensive and long-term hazard management program. In this regard, it is important to consider ways that communities and regions affected by disasters can develop strategies for reducing future losses. For example, what types of measures can be utilized for reducing losses to the existing infrastructure and lifelines that have an impact on the welfare of the residents in hazard-prone areas? One should also consider the positive externalities associated with risk reducing measures for natural disasters. For example, strengthening property against floods, earthquakes and hurricanes may have side-benefits such as providing added protection against terrorism attacks.

Finally when developing a hazard management strategy it is important to take into account the current institutional arrangements and the types of information individuals, firms and organizations in the private and public sectors utilize on the risk. Without a clear understanding of the political and social landscape as well as how choices are actually made, we are likely to develop policies and programs that will not achieve their desired impacts.

Hurricane Katrina offers us an opportunity to learn from past mistakes and develop programs and policies that have a chance of reducing future losses by bringing theory and practice closer together. This chapter and others in this book examine the important roles of risk assessment and risk perception in developing risk management strategies for reducing future disaster losses and rebuilding stricken communities. We need to capitalize on the interest by the public and private sectors in taking steps to address these problems today rather than waiting until next large-scale disaster to occur.

Notes

Thanks to James Ament, Debra Ballen, Hannah Chervitz, Ronald Daniels, Gary Grant, Scott Harrington, Robert Hartwig, David Hays, Chris Lewis, Erwann Michel-Kerjan, Frank Nutter, Mark Pauly, Peter Schmeidler, Jason Schupp, and Richard Thomas for helpful comments and discussion on an earlier draft of this paper. Support from NSF Grant Award # CMS-0527598 and the Wharton Risk Management and Decision Processes Center is gratefully acknowledged.

1. A homeowners policy does cover some water damage if it is caused by the wind such as from wind driven rain or from the wind creating a hole in the roof or breaking a window.

2. For more details, see Pasterick (1998). See also http://www.fema.gov/nfip.

3. More detail on these federal commitments can be found at http://www.oes .ca.gov/Operational/OESHome.nsf/PDF/Katrina%20PDFs/$file/TransHous-Prog10-4.pdf

4. The annual interest rate on the home loans is either 2.687% or 4%, respectively depending on whether the victim does not or does have credit available elsewhere. For SBA business loans, the interest rates for those without and with credit are 4% and 6.557% respectively. Either business or home loans can be for a maximum of 30 years. For more information on the SBA disaster loan program go to www.sba.gov/disaster

5. For simplicity I am assuming that this is the only hurricane that will cause damage to the Lowes' house.

6. I assume that the coverage limit on the insurance policy is high enough to cover the losses above the deductible.

7. This subsection draws on material in Kunreuther (1996).

8. With the passage of the 1994 National Flood Insurance Reform Act lenders who fail to enforce the flood insurance requirement can be fined up to $350. Prior to that time no penalties were imposed.

9. This subsection draws on material in Kunreuther and Pauly (2006).

10. A notable exception was the Oakland, CA fire of 1991, which destroyed 1941 single-unit dwellings and damaged 2069 others.

11. In many states premiums are subject to prior approval by the Insurance Department. There is a mechanism that would enable an underwriter to charge a different premium than the one on file and approved but the procedure is quite cumbersome and time consuming so it generally not done for personal lines of insurance such as homeowners policies. I am grateful to Gary Grant and David Hayes for pointing this out to me.

12. This behavior reinforces the importance of distinguishing between risk and uncertain outcomes, a concept first introduced by Knight (1921) and then examined empirically forty years later by Ellsberg (1961).

13. The FHCF operates as a tax exempt source of reimbursement to property insurers above a given retention limit should industry hurricane losses exceed $4.5 billion. Reimbursement is limited to available assets (retained earnings) and bor-

rowing ability of the Fund. Each insurer has an individual deductible, which is its proportionate share of the $4.5 billion industry aggregate. Insurers can choose from three reimbursement options for their losses (45%, 75% or 90%) depending on how much they want to pay for reinsurance to the Florida Cat Fund (King 2005).

14. Trebilcock and Daniels (2006) discuss alternative philosophical position as to who should be responsible for the costs of disaster ranging from libertarianism to paternalism.

15. For more details on each of these insurance programs see Kunreuther and Roth (1998).

16. There is a private insurance market for those who would like to purchase higher coverage limits.

17. If a home that is mitigated can suffer damage from a neighboring structure that is not, then the insurer should this into account when determining the premium discount. This type of interdependency creating negative externalities provides a justification for well-enforced building codes.

18. This section is based on Grossi and Kunreuther, chapter 2 (2005). A more detailed discussion of the use of exceedance probability curves in estimating risks from earthquakes and hurricanes can be found in other chapters in this book.

19. For more details on the reasons why investors are concerned with investing in cat bonds see Bantwal and Kunreuther (2000).

20. Harrington (2006) points out that specific Congressional proposals to date have involved low thresholds such as $2 billion that would substantially crowd out private sector coverage.

21. See Harrington (2006) for a more detailed discussion on how the federal government could provide reinsurance against large catastrophic losses.

Rethinking Disaster Policy After Hurricane Katrina

Scott E. Harrington

The approach of Hurricane Katrina and the ensuing devastation in New Orleans and the Gulf Coast riveted the nation's attention. Estimates of privately insured losses from Hurricane Katrina and subsequent storms Rita and Wilma approach $60–$70 billion (Mallion 2005). Losses insured under federal flood insurance are expected to be near $25 billion, compared to $15 billion over the program's entire prior history (Schroeder 2005). The total cost of federal disaster assistance could approach $100 billion; some estimates suggest a much higher figure. These events punctuate an increase in the frequency and severity of losses from natural catastrophes in the U.S. since the late 1980s, including four major hurricanes that produced almost $25 billion of insured losses in 2004. Fortunately, the experience in 2004–2005 accompanied strong profitability growth, apart from catastrophe losses, in the property-casualty insurance (Hartwig 2005). Insurers and reinsurers generally had ample resources to meet their obligations, and strong profits apart from catastrophe coverage also will very likely reduce the scope and intensity of short-run supply contractions and rate increases due to the catastrophe losses.

Even before recent events, growing losses from natural catastrophes led to large government outlays for disaster assistance and substantial increases in premiums for catastrophe insurance. Some states, including California, Florida, Hawaii, and Louisiana, created government or quasi-government catastrophe insurance mechanisms in an attempt to make coverage more affordable and available in hazard-prone regions.[1] The U.S. Congress considered legislation to create some mechanism for federally-backed catastrophe insurance to augment the federal flood and crop insurance programs, in part to reduce the cost of federal disaster assistance. It appears poised to extend a modified version of the Terrorism Risk Insurance Act, which was enacted in 2002 to provide federal reimbursement for specified losses from terrorism. Direct government provision of catastrophe insurance/reinsurance or other government intervention in private catastrophe insurance markets is often justified as necessary to overcome private insurance market "failure," to reduce costs providing "free" disaster assistance, and to promote incentives for risk mitigation and other forms of risk management.

This paper considers appropriate public policy regarding government assistance and insurance coverage for losses from natural catastrophes and other extreme events in the light of recent experience.[2] I first summarize the major factors that affect the insurability of catastrophe risk in the private sector. I then review how the U.S. corporate income taxation of insurers makes catastrophe insurance more expensive and less available, which very likely increases both the cost of disaster assistance and pressure for government regulation and provision of catastrophe insurance. Following a brief discussion of short-run influences on the private sector's capacity to provide catastrophe insurance following large insured losses, I briefly consider the efficacy of prior government responses to problems in catastrophe insurance markets, including the direct provision of insurance.

I conclude by outlining reforms that would significantly expand private sector risk sharing and improve private sector incentives for risk management. The reforms include:

- Allowing private catastrophe insurance premium rates and availability of coverage to be determined by competition among insurers rather than by government regulation—except in certain well-defined and narrow circumstances.
- Reducing corporate tax disincentives for supplying private insurance against large losses from extreme events.
- Developing some method of constraining *ex post* disaster assistance, even if only marginally, to reduce its direct costs and dulling effects on *ex ante* risk management.

If such changes proved inadequate, consideration could be given to adopting, as a last resort, a national risk-spreading mechanism for *extreme* catastrophe losses. I outline possible characteristics of a program that would likely expand rather than crowd out private sector risk-bearing capacity, with minimal adverse effects on incentives for risk mitigation.

Insurability of Catastrophe Risk in the Private Sector

The basic economic theory of the demand for insurance predicts that risk-averse parties who would otherwise bear the full cost of losses are willing to pay an insurance premium greater than the expected indemnity (that is, greater than the statistical expected value of the losses to be paid by the insurance, which equals the expected frequency or probability of loss times the expected average severity of loss). The welfare enhancing effects of insurance have naturally led to investigation of whether private markets produce socially adequate levels of insurance and, if not, whether government insurance can improve welfare. Unless prevented by regulation, private insurance markets develop when prices that potential insurance buyers are willing to pay exceed the prices that insurers need to supply coverage. A particular risk's insurability depends on whether a number of factors that reduce supply and/or demand largely or completely exhaust potential gains from trade.[3]

Premiums generally must exceed the discounted value of expected payments to policyholders to cover insurers' necessary sales, administrative and capital costs, thus reducing the attractiveness of insurance.[4] Insurance buyers also incur indirect costs in arranging insurance, such as the time and effort involved in selecting an insurer and specific coverages and terms. These direct and indirect costs generally make partial insurance coverage desirable (through deductibles and other loss-sharing arrangements), as opposed to full coverage, and they may make some risks uninsurable.

Insurance generally involves moral hazard: policyholders have less incentive to mitigate risk—either *ex ante* (before loss) or *ex post* (after loss)—because insurance rates cannot be adjusted with complete accuracy to reflect policyholders' risk mitigation efforts. Moral hazard inflates expected claim costs and premiums, thus reducing gains from trade. A variety of private insurance contract provisions and other mechanisms mitigate moral hazard, including deductibles and other loss-sharing between insured and insurer, experience rating (basing premiums on the insured's prior loss experience), and insurers' investigation of claims. In the case of catastrophe insurance, policyholders' inability to influence the probability of a disaster-causing storm or event reduces *ex ante* moral hazard, but catastrophe insurance reduces incentives to mitigate risk through location and construction choices. Although government can mandate risk mitigation through restrictions on use and building codes, it has no comparative advantage in controlling moral hazard through insurance contracting mechanisms. Instead, guaranteed availability of coverage at subsidized rates under government insurance aggravates moral hazard, especially for high-risk buyers, and generally lower incentives for government programs to control costs compared with the private sector likely reduce the use of mechanisms that mitigate *ex ante* and *ex post* moral hazard (Priest 2003).

Adverse selection also reduces gains from trade in insurance. It arises when the risk of loss varies across potential buyers in ways that are at least partially known to buyers but unobservable to insurers. At a given premium rate, "high-risk" buyers then are likely to purchase more insurance than "low-risk" buyers, which increases insurers' average cost of paying claims and thus premiums needed to supply coverage. Private insurers have correspondingly strong incentives to group buyers into classes based on all information that helps predict differences in expected claim costs across buyers and that can be acquired (or observed) by insurers at relatively low cost, thus reducing adverse selection and improving incentives for buyers to take efficient steps to mitigate risk.

Adverse selection might make some types of insurance infeasible. Low-risk buyers might be unwilling to buy any coverage at a premium rate large enough for the insurer to cover average expected costs for heterogeneous risk classes. Transactions costs and other factors might make high-risk buyers unwilling to buy any coverage unless their premium rates are subsidized by low-risk buyers. Compulsory insurance requirements constrain adverse selection by forcing low-risk buyers to buy coverage at rates that subsidize high-risk buyers.

Some observers argue that adverse selection is pronounced for some forms of catastrophe insurance. Some studies in the crop insurance literature, for example, suggest that adverse selection could make private insurance for crop damage from weather and related causes infeasible because producers with low or moderate risk of loss will not be willing to buy coverage at rates that include subsidies for higher-risk producers (see Goodwin and Smith 1995 for discussion and references). Before the creation of the federal flood insurance program in 1968, adverse selection was often blamed for the dearth of private flood insurance on residential properties, because there was little demand for coverage outside of flood-prone areas and many insurers apparently felt that they could not distinguish adequately between risks in high- and low-risk areas.

Whether adverse selection played the predominant role in preventing viable private insurance markets when the federal crop and flood insurance programs were created is uncertain. Many characteristics and decisions that affect the risk of loss are observable to insurers and can be reflected in premiums, and on-going improvements in information technology have produced more refined risk classification in many types of insurance over the past several decades. Hartwig (2005) notes that privately insured losses for flood damage (primarily for commercial risks) from Hurricanes Katrina, Rita, and Wilma are expected total about $15 billion, which certainly indicates a substantial private market for flood coverage for commercial risks. In addition, a number of major insurers have begun to offer private flood insurance on high-valued residential properties.

A failure of parties with relatively little exposure to loss to buy catastrophe insurance does not necessarily imply adverse selection or prevent a viable private insurance market for parties with significant exposure. It does, however, imply that parties with significant exposure will have to pay rates that reflect their risk of loss without significant subsidization by parties with little exposure. Compulsion aside, government insurance has no comparative advantage in mitigating adverse selection but instead generally aggravates adverse selection by employing relatively crude pricing and risk classification compared to private insurance, as is well known to be true, for example, for the federal crop and flood insurance programs (see below and Harrington 2000; Priest 2003).

On the supply side, insurers' comparative advantage in bearing risk arises from an ability to diversify losses across many policies (and often investors). Because risk at the level of the individual insurer generally cannot be eliminated through diversification, insurers hold capital (assets in excess of expected claim liabilities) to bond their promises to pay unexpectedly high losses. Private insurance premiums must therefore increase to compensate the insurer for the costs of holding this capital (that is, to provide a reasonable expected profit as compensation for holding capital). When losses are uncorrelated across contracts, insurers can substantially eliminate risk by selling large numbers of contracts. When losses are positively correlated across policyholders—the essence of catastrophe risk—more capital must be held, increasing premiums and reducing gains from trade.[5] Similarly, insurers may sometimes have little information to estimate loss distributions with reasonable accuracy (a problem known as "parameter uncertainty" or "ambiguity"), increasing the likelihood of large, and positively-correlated forecast errors.[6] Because an insurer's comparative advantage declines when losses are positively correlated and/or loss distributions are poorly estimated, a point may be reached where private sector coverage becomes infeasible.

Insurers are often able to achieve substantial risk reduction in the presence of these problems by diversifying catastrophe risk globally through world reinsurance markets. Financial market instruments, such as catastrophe bonds, in principle have the potential to spread the risk of large losses more broadly among investors. But the large amount of capital needed by insurers and reinsurers to support the sale of coverage nonetheless significantly impedes broader private sector coverage of catastrophe losses. I return to this issue below.

The demand for catastrophe insurance appears to be soft in many instances, even when government intervenes to lower the average price of coverage. It is well known, for example, that many property owners eligible for federal flood insurance eschew coverage (Hartwig 2005; Kunreuther 2006). Similarly, a large majority of California property owners eschew earthquake coverage (see Jaffee and Russell 2003; Cummins

2005). A variety of influences can reduce the willingness of risk-averse parties to pay for insurance in general and catastrophe insurance in particular:

- The possibility of relatively frequent losses of small or modest size may not pose sufficient risk to justify buying insurance.
- Consumers' willingness to pay relatively high premium loadings to insure potentially large but exceedingly rare catastrophe losses may be relatively low.
- Property-owners generally do not bear the full cost of uninsured losses due to (a) tax deductibility of uninsured losses, (b) limited liability and bankruptcy law, and (c) the availability of disaster assistance or private charity/relief.
- Other risk management methods can reduce the attractiveness of insurance, including risk mitigation (such as, locating property in less hazard prone areas). Beyond some point, higher expected claim costs and insurance premiums in relation to property values can make insurance unattractive at market-determined rates. The preferred risk management strategy is risk avoidance (such as building a home is a safe area).
- Some parties are naturally hedged against certain losses. Many agricultural producers, for example, are partially hedged against crop losses from weather conditions because lower yields reduce supply, thereby increasing crop prices.
- Some consumers may underestimate the risk of loss or be unaware of the availability of insurance.[7]

The economic literature and policy debate stresses the possible effects of *ex post* disaster assistance on *ex ante* insurance demand. Even apart from the possibility of special, ad hoc grants to victims, the availability of disaster assistance to property owners in the form of heavily subsidized loans could significantly reduce the demand for insurance.[8] Although there is relatively little direct empirical evidence that this is the cause of low demand (see Kunreuther 2006, but also see van Asseldonk et al. 2002), it could be difficult to identify empirically identify such an effect. Large and highly publicized payments following Hurricane Katrina could aggravate any reduction in demand going forward (Kunreuther 2006). In any case, the well-below market borrowing rate on long-term loans for disaster losses greatly reduces the effective cost of a disaster loss to a property-owner, even apart from the tax deductibility of such losses. Eligibility rules are not restrictive, and repayment schedules are flexible. In some instances, homeowners that experience a large loss can borrow at the subsidized rate to repair the damage and to refinance an existing loan. Some homeowners may be able to extinguish existing previous loans through bankruptcy and then borrow funds to rebuild at subsidized rates.

High Tax Costs Impede Private Catastrophe Insurance Markets

There are three main sources of costs of holding large amounts of capital on insurance company balance sheets to back the sale of catastrophe coverage: (1) the possibly limited ability of ultimate investors to diversify risk associated with catastrophe losses, which could increase insurers' cost of capital; (2) tax costs; and (3) "agency" costs associated with how the capital is invested and managed, which could reduce returns to investors.[9] The first source generally is considered modest if not negligible. Relatively little is known about the magnitude of agency costs. Evidence suggests that tax costs could be very large for catastrophe coverage due to the large amounts of capital that must be held in relation to expected claim costs (see Harrington and Niehaus 2003).

In particular, U.S. federal tax policy significantly increases the costs of supplying catastrophe coverage.[10] Insurers cannot establish tax deductible reserves for losses until they have occurred. Premiums are taxed up front, leading to high taxes in years where losses from catastrophes or other extreme events are relatively low, with limited write-offs from net loss carry-back and carry-forward provisions in the tax code when losses are high. More important and as indicated above, providing insurance against rare but potentially enormous losses requires insurers to hold large amounts of equity (non-debt) capital. This capital is primarily invested in marketable securities. Investors can easily purchase such securities directly or through investment funds, where investment returns are subject to personal taxes only (given "pass through" treatment of investment fund returns). When held by an insurer to back the sale of policies, investment returns are taxed twice, at the corporate level and personal level, because insurers cannot hold such capital on a tax-favored basis.

In order for securities to be held as capital by insurers to back the sale of policies, premiums must be high enough to compensate investors for the extra layer of taxes.[11] The total cost can be very large for the amounts of capital that must be invested to back the sale of insurance for losses from relatively rare but potentially extreme events. To illustrate simply, let p denote the probability of a major catastrophe (such as a major hurricane), L is the loss if the event occurs (for instance, $40 billion, $50 billion, or more), S is the additional amount of capital (surplus) that insurers (or reinsurers) would desire to hold to insure the event (without increasing their default risk), and c is the incremental tax cost (as a proportion of S) of holding securities as capital. Ignoring all other costs, the premium P needed for investors to achieve an expected return equal to direct investment (or investment through an investment fund with pass-through treatment) is simply:

$$P = pL + cS.$$

The essence of insurance against catastrophe losses and other extreme events is that S is large in relation to L, given limited diversification of the risk, and that p is relatively small. Letting s denote S/L, the ratio of the additional capital to amount of potential loss, then

$$P = pL + csL.$$

The (gross) premium "loading" factor is the ratio of the premium to the expected loss:

$$P / pL = 1 + cs / p.$$

Given this setup, simple calculations indicate that the tax loading can be substantial. For example, with $s = 0.5$ (the amount of extra capital held equals 50 percent of the potential loss), $p = 0.01$ (the probability of the event in a given year in 1 percent), and $c = 0.02$ (corporate taxes on investment returns of 200 basis points), the premium loading factor, which only exceeds one due to taxes, is 2.[12] If $s = 0.5$, $c = 0.02$, and $p = 0.001$ (the probability of the event is 0.1 percent), the loading factor is 11. Much more realistic models and calibration support the conclusion that the effects of U.S. corporate taxation of returns on invested capital can be large (for example, tax costs equal to 100 percent of expected indemnities or higher) for coverage against extreme losses.[13]

A variety of mechanisms reduce the tax costs of holding capital to back the sale of insurance, including insurer investment in tax-exempt securities (with, however, lower pre-tax yields than comparable taxable securities), some degree of debt financing by insurers or insurance holding companies (where the interest is deductible under the corporate income tax, which in effect allows a pass through to investors of income from the securities backing the debt), and the purchase by domestic insurers and reinsurers of reinsurance from off-shore entities that are governed by tax rules that impose lower costs.[14] These devices entail their own costs.

As noted above, another, albeit quantitatively less important, tax-related impediment to providing insurance against extreme events for U.S. insurers and reinsurers is higher expected costs imposed by having to pay taxes on underwriting income in the (typical?) years where severe events do not occur. This presents a problem because insurers and reinsurers may have limited ability to deduct all losses immediately in the years when their losses are high and taxable income is negative.

Corporate tax policy also increases the costs of alternative risk spreading arrangements, at least indirectly (see Cummins 2005). It generally is recognized, for example, that mechanisms such as catastrophe bonds cannot be cost effective unless the investment income on securities held to back the bonds is not taxed at the entity level. Achieving that tax status typically requires the creation of special purpose vehicles in tax-favored jurisdictions, which increases transactions costs, and might help explain their limited role to date in managing catastrophe risk.

Insurance Market Capacity Constraints and Short-Run Supply

Models of short-run insurance pricing when capital (capacity) is constrained posit that (1) industry supply depends on the amount of insurer capital, and (2) industry supply shifts backwards and is sharply upward sloping following large negative shocks to capital due to the greater costs of raising external capital compared with internal capital.[15] The main implication (subject to some theoretical ambiguity), is that large, negative shocks to capital (such as from catastrophe losses) can produce short-run increases in prices above and beyond changes implied by possible revisions in insurers' forecasts of claim costs for new and renewal business.[16]

If insurers could freely restore capital to its pre-shock level (or any new desired level), prices (premium-cost margins) would not increase, and premium rates would increase commensurately with revisions in expected claim costs But because the cost of obtaining capital increases following the shock, the post-shock short-run supply curve shifts backwards, increasing prices and premium rates. The price increases in turn help insurers to replenish capital through retained earnings, which, along with issues of new capital, gradually eliminates the effects of the shock on supply.

Because rate increases would be expected during temporary capacity shortages, rate regulation to hold down such rate increases would discourage necessary capacity adjustments and reduce availability of coverage. However, the possibility of short-run but acute reductions in coverage availability could make some government intervention to ensure availability economically efficient (that is, it produce benefits that exceed the costs). Any factors that increase the costs of holding capital (such as the corporate tax code), raising new capital, or entry of new firms will make rate changes more volatile.

Empirical evidence on the capacity constraint model is inconclusive.[17] If short-run capacity constraints following large catastrophe losses increase insurance rates, it generally will be difficult to quantify such effects, given the possibility that insurers' expectations of future catastrophe losses will be revised upward in response to new information about the likelihood and/or scope of future potential losses.[18] In the context of catastrophe losses during the past two years, it generally is agreed that upward pressure on prices has been tempered by robust profitability of property-casualty insurers apart from catastrophe experience (see Mallion 2005; Hartwig 2005). That profitability reflects favorable claims experience for non-catastrophe exposures and substantial rate increases, primarily during 2001–2003, following a prolonged "soft" market for commercial property-casualty insurance during the 1990s.

Government Responses to Catastrophe Insurance Market Problems

In the long-run context—and ignoring for the moment the effects of government intervention on private sector capacity—high prices for private catastrophe insurance reflect the high costs of supply. High prices, in combination with the limited willingness of many consumers to pay for insurance when they have voluntary choice, reduce the scope of protection, which in turn leads to some increase in reliance on disaster assistance and greater cost to taxpayers of providing such assistance. High long-run costs to insurers and low demand for catastrophe coverage also increase pressure for creating federal insurance programs with subsidized rates (or even "free" coverage), such as the federal flood and crop insurance programs, the federal backstop for terrorism risk insurance under TRIA, and proposals for federal insurance for other losses from natural catastrophes. As illustrated by programs in California, Florida, Hawaii, Louisiana, and a number of other states, state governments have an incentive to cap private market insurance rates, mandate supply, and create state pools to provide catastrophe reinsurance coverage at subsidized rates, especially given that state pools are permitted to accumulate tax-exempt reserves. This is true even though such mechanisms may expose policyholders to significant risk of rate increases and surcharges to fund catastrophe pools following large losses (as is occurring in Florida and Louisiana, see Hartwig and Wilkerson 2005), as well as increased risk that taxpayers could have to fund part of any losses.

Given tax costs, other costs of capital, and relatively low demand for catastrophe coverage, insurers will hold less capital to back catastrophe coverage, which at the margin increases their insolvency risk and vulnerability to natural disasters. Large disasters therefore have the potential to disrupt insurance markets more severely in the short run, with more insurer insolvencies, higher price increases, more cancellations and non-renewals, and greater pressure on state governments to cap rates and mandate supply. The risk that large catastrophe losses will produce government intervention that limits their ability to charge adequate prices or control their exposure reduces insurers' incentives to expand coverage in disaster prone areas and/or requires them to charge yet higher prices. Given these problems, a point can be reached where direct government provision of coverage or substantial government reinsurance of private sector coverage becomes likely.

The cost and incentive effects of disaster assistance alone are often argued to justify some form of government insurance.[19] The basic story is:

- Disaster assistance is a form of free insurance that is costly to taxpayers.
- Disaster assistance represents an inefficient form of protection compared to formal insurance because its benefits are less certain and less complete.
- The availability of disaster assistance inefficiently distorts incentives of property-owners, producing deadweight losses from excessive levels of activity (location of property in hazardous areas) and inadequate levels of care to prevent and reduce loss (such as more damage prone construction).
- While catastrophe losses cannot be fully diversified across insurance buyers, they can be diversified further over time (that is, by allowing low losses in "good years" to offset high losses in "bad" years). Given its taxing and borrowing authority, the government may have a theoretical advantage in bearing the "timing risk" associated with disasters.
- Appropriately priced and perhaps mandatory government insurance reduces reliance on disaster assistance, provides superior protection against risk, and improves incentives for risk mitigation.

In principle (that is, ignoring the politics and practice of existing programs), government catastrophe insurance (or reinsurance) offers potentially lower deadweight costs from excessive development and inadequate risk mitigation in catastrophe-prone areas. Absent government intervention (and widespread myopia), property development decisions should reflect the private costs and private benefits to decision-makers. Hazard-prone areas will be developed to the point at which marginal private benefits equal marginal private costs. Free disaster assistance causes marginal private costs to be less than total (social) marginal costs. The result is excessive development: development for which the benefits do not exceed the total cost, as many persons believe has occurred, for example, in Florida.[20]

Deadweight losses from excessive development and inadequate precautions would decline if the government could credibly commit to shrinking disaster assistance. Given that such commitment is generally viewed as infeasible, government insurance in hazard-prone regions is advocated as the preferred alternative for promoting efficient risk management. Appropriately priced insurance—perhaps subject to a mandatory purchase requirement—will cause property-owners and developers to internalize more of the costs of hazards in their decisions, thereby deterring excessive development and encouraging efficient risk mitigation.

Despite its conceptual foundations, this view of efficient government insurance is difficult to reconcile with the underlying causes of limited private insurance protection and with the design and performance of existing government insurance programs. The premise that disaster assistance reduces incentives to insure and incentives for risk mitigation is sound, at least in theory. In practice, however, political pressures that produce generous disaster assistance will likely prevent property owners and developers from being required to insure at prices that reflect the full costs of coverage. Given low demand, the cost of government insurance must be subsidized significantly and/or property-owners must be forced to purchase coverage.

Adoption and enforcement of mandatory coverage, however, are politically unattractive, even if rates are subsidized. Since 1973, for example, the federal flood insurance program has required owners of properties in specified flood zones with federally insured loans to buy flood insurance. This requirement was flouted for many years, with many policyholders either failing to buy any coverage or dropping coverage soon after obtaining a mortgage.[21] In the case of federal crop insurance, legislation enacted in 1994 required farmers to pay a nominal fee for compulsory coverage of catastrophic crop losses. The compulsory requirement was dropped in 1996. Farmers were allowed to opt out if they agreed to be ineligible for disaster assistance. The restriction on eligibility for disaster assistance was eliminated in 1998 (see Harrington 2000).

The politically attractive alternative to mandatory, risk-rated coverage is for the government to offer subsidized insurance with limited compulsion and/or the hope that many parties will be induced to purchase coverage, in conjunction with the adoption of some direct controls on development in hazardous regions (such as strict building codes or outright prohibitions on building in very high-risk regions). As a result, the main features of private insurance that help promote efficient risk management, including pricing that is closely tailored to perceived risk of loss, generally do not characterize government insurance. Subsidized rates and limits on underwriting and risk classification under government insurance dull its ability to provide incentives for risk mitigation.

Federal crop insurance premiums are heavily subsidized. The government pays direct subsidies as percentages of premiums collected and pays the expenses of private insurers who issue and service policies on behalf of the government. Higher risk farmers receive larger absolute subsidies under this system. Until this year, the federal flood insurance program had been largely self-sustaining. The program now faces a massive deficit, raising the possibility that rates were too low on average in relation to expected claim costs prior to recent losses, and that its historical experience might reflect fortuity rather than a pricing methodology designed to produce self-sustaining rates over the long run. Premiums have always been heavily subsidized for properties in existence when the program was created, which represent roughly one-third of all insured properties. Given large subsidies to higher risk properties, it seems likely that significantly higher premiums were charged to other property-owners in order to keep the overall program from running large deficits until this year. Those higher premiums would reduce demand by lower risk properties, which might help explain why many eligible homes do not have flood coverage.

While government insurance would be expected to produce some reduction in *ex post* disaster assistance, the magnitude of any reduction is not clear and could be modest. Even before Katrina, the U.S. government appeared incapable of withholding disaster assistance to persons who fail to buy private or, when available, government insurance. In the case of crop insurance, the Congress has repeatedly provided disaster assistance to both insured and uninsured farmers. Any potential savings from government insurance in the form of reduced costs of disaster assistance should be compared with the increased costs that tend to result from subsidized premiums in government catastrophe insurance programs. Subsidies involve direct costs. The scope of losses covered by subsidized government insurance could significantly exceed the scope of losses covered by disaster assistance. Moreover, subsidized rates for government catastrophe insurance inevitably crowd out some amount of private insurance. In any case, subsidized insurance and the ability of property-owners to forego insurance and remain eligible for disaster assistance undercut any efficiency rationale for government catastrophe insurance. Improvements in incentives for efficient risk management are substantially attenuated compared to what would be true with private insurance.

Enhancing Private Markets for Catastrophe Insurance

Policy changes that encourage private sector supply of catastrophe insurance with risk-based pricing and that recognize the weaknesses of government insurance (or government controls on private sector pricing) are the best approach to enhancing efficiency in catastrophe insurance markets and catastrophe risk management. Appropriate policy changes should focus specifically on the following:

1. Allowing private catastrophe insurance premium rates and availability of coverage to be determined by primarily by competition among insurers rather than by government regulation and mandate—except in well-defined and narrow circumstances.
2. Reducing corporate tax disincentives for supplying insurance (and alternative forms of protection) against large losses from extreme events.

3. Tempering the ethos—and changing the practice—of providing generous, ad hoc disaster assistance based in large part on the number of persons harmed from an event, regardless of their pre-loss risk management.

If such changes proved inadequate, consideration could be given to adopting, as a last resort, a government *ex post* reinsurance program that would attach at truly high levels of catastrophic loss. I outline possible characteristics of such a program following brief discussion of these three changes.

1. Except in certain narrowly defined circumstances, rate regulation is unnecessary and counter-productive, especially when it discourages private sector supply and risk-based pricing. To the extent that short-run capacity constraints and associated insurance market dislocations following significant catastrophes favor some governmental or regulatory mechanism to encourage supply, well-designed "beach and windstorm" plans represent a sensible response that reduce the scope of crowd-out, subsidized rates, and disincentives for mitigation, in part by helping to ensure that subsidized rates are narrowly targeted to high risk regions (beachfronts) where possible positive spillovers from economic development may be most likely.

Under these plans, properties within specified distances of the ocean are eligible for windstorm coverage from the plan at regulated rates. All insurers writing residential property insurance within the state share responsibility for any plan deficits. Insurers are motivated to charge premiums for voluntary coverage that reflect the expected cost of any expected assessments for plan deficits. While such arrangements involve some cross-subsidization from low-risk to high-risk areas within a state, the extent of cross-subsidization is inherently lower than from more intrusive mechanisms, such as government sponsored insurance, because pressure to increase the scope of subsidies is naturally counter-balanced by pressure against rate increases that would be required in lower-risk areas in the state.

2. The current tax on private sector investment of capital to back catastrophe insurance is counter-productive. Opposition to reducing this burden reflects a variety of beliefs and sentiments, including (1) ignorance of the burden's deleterious effects, (2) preoccupation with possible short-run loss of tax revenues from corrective action, (3) concerns about possible gaming by insurers (such as artificially inflating the amount of capital or premiums allocated to catastrophe exposures to avoid tax) if the rules are modified to reduce the burden, (4) opposition to sector-specific tax relief in principle and because it could undermine pressure for wholesale modification of the U.S. tax code, (5) opposition by some players in the insurance/reinsurance industry, such as some reinsurers who might fear

a loss of business if holding capital on primary insurers' balance sheets became significantly less expensive, and (6) a preference among some parties for government insurance as opposed to a more robust private market.

I am sympathetic to general arguments against sector-specific tax changes, but I worry in practice that such arguments might let the desire for the perfect (fundamental tax reform) prevent achievement of the good (expanded private sector provision of catastrophe coverage following suitable sector-specific tax changes). A sensible system of tax-deferred reserves would help correct the current chilling effect of federal tax law on the supply of catastrophe insurance. A potentially superior approach, which also would reduce concern with potential gaming, would be to replace the federal income tax for property-casualty insurers with a federal premium tax (which might be designed to be revenue neutral vis-à-vis current taxation). A premium tax would spread the federal insurance tax burden in relation to expected claim costs (the primary determinant of premiums by line of business and geographic region, and thus of the tax burden under a premium tax), as opposed to uncertainty in claim costs and the amount of capital held to achieve safety and soundness under the current tax system.

3. Disaster assistance reflects the classic Samaritan's dilemma. An important question is whether and how the government can commit *ex ante* to levels of disaster assistance *ex post* that respond to inevitable demands—both compassionate and self-interested—to help victims, without significantly undermining incentives for *ex ante* risk management. I have no clever suggestions for addressing this conundrum. It is possible, however, that a systematic attempt at educating the citizens (and media) about the corrosive effects of *ex post* government largesse on *ex ante* incentives and total costs over time could help. In any case, the notion that generous disaster assistance represents an entitlement should be strongly resisted.

If such changes proved inadequate, consideration could be given to adopting, as a last resort, a government reinsurance program that would attach at truly high levels of catastrophic loss. Given the government's potential theoretical advantage in bearing "timing risk" due to its taxing and borrowing authority, federal reinsurance for truly large catastrophe losses has some conceptual appeal. While the devil is certainly in the details, an *ex post* catastrophe reinsurance program with the following components might be able to suitably balance this advantage against the risk of crowding out viable private sector supply:

- The federal government as reinsurer would reimburse a percentage of insured losses (such as 80–90%) from catastrophes during a year in excess of a large aggregate retention (such as $30 billion, indexed for inflation). Consideration could be given to having different retentions for different hazards (hurricane, earthquake, terrorism) and to having a higher federal share once losses exceed a higher aggregate threshold (such as 80% of losses above $30 billion and 90% once losses exceed $50 billion).

- If the aggregate retention were reached, federal reimbursement would be based on net (after reinsurance) losses. Thus, reinsurers—both domestic and foreign—would receive reimbursement in relation to the amount of losses assumed. Consider, for example, the case of a $30 billion aggregate retention with 80 percent reimbursement. If losses during the year totaled $40 billion, each insurer and reinsurer would be reimbursed in the amount of $0.20 per dollar of net loss [0.8 x ($40 billion – $30 billion) / $40 billion]. Hence, an insurer with $1 billion of losses after reinsurance would receive $200 million. If insured losses totaled $60 billion, reimbursement would be $0.40 per dollar of net loss [0.8 x ($60 billion – $30 billion) / $60 billion]. Primary and reinsurance prices and capacity would adjust to reflect that the federal government would be bearing much of the risk of losses beyond the threshold. A catastrophe reinsurer would know, for example, that if aggregate losses reached $60 billion, then 40 percent of its assumed losses would be funded by the government, and it would consider that possibility when pricing its catastrophe treaties.

- Insurers and reinsurers would not be forced to offer catastrophe coverage as part of property insurance policies and programs (apart from traditional state regulation of policy forms). The ability to negotiate inclusion / exclusion of catastrophe losses is especially important for reinsurance, where coverage arrangements are customized and negotiated between sophisticated parties.

- With a suitably high aggregate private sector retention, the extent of the federal (taxpayer) subsidy would be modest. The federal reinsurance would be "free" to insurers / reinsurers, with the benefits of the federal subsidy inuring in large part to policyholders. Insurers / reinsurers would not be charged; there would be no assessments of policyholders. Charging premiums for federal protection is that coming up with appropriate prices could be highly political. Moreover, even apart from political pressures, if the thresholds for government reimbursement were high enough to avoid crowding out viable private sector capacity (such as an aggregate annual threshold of $30 billion or more), the *potential* funding and incentive benefits of charging for protection might not outweigh the necessary transaction and administrative costs (such as the costs of developing rates linked to measures of risk assumed, possibly for numerous coverages of different types in different regions, and in writing and issuing contracts).

- If technically feasible, reimbursement might be extended to investors in catastrophe bonds and related instruments, to the extent that they are responsible for funding catastrophe losses during a given year. That might avoid biasing transactions toward insurance and away from alternative capital market arrangements.

A conceptually attractive alternative to "free" aggregate excess of loss federal reinsurance would be for the federal government to sell (auction) excess of loss reinsurance contracts for catastrophe losses (see Lewis and Murdoch 1996; also see Cummins 2005). Specific Congressional proposals, however, generally involve relatively low thresholds for government payoffs that would substantially crowd out private sector capacity and coverage (such as $2 billion of loss from one event under H.R. 21, the Homeowners Insurance Availability Act of 1999, approved in 1999 by the House Committee on Banking and Financial Services). Moreover, regardless of any initial safeguards to reduce the likelihood that coverage would be under-priced in such a program, pressure would likely mount over time for artificially low prices and program expansion, with adverse effects on costs to taxpayers, on incentives for efficient risk spreading by insurers and reinsurers, and on incentives for efficient risk management by policyholders.[22]

Conclusions

Hurricane Katrina, other severe storms during 2004–2005, and the policy debate over terrorism risk insurance have focused renewed attention on the appropriate roles of the private and public sectors in managing and spreading risk associated with extreme events. Before adopting any new public insurance programs, it is desirable to make a number of policy changes that would significantly expand private sector risk sharing and improve private sector incentives for risk management. First, it is fundamentally important to allow private catastrophe insurance premium rates and availability of coverage to be determined by competition among insurers rather than by government regulation—except in certain well-defined and narrow circumstances. Second, a reduction in corporate tax disincentives for supplying private insurance against large losses from extreme events would likely significantly expand the availability of catastrophe coverage at lower rates. Third, the development of some method of constraining *ex post* disaster assistance, even if only marginally, would reduce its direct costs and dulling effects on *ex ante* risk management. If, after pursuing such changes, it appears that additional government intervention could help expand private catastrophe insurance markets, such as the adoption, as a truly last resort, a national risk-spreading mechanism for *extreme* catastrophe losses that would likely enhance rather than crowd-out private sector risk-bearing capacity.

Notes

I thank Howard Kunreuther for detailed comments and suggestions.

1. Florida created a state-mandated catastrophe fund following Hurricane Andrew in 1992. California created a state-mandated mechanism to provide earthquake coverage following the Northridge earthquake in 1994. See Cummins (2005), Hartwig (2005), and Kunreuther (2006) for further details on state catastrophe programs.
2. I have previously considered these issues in several articles. My treatment here draws heavily from Harrington (2000). Other analyses with broadly similar perspectives on the performance of private catastrophe insurance markets and the potential benefits and costs of increased government insurance of such losses include Priest (2003) and Jaffee and Russell (2003). Also see Froot (2001), Niehaus (2002), and Cummins (2005). Moss (1999) provides insightful historical background on disaster policy in the U.S.
3. A large literature considers the insurability of risk. Cummins (2005) provides a recent treatment. Also see Kunreuther (2006).
4. The "discounted" (or "present") value of expected claim payments equals the amount the insurer would need to charge up front to fund expected claim payments, recognizing its ability to invest and earn investment income on those funds prior to paying claims.
5. Losses also can be higher than predicted for many policyholders at once due to unexpected growth in the costs of repairing property, medical costs, and jury awards.
6. Actuarial, economic, and behavioral literatures consider the ambiguity (parameter uncertainty) issue. My perspective is that ambiguity primarily affects supply through its direct upward impact on insurers' costs of providing coverage. Ambiguity therefore increases the amount of capital that insurers must hold to achieve a given probability of being able to honor their promises and thus the total costs of holding capital. Ambiguity might also reduce the supply of coverage and/or reduce rates for behavioral reasons (Kunreuther 2006; Kunreuther, Hogarth, and Meszaros 1993).
7. A set of behavioral factors might lead to underestimation of risk (see Kunreuther 1996, 2006).
8. Demand in theory could still be low in some cases, such as low-value properties owned by persons with low income, even if disaster assistance were not available and consumers did not underestimate risk.
9. Specifically, the "agency" costs of holding capital include the costs of monitoring managers, the costs to the firm of actions to help ensure investors of incentive-compatible behavior by managers, and any residual reduction in (risk-adjusted) returns arising from managers pursuing their own interests rather than those of capital providers (see Jensen and Meckling 1976).
10. This discussion draws from material I prepared for chapter 5 of the report *TRIA and Beyond* (2005).
11. The extra tax hits any corporation, not just insurers, that invests in marketable securities (unless offset by corporate borrowing). The same principle

applies to any incremental cost of holding large amounts of securities as capital in any company, such as agency costs.

12. Two hundred basis points approximate the tax on bonds with a taxable coupon rate of 6 percent at the corporate tax rate of 35%.

13. See Harrington and Niehaus (2003), which also suggests that the effects of the taxation of investment income on capital dwarf those of limitations on loss carry-back and carry-forward provisions. Also see Harrington and Niehaus (2001b).

14. The relevant tax regimes in other major jurisdictions are summarized in U.S. GAO (2005).

15. Winter (1988, 1994) and Gron (1989, 1994) developed the basic capacity constraint model, assuming respectively that insurers were constrained to have zero insolvency risk or meet a regulatory constraint mandating a low probability of insolvency.

16. When demand is sensitive to insolvency risk, Cagle and Harrington (1995) show that any post-shock price increases will be lower than when demand is risk insensitive. Cummins and Danzon (1997) stress that prices need not increase and could decrease if demand is sufficiently risk sensitive.

17. I provide a brief review elsewhere (Harrington 2004). Also see Harrington and Niehaus (2001a).

18. Froot and O'Connell (1997a, 1997b) analyze the relation over time between catastrophe reinsurance premiums and simulated values of expected claim costs parameterized using historical data on U.S. catastrophe losses to provide evidence of whether costly external finance aggravates reinsurance rate changes following large catastrophe losses. They argue (1997a) that changes in expected claim costs ("probability updating") following loss shocks should primarily occur for hazards (such as a hurricane or earthquake) and regions that are closely related to prior loss shocks. They present evidence that reinsurance rate increases following large catastrophe losses during the early 1990s were broader than implied by revisions in expected claim costs, thus providing indirect evidence that loss shocks reduced capacity with an attendant effect on rates.

19. See, for example, Kaplow (1991) and, more recently, Innes (2003) and Schwarze and Wagner (2002). Examples of opposite views include Harrington (2000) article and Priest (2003).

20. Similarly, when making construction (or other risk mitigation) decisions, property-owners will weigh the private benefits and private costs of precautions, such as damage resistant construction. Private benefits are less than total benefits, which include reductions in expected disaster assistance. Investments are foregone for which the total marginal benefit (including the benefit to taxpayers) exceeds the marginal cost to the property-owner. Too little investment in loss control results; property is excessively vulnerable to damage.

21. See Kunreuther (2006) for further discussion. Enforcement ultimately was beefed up in 1994, including penalties for lenders who fail to ensure that flood coverage is procured, and FEMA eventually required private insurers that issue and service federal flood policies to report policy cancellations and non-renewals.

22. David Moss (2006) has proposed linking the price of reinsurance in a pre-funded federal catastrophe reinsurance program to prices charged by the underlying insurers / reinsurers. An important issue is whether such an approach could be used in practice (given complex private sector contracting) without low attachment points for government reinsurance that would displace a large amount of viable, private sector coverage.

Providing Economic Incentives to Build Disaster-Resistant Structures

HARVEY G. RYLAND

As the nation faces up to the challenges of rebuilding in the aftermath of Hurricane Katrina, it also needs to face up to something it has long avoided: the need to help homeowners and business people construct buildings and retrofit existing structures in ways that will help resist future severe storms and other natural calamities.

Katrina heavily damaged New Orleans and other parts of Louisiana, Mississippi and Alabama when it roared ashore August 29, 2005. Congress has already approved more than $62 billion for disaster relief, and White House officials have said total federal disaster relief costs could reach $200 billion (Schor 2005). This amount does not include state and local costs, insurance payments, and costs borne by individuals and businesses.

However, this situation did not have to occur, because we know how to significantly reduce the damage to homes and businesses, and corresponding costs, from hurricanes as well as from other types of disasters, but are not fully applying this knowledge to protect people and structures.

Though hurricanes have been in the news a lot lately, they are not the only disasters that could be made less destructive and deadly if structures were built using better construction techniques and materials, such as disaster-resistant doors and windows. Earthquakes, floods, wildfires, tornadoes, hailstorms and blizzards are all major threats. In any year several natural disasters are bound to make national headlines.

Across the country, when new building codes aimed at improving construction techniques and materials are proposed, objectors often cite higher costs as a reason for opposition. They prefer the immediate benefits of slightly lower construction costs to the delayed benefits of a building whose special features might not be needed until the occurrence of a natural disaster years in the future. The concept of "delayed gratification" is probably also a factor with many consumers; that is if they have $3,000 to spend, they would experience immediate gratification by using the funds to buy a new plasma television set, but might have to wait years for the gratification of having less damage from a disaster.

To overcome this reluctance to embrace measures that would make homes and businesses better able to withstand natural disasters, financial incentives need to be offered. Incentives can come from private businesses and local, state and federal governments. Unpublished consumer opinion research conducted for the Institute for Business and Home Safety indicated that many consumers (homeowners and tenants, and business owners and managers) will not spend money to take protective actions, except under two conditions:

1. If their children come home from school and tell their parents that the family has to take protective actions;
2. If they will receive financial incentives for taking these actions.

Thus, the purpose of this paper is to present the case for providing financial incentives (other than from insurance) to encourage consumers to take disaster protective actions that can help reduce injuries and deaths, as well as damage to homes and businesses, and help preserve jobs by keeping businesses open.

Types of Financial Incentives

Every level of government and every commercial entity that sells a product or service to a home or business could offer an incentive when that home or business has taken actions to become "disaster- resistant." And it is postulated that it is in the financial interest of each such government or entity to provide such incentives.

For example, it is in the best interest of federal, state and local governments, lending institutions, utility companies, retailers and service organizations to promote the construction of disaster resistant homes and businesses, and the retrofitting of existing structures to reduce risk from natural disasters. Examples of financial incentives and the corresponding justification are discussed in the following sections.

Government Institutions

All levels of government have good reasons to offer incentives. New Orleans presents a stark example why. Destroyed buildings and abandoned neighborhoods have resulted in reduced tax revenues, forcing the City to lay off thousands of employees. The Louisiana state government has also seen its revenue decline, at the very time when its residents are most in need of help (Kaufman 2005). Government incentives can take many forms.

There is already precedent for federal government incentives that encourage disaster mitigation. The National Flood Insurance Program, operated by the federal government, discounts insurance premiums in cities and villages in the Community Rating System, a voluntary incentive program that recognizes and encourages community floodplain management activities that exceed the minimum NFIP requirements. The size of the discount depends on the amount of flood risk reduction and related efforts, such as dissemination of flood information to the public. Discounts up to 45 percent are possible.[1]

The federal Energy Policy Act of 2005 includes tax incentives for consumers in 2006 and 2007 for the purchase of energy efficient homes and appliances such as air conditioners, water heaters, boilers, and furnaces. Similar incentives could be granted for construction that provides a high degree of disaster resistance.

Promoting disaster resistant homes and businesses would be of significant benefit to the federal government because every such protected structure could reduce the need for disaster relief provided by the Federal Emergency Management Agency, Small Business Administration, Department of Housing and Urban Development, and other agencies. These structures would also benefit the federal government by helping to reduce the amount of income and other tax revenue that it might otherwise lose following a disaster.

State and local incentives are discussed together, as the authority to offer these incentives might in some cases reside at the state level, while in other cases local governments have such authority.

Cities or counties that issue building permits could reduce permit fees on structures that are built to be disaster-resistant. Or they could do something as simple as move applicants to the head of the line for permit issuance and inspections. Time is often big money in the construction industry. Many builders would appreciate an expedited issuance and inspection process.

Property tax assessors could be instructed not to include disaster-resistant features in the value of a piece of property. Local officials who rely on property tax money to run their units of government may argue against "giving up" tax revenue. But they really would not be giving up any revenue, because without incentives, disaster resistance probably would not be built into the structure.

California's Proposition 127, passed in 1990 barred increases in the property tax on structures that were retrofitted to withstand earthquake damage between January 1, 1991 and July 1, 2000, unless the property changed ownership. As Kunreuther, Meyer and van de Bulte point out "The state concluded that these improvements constitute such a significant reduction in the risks to life and safety, they should be exempt from additional property tax" (Kunreuther et al. 2004).

Communities have also developed economic incentives, such as tax relief for those who retrofit and public awareness and training programs. The city of San Leandro, California has set priorities to retrofit both unreinforced masonry buildings and older wood-frame houses for earthquake survival. The program includes earthquake-strengthening workshops for residents, a list of available earthquake contractors, as well as a tool-lending library for homeowners should they wish to do the work themselves (Kunreuther et al. 2004).

States could also refrain from collecting sales tax on disaster-resistant windows, doors, or related disaster protection materials. The State of Florida established a "tax holiday" during the period June 1–12, 2005 for certain hurricane preparedness items. During this period, sales tax was not charged on such items as inexpensive as flashlights and batteries and as expensive as generators, which were in great demand during the "holiday." This was a lost opportunity to allow the tax holiday for disaster protection materials. However, it does provide a precedent for a program that would provide significant incentives for home and business protection (Florida Department of Revenue 2005).

In exchange for such incentives, the local, state and federal governments would be gaining the economic sustainability of communities. They would also be reducing the costs of responding to disasters, as fewer people would need to be protected, sheltered and housed at government expense.

Lending Institutions

Mortgage companies could lower interest rates, reduce closing costs or give other kinds of preferred treatment for loans on disaster-resistant structures and related home improvement projects. Such loans could include mortgages, construction financing, home improvement loans, and business development loans.

Skeptical lenders may say they see no benefit in giving such preferred treatment, because if the property is heavily damaged and the owner abandons it, the lender will get the property back and an insurance check to pay for repairs. However, the lender would first have to go through foreclosure to obtain the property. This costs time and money. It would then have to oversee repairs (more time and money) to prepare the property for sale (still more time and money).

In a large-scale disaster like Katrina, damage could be so widespread that months will pass before repairs can begin. Those are months during which the lender is responsible for whatever happens on that property. This is a risk lenders usually try to avoid.

Far more preferable, from a lender's standpoint, would be the receipt of monthly mortgage payments on a well-maintained piece of property that is increasing in value. A lender is more likely to have that income by approving loans on disaster-resistant structures and for related improvements to existing buildings.

If homeowners are reluctant to incur the upfront cost of mitigation due to budget constraints, then long-term loan may provide a financial incentive for adopting cost-effective measures. The bank holding the mortgage on the property could provide funds for this purpose through a home improvement loan with a payback period identical to the life of the mortgage (Kunreuther 2006). For example, a 20-year loan for $1,500 at an annual interest rate of 10% would result in payments of $145 per year. If the value of expected annual benefits from the mitigation measure exceed this amount the homeowner would be better off by experiencing the increased level of protection for a home or business. By tying mitigation and corresponding financial incentives to a loan, one makes small payments each month and avoids the possibility of a much larger loss should a disaster occur.

Retailers and Utilities

Lenders are by no means the only businesses that could offer incentives. Utility companies, such as energy, telephone and cable, could offer discounts to owners of disaster-resistant homes. They might, for example, offer a 5% discount on monthly service fees. So could appliance stores, moving companies, lawn maintenance firms and other businesses that sell products or services to homeowners.

It is in their interest to do so. Our research shows that 25 percent of businesses go out of business after closing because of a natural disaster (Insurance Information Institute 2005). Many times they close not because of direct damage but because of the loss of customers who were affected by the disaster. Hundreds of thousands of residents of New Orleans and nearby areas still have not returned to their homes. Customers are gone. Many of the closed businesses will never reopen because they do not have the resources to last until their customers return.

Research by the Public Entity Risk Institute that shows "following any large scale disaster in a community, things never get 'back to normal.' The community almost always changes permanently, creating a new business environment in which doing business the old way often results in operating at a loss for years and, then, when all equity in the business is used up, going out of business" (Alesch et al. 2005).

Conclusions

We know how to better protect homes and businesses from natural disasters, but economic incentives are needed as one tool to encourage many consumers to take action. Furthermore, incentives from a single source will probably not be sufficient to motivate consumers. A package of incentives from government and business sources will generally be required to ensure that protective action is taken by the largest number of consumers.

Proof of the effectiveness of disaster resistant construction techniques and materials can be seen in Florida, where building codes were strengthened after Hurricane Andrew roared through the state in 1992, causing more than $20 billion of insured damage. Most of the homes and businesses built since those improved codes (and code enforcement) were enacted have withstood the multiple hurricanes that have since battered Florida with little or no damage. Many older structures have been seriously damaged or destroyed.

A preliminary review of wood-frame houses that withstood the 130 mile per hour winds of Katrina shows they also survived in large part because they were built using good construction standards and materials. Strong foundations, installation of "hurricane straps" that help secure roofs to walls, and storm-grade windows and doors protected lives and reduced structural damage (Witt 2005)

Unfortunately, existing structures built to those higher standards are few and far between. Building codes that call for disaster resistance in new construction can have an impact over time, but most existing structures do not have disaster-resistant features.

By offering incentives to encourage people to replace old windows and doors with storm-resistant ones, install hurricane straps to walls and roofs, and take other steps to make their homes and businesses more structurally sound, businesspeople and government officials can expect to see more viable communities, stronger economies, and lower disaster relief costs.

In 2002 the Wharton Risk Management and Decision Process Center and the Institute for Business and Home Safety held a roundtable discussion with nearly 50 participants representing the private and public sectors and academia. Suggestions included launching pilot incentive programs in several communities in disaster-prone areas. That work is ongoing (Final Summary 2002).

Note

1. Information on the National Flood Insurance Program Community Rating System is available at <http://www.fema.gov/nfip/crs.shtm>.

Part Four

The Government's Role in Disaster Preparedness and Response

Role of Public Health and Clinical Medicine in Preparing for Disasters

BRIAN STROM

While originally connected, public health and clinical medicine have evolved as different fields, with clinicians focusing on the needs of the individual, and public health professionals focusing on the needs of the community. Their education has even drifted into different schools (schools of medicine, nursing, dentistry, and veterinary medicine, vs. schools of public health), with different accreditations, and different professional organizations. Indeed, the degree of difference between clinical medicine and public health is sometimes sufficiently broad that the gap has been referred to as a schism (White 1991). In recent decades, there have been attempts to heal that schism (White 1991), ranging from the clinical epidemiology movement (Terris 1986), to the funding by the Robert Wood Johnson Foundation of programs to foster cooperation (RWJF 2005), to activities conducted jointly by the American Medical Association and the American Public Health Association (Elster 2002). The need for this coordination is brought into sharpest focus in a situation like disaster planning.

It is important to keep in mind that the field of public health is, by design, extraordinarily decentralized, as are other levels of government. This leads to a need for multiple levels of coordination, horizontal and vertical, as well as a need for coordination with multiple levels of non-governmental charity and rescue organizations (Landesman 2001; Landesman 2001a). Many localities have their own health departments. There are also county health departments, and state health departments. The structure and coordination of these hierarchical departments are determined by and vary among different states. State health departments must, in turn, coordinate federally with the Centers for Disease Control and Prevention (CDC), which provides funding but not control over what happens locally. In addition, there is a separate quasi-military public health service corps within the Department of Health and Human Services, which is led by the Surgeon General. In the event of any disaster, these agencies must also coordinate with the Department of Homeland Security, as well as with the Red Cross and other non-profit and for-profit organizations seeking to provide assistance. Equivalent coordination is needed locally with local and state police departments, National Guard units, and other organizations. The responsibilities among such disparate organizations are often unclear, and even conflicting. Policy coordination is almost completely ad hoc.

Clinical medicine is even more decentralized and lacking in coordination. Most of it is private, but some public. Most primary care practices are completely independent of the specialists they use, as well as the hospitals they admit to, which in turn are independent of nursing homes, pharmacies, and other clinical medicine sites. Even within each profession, there are issues of credentialing, including licensure by state and privileges by hospital, such that practitioners in one state cannot come to the aid of practitioners in an adjacent state, or even an adjacent hospital, if they are not licensed and/or privileged to do so, and most are not.

It is perhaps useful to reconsider such relationships and strictures in the context of recent disasters, and contemplate how we should be planning for future disasters. From both a public health point of view and a clinical point of view, for example, Hurricane Katrina can be seen as a test of preparedness. And it showed a terrible failure. In this paper, I will present a conceptual framework for viewing disasters from a health point of view, a summary of the health risks that disasters represent, possible solutions, and some general conclusions. Much of this comes from modern plans for public health preparedness (Landesman 2001; Novick 2001), but hopefully it will become very clear how integrated the clinical system must be in that preparedness. This proposed plan calls for massive change in the coordination of health efforts, one that the United States seems traditionally unable to effect.

Conceptual Framework

Quantitatively and qualitatively, disasters are by definition different from minor emergencies and everyday crises (Quarantelli 1996, 2005). They can, however, be of multiple different types, which in turn dictate different approaches to preparedness.

One dichotomy to consider is the acute onset vs. slow onset disaster. Examples of acute onset disasters include blizzards, earthquakes, tornadoes, and of course hurricanes. Examples of chronic disasters include droughts, heat waves, and avian flu (Landesman 2001; CDC 2004, 2005f; Emanuel 2005).

In addition, disasters can be categorized as natural vs. unintentional technological vs. deliberate. All of the examples in the previous paragraph are natural disasters. Instances of acute, unintentional technological disasters include transportation crashes, nuclear accidents, bridge collapses, and of course levee collapses. In contrast, examples of chronic, unintentional technological disasters include desertification and deforestation. Bombings and acts of bioterrorism are examples of deliberate disasters.

The biological effects of disasters can be separated into acute biological effects vs. ongoing effects. Examples of the former would be an anthrax attack, which affects only those directly exposed to the anthrax spores (IOM 2002). In contrast, smallpox also has chronic effects, because it is contagious (IOM 2005).

A critically important dichotomy differentiates agent-generated demands vs. response-generated demands. Agent-generated demands reflect the need to respond to the exposure causing the disaster, such as radiation, infection, earthquake, or of course flooding. These are unique to each different type of disaster. In contrast, response-generated demands are common to all disasters, and thereby can be better planned for in advance. Planning should focus especially on such demands, because they will cut across all disasters. This will be discussed more below.

Finally, it is important to consider the different organizational roles in disasters. Some people and organizations have the same roles in disaster that they have in normal times, such as firefighters and police. In contrast, others have completely new roles in disasters. Examples are members of relief organizations, who shift from fundraising and administration to direct disaster recovery; people mobilized from their normal occupations to assist with search and rescue; people who shift from their normal occupations to spend their time distributing relief supplies; or members of the National Guard. A different type of example is the role of ambulances vs. bystanders. In normal times, primary emergency care is given by emergency medical technicians in ambulances. In a true disaster, ambulances often cannot access people needing help, who then must rely on bystanders for assistance.

Health Risks Presented by Disasters

Consistent with the above conceptual framework, it is useful to differentiate between specific risks presented by bio-events, and general health risks presented by all major disasters. The specific risks are the health outcomes from the initiating agent and the type of outcome differs depending on the agent. Such risks can be posed by deliberate disasters, such as bioterrorism with anthrax or smallpox (Landesman 2001). Alternatively, they could be natural and unintentional, such as severe acute respiratory syndrome (SARS) or avian flu. In each case, the health effect is specific to the agent: clinical anthrax (which is not contagious), smallpox (which does spread to others), SARS (which spreads only to those with close contact), and avian flu.

In contrast, there are a series of general health risks presented by *all* major disasters. One category results from loss of access to uncontaminated water and food. The waterborne illnesses that result include multiple forms of diarrheal disease (including typhoid, cholera, and giardiasis) and hepatitis A as well as insect-borne diseases, especially mosquito-borne diseases (such as malaria and viral encephalitis). Also resulting from a lack of uncontaminated water are dehydration and heat stroke. Microorganisms growing in unclean water lead to an increase in wound infections, particularly problematic of course in situations where there are increased numbers of wounds (see below). Finally, in the absence of adequate uncontaminated food, if protracted, people begin to suffer from malnutrition.

Another general category of health risks emerges from other environmental exposures. Included are toxic chemical exposures; acute injuries from the agent (such as drownings, electrocution, lacerations, fractures); tetanus; animal exposures (like rodents carrying plague and other illnesses, snakes, biting insects); acute illness secondary to the indirect impact of the situation (including myocardial infarctions resulting from stress or exertion); pediatric poisonings; injury from recovery machinery (such as mechanical injuries from saws and heavy equipment); carbon monoxide poisonings from generators; fires; crush injuries; and other like events.

Another general risk is airborne illness, such as tuberculosis, influenza, chicken pox, and measles, all of which are passed by close contact. Insect infestations (like lice and scabies) are also transmitted by close physical contact.

Additional risk emerges from violence, and the need to treat its sequelae. Further risk comes from panic, and post-traumatic stress disorder. A major problem associated with large-scale disasters on the order of Hurricane Katrina is the loss of access to lifesaving acute medical care, such as ventilators and intensive care units. Modern medical care is highly technological, and loss of electrical power will result in deaths. Further, there is a loss of access to life-sustaining chronic medical care, including insulin, anti-epileptic drugs, and treatments for asthma, cardiac disease, HIV, tuberculosis, and so forth. Lifesaving procedures like dialysis are also lost in such crises. Indeed, as of 10 days after Katrina, 50% or more of those on dialysis in the New Orleans area had not yet been located (Cohen 2005).

Other risks emerge from loss of access to medical facilities. This is especially the case in the current climate, where there is no unused reserve in the health care system. Thus, it would not require loss of a facility for this to be a problem, but simply a surge in need for medical care. In response, patients would go untreated, as the absence of surge capacity would mean they could not be cared for. A loss of medical personnel due to illness, transportation difficulties, or simply fear of coming to work, would compound that markedly. Loss of a physical facility (such as the loss of Charity Hospital, as happened with Hurricane Katrina), would significantly aggravate an already dire situation. Other problems would result from a loss of hard copy medical records, and the knowledge thereby to provide proper medical care. Further, while increasing computerization protects against the complete loss of medical records, insofar as "lost" records could eventually be reconstructed, inoperative computers from lack of electricity would lead to a devastating impact on medical infrastructures that depend on them (such as in the event that the hospital order entry systems would not function, severely hampering the capabilities of already-stressed hospitals). Mobility for the many patients who are non-ambulatory would also be greatly challenged by the effects of disasters on medical facilities. Of course, all of these problems, including lack of medical supplies, will emerge in the context of unorganized health care workers self-deploying to the scene to attempt to provide help.

Overall Approach to Solutions

Given the wide array of health risks posed by a disaster, some agent-specific but most common to any disaster, it is critical to take an "all-hazards approach" to preparedness, that is an approach designed to be useful regardless of the agent. It is difficult to prepare for agent-specific risks, since the range of possible agents is enormous, and the preparation for one agent is largely unhelpful in disasters resulting from other agents. For example, vaccinating against smallpox does not help in the slightest against an attack from anthrax, or the spread of avian flu. While there was probably some gain in general preparedness resulting from the recent smallpox vaccine program, there also was a massive diversion of resources from other initiatives to work on this vaccine program (IOM 2005).

In addition, it is important to recognize that public health and clinical medicine *both* need to be central aspects of any disaster response, thus central aspects of any disaster planning. The former is responsible for planning and response, but is inevitably insufficient given the list of risks above; the latter is among the first responders. In contrast to disasters such as plane crashes or earthquakes, if the agent of the disaster is biologic, the first cases will be seen in emergency rooms and physicians' offices. Further, practicing clinicians serve as the effector arm of public health planners, as they seek to have the public vaccinated, treated, educated, or assisted through almost any other health intervention. As such, it is even more critical for disaster planning than for other reasons that we break down the artificial and archaic cultural barriers between public health and clinical medicine, described above.

Planning

In order to achieve adequate preparedness for disasters, multiple levels of planning are needed. Disaster planning usually includes a written disaster plan, specifically outlining who does what in what circumstance. Proper organization is critical. Should there be a command and control infrastructure? This is expected in most public health plans (Landesman 2001), based on military and emergency medical services experience. However, others argue against command and control, but recommend planned coordination (Quarantelli 1997). As part of that planning it is important to recognize that disaster victims will not be passive in the process. In other words, some will be actively seeking help, sometimes getting in the way. Others will be providing help, and indeed the first help available in disasters will nearly always be from bystanders.

Also critical is a communications infrastructure. Communicating with the public is vital. Educational campaigns should inform people of the preparations for disaster, before it even occurs. Adequate communication with the public also would entail providing an early warning system, such as when a hurricane approaches. Communication is needed between governmental agencies and the individuals counted on as aid workers. For example, if there were a smallpox attack, is there a beeper system to notify vaccinated individuals to be able to ask them to provide care? Close communication is needed within government, across agencies. Close communication is also needed among governments, whether in geographically adjacent areas, and/or vertical communication between local, county, and state health departments and the CDC. In addition, how do any of these entities communicate with the health care workers who will be expected to implement public health recommendations? Analogous communication is needed between government and the many nongovernmental organizations that will be partners in response to any disaster.

A key step in disaster planning is risk assessment, that is, identifying potential outbreaks, hazards, and vulnerable populations, and modeling the resulting risks. Accordingly, one needs to identify the range of possible problems that may occur and a range of possible solutions for each. For example, if there were a case of smallpox, would you plan to implement mass vaccination or "ring vaccination," that is vaccinating contacts of cases, and contacts of those contacts (IOM 2005)? If there were another anthrax attack, would we again distribute ciprofloxacin? From where?

What about use of a tetracycline instead? What role will anthrax vaccine play in the response, if any (IOM 2002)?

Also needed for coping and recovering from a disaster is planning for sufficient facility infrastructure, including surge capacity. It is difficult and sometimes cost prohibitive to plan for unused facilities, but sometimes a community can plan for facilities to be used only in the case of a disaster, such as a stadium for storage of corpses, temporary military-style hospitals for use for acute care, and other such contingencies. Such plans need to be explicit, however, and still require expenditures to provide for access to such temporary facilities, when needed. A plan to develop and access pre-positioned equipment and supplies is critical.

Key for such planning is to assure adequate human resources for a response. This entails identifying the likely first responders, who will be health care workers in many situations, training them, and having plans to access them, such as a beeper system that could contact them in the face of an emergency.

Inevitably, though, systems under stress cannot mobilize enough people to meet their needs. Toward that end, of great importance are mutual aid agreements, whereby one locality will come to assist another. This also requires planning and often legislation or regulation (such as for licensure and hospital privileges), so those coming to assist have the legal right to provide such assistance. Licensure and privileges are local decisions, so such planning must be local and based in the states. However, the federal government must play a central role in making sure it happens, as will be discussed more below.

A related issue is modern public health law. If there is an epidemic, for example, either as the primary agent or secondary to a different type of disaster, the public health community needs the authority to establish and enforce quarantines. This is a power that is applied reluctantly, as no one seeks to breach civil liberties unnecessarily. This requires close coordination, obviously, with police jurisdictions, but is critical to protecting the public, especially in situations where there is no other alternative approach, such as SARS and, for now at least, avian flu. State public health laws are now in place, but only some have been updated to the "model public health law" that has been agreed upon.

As disasters occur, it is critical to have plans for data collection during the event. This includes surveillance for infectious diseases. It also includes tabulation of mortality and morbidity, so family members can know the outcomes of their loved ones. In addition, laboratory capacity to detect the diseases is an essential component in the need for data collection during a disaster. Collecting data on the processes used to respond to the disaster, and the outcomes associated with them, so that preparedness could be improved even further in the future is also important.

Finally, it is clear that a central part of planning is to test one's preparation for the next disaster. There are many ways to accomplish this. One is modeling, such as using mathematical models to project events that may occur under different circumstances, based on different assumptions. In this way, one can determine via sensitivity analysis which assumptions are most important to changing health outcomes, and focus subsequent efforts on those areas. Another option is so-called tabletop exercises, which are basically exercises in role-playing given certain assumptions, to determine how different stakeholders would respond. This is essentially the exercise performed regarding New Orleans, in which predictions came remarkably close to what ultimately happened with Hurricane Katrina (FEMA 2004; ADCIRC 2004). Another option is the use of operational exercises, either announced or, better, unannounced. Thus, someone could show up in an emergency room declaring that they have smallpox, and let events play out as they would have, were it a real case. Finally, we can learn much from proxy events, in the case of epidemics like SARS, monkeypox, annual influenza epidemics, and others. By evaluating what are essentially "after action reports," we can learn how recovery efforts could have been better conducted. Thus, for example, the smallpox preparedness program undoubtedly helped enormously in our preparedness for a possible smallpox attack. Yet, when a case of monkeypox occurred, which appears clinically very much like smallpox, it took a full 13 days before the CDC was notified (IOM 2005). If that had been a case of smallpox, the results could have been catastrophic.

Thus, there is a considerable need for planning prior to any possible disaster that must be closely coordinated between the public health department, which designs the plan, and the clinical facilities, such as hospitals, which ultimately will need to implement it. Once again, such planning needs to be performed locally but, as will be discussed more below, will require federal oversight and funding to make sure it happens, and meets uniform standards.

Prevention

The ultimate goal of disaster planning is to prevent bad health outcomes. Prevention is commonly divided conceptually into primary prevention, secondary prevention, and tertiary prevention, a conceptualization that is useful in this context, as well. *Primary prevention* is undertaken before an event occurs, to avoid adverse outcomes should an event later occur. Examples include: immunization against infectious agents of concern, whether they are the primary agent (such as smallpox) or a complication of all disasters (like hepatitis A). Other examples entail the control or prevention of routine endemic disease outbreaks, so that they will not become epidemic in the face of disaster, like cholera. Related is the maintenance of effective sanitation and first aid systems, and the development of stockpiles of needed supplies, in case an event occurs. Also included in primary prevention are initiatives undertaken to protect against previously identified risks, and to reduce the impact of those risks when they do occur, such as "earthquake-proof" buildings, and building stronger levees in areas prone to flooding. Finally, primary prevention would include community education regarding personal hygiene, how long food remains unspoiled in a refrigerator without power, how long to boil unclean water, and so forth. Such interventions are often useful regardless of the agent of the future disaster, and also serve to reduce the risk of future panic, with all of its attendant problems.

Secondary prevention is undertaken in response to an event in order to prevent adverse health outcomes. Included are emergent efforts to identify and extricate victims, remove healthy individuals from risk of harm (evacuation), quarantine/isolate infected individuals, and ration key supplies. Also included are efforts to deploy relief supplies and personnel, coordinate donations, manage the media, and establish infectious disease control and surveillance, including, where relevant, mosquito and vector control. In addition, secondary prevention would include the provision of emergency medical care, and conducting short-term counseling/mental health interventions. Given this wide range of activities, performed by many different types of people and professions, efforts are also needed to organize health care and other services and treatment, including coordinating with other governmental bodies. Toward that end, it is often useful to have an emergency operations center, with representatives of each organization present at the center.

Finally, *tertiary prevention* focuses on recovery from the event, that is, preventing adverse health outcomes after the event is over. Included is a need to dispose of waste, debris, human and animal bodies; manage ongoing emergency medical care; manage injuries; and re-establish normal health services as soon as possible, so patients do not die from a lack of acute or chronic lifesaving medications or technology. Re-establishing surveillance systems is also necessary as is continuing to manage the media. Finally, this is the opportunity to use the records of the event to learn how to better prepare for the next event.

Thus, while public health focuses on prevention, it is clear that clinical medicine must be mobilized to achieve prevention and, indeed they need to be closely coordinated.

Conclusions

In many ways, the experience with Hurricane Katrina clearly illustrated this need for coordination. Previous planning identified the risk of rupture of the New Orleans levees in the face of a strong hurricane (Gilgoff 2005; Travis 2005), and tabletop exercises confirmed that the levees would break, the city would flood, and a catastrophic human and economic toll would be exacted (FEMA 2004; ADCIRC 2004). Subsequent events revealed cholera-like vibrio, other infectious diarrheal disease, infected wounds, numerous arthropod bites (probably mites), pertussis (whooping cough), tuberculosis, other respiratory diseases, rashes, heat-related illness, carbon monoxide poisoning from use of portable generators and other gasoline-powered appliances, other toxic exposures, falls, motor vehicle crashes, intentional injuries, other unintentional injuries, and complications from renal disease, diabetes, cardiovascular conditions, obstetric/gynecologic conditions, dental problems, and so forth. (CDC 2005a–e). Of note, these health problems occurred in New Orleans residents and rescuers. Further, they occurred in a context where there was near total collapse of the health care infrastructure of the city. As noted above, 10 days after Katrina, 50% of those on dialysis in the New Orleans area still had not yet been located (Cohen 2005). The number of people who died due to lack of medications and other care, even after rescue, remains unknown.

How could this have been prevented, and how can we prepare better for the next disaster? Many of the initiatives described above need to be local, and so primary responsibility must lie with the states, and the local governments and health departments they control. Indeed, most disasters are local, such as earthquakes and tornadoes. Yet, often local governments do not have the resources, or expertise, to achieve appropriate preparedness. Further, even those disasters that are primarily local, can have national impact through their economic repercussions, such as Hurricane Katrina. In addition, there is a need for clarity on when the capacity of local governments is expected to be exceeded, and the federal government needs to step in. Still other disasters will have immediate national impact, and this will be the case with most contagious biologic agents. Indeed, most such disasters are likely to be international in scope and importance, and origin, such as SARS and pandemic flu.

Ultimately, therefore, the only way to assure preparedness throughout the country, to the degree it is needed, will be the strong intervention of the federal government. Our federal government, preferably through the CDC, must provide strong support to other countries in their development of a public health infrastructure, including effective surveillance practices. It also needs to assure that localities in the US provide an adequate public health infrastructure, as well. It should establish a clear set of plans and rules for coordination in the face of disasters, including a plan for what needs to be carried out on a local level and what triggers immediate federalization of the event. It also must provide to hospitals and other health care facilities sufficient resources to be able to provide surge capacity in the face of disasters, conditional of course on the needed planning. This array of requirements must be institutionalized within a new, model public health law for states to pass. Finally, to permit all this, and to enforce it, the federal government, preferably through the CDC, should create an ongoing granting program, providing to the states the resources to perform this ambitious but necessary task, resources which would only be received if the states meet the specified standards. This is analogous to the funding provided to induce states to create and carry out a smallpox vaccination program, but would be focused on all-hazards preparedness, rather than simply vaccination against a single biologic agent (IOM 2005). Of note, this is in great contrast to the recent past, where public health infrastructure funding has been cut, and resources for clinical medicine have been provided by agencies different from public health funding. Even in the current proposal to prepare for the avian flu, the administration plan provides little funding to other countries, requires states to pay 75% of the cost of anti-viral medications, and provides little for surveillance or hospital capacity (*New York Times* 2005).

It is clear that public health will always play a role in disasters, whether or not the events are primarily biological in origin. All-hazards planning is needed and such planning must be tested. Proper public health planning for disasters is feasible, and critically needed. Our nation's public health infrastructure has been starved in recent years, and we are seeing some of the costs in recent disasters. However, public health planning for disasters requires close coordination with clinical medicine as a partner, as both will operate via the other. Hurricane Katrina demonstrated the multi-level failure of the system, and future investment is needed in a better infrastructure, and better planning.

Finally, and of note, relatively little of the above is based on formal research (mainly in the social science literature) and much more is needed. This is a role for a multidisciplinary effort of the type that can emerge uniquely from an integrated university.

Hurricane Katrina as a Bureaucratic Nightmare

VICKI BIER

Since Hurricane Katrina in August 2005, there has been extensive public discussion about the reasons for the disastrous emergency planning and response. Many people and organizations have been blamed for the disaster, ranging from the Federal Emergency Management Agency (FEMA) to Mayor Nagin of New Orleans.

Of course, all analyses of Hurricane Katrina at this point are necessarily preliminary, especially in light of the voluminous records that were recently released (CNN December 3, 2005; Associated Press 2005), and scholars will undoubtedly be poring over what went wrong before and after Katrina for many years to come. However, given the complexity of the disaster, even a preliminary analysis can be useful in interpreting the press coverage of the event and making sense of what happened. Moreover, existing information about how organizations work (and why they fail to work)—see for example Clarke (1999), Druckman et al. (1997), Pandey and Moynihan (2006), Reason (1997), Roberts (1993), Vaughan (1996), and Westrum (1999, 2004)—can help to create meaning from the flood of information about the hurricane.

My contention here, in particular, is that many of the problems observed in the aftermath of Katrina were not due to any one person or organization, but rather were problems of coordination at the interfaces *between* multiple organizations and multiple levels of government (Kettl 2006). In retrospect, this is not surprising. For example, probabilistic risk analyses of nuclear power plants have frequently found that plants designed according to current engineering practice often have "latent" failure modes at the interfaces between systems. In other words, even if every individual system in the power plant operates as designed, accidents and disasters can still occur, because the interfaces and dependencies among those systems have often not been thought through and debugged sufficiently carefully (see for example Perrow 1984).

The remainder of this paper will discuss some of the failures and problems observed after Katrina, and document the ways in which they represent failures of coordination. I will distinguish roughly between failures of coordination in emergency planning and failures of coordination in emergency response. However, the two are of course closely related, since failures at the planning stage can easily give rise to failures in emergency response.

Failures of Planning

The experiences in New Orleans after Hurricane Katrina made it clear that New Orleans had prepared for the hurricane, but not the subsequent flood. This is rather remarkable, given that the potential for catastrophic levee failure after a major hurricane had been well known and highly publicized (Fischetti 2001; *Times-Picayune* 2002). A weeklong simulation or elaborate "tabletop exercise" conducted by FEMA (2004; see also *Times-Picayune* 2004; Fournier and Bridis 2005), Hurricane Pam, tested the ability of federal, state, and local responders to cope with similar flooding (due to overtopping rather than breach of the levees), and identified many of the problems that actually occurred, such as the fact that many residents would not be able to evacuate New Orleans due to lack of transportation, as well as the challenges of dealing with "human and animal corpses . . . ; and a mix of toxic chemicals." In fact, McPhee (1990) had even alerted the general reading public to the possible destruction of New Orleans from flooding fifteen years before Hurricane Katrina hit.

The failure of New Orleans to plan seriously for the possibility of flooding is clearly demonstrated by the fact that the Superdome had been designated a "refuge of last resort." Some have taken the fact that the Superdome was provided with only "90,000 liters of water and 43,776 military meals" (Salopek and Horan 2005) as a sign of inadequate planning, since the Superdome eventually came to hold over 10,000 people for a period of several days. However, the applicable Emergency Operations Plan (State of Louisiana 2000) states that "The definition of Last Resort Refuge is a place for persons to be protected from the high winds and heavy rains from the storm. Unlike a shelter, there may be little or no water or food and possibly no utilities. A Last Resort Refuge is intended to provide best available survival protection for the duration of the hurricane only." The Superdome actually performed reasonably well as a refuge of last resort during the hurricane; there was some damage to the roof during the hurricane (CNN August 29, 2005), but the structure largely withstood the hurricane, and conditions inside were not too bad at that time. It was only the subsequent flood (resulting in the loss of water and electric power, and the need to house larger numbers of people for longer periods of time) that led to the deplorable conditions there that were so graphically described as "hell" only a couple of days later (Gerhart 2005).

In light of what is known from the social-science literature on accidents and disasters, the fact that the city government of New Orleans prepared only for the hurricane and not the flood is perhaps not quite so surprising. Such tunnel vision has contributed to numerous other disasters and potential disasters, including: the inability of the National Aeronautics and Space Administration to anticipate and prevent the failures of the Challenger (Vaughan 1996) and Columbia space shuttles; the failure of the Federal Aviation Administration (and the federal government as a whole) to anticipate and prevent the terrorist attacks on September 11, 2001; and the lack of urgency placed on preparing for a possible influenza pandemic until just recently. Kunreuther (1996, 2006) has discussed similar myopia on the part of individuals. However, this tunnel vision on the part of emergency planning for New Orleans does appear to represent a failure of coordination, since a senior FEMA official reported skepticism about plans for use of the Superdome long before Katrina hit: "We used to stare at each other and say, 'This is the plan? Are you really using the Superdome?' People used to say, what if there is water around it? They didn't have an alternative" (Glasser and White 2005).

Westrum (2004) has observed that "Bureaucratic organizations . . . typically fail because they have neglected potential problems or have taken on tasks for which they do not have the resources to do well." In other words, it is a natural organizational (and human) tendency to ignore problems for which there are currently no good solutions, rather than having to admit publicly that a solution is not yet available (or will be prohibitively expensive). This was clearly the case with Katrina. In fact, Glasser and Grunwald (2005) quoted Ebbert, director of emergency management for New Orleans, as saying "We always knew we did not have the means to evacuate the city."

In fact, the state of emergency planning for Hurricane Katrina in New Orleans can be crudely summarized as "We tell you when to leave; you take your car and your credit cards, and look after yourself." That does *not* describe the status of emergency planning in the country as a whole. However, in the U.S., emergency planning is primarily a state and local responsibility. The result is almost literally a patchwork quilt of varying levels of preparedness, with some communities having a hodgepodge of loosely connected plans that could easily come unraveled in an actual emergency, and others having plans that are elaborately embroidered and carefully stitched together. For example, Tierney (2005) cites Newport News, Virginia, as an example of an area where "Officials have plans . . . to evacuate those without cars, . . . keep registries of the people who need special help . . . [and] go door to door" to encourage holdouts to evacuate.

Note that these patchwork levels of preparedness will most likely apply to avian influenza just as they do to hurricanes. For example, in response to the plan for pandemic influenza recently released by the U.S. Department of Health and Human Services (HHS 2005), the *New York Times* (2005) observed that according to the plan, "The real responsibilities wind up on the shoulders of state and local health agencies and individual hospitals, none of which are provided with adequate resources to handle the job." Similarly, there will be a need for close coordination even beyond the healthcare field; for example, school closures may be advisable for reasons of public health, but create problems for essential employees that depend on the schools as a source of childcare.

It is certainly possible to plan and implement vastly better emergency response than that observed in New Orleans, even for communities in which many people do not have private vehicles. The massive evacuation of coastal communities in Cuba before Hurricane Ivan (CNN 2004) has been held up as one successful example. For instance, Parenti (2005) has asserted that before Ivan, "the Castro government, abetted by neighborhood citizen committees and local Communist party cadres, evacuated 1.5 million people, more than 10 percent of the country's population. The Cubans lost 20,000 homes to that hurricane—but not a single life was lost." The evacuation of millions of people in Florida before Hurricane Frances (Wikipedia 2005) is sometimes also held out as a success story. However, that evacuation might not have seemed as successful in retrospect if Frances had been as damaging as Katrina (for example, if Florida were below sea level, and had therefore endured extensive flooding), since presumably many people did not actually evacuate; moreover, the fraction of residents without their own means of transportation may also have been much smaller.

One of the reasons for the inadequate planning in New Orleans was undoubtedly a lack of seriousness about the possibility of a major flood— the phenomenon of "it cannot happen to me" documented by Kunreuther (1996) for individuals, and by Vaughan (1996) for organizations, writ on a larger canvas. Another reason, however, was a mismatch of expectations about how soon federal relief could be expected after a major disaster. Ebbert said the emergency plan for New Orleans was basically to "hang in there for 48 hours and wait for the cavalry" (Glasser and Grunwald 2005). Similarly, Maestri, Emergency Preparedness Director for Jefferson Parish (JP), stated: "We had been told we would be on our own for 48 hours . . . Prepare to survive and in 48 hours the cavalry would arrive" (Schleifstein 2005). Elsewhere, Maestri claimed that FEMA had actually signed a written commitment to respond within "48 to 60 hours" (Frontline 2005).

However, according to Glasser and White (2005), "federal and state officials pointed to Louisiana's failure to measure up to national disaster response standards, noting that the federal plan advises state and local emergency managers not to expect federal aid for 72 to 96 hours, and base their own preparedness efforts on the need to be self-sufficient for at least that period." The preparations made by New Orleans and the surrounding parishes would have seemed much more reasonable if substantial FEMA assistance had arrived within 48 to 60 hours. Similarly, the actual FEMA response, while still perhaps unacceptable in the face of a major disaster like Katrina, seems somewhat less dreadful if measured against a goal of responding within 72 to 96 hours. (In the next section, I discuss the separate question of why FEMA's response was not dramatically expedited once the catastrophic nature of the situation had become clear.)

Interestingly, a former employee of Innovative Emergency Management, Inc. (which helped create the simulation exercise for Hurricane Pam), writing under the name of "suspect device" (2005), confirmed that during that exercise, FEMA "promised the moon and the stars. They promised to have 1,000,000 bottles of water per day coming into affected areas within 48 hours. They promised massive prestaging with water, ice, medical supplies and generators. Anything that was needed, they would have either in place as the storm hit or ready to move in immediately after. All it would take is a phone call from local officials to the state, who would then call FEMA, and it would be done." This suggests that FEMA may have been more concerned with using Hurricane Pam for public relations (as an opportunity to make the agency "look good") than with identifying actual weaknesses in agency planning and capabilities, so that they could be remedied. In any event, Fournier and Bridis (2005) note that "A followup conference, to iron out difficulties in some of the individual plans . . . was cancelled at the last minute, due to lack of funding."

The actual explanation for the discrepancy in expectations as to FEMA's response time is not entirely clear. To my knowledge, neither the National Incident Management System (U.S. Department of Homeland Security March 2004) nor the National Response Plan (December 2004) actually cites a specific number of hours or days by which the FEMA response is supposed to be effective. However, briefing material on these documents (U.S. Department of Homeland Security August 2004) does make clear that federal emergency planning envisions a "layered response strategy," suggesting that short-term federal assistance in the immediate aftermath of a disaster is anticipated to arrive only if and when local, regional, and state responders and resources become overwhelmed or exhausted. Similarly, it now appears that much of the federal assistance that had been promised immediately after Katrina may never materialize (Easton 2005), in part due to congressional inaction.

In addition to a lack of serious planning for the possibility of a flood, and uncertainty about how quickly federal resources could be expected, there was also apparently a lack of consistency regarding which areas of the city were considered to be at risk. While one group within FEMA was conducting emergency exercises for a breach of the levees and expressing concern about the possibility that the Superdome could be surrounded by water, the FEMA maps indicating the "special flood hazard areas" (in which flood insurance is required) had implicitly assumed that "the levees and flood walls protecting the [Lower Ninth Ward] from inundation would remain intact" (Whoriskey 2005). Insurance recommendations were based on potential rainfall amounts in a "100-year storm," but had apparently not considered the possibility of levee failure.

Despite the unique topography of New Orleans, difficulties with flood insurance are unfortunately not unique. Problems with FEMA's flood maps had been identified even before Hurricane Katrina; for example, Berginnis (2005) had testified before Congress that "fully one-third of flood insurance claims . . . [and] approximately 25% of properties that have received multiple claims are located outside of areas mapped as flood-prone." Kunreuther (2006) discusses other reasons for underinsurance. The result of such problems was that even a neighborhood lying below sea level was apparently considered to be "relatively safe" (Whoriskey 2005) by the agency charged to help "prepare the nation for all hazards" (FEMA 2005).

Failures of Response

Even ignoring the poor emergency planning for Hurricane Katrina on the part of New Orleans, it is at first baffling that the federal response was so slow in the face of what was clearly an overwhelming catastrophe. Again, however, I will argue that one reason for the delayed federal response was due to miscommunication, differing assumptions, and failures of coordination among different agencies and different levels of government.

One such area of missed coordination concerned which resources FEMA should supply to Louisiana. Before Katrina struck, Governor Blanco had filed a formal request with FEMA for "emergency protective measures, direct Federal Assistance, Individual and Household Program . . . assistance, Special Needs Program assistance, and debris removal" (Blanco 2005). This was in keeping with FEMA's ordinary mode of doing business, in which it provided support to state and local government, in response to explicit requests.

After the breach of the levees, FEMA was initially still in normal operating mode, waiting for itemized requests of needed supplies and support.

Brown reported that he had asked officials in Louisiana: "'What do you need? Help me help you.' . . . I never received specific requests for specific things that needed doing" (Kirkpatrick and Shane 2005).

In fact, it appears that such itemized requests were actually made. For example, Maestri of Jefferson Parish stated, "We were flabbergasted by some statements made by high FEMA officials . . . that FEMA didn't come because the locals didn't ask . . . The locals did ask" (Frontline 2005). However, Governor Blanco and other state and local officials were clearly exasperated with even the request for an itemized list of needs, since Louisiana's emergency responders were overwhelmed and lacked adequate communication systems. In a conversation with President Bush, she is reported to have said simply: "Mr. President, we need your help. We need everything you've got" (Thomas 2005). Members of Blanco's staff summarized the frustration similarly: "It was like walking into an emergency room bleeding profusely and being expected to instruct the doctors how to treat you" (Kirkpatrick and Shane 2005); "We wanted soldiers, helicopters, food and water . . . They wanted to negotiate an organizational chart" (Shane 2005).

This provides the context for Chertoff's remarks about "breaking the mold" for emergency response: "The fact of the matter is, this set of catastrophes has broken any mold for how you deal with this kind of weather devastation, and so we're going to break the mold in terms of how we respond. The federal government is not going to play merely its customary role in giving all necessary support to first responders. The federal government is going to step up and take a primary role, working with state and locals to deal with the outcome of this tragedy" (Chertoff 2005). In other words, for FEMA to actually initiate emergency efforts without first "negotiating an organizational chart" was apparently viewed as "breaking the mold"—a decision that was not implemented until September 3 (roughly five days after the request for "everything you've got"). Note, on this point, that the plan resulting from Hurricane Pam, "which was never put into effect, envisions giving the federal government authority to act without waiting for an SOS from local officials" (Fournier and Bridis 2005).

While FEMA eventually did break the mold in initiating emergency efforts, the government was frequently unable to waive requirements that did not appear to make sense in a catastrophic situation. The most famous (or infamous) example was requiring routine training on issues like sexual harassment before sending first responders out into the field (Rosetta 2005). However, similar "red tape" also resulted in international food aid going unused (Connolly 2005), physicians being unable to practice medicine (see for example Anderson 2005), bus drivers being allowed to drive for only their 12-hour customary shifts (Louisiana Office of the Governor

2005), buses being turned away for lack of air conditioning and toilet facilities (Alpert 2005), FEMA refusing donated supplies in order to honor prearranged contracts with other vendors ("suspect device" 2005), and voluntary organizations such as the Red Cross and the Salvation Army being impeded from providing support (American Red Cross 2005; Young and Borenstein 2005). See also the discussion on the inherent tensions between bureaucratic regulations and "superior performance" by Kettl (2006), and the observation that "federal law, FEMA regulations, and FEMA policy limited the agency's ability to anticipate disasters for which there was adequate warning" in the case of Hurricanes Hugo and Andrew (Daniels and Clark-Daniels 2000).

Perhaps most disturbingly, FEMA was apparently unable to waive its requirement for signed original requests for assistance, even in the face of an overwhelming emergency that severely disrupted normal mail service, Federal Express, and so forth. Recently released documents show that "Three days after the storm, Blanco . . . had already requested 40,000 more troops; ice, water and food; buses, base camps, staging areas, amphibious vehicles, mobile morgues, rescue teams, housing, airlift and communications systems" (Associated Press 2005), and sent an itemized request for "generators, medicine and healthcare workers" (CNN 2005). The administration responded that it had not received a formal application: "We found it on the governor's Web site, but we need 'an original' for our staff secretary to formally process the requests" (Associated Press 2005). (It is not yet clear whether FEMA actually had a rule requiring signed originals before taking action, or if this was an after-the-fact explanation for not having acted more promptly.)

Further lack of coordination was exhibited by the problems of truckloads of ice and other supplies circling the country for days, much of it never used for purposes of emergency response. Some of the ice eventually ended up in Tucson, Arizona, where it provided a treat for some polar bears in the local zoo (Kelly 2005). Helferich (2005) has raised similar concerns regarding the distribution of food supplies after Katrina, and emphasized the importance of collaborative programs involving government, voluntary organizations, and private-sector food providers in improving food preparedness and resilience. Such collaborative planning efforts can make the difference in knowing whom to call during a long holiday weekend to arrange food deliveries or debug problems—a factor that turned out to be important in this instance, since Hurricane Katrina hit a week before Labor Day.

There were also major conflicts between the federal and state governments over the role of the National Guard and the use of military power. The Bush administration "sent Blanco a legal memo seeking to federalize Louisiana law enforcement under the Insurrection Act, which is used to suppress civil disobedience that threatens to turn into anarchy . . . Rather than cede control, Blanco . . . named James Lee Witt, who ran the Federal Emergency Management Agency under Clinton, to help run relief efforts" (Millhollon and Ballard 2005). According to Walsh et al. (2005), Blanco was concerned that "They wanted to take over my National Guard."

The Insurrection Act of 1795 "permits the use of federal troops on U.S. soil to put down violence" (Yaukey 2005). However, the 1878 Posse Comitatus Act (literally, "power of the county") "forbids the military from performing civilian law enforcement without congressional approval" (McDonnel 2005). Thus, it would have been politically risky for Bush to send in federal troops to maintain order without formal authorization from Blanco. (Note also that the Posse Comitatus Act was passed specifically to address the frustrations of the South over the extended federal military presence after the Civil War. Therefore, Bush might have been risking not only the ire of Democrats such as Blanco and her supporters, but quite possibly also the resentment even of some conservative Republicans who viewed themselves as patriotic Southerners.)

Walsh et al. (2005) observe that "The [resulting] parallel command structure [with both federal and state personnel] in Louisiana isn't without precedent." For example a similar parallel command involving both federal troops and the Florida National Guard was used after Hurricane Andrew in 1992, largely without incident; Kettl (2006) also notes that Mayor Giuliani of New York City had functioned effectively as "the conductor of a large and hugely complex symphony" under similar circumstances after the events of September 11, 2001. However, in the aftermath of Katrina, struggles over "who is in charge" greatly complicated the coordination of emergency response. As stated by Kettl, "Someone has to be in charge of the response to events like Katrina. But that does not require a civil war among levels of government and between government organizations over just who that ought to be . . . A coordinated response requires the subtle weaving together of forces from a vast array of functional areas and from different levels of government, not hierarchical control."

Note that similar issues are likely to remain problematic in future emergencies. For example, in discussing the Bush plan for an influenza pandemic, the *New York Times* (2005) notes that "The chain of command is unclear, with myriad agencies and multiple levels of government playing a role." Kettl (2006) also points out that future hurricanes, earthquakes, or terrorist events may be even more severe than those we have confronted so far. Thus, problems similar to those observed after Katrina are likely to arise again in the future, unless improvements are achieved in the ability to coordinate multiple agencies and levels of government.

Summary

The net result of the types of communication and coordination problems documented above was a slow response to the hurricane and especially the flood. For example, Lipton et al. (2005) note that the number of people in the Superdome in New Orleans was reported to have reached 20,000 by August 31 (two days after Katrina hit the city), but it wasn't until September 3 that the National Guard achieved its full strength there. FEMA and the Department of Defense were similarly slow in achieving a substantial presence in New Orleans.

By contrast, the Coast Guard (an organization reputed for its capabilities in emergency response) had rescued over a thousand people by August 30 (Lipton et al. 2005), and was responsible for approximately 20,000 rescues in the Gulf area during the week after Katrina (Barr 2005). A representative of the Coast Guard attributed the organization's success after Hurricanes Charley, Frances, and Ivan in 2004 to "training, readiness and flexibility" (Silverstein 2004). Interestingly, the organization had earned high marks for effective management five years ago (*Government Executive* 2000), receiving an A grade overall, and an A on "managing for results"; *Government Executive* noted specifically that "Top-notch planning and performance budgeting [had helped the agency] overcome short staffing and fraying equipment."

Many of the problems that were observed after Katrina appear to be due to the difficulties of coordinating within and among large bureaucracies. Bureaucracies are widely noted in the literature on organizational design (and especially contingency theory) as being inflexible and not well suited to coping with rapidly changing situations. For example, Druckman et al. (1997) summarize the finding that "organizations with low levels of centralization and formalization are more effective in turbulent environments, whereas organizations with high levels of centralization and formalization are more effective in placid environments." Similarly, Westrum (2004) has observed that "The bureaucratic culture . . . is oriented toward following rules and protecting the organization's 'turf.'" In fact, the common-sense observation that bureaucracies can be slow and cumbersome led Representative Foley of Florida to argue that "FEMA should not be hindered by a top-heavy bureaucracy when they are needed to act swiftly to save lives," and to suggest removing it from the Department of Homeland Security (Young and Borenstein 2005).

Effective emergency response, like safety, would seem to call for resilient and flexible organizations, since it is not possible to anticipate all possible problems (Carroll 2004). For example, high-reliability organizations are noted as being able to "quickly move from completely centralized decision making and hierarchy during periods of relative calm to completely decentralized and flat decision structures during 'hot times'"

(Mannarelli et al. 1996), and having a "flexible delegation of authority and structure under stress (particularly in crises and emergency situations)" (Rochlin 1996).

Unfortunately, emergency response as currently implemented in the U.S. is a complex interlocking network of bureaucratic organizations. In fact, a graphic apparently produced by the Monterey Institute of International Studies (2001), and available on the web at <http://russnelson.com/why-red-cross.html>, identifies well over a hundred government officials and agencies that may need to be involved in some way in emergency planning and response for terrorism and natural disasters.

Pandey and Moynihan (2006) note that "bureaucratic red tape is widely viewed as the most significant performance barrier for public organizations," and identify several factors that appear to improve the ability of bureaucratic organizations to cut through red tape and perform effectively. One is an organizational culture that facilitates the "flow of information" and rewards "risk-taking, flexibility and innovation"—basically, what Westrum (2004) would describe as a "generative" rather than a bureaucratic culture (even if the structure of the organization remains bureaucratic and hierarchical). The Coast Guard appears to be one example of such an organization in the area of emergency response. In fact, Baron (2005) noted that "The Coast Guard is one of very few agencies to win plaudits for response and public information in Hurricane Katrina," suggesting that further study should be devoted to identifying what the agency did well.

A second factor contributing to effective performance is "high levels of political support" (such as, from elected officials). Similarly, Daniels and Clark-Daniels (2000) emphasize specifically that in transforming government to achieve more effective performance, it is important to "leverage the presidency." From this perspective, it is instructive to note that FEMA was marginalized when it was incorporated in the Department of Homeland Security (Holderman 2005; Young and Borenstein 2005). Not only did its all-hazards approach not accord well with the department's primary emphasis on terrorism, but it also lacked effective leadership with a background in emergency preparedness (such as Witt), and lost its cabinet status. In light of the findings of Pandey and Moynihan, FEMA's lack of political support after the terrorist attacks of September 11 may have contributed to its disastrous response by creating not only a lack of money, expertise, and capability, but also a lack of initiative—an agency that was too afraid of possible political repercussions to act swiftly and decisively in a disaster.

Finally, Pandey and Moynihan suggest that formal efforts at reinventing government, such as the reforms introduced by Witt after Hurricane Andrew, when he was appointed director of FEMA (Worth 1998), and the associated "development of a proactive strategy for disaster response" (Daniels and Clark-Daniels 2000), can also be effective. Thus, there is hope that post-Katrina reforms may lead to more effective emergency planning and response in future, particularly if coupled with greater political support for the agency and its mission, and restoration of FEMA to its former independent status as a cabinet-level agency.

However, the natural bureaucratic tendency to ignore intractable problems can still lead to disastrous consequences. For example, even though HHS Secretary Leavitt remarked recently that "What we all learned from (Hurricane) Katrina is sometimes we have to think clearly about the unthinkable" (Yen 2005), official HHS estimates for the numbers of fatalities that could occur in a pandemic of avian influenza seem remarkably low. In particular, Gerberding (2005), director of the Centers for Disease Control and Prevention, has presented fatality estimates on the order of only 200,000 people or less for the U.S., for a disease that she estimates to have a fatality rate of 55% and could well be roughly as infectious as the seasonal flu.

Therefore, in addition to reforms at FEMA and improved cross-agency coordination, better emergency preparedness also requires a willingness to consider what Clarke (2005), a sociologist, has called "worst cases." This is a significant challenge. As a society, we cannot consider and prepare for all "worst cases," yet must find effective ways to counter the natural tendency to dismiss or ignore them. This suggests a need for research (possibly including methodologies such as benefit/cost analysis, probabilistic risk assessment, and decision analysis) to help in determining which actions to take in advance of disasters to deal with potential catastrophic events, and what levels of preparedness are appropriate. While Clarke (2005) argues against overemphasis on probability in making decisions about emergency preparedness, the probability of an event such as Hurricane Katrina clearly needs to be taken into account when assessing possible protective actions, and most likely would have supported vastly greater investments in emergency preparedness than were in fact made. As suggested by Romano (2005), "Probability theory and risk analysis may not be the jazziest topics to wrestle with in Katrina's wake, but more people should try."

Note

This research was supported by the U.S. Department of Homeland Security through the Center for Risk and Economic Analysis of Terrorism Events (CREATE) under grant number EMW-2004-GR-0112, and by the U.S. Army Research Laboratory and the U.S. Army Research Office under grant number DAAD19-01-1-0502. However, any opinions, findings, and conclusions or recommendations in this paper are those of the author and do not necessarily reflect the views of the sponsors.

The Katrina Breakdown

JONATHAN WALTERS AND DONALD F. KETTL

When Hurricane Katrina hit New Orleans, only one thing disintegrated as fast as the earthen levees that were supposed to protect the city, and that was the intergovernmental relationship that is supposed to connect local, state and federal officials before, during and after such a catastrophe.

In sifting through the debris of the disaster response, the first question is why intergovernmental cooperation broke down so completely. While it's hard even at this point to get an official accounting of exactly what happened, clearly there were significant communication and coordination problems at all levels of government. At the moment, much time and effort is being spent assigning culpability—for a lack of preparation, delayed decision making, bureaucratic tie-ups and political infighting—to individuals and agencies. But in the end, such investigations may produce little that is of widespread practical use.

What is more critical, and has significant implications for the future of emergency management in the United States, is the need to explicitly and thoroughly define governments' roles and responsibilities so that officials in other jurisdictions don't suffer the same sort of meltdown in the next natural or man-made disaster. The lurching tactical responses to the terrorist attacks of 2001 and this year's rash of major hurricanes only underline the truly fundamental issue: how to sort out who should do what—and how to make sure the public sector is ready to act when the unexpected but inevitable happens.

It won't be easy. Some in the federal government clearly feel that if they're going to be blamed for failures—failures that they ascribe at least in part to state and local officials—then they'd prefer a system where the federal government has the option of being much more preemptive in handling large-scale domestic disasters. States as a whole, though, are not going to go along with any emergency management plan that involves the feds declaring something like martial law. They would much prefer that existing protocols be continued and the Federal Emergency Management Agency regain its independence from the Department of Homeland Security and be led by experienced professionals rather than political appointees.

A Growing Federal Role

In fact, the history of disaster response and recovery in the United States has witnessed an ever-increasing federal role. On April 22, 1927, President Calvin Coolidge named a special cabinet-level committee headed by Commerce Secretary Herbert Hoover to deal with the massive flooding that was ravaging communities up and down the Mississippi River Valley that year. The scene, described in John M. Barry's highly topical chronicle, *Rising Tide: The Great Mississippi Flood of 1927 and How It Changed America,* arguably represents the beginning of the modern era of intergovernmental disaster response. (It also represents the first clear attempt to politicize federal disaster response, with Hoover consciously riding his performance during the disaster all the way to the White House.)

In 1950, the federal government began trying to formalize intergovernmental roles and responsibilities through the Federal Civil Defense Act, which defined the scope and type of assistance that the federal government would extend to states and localities after certain kinds of disasters or emergencies (although Congress had been offering financial aid to states and localities in a piecemeal fashion since the early 1800s). In 1979, President Jimmy Carter created the Federal Emergency Management Agency, largely in response to governors' complaints about the fragmented nature of federal disaster planning and assistance. And in 1988, Congress, passed the Robert T. Stafford Disaster Relief Act, which outlined the protocols for disaster declaration and what sort of intergovernmental response would follow.

From 1989 to 1992, a succession of disasters, including the Loma Prieta earthquake in California and Hurricanes Hugo in South Carolina and Andrew in Florida put the whole issue of intergovernmental emergency response in the public hot seat, notes Tom Birkland, director of the Center for Policy Research at the Rockefeller College of Public Affairs and Policy. In particular, the disasters highlighted the federal government's slow-footed and bureaucratic response in the wake of such catastrophic events. (To be sure, such events were also teaching state and local governments plenty about *their* emergency response capabilities). That, in turn, led to a major turnaround at FEMA, with the appointment of James Lee Witt, the first FEMA director to arrive on the job with actual state emergency management experience.

In general, two things were going on around the increasing federal role in emergency readiness and response, Birkland says. States and localities were getting hooked on federal money—especially for recovery. But American presidents were also discovering the political benefits of declaring disasters, which allowed them to liberally sprinkle significant amounts of cash around various states and localities in distress. "That spending grew considerably under the Clinton administration," says Birkland. "And it created the expectation of federal government largesse. Federal spending, however, was always meant to supplement and not supplant state and local spending."

Local Response

But if the federal role in disaster response and recovery has increased—along with expectations of federal help—emergency management experts at all levels still agree on the basics of existing emergency response protocol: All emergencies are, initially at least, local—or local and state—events. "For the first 48 to 72 hours, it's understood that local and state first responders are principally responsible," says Bill Jenkins, director of the Homeland Security and Justice Issues Group, which is currently looking into the intergovernmental response to Katrina. "The feds come in as requested after that."

The extent to which the local-state-federal response ramps up depends on a host of factors, including the size of the incident and what plans and agreements are in place prior to any event. It also very much depends on the capacity of the governments involved. Some local and state governments have the ability to deal with disasters on their own and seem less inclined to ask for outside help. Others seem to hit the intergovernmental panic button more quickly. But whichever it is, say those on the front line of emergency response, how various governmental partners in emergency response and recovery are going to respond shouldn't be a surprise-filled adventure. Key players at every level of government should have a very good idea of what each will be expected to do or provide when a particular disaster hits.

Most important to the strength of the intergovernmental chain are solid relationships among those who might be called upon to work closely together in times of high stress. "You don't want to meet someone for the first time while you're standing around in the rubble," says Jarrod Bernstein, spokesman for the New York City Office of Emergency Management. "You want to meet them during drills and exercises." In New York, notes Bernstein, the city has very tight relationships with state and federal officials in a variety of agencies. "They're involved in all our planning and all our drills. They have a seat at all the tabletop exercises we do."

During those exercises, says Bernstein, federal, state and local officials establish and agree on what their respective jobs will be when a "big one" hits. Last summer, for example, the city worked with FEMA, the U.S. Department of Health and Human Services, the Federal Bureau of Investigation and New York State health and emergency response officials on an exercise aimed at collecting 8 million doses of medicine and distributing them throughout the city in a 48-hour window. "What we were looking at is how we'd receive medical stockpiles from the federal government, break them down and push them out citywide. There is a built-in federal component to that plan," Bernstein says.

No Plan B

While pre-plans and dry runs are all well and good, they're not much use if not taken seriously, however. In 2004, FEMA and Louisiana's Office of Homeland Security and Emergency Preparedness conducted a tabletop exercise, called Hurricane Pam, that simulated a Category 3 storm hitting and flooding New Orleans. It identified a huge gap in disaster planning: An estimated 100,000 people wouldn't be able to get out of the city without assistance. As is standard in emergency management practice, it is the locality's responsibility—at least initially—to evacuate residents, unless other partners are identified beforehand.

Critics of Mayor Ray Nagin say he failed to follow up aggressively on the finding. Last spring, the city floated the notion that it would rely primarily on the faith-based community to organize and mobilize caravans for those without cars or who needed special assistance getting out of the city. The faith-based community balked, however, citing liability issues. The city never came up with a Plan B.

Meanwhile, the Department of Homeland Security had great confidence in its 426-page "all-hazards" National Response Plan. Unveiled last January, it "establishes standardized training, organization and communications procedures for multi-jurisdictional interaction; clearly identifies authority and leadership responsibilities; enables incident response to be handled at the lowest possible organizational and jurisdictional level; ensures the seamless integration of the federal government when an incident exceeds state or local capabilities; and provides the means to swiftly deliver federal support in response to catastrophic incidents."

Katrina was its first test. And in the wake of the Category 4 storm and subsequent flooding, the city's vital resources—communications, transportation, supplies and manpower—were quickly overwhelmed. But DHS Secretary Michael Chertoff waited until 24 hours after the levees were breached to designate the hurricane as an "incident of national significance—requiring an extensive and well-coordinated response by federal, state, local tribal and nongovernmental authorities to save lives, minimize damage and provide the basis for long-term community and economic recovery."

The nation—indeed the world—bore painful witness to its failure. "There are mechanisms and protocols set up as part of the National Response Plan, and those were not followed," says John R. Harrald, director of the Institute for Crisis, Disaster and Risk Management at George

Washington University. Harrald notes that under the response plan, one of the first things that's supposed to happen is the rapid activation of a joint operations center to coordinate the intergovernmental response. In Louisiana, that didn't happen quickly enough, he says.

Calling in the Troops

As a result of Katrina, and to a lesser extent Hurricanes Rita and Wilma, the general citizenry and elected leaders at all levels of government, as well as emergency responders up and down the chain of command, are demanding a comprehensive review of how local, state and federal governments work (or don't work) together.

Part of that discussion has to include what to do when a state or local government's ability to prepare, respond or to ask for help is either impaired or wiped out altogether. "The question is what do you do when state and local capacity fails for one reason or another, either because they're overwhelmed or they're incompetent," says GWU's Harrald. "Do we have a system that allows us to scale up adequately or do we need a system where we can bring the military in sooner but that doesn't give away state and local control?"

Bill Leighty, Virginia Governor Mark Warner's chief of staff, who volunteered to spend two weeks in Louisiana helping manage the state response to Katrina, says he thinks there needs to be a serious intergovernmental discussion about when, for example, it might be appropriate to involve the military more directly in a domestic crisis. It is a position born of watching FEMA in action, versus what he saw of the military while he was in New Orleans. FEMA's bureaucratic approach to every item it provided or action it took was, at times, brutally exasperating, says Leighty. "But when you tell the 82nd Airborne, 'Secure New Orleans,' they come in and they know exactly what to do and it gets done."

Even some long-time New Orleans residents, who watched helplessly as looters rampaged through parts of the city, say they wouldn't have minded at all if the military had stepped in to restore order. "There are times when people are overwhelmed," says Frank Cilluffo, director of the Homeland Security Policy Institute at George Washington University, "and they don't care what color uniform is involved in coming to the rescue—red, blue or green." Governors were aghast at the idea, suggested by President Bush, that the military would become America's first responders.

However, both Kathleen Babineaux Blanco, the Democratic governor of Louisiana, and Haley Barbour, the Republican governor of Mississippi, strenuously objected to requests from the White House to give the Pentagon command over their states' National Guard troops. And President George W. Bush's suggestion of a quick resort to the military in future disasters stunned many observers, including those in his own party. In a tele-vision address from New Orleans, he argued that only the armed forces were "capable of massive logistical operations on a moment's notice."

But governors were aghast at the idea that the military would become America's first responders. In a *USA Today* poll, 36 of 38 governors (including brother Jeb Bush) opposed the plan. Michigan Governor Jennifer Granholm put it bluntly: "Whether a governor is a Republican or Democrat, I would expect the response would be, 'Hell no.'" For one blogger, the worry was "How long before a creek flooding in a small town in Idaho will activate the 82d Airborne Division?"

Bush grabbed the military option in part because of the poor performance of state and local governments. Indeed, everyone breathed a sigh of relief when Coast Guard Admiral Thad Allen arrived to assume command.

Part of the explanation also lies in public opinion polls. A Pew Research Center survey just after the storm revealed that nearly half of those surveyed believed state and local governments had done a fair or poor job— and there was no partisan difference on that conclusion. That meant the smart political play for Bush, although he didn't fare much better in the poll, was to suggest that the military might have to do what state and local governments could not.

That idea, of course, could scarcely be further from the strategy the Republicans had spent a generation building. The Richard Nixon–Ronald Reagan model of new federalism revolved around giving the states more autonomy and less money. But faced with the need to do something—and lacking any alternative—Bush reached back to Lyndon Johnson's Great Society philosophy of an expanded role for the federal government.

But Bush's plan to push the military into a first-response role was clearly less a broad policy strategy than a tactic to find a safe haven in the post-Katrina blame game. That became clear in November, when he announced his avian flu initiative. In that plan, he penciled in a heavy role for state and local public health officials.

Control and Contention

Some believe there is a middle ground when it comes to issues of authority and autonomy. James A. Stever, director of the Center for Integrated Homeland Security and Crisis Management at the University of Cincinnati, says he and colleagues had forwarded a paper to the former head of Homeland Security, Tom Ridge, outlining the concept of "homeland restoration districts." The idea is to have established criteria for when a more robust federal disaster response might be appropriate. Recovery districts would allow for ad hoc federal takeovers of specific geographic areas when appropriate, says Stever, rather than creating some new, overriding national response protocol that calls for broad federal preemption of local and state authority.

But sifting through such ideas—and the others that are sure to surface—is going to mean rekindling the sort of conversation about intergovernmental coordination and cooperation that Washington hasn't seen in a long time. Whether the current Congress and administration will be willing to conduct that conversation isn't clear. State and local officials, for their part, have been called in by Congress to testify on how the intergovernmental response to disasters ought to go. But such sessions have frequently had the familiar ring of both state and local tensions over who controls federal funding, as well as a little tin-cup rattling.

For example, in testimony before the House Homeland Security Committee, David Wallace, mayor of Sugar Land, Texas, argued that the first lesson learned in the wake of Katrina is that local governments should have more control over how federal homeland security first-responder money should be spent. "There was a real concern from the beginning that an over-reliance by the federal government on a state-based distribution system for first responder resources and training would be slow and result in serious delays in funding reaching high-threat, high-risk population areas." Wallace concluded his testimony with a request for federal funding for what he describes as Regional Logistics Centers, designed to bring local regional resources to bear in the immediate aftermath of disasters.

Nor is it only touchy issues of funding and control related to readiness and response that need discussing, points out Paul Posner, who spent years as a GAO intergovernmental affairs analyst. "There's other knotty issues that cause a lot of intergovernmental friction, like federal insurance policies, local building codes and state land use policies." These are key issues that Posner points out all influence how vulnerable certain places are to disasters in the first place.

From hurricanes and pandemics and to earthquakes and terrorism, the United States is grappling with the prospect of a host of cataclysmic events. Taken individually, most communities face a small chance of being hit, but experts agree that its not a matter of "if" but "when" another large-scale disaster will occur somewhere in the United States. As Katrina so powerfully illustrated, a fragmented intergovernmental response can be disastrous.

Bibliography

Ackerman, B. and A. Alstott. 1999. *The Stakeholder Society*. New Haven: Yale University Press.

Adler, M. D. 2000. "Beyond Efficiency and Procedure: A Welfarist Theory of Regulation." *Florida State University Law Review* 28.

———. 2003. "Risk, Death and Harm: The Normative Foundations of Risk Regulation." *Minnesota Law Review* 87.

———. 2005. "Against 'Individual Risk': A Sympathetic Critique of Risk Assessment." *University of Pennsylvania Law Review* 153.

———. 2006. "Equity Analysis and Natural Hazards Policy. In Daniels, R. J., D. F. Kettl, and H. Kunreuther, eds., *On Risk and Disaster: Lessons from Hurricane Katrina*. Philadelphia: University of Pennsylvania Press.

Adler, M. D. and E. A. Posner. 1999. "Rethinking Cost-Benefit Analysis." *Yale Law Journal* 109.

———. 2001. "Implementing Cost-Benefit Analysis when Preferences Are Distorted." In M. D. Adler and E. A. Posner, eds., *Cost-Benefit Analysis: Legal, Economic, and Philosophical Perspectives*. Chicago: University of Chicago Press.

———. 2006. *New Foundations of Cost-Benefit Analysis*. Cambridge, Mass: Harvard University Press.

ADCIRC (Advanced Circulation Model Development Group). 2004. *Advanced Circulation Model Example: Hypothetical Hurricane Pam*. <http://www.nd.edu/~adcirc/pam.htm> (accessed December 16, 2005).

Alesch, D. J., J. N. Holly, E. Mittler, and R. Nagy. "After the Disaster . . . What Should I Do Now?" Public Entity Risk Institute. <http://www.riskinstitute.org>

Alesch, D. J. and W. J. Petak. 1986. *The Politics and Economics of Earthquake Hazard Mitigation: Unreinforced Masonry Buildings in Southern California*. Boulder, Colo: University of Colorado, Natural Hazards Research and Applications Information Center.

Alkire, S. 2002. *Valuing Freedoms: Sen's Capability Approach and Poverty Reduction*. Oxford: Oxford University Press.

Alpert, B. 2005. "State Couldn't Keep up with Aid Offers." *Times-Picayune* (December 4). <http://www.nola.com/news/t-p/frontpage/index.ssf?/base/news-4/113368322767800.xml>

American Red Cross. 2005. "Hurricane Katrina: Why Is the Red Cross not in New Orleans?" <http://www.redcross.org/faq/0,1096,0_682_4524,00.html>

Anderson, L. S. 2005. "Doctor Says FEMA Ordered Him to Stop Treating Hurricane Victims." *Advocate* (September 16). <http://www.2theadvocate.com/stories/091605/new_doctorordered001.shtml>

Arneson, R. J. 2000. "Welfare Should Be the Currency of Justice." *Canadian Journal of Philosophy* 30.

Associated Press. 2005. "Governor's Papers Show Political Storm." *Indianapolis Star* (December 14). <http://www.indystar.com/apps/pbcs.dll/article?AID=/20051204/NEWS06/512040513/1012/NEWS06>

Balestrino, A. 1996. "A Note on Functioning-Poverty in Affluent Societies," *Notizei di Politeia* 12.

Bantwal, V. and H. Kunreuther. 2000. "A Cat Bond Premium Puzzle?" *Journal of Psychology and Financial Markets,* 1: 76–91.

Baron, G. 2005. "Now Is Too Late: Why You Have the Black Hat on and What You Can Do about It." Presented at the Washington State Emergency Management Association Conference. <http://news.audiencecentral.com/go/doc/6/83899>

Barr, S. 2005. "Coast Guard's Response to Katrina a Sliver Lining in the Storm." *Washington Post* (September 6).

Barras, J., S. Beville, D. Britsch, S. Hartley, S. Hawes, J. Johnston, P. Kemp, Q. Kinler, A. Martucci, J. Porthouse, D. Reed, K. Roy, S. Sapkota, and J. Suhayda. 2003. *Historical and Projected Coastal Louisiana Land Changes: 1978–2050.* USGS Open File Report 03-334 (revised January 2004).

Barry, J. 1997. *Rising Tide: The Great Mississippi Flood of 1927 and How It Changed America.* New York: Simon and Schuster.

Barton, A. H. 1969. *Communities in Disaster: A Sociological Analysis of Collective Stress Situations.* Garden City: Doubleday.

Bedford, T. and R. Cooke. 2001. *Probabilistic Risk Analysis: Foundations and Methods.* New York: Cambridge University Press.

Been, V. 1993. "What's Fairness Got to Do with It? Environmental Justice and the Siting of Locally Undesirable Land Uses." *Cornell Law Review* 78.

Benson, C. and E. J. Clay. 2004. *Understanding the Economic and Financial Impacts of Natural Disasters.* Washington, DC: The World Bank.

Berginnis, C. 2005. "Testimony, Association of State Floodplain Managers, Inc., before the Subcommittee on Housing and Community Opportunity, House Committee on Financial Services: Bunning-Bereuter-Blumenauer Flood Insurance Reform Act Implementation and Flood Insurance Claims Issues." <http://www.floods.org/PDF/ASFPM_Testimony_FIRA2004_4-14-05.pdf>

Berke, P. R. et al. 1993. "Recovery after Disaster: Achieving Sustainable Development, Mitigation and Equity." *Disasters* 17.

BestWire. 2005. "Florida's Last-Resort Homeowners Insurer to Raise Rates 15%." (November 22).

Bier, V. 2006. "Hurricane Katrina as a Bureaucratic Nightmare." In Daniels, R. J., D. F. Kettl, and H. Kunreuther, eds., *On Risk and Disaster: Lessons from Hurricane Katrina.* Philadelphia: University of Pennsylvania Press.

Blaikie, P., T. Cannon, I. Davis, and B. Wisner. 1994. *At Risk: Natural Hazards, People's Vulnerability, and Disasters.* London: Routledge.

Blanco, K. B. 2005. "Letter to President Bush." (August 28). <http://rawstory.com/news/2005/La._Governors_August_27_request_for_assista_0906.html>

Block, L. G. and P. Williams. 2002. "Undoing the Effects of Seizing and Freezing: Decreasing Defensive Processing in Personally-Relevant Messages." *Journal of Applied Social Psychology* 32.

Blumenthal, R. and D. Barstow. 2005. "'Katrina Effect' Pushed Texans into Gridlock." *New York Times.* (September 24).

Bojer, H. 2003. *Distributional Justice: Theory and Measurement.* London: Routledge.

Bonomi, A. et al. 2000. "Validation of the United States' Version of the World Health Organization Quality of Life (WHOQOL) Instrument." *Journal of Clinical Epidemiology* 53.

Bourne, J. 2000. "Louisiana's Vanishing Wetlands: Going, Going." *Science* 289 (5486).

Bourne, J. K., Jr. 2004. "Gone With the Water." *National Geographic.* (October).

Britsch, L. D. and J. B. Dunbar. 1993. "Land Loss Rates: Louisiana Coastal Plain." *Journal of Coastal Research* 9 (2).

Brown, M. J. and R. E. Hoyt. 2000. "The Demand for Flood Insurance: Empirical Evidence." *Journal of Risk and Uncertainty* 20 (3).

Buehler, R., D. Griffin, and M. Ross. 1994. "Exploring the Planning Fallacy: Why People Overestimate their Task Completion Times." *Journal of Personality and Social Psychology* 67.

Bumiller, K. 1998. *The Civil Rights Society: The Social Construction of Victims.* Baltimore: Johns Hopkins University Press.

Burby, Raymond J. with Beverly A. Cigler, Steven P. French, Edward J. Kaiser, Jack Kartez, Dale Roenigk, Dana Weist, and Dale Whittington. 1991. *Sharing Environmental Risks: How to Control Governments' Losses in Natural Disasters.* Boulder, Colo: Westview.

Burger, J. M. and M. L. Palmer. 1992. "Changes in and Generalization of Unrealistic Optimism Following Experiences with Stressful Events: Reactions to the 1989 California Earthquake." *Personality and Social Psychological Bulletin* 18.

Burkett, V. R., D. B. Zilkoski, and D. A. Hart. 2003. "Sea-level Rise and Subsidence: Implications for Flooding in New Orleans, Louisiana." In Prince, K. R. and D. L. Galloway, eds., *U.S. Geological Survey Subsidence Interest Group Conference, Proceeding of the Technical Meeting.* <http://www.nwrc.usgs.gov/hurricane/Sea-Level-Rise.pdf>

Burton, I., R. Kates, and G. White. 1978. *The Environment as Hazard.* Oxford: Oxford University Press.

———. 1993. *The Environment as Hazard.* 2nd ed. New York: Guilford.

Cabinet Office. 2002. *Risk and Uncertainty.* London: Author.

Cagle, J, and S. Harrington. 1995. "Insurance Supply with Capacity Constraints and Endogenous Insolvency Risk." *Journal of Risk and Uncertainty* 11.

Camerer, C., S. Issacharoff, G. Lowenstein, T. O Donoghue, and M. Rabin. 2003. "Regulation for Conservatives: Behavioral Economics and the Case for 'Asymmetric Paternalism.'" *University of Pennsylvania Law Review* 151.

Canadian Standards Association. 1997. *Risk Management Guidelines for Decision Makers* (Q850). Ottawa: Author.

Carroll, J. S. 2004. "Knowledge Management in High-Hazard Industries: Accident Precursors as Practice." In Phimister, J. R., V. M. Bier, and H. C. Kunreuther, eds., *Accident Precursor Analysis and Management: Reducing Technological Risk through Diligence.* Washington, DC: National Academies Press.

Centers for Disease Control and Prevention (CDC). 2004. "Outbreaks of Avian Influenza A (H5N1) in Asia and Interim Recommendations for Evaluation and Reporting of Suspected Cases—United States, 2004." *Morbidity and Mortality Weekly Report* 53 (05).

———. 2005a. "Vibrio Illnesses after Hurricane Katrina—Multiple States, August–September 2005." *Morbidity and Mortality Weekly Report* 54 (37).

———. 2005b. "Carbon Monoxide Poisoning after Hurricane Katrina—Alabama, Louisiana, and Mississippi, August–September 2005." *Morbidity and Mortality Weekly Report* 54 (39).

———. 2005c. "Surveillance for Illness and Injury after Hurricane Katrina—New Orleans, Louisiana, September 8–25, 2005." *Morbidity and Mortality Weekly Report* 54 (40).

———. 2005d. "Infectious Disease and Dermatologic Conditions in Evacuees and

Rescue Workers after Hurricane Katrina—Multiple States." *Morbidity and Mortality Weekly Report* 54 (38).

———. 2005e. "Norovirus Outbreak Among Evacuees from Hurricane Katrina—Houston, Texas, September 2005." *Morbidity and Mortality Weekly Report* 54 (40).

———. 2005f. "Update: Influenza Activity—United States and Worldwide, May 22–September 3, 2005, and 2005–06 Season Vaccination Recommendations." *Morbidity and Mortality Weekly Report* 54 (36).

Chandler, C. C., L. Greening, L. J. Robison, and L. Stoppelbein. 1999. "It can't happen to me . . . or can it? Conditional Base Rates Affect Subjective Probability Judgments." *Journal of Experimental Psychology: Applied* 5 (4).

Chertoff, M. 2005. "Briefing, September 3, 2005." CNN. <http://transcripts.cnn.com/TRANSCRIPTS/0509/03/cst.04.html>

Chowdhury, A., R. Mushtaque, A. U. Bhuyia, A. Yusuf, and R. Sen. 1993. "The Bangladesh Cyclone of 1991: Why So Many People Died." *Disasters* 17 (4).

Clarke, L. 1999. *Mission Improbable: Using Fantasy Documents to Tame Disaster.* Chicago: University of Chicago Press.

———. 2005. *Worst Cases: Terror and Catastrophe in the Popular Imagination.* Chicago: University of Chicago Press.

Clayton, M. and A. Williams, eds. 2000. *The Ideal of Equality.* Basingstoke: Palgrave.

CNN. 2004. "Hurricane Ivan Passes Battered Cuba." (September 13). <http://www.cnn.com/2004/WEATHER/09/13/hurricane.ivan/>

———. 2005. "Katrina Batters Roof of Superdome." (August 29). <http://www.cnn.com/2005/WEATHER/08/29/superdome/>

———. 2005. "Katrina Documents Released." (December 3). <http://www.cnn.com/2005/US/12/03/katrina.docs.ap/>

Cochrane, H. C. 1975. *Natural Hazards and Their Distributive Effects.* Boulder, CO: National Technical Information Service.

Cohen, A. J. 2005. "Hurricane Katrina: Lethal Levels." *New England Journal of Medicine* 353 (15).

Cohen, L. and R. Noll. 1981. "The Economics of Building Codes to Resist Seismic Structures." *Public Policy* (Winter).

Combe, J. 2002. "Interview with American RadioWorks." <http://americanradioworks.publicradio.org/features/wetlands/hurricane2.html>

Comerio, M. C. 1998. *Disaster Hits Home: New Policy for Urban Housing Recovery.* Berkeley: University of California Press.

Committee on Assessing the Costs of Natural Disasters. 1999. *The Impacts of Natural Disasters: A Framework for Loss Estimation.* Washington, DC: National Academy Press.

Conlin, M., T. O Donoghue, and T. J. Vogelsang. 2005. "Projection Bias in Catalog Orders." Working paper, Department of Economics, Cornell University.

Connolly, C. 2005. "Katrina Food Aid Blocked by U.S. Rules: Meals from Britain Sit in Warehouse." *Washington Post* (October 15).

Crisp, R. 2003. "Equality, Priority, and Compassion." *Ethics* 113.

Cropper, M. L. 2000. "Has Economic Research Answered the Needs of Environmental Policy?" *Journal of Environmental Economics and Management* 39.

Cross, J. A. 2001. "Megacities and Small Towns: Different Perspectives on Hazard Vulnerability." *Environmental Hazards* 3.

Crosson, P. and K. Frederick. 1999. "Impacts of Federal Policies and Programs on Wetlands." Discussion Paper 99–26. Washington, DC: Resources for the Future.

Cummins, J. D. 2005. "Should the Government Provide Insurance for Catastrophes." Paper presented at the 30th Annual Economic Policy Conference, Federal Credit and Insurance Programs, Federal Reserve Bank of St. Louis, October 20–21.

Cummins, J. D. and P. M. Danzon. 1997. "Price, Financial Quality, and Capital Flows in Insurance Markets." *Journal of Financial Intermediation* 6.

Cummins, J. D., N. Doherty, and A. Lo. 2002. "Can Insurers Pay for the 'Big One'? Measuring the Capacity of the Insurance Market to Respond to Catastrophe Losses." *Journal of Banking and Finance* 26.

Cutter, S. L. 2005. "The Geography of Social Vulnerability: Race, Class, and Catastrophe." New York: Social Science Research Council forum on "Understanding Katrina: Perspectives from the Social Sciences." <http://understandingkatrina.ssrc.org/cutter>

Cutter, S. L., ed. 2001. *American Hazardscapes: The Regionalization of Hazards and Disasters.* Washington, DC: Joseph Henry Press.

Cutter, S. L., B. J. Boruff, and W. L. Shirley. 2003. "Social Vulnerability to Environmental Hazards." *Social Science Quarterly* 84 (1).

Cutter, S. L., J. T. Mitchell, and M. S. Scott. 2000. "Revealing the Vulnerability of People and Places: A Case Study of Georgetown County, South Carolina." *Annals of the Association of American Geographers* 90 (4).

Dahlhamer, J. 1992. "Small Business and the Whittier Narrows Earthquake: Loan Request Outcomes in the U.S. Small Business Administration Disaster Loan Program for Businesses." MA thesis, University of Delaware, Department of Sociology and Criminal Justice, Disaster Research Center.

Daily, G. C. 1997. *Nature's Services: Societal Dependence on Natural Ecosystems.* Washington, DC: Island Press.

Dale, V. H., F. J. Swanson, and C. M. Crisafulli. 2005. *Ecological Responses to the 1980 Eruption of Mt. St. Helens.* New York: Springer-Verlag.

Daniels, N. 1996. *Justice and Justification: Reflective Equilibrium in Theory and Practice.* Cambridge: Cambridge University Press, 1996.

Daniels, R. J., D. F. Kettl, and H. Kunreuther, eds. 2006. *On Risk and Disaster: Lessons from Hurricane Katrina.* Philadelphia: University of Pennsylvania Press.

Daniels, R. and M. Trebilcock. 1996. "Private Provision of Public Infrastructure: An Organizational Analysis of the Next Privatization Frontier." *University of Toronto Law Journal* 46.

Daniels, R. and M. Trebilcock, M. 2005. *Rethinking the Welfare State: The Prospects for Government by Voucher.* Routledge, London.

Daniels, R. S. and C. L. Clark-Daniels. 2000. "Transforming Government: The Renewal and Revitalization of the Federal Emergency Management Agency." PricewaterhouseCoopers Endowment for the Business of Government (April). <http://www.fema.gov/pdf/library/danielsreport.pdf>

Dao, J. 2005. "Louisiana Sees Faded Urgency in Relief Effort." *New York Times* (November 22).

Dash, N., W. G. Peacock, and B. H. Morrow. 1997. "And the Poor Get Poorer: A Neglected Black Community." In Peacock, W. G., B. H. Morrow, and H. Gladwin, eds., *Hurricane Andrew: Ethnicity, Gender and the Sociology of Disasters.* London: Routledge.

Davis, M. and A. Fontenot. 2005. "Hurricane Gumbo." *The Nation* (November 7). <http://www.thenation.com/doc/20051107/davis>

De Laney, T. A. 1995. "Benefits to Downstream Flood Attenuation and Water Quality as a Result of Constructed Wetlands in Agricultural Landscapes." *Journal of Soil and Water Conservation* 50 (6).

Diamond, P. A. 1967. "Cardinal Welfare, Individualistic Ethics, and Interpersonal Comparisons of Utility: Comment." *Journal of Political Economy* 75.

Doherty, N., A. Kleffner, and L. Posey. 1992. *Insurance Surplus: Its Function, Its Accumulation and Its Depletion.* Boston: The Earthquake Project.

Doherty, N., P. Kleindorfer, and H. Kunreuther. 1990. "Insurance Perspectives on an Integrated Hazardous Waste Management Strategy." *Geneva Papers on Risk and Insurance* 27.

Doherty, N. and L. L. Posey. 1997. "Availability Crises in Insurance Markets: Optimal Contracts with Asymmetric Information and Capacity Constraints." *Journal of Risk and Uncertainty* 15.

Drabek, T. E. 1986. *Human System Responses to Disaster: An Inventory of Sociological Findings.* New York: Springer-Verlag.

Druckman, D., J. E. Singer, and H. Van Cott, eds. 1997. *Enhancing Organizational Performance.* Washington, DC: National Academy Press.

Drye, W. 2002. *Storm of the Century: The Labor Day Hurricane of 1935.* Washington, DC: The National Geographic Society.

Dunn, G. E. and B. I. Miller. 1964. *Atlantic Hurricanes.* Baton Rouge: Louisiana State University Press.

Dworkin, R. N. 2000. *Sovereign Virtue: The Theory and Practice of Equality.* Cambridge: Harvard University Press.

Dynes, R. R. 1970. *Organized Behavior in Disaster.* Lexington, MA: Heath Lexington Books.

Earthquake Engineering Research Institute. 1998. *Incentives and Impediments to Improving the Seismic Performance of Buildings.* Oakland, Calif: Earthquake Engineering Research Institute.

Easton, N. J. 2005. "Katrina Aid Falls Short of Promises." *Boston Globe* (November 27). <http://www.boston.com/news/nation/washington/articles/2005/11/27/katrina_aid_falls_short_of_promises/>

The Economist. 2005a. (September 10).

———. 2005b. (September 17).

Ellet, C., Jr. 1852. "Report on the Overflows of the Delta of the Mississippi." In Heyand, D. L. and N. S. Phillipi, *Reinventing a Flood Control Strategy.* Chicago: The Wetlands Initiative, 1994.

Ellsberg, D. 1961. "Risk, Ambiguity and the Savage Axioms." *Quarterly Journal of Economics* 75.

Elster, A. B., and C. M. Callan. 2002. "Physician Roles in Medicine-Public Health Collaboration: Future Directions of the American Medical Association." *American Journal of Preventative Medicine.* 22 (3).

Elster, J. 1984. *Ulysses and the Sirens.* Cambridge: Cambridge University Press.

Emanuel, K. A. 2005. *Divine Wind: The History and Science of Hurricanes.* New York: Oxford University Press.

Enarson, E. and B. H. Morrow. 1998. *The Gendered Terrain of Disaster: Through Women's Eyes.* Westport, CT: Praeger.

Environmental Protection Agency. (2005). "Background on Lower Mississippi River Basin." <http://www.epa.gov/msbasin/subbasins/lower/>

Ewing, B. T. et al. 2005. *Economics and the Wind.* New York: Nova Science Publishers.

Executive Order No. 12,291. 1982. *Code of Federal Regulations* 3 (replaced by Executive Order No. 12,866).

Executive Order No. 12,866. 1994. *Code of Federal Regulations* 3.

Executive Order No. 12,898. 1995. *Code of Federal Regulations* 3.

Faber, S. 1996. *On Borrowed Land: Public Policies for Floodplains.* Cambridge, Mass: Lincoln Land Institute of Land Policy.

Federal Emergency Management Agency (FEMA). 2004. "Region VI. Hurricane

Pam Exercise Concludes." Release date: July 23, 2004. Release number: R6-04-093. <http://www.fema.gov/news/newsrelease_print.fema?id=13051>

FEMA. 2005. "About FEMA." (July 5). <http://www.fema.gov/about/>

Final Summary, 2002. "The Wharton Risk Management and Decision Process Center and Institute for Business and Home Safety Roundtable on Economic Incentives for Building Safer Communities." (June 11).

Finkel, A. M. 1996. "Comparing Risks Thoughtfully." *Risk* 7.

Fischetti, M. 2001. "Drowning New Orleans." *Scientific American* (October).

Fischhoff, B. 1977. "Cost-Benefit Analysis and the Art of Motorcycle Maintenance." *Policy Sciences* 8.

———. 1980. Clinical Decision Analysis. *Operations Research* 28.

———. 1989. "Eliciting Knowledge for Analytical Representation. *IEEE Transactions on Systems, Man and Cybernetics* 13.

———. 1994. "What Forecasts (seem to) Mean." *International Journal of Forecasting* 10.

———. 1995. "Risk Perception and Communication Unplugged: Twenty Years of Process." *Risk Analysis* 15.

———. 2000. "Scientific Management of Science?" *Policy Sciences* 33.

———. 2005. "Decision Research Strategies." *Health Psychology* 21 (4).

———. 2006. "Behaviorally Realistic Risk Management." In Daniels, R. J., D. F. Kettl, and H. Kunreuther, eds., *On Risk and Disaster: Lessons from Hurricane Katrina.* Philadelphia: University of Pennsylvania Press.

———. In press. "Cognitive Issues in Stated Preference Methods." In K-G. Mäler and J. Vincent, eds., *Handbook of Environmental Economics.* Amsterdam: Elsevier.

Fischhoff, B., A. Bostrom, and M. J. Quadrel. 2002. "Risk Perception and Communication." In R. Detels, J. McEwen, R. Beaglehole, and H. Tanaka, eds., *Oxford Textbook of Public Health.* London: Oxford University Press.

Fischhoff, B., R. Gonzalez, D. Small, and J. Lerner. 2003. "Evaluating the Success of Terror Risk Communication." *Biosecurity and Bioterrorism: Biodefense Strategy, Practice, and Science* 1 (4).

Fischhoff, B., S. Lichtenstein, P. Slovic, S. L. Derby, and R. L. Keeney. 1981. *Acceptable Risk.* New York: Cambridge University Press.

Fischhoff, B., P. Slovic, and S. Lichtenstein. 1983. "Lay Foibles and Expert Fables in Judgments About Risk. *American Statistician* 36.

Fischhoff, B., S. Watson, and C. Hope. 1984. "Defining Risk." *Policy Sciences* 17.

Fischhoff, B., and S. Wesseley. 2003. "Managing Patients with Inexplicable Health Problems." *British Medical Journal* 326.

Fiss, O. et al. 2003. *A Way Out: America's Ghettos and the Legacy of Racism.* Princeton: Princeton University Press.

Florida Department of Revenue. 2005. Tax Information Publication 05A01. (May 10).

Flynn, J., P. Slovic, and C. K. Mertz. 1994. "Gender, Race, and Perception of Environmental Health Risks." *Risk Analysis* 14.

Folkes, V. 1988. "The Availability Heuristic and Perceived Risk." *Journal of Consumer Research* 15 (1).

Foster, K. R. and R. Giegengack. 2006. "Planning for a City on the Brink." In Daniels, R. J., D. F. Kettl, and H. Kunreuther, eds., *On Risk and Disaster: Lessons from Hurricane Katrina.* Philadelphia: University of Pennsylvania Press.

Fothergill, A. 1998. "The Neglect of Gender in Disaster Work." In Enarson, E. and B. H. Morrow, eds., *The Gendered Terrain of Disaster: Through Women's Eyes.* Westport, CT: Praeger.

Fothergill, A. et al. 1999. "Race, Ethnicity and Disasters in the United States: A Review of the Literature." *Disasters* 23.

Fothergill, A. 2004. *Heads Above Water: Gender, Class, and Family in the Grand Forks Flood.* Albany: State University of New York Press.

Fothergill, A. and L. A. Peek. 2004. "Poverty and Disasters in the United States: A Review of Recent Sociological Findings." *Natural Hazards* 32.

Fournier, R. and T. Bridis. 2005. "'Hurricane Pam' Depicted Direct Hit on New Orleans." *Star Tribune* (September 10). <http://www.startribune.com/stories/125/5606659.html>

Frankfurt, H. 1987. "Equality as a Moral Ideal." *Ethics* 98.

Freeman, P. and K. Scott. 2005. "Comparative Analysis of Large Scale Catastrophe Compensation Schemes." In *Catastrophic Risks and Insurance.* Paris: Organization for Economic Cooperation and Development (OECD).

Fritz, C. E. 1961. "Disasters." In Merton, R. K. and R. A. Nisbet, eds., *Contemporary Social Problems.* New York: Harcourt.

Fritz, C. E. and E. Marks. 1954. "The NORC Studies of Human Behavior in Disaster." *Journal of Social Issues* 10.

Frontline. 2005. "Interview: Walter Maestri." (November 22). <http://www.pbs.org/wgbh/pages/frontline/storm/interviews/maestri.html>

Froot, K. 2001. "The Market for Catastrophe Risk: A Clinical Examination." *Journal of Financial Economics* 60.

Froot, K. and P. O'Connell. 1997a. "The Pricing of U.S. Catastrophe Reinsurance." Working Paper 6043. National Bureau of Economic Research.

———. 1997b. "On the Pricing of Intermediated Risks: Theory and Application to Catastrophe Reinsurance." Working Paper 6011. National Bureau of Economic Research.

Fukuda-Parr, S. 2003. "The Human Development Paradigm: Operationalizing Sen's Ideas on Capabilities." *Feminist Economics* 9.

Gerhart, A. 2005. "And Now We Are in Hell." *Washington Post* (September 1).

Gilbert, D., E. C. Pinel, T. D. Wilson, S. J. Blumberg, and T. P. Wheatley. 1998. "Immune Neglect: A Source of Durability Bias in Affective Forecasting." *Journal of Personality and Social Psychology* 75 (3).

Gilgoff D, A. C. Marek, S. Brush, and A. Kingsbury. 2005. "Understanding Katrina." *U.S. News and World Report* 139 (9).

Glaeser, E. 2005. "Should the Government Rebuild New Orleans or Just Give Residents Checks?" *The Economists Voice* 4.

Glass, R. I., J. J. Urrutia, S. Siboney, H. Smith, B. Garcia, and L. Rizzo. 1977. "Earthquake Injuries Related to Housing in a Guatemala Village." *Science* 197.

Glass, T. A. and M. Spoch-Spana. 2002. "Bioterrorism and the People: How to Vaccinate a City Against Panic." *Clinical Infectious Disease* 34.

Glasser, S. B. and M. Grunwald. 2005. "Steady Buildup to a City's Chaos." *Washington Post* (September 11).

Glasser, S. B. and J. White. 2005. "Storm Exposed Disarray at the Top." *Washington Post* (September 4).

Glenn, D. 2005. "Disaster: Sociologists Study What Went Wrong in the Response to the Hurricanes, But Will Policy Makers Listen?" *Chronicle of Higher Education* (September 29).

Goodwin, B. and V. H. Smith. 1995. *The Economics of Crop Insurance and Disaster Aid.* Washington, DC: American Enterprise Institute.

Gordon, P. et al. 2005. "The Economic Costs of Port Closure in the United States." Paper presented at the Second National Symposium on the Economic Costs of Terrorism. University of Southern California, Los Angeles.

Gosselin, P. G. 2006. "On Their Own in Battered New Orleans." In Daniels, R. J., D. F. Kettl, and H. Kunreuther, eds., *On Risk and Disaster: Lessons from Hurricane Katrina.* Philadelphia: University of Pennsylvania Press.

Government Executive. 2000. "Government Performance Project Report Card." <http://www.govexec.com/gpp/reportcard.htm>

Greenwald, B. and J. Stiglitz. 1990. "Asymmetric Information and the New Theory of the Firm; Financial Constraints and Risk Behavior." *American Economic Review: Papers and Proceedings* 80.

Gregory, R., B. Fischhoff, and T. McDaniels. 2005. "Acceptable Inputs: Decision Analytic Standards for Participatory Processes. *Decision Analysis* 2.

Gron, A. 1994. "Capacity Constraints and Cycles in Property-Casualty Insurance Markets." *RAND Journal of Economics* 25 (1).

———. 1994. "Evidence of Capacity Constraints in Insurance Markets." *Journal of Law and Economics* 37.

Groot, W. "Time for a Check-Up: The Netherlands and the Perils of Water." Radio Netherlands <www2.rnw.nl/rnw/en/currentaffairs/region/Netherlands/ned050923>

Grossi, P. and H. Kunreuther. 2005. *Catastrophe Modeling: A New Approach to Managing Risk.* New York: Springer.

Grunwald, M. 2003. "River Blindness." (November 10). <slate.msn.com>

———. 2005. "Canal May Have Worsened City's Flooding." *Washington Post* (September 14).

Hammond, P. J. 1982. "Utilitarianism, Uncertainty and Information." In Sen, A. and B. Williams, eds., *Utilitarianism and Beyond.* Cambridge: Cambridge University Press.

Handmer, J. W. 1995. "Managing Vulnerability in Sydney: Planning or Providence?" *GeoJournal* 37.

Harrington, S. E. 2000. "Rethinking Disaster Policy." *Regulation: Cato Review of Business and Government.*

———. 2004. "Tort Liability, Insurance Rates, and the Insurance Cycle." In Herring, R. and R. Litan, eds., *Brookings-Wharton Papers on Financial Services: 2004.* Washington, DC: Brookings Institution Press.

———. 2006. "Rethinking Disaster Policy After Hurricane Katrina." In Daniels, R. J., D. F. Kettl, and H. Kunreuther, eds., *On Risk and Disaster: Lessons from Hurricane Katrina.* Philadelphia: University of Pennsylvania Press.

Harrington, S. E. and G. Niehaus. 2001. "Cycles and Volatility." In G. Dionne, ed., *The Handbook of Insurance.* Boston: Kluwer.

———. 2001. "Government Insurance, Tax Policy, and the Availability and Affordability of Catastrophe Insurance." *Journal of Insurance Regulation* 19.

———. 2003. "Capital, Corporate Income Taxes, and Catastrophe Insurance." *Journal of Financial Intermediation* 12.

Hartwig, R. 2005. "Hurricane Season of 2005: Impacts on US P/C Insurance Markets in 2006 and Beyond." (December 1). <http://www.disasterinformation.org/disaster2/facts/presentation>

———. 2005. "Hurricanes Katrina, Rita and Wilma: Impacts on the Property/Casualty Insurance and Reinsurance Industries." Insurance Information Institute. (October 25). <http://www.disasterinformation.org/disaster2/facts/presentation/>

Hartwig, R. and C. Wilkinson. 2005. "Public/Private Mechanisms Handling Catastrophic Risk in the Unites States." New York: Insurance Information Institute.

Helferich, O. K. 2005. "Supply Chain Assessment, Compliance and Corrective Action: Application to Catastrophic Incident Planning and Response." Paper presented at the First Annual Food Protection and Defense Research Conference, Institute of Food Technologists, Atlanta, GA.

Hey, D. L. 2001. "Modern Drainage Design: The Pros, the Cons, and the Future." Paper presented at the Annual Meeting of the American Institute of Hydrology, Hydrologic Science: Challenges for the 21st Century. Bloomington, MN.

Hey, D. L., D. L. Montgomery, L. S. Urban, T. Prato, A. Forbes, M. Martell, J. Pollack, Y. Steele and R. Zarwell. 2004. *Flood Damage Reduction in the Upper Mississippi River Basin: An Ecological Alternative.* Chicago: The Wetlands Initiative.

Hey, D. L. and N. S. Philippi. 1995. "Flood Reduction through Wetland Restoration: The Upper Mississippi River Basin as a Case History." *Restoration Ecology* 3 (1).

Hirsch, F. 1976. *Social Limits to Growth.* Cambridge: Harvard University Press.

H. John Heinz III Center for Science, Economics and the Environment, The. 2000. *The Hidden Costs of Coastal Hazards: Implications for Risk Assessment and Mitigation.* Washington, DC: Island Press.

HM Treasury. 2005. *Managing Risks to the Public: Appraisal Guidance.* London: Author.

Hoch, S. J. 1998. "Who Do We Know: Predicting the Interests and Opinions of the American Consumer." *Journal of Consumer Research* 15.

Hogarth, R. and H. Kunreuther. 1989. "Risk, Ambiguity and Insurance." *Journal of Risk and Uncertainty* 2.

Holderman, E. 2005. "Destroying FEMA." *Washington Post* (August 30).

Holmes, D. S. 1968. "Dimensions of Projection." *Psychological Bulletin* 69 (4).

Hood, J. 2005. "A Policy of Deceit." *New York Times* (November 19).

Horswell, C. and E. Hegstrom. 2005. "Evacuation Lessons Come at a High Cost: 107 Lives." *Houston Chronicle* (September 29).

Hunt, C. E. 1997. *A Natural Approach for Flood Damage Reduction and Environmental Enhancement, Long Term Resource Monitoring Program, Special Report 97-S005.* Onalaska, WI: Environmental Management Technical Center.

Iacobucci, E., M. Trebilcock, and H. Haider. 2001. *Economic Shocks: Defining a Role of Government.* Toronto: C. D. Howe Institute.

Iacobucci, E., M. Trebilcock, and R. Winter. 2005. "The Political Economy of Deregulation." (September 28).

Ichniowski, T. 2005. "Reports of Malfeasance in New Orleans Levee Construction." *New Orleans Sun* (November 3). <http://story.neworleanssun.com/p.x/ct/9/id/f80fa4f90e926cc9/cid/aa408b759025f381>

Innes, R. 2003. "Crop Insurance in a Political Economy: An Alternative Perspective of Agricultural Policy." *American Journal of Agricultural Economics* 85.

Institute of Medicine (IOM). 1998a. *Scientific Opportunities and Public Needs.* Washington, DC: National Academy Press.

———. 1998b. *Toward Environmental Justice.* Washington, DC: National Academy Press.

———. 2002. Committee to Assess the Safety and Efficacy of the Anthrax Vaccine, Medical Follow-up Agency. Joellenbeck, L. M., L. L. Zwanziger, J. S. Durch, and B. L. Strom, eds. *The Anthrax Vaccine: Is It Safe? Does It Work?* Washington, DC: National Academy Press.

———. 2005. Committee on Smallpox Vaccination Program Implementation, Board on Health Promotion and Disease Prevention. Baciu, A, A. P. Anason, K. Stratton, B. Strom, eds. *The Smallpox Vaccination Program: Public Health in an Age of Terrorism.* Washington, DC: The National Academies Press.

Insurance Information Institute. 2005. "Can Your Business Survive This Year's Active Hurricane Season?" (August 1). <http://www.iii.org/media/updates/press.742201/>

———. 2005. "Flood Insurance: Facts and Figures." (November 15).

Jaffee, D. 2005. "Comments on Cummins, J. D." Paper presented at the 30th Annual Economic Policy Conference, Federal Credit and Insurance Programs, Federal Reserve Bank of St. Louis.

———. 2005. "The Role of Government in the Coverage of Terrorism Risks." In *Terrorism Risk Insurance in OECD Countries.* Paris: Organisation for Economic Cooperation and Development (OECD).

Jaffee, D. and T. Russell. 2003. "Markets Under Stress: The Case of Extreme Event Insurance." In Arnott, R. et al., eds., *Economics for an Imperfect World: Essays in Honor of Joseph E. Stiglitz.* Cambridge: MIT Press.

Janis, I. L. 1951. *Air War and Emotional Stress.* Westport, CT: Greenwood Press.

Jensen, M. and W. Meckling. 1976. "Theory of the Firm: Managerial Behavior, Agency Cost and Ownership Structure." *Journal of Financial Economics* 3.

Jordan, L. J. 2005. "FEMA Official Warned About Unprepared Teams." Associated Press. (December 8).

Just, R. E. et al. 2004. *The Welfare Economics of Public Policy.* Cheltenham: Edward Elgar.

Kagan, S. 1998. *Normative Ethics.* Boulder: Westview Press.

Kahn, B. E., and M. F. Luce. 2005. "Repeated-Adherence Protection Model (RAP), I'm Ok and It's a Hassle." *Journal of Public Policy and Marketing.*

Kahneman, D. and D. Lovallo. 1993. "Timid Choices and Bold Forecasts: A Cognitive Perspective on Risk Taking." *Management Science* 39 (1).

Kahneman, D. and A. Tversky. 1973. "The Psychology of Prediction." *Psychological Review* 89 (4).

———. 1979. "Prospect Theory: An Analysis of Decision Under Risk." *Econometrica* 47 (2).

Kaplow, L. 1986. "An Economic Analysis of Legal Transitions." *Harvard Law Review* 99.

———. 1991. "Incentives and Government Relief for Risk." *Journal of Risk and Uncertainty* 4.

Kaufman, S. 2005. "New Orleans Mayor Says Improved Levees Will Help Spur Recovery." U.S. Department of State International Information Programs. (November 4).

Kazmann, R. G. and D. B. Johnson. 1980. "If the Old River Control Structure Fails? (The Physical and Economic Consequences)." *Louisiana Water Resources Research Institute Bulletin* 12. <http://www.lwrri.lsu.edu/downloads/LWRRI_Bulletins/May2005/LWRRI_B12_1980.pdf>

Keeney, R. 1992. *Value-Focused Thinking: A Path to Creative Decisionmaking.* Cambridge: Harvard University Press.

Keeney, R. and H. Raiffa. 1976. *Decisions with Multiple Objectives.* New York: Wiley.

Keeney, R. and D. von Winterfeldt. 1989. "On the Uses of Expert Judgment on Complex Technical Problems." *IEEE Transactions on Engineering Management* 36.

Kelly, A. 2005. "How Nice! Tons of Ice." *Arizona Daily Star* (September 20). <http://www.azstarnet.com/dailystar/metro/94060.php>

King, Rawle. 2005. *Hurricanes and Disaster Risk Financing Through Insurance: Challenges and Policy Options.* Washington, DC: Congressional Research Service.

Kirkpatrick, D. D. and S. Shane. 2005. "Ex-FEMA Chief Tells of Frustration and Chaos." *New York Times* (September 15).

Klasen, S. 2000. "Measuring Poverty and Deprivation in South Africa." *Review of Income and Wealth* 46.

Kleindorfer, P. and H. Kunreuther. 1999. "The Complimentary Roles of Mitigation and Insurance in Managing Catastrophic Risks." *Risk Analysis* 19.

Klinenberg, E. 2002. *Heat Wave: A Social Autopsy of Disaster in Chicago.* Chicago: University of Chicago Press.

Kousky, C. and R. Zeckhauser. 2006. "JARring Actions That Fuel the Floods." In Daniels, R. J., D. F. Kettl, and H. Kunreuther, eds., *On Risk and Disaster: Lessons from Hurricane Katrina.* Philadelphia: University of Pennsylvania Press.

Krisher, H.P., III, S. A. Darley, and J. M. Darley. 1973. "Fear-provoking Recommendations, Intentions to Take Preventive Actions, and Actual Preventive Actions." *Journal of Personality and Social Psychology* 26.

Kreuter, M. W. and V. J. Strecher. 1995. "Changing Inaccurate Perceptions of Health Risk: Results from a Randomized Trial." *Health Psychology* 14 (1).

Kuklys, W. 2005. *Amartya Sen's Capability Approach: Theoretical Insights and Empirical Applications.* Berlin: Springer.

Kunreuther, H. 1973. *Recovery from Natural Disasters: Insurance or Federal Aid?* Washington, DC: American Enterprise Institute for Public Policy Research.

———. 1989. "The Role of Actuaries and Underwriters in Insuring Ambiguous Risks." *Risk Analysis* 9.

———. 1996. "Mitigating Disaster Losses through Insurance." *Journal of Risk and Uncertainty* 12.

———. 2005. "Disaster Mitigation and Insurance: Learning from Katrina." *Special Issue of The Annals on Hurricane Katrina.*

———. 2006. "Has the Time Come for Comprehensive Natural Disaster Insurance?" In Daniels, R. J., D. F. Kettl, and H. Kunreuther, eds., *On Risk and Disaster: Lessons from Hurricane Katrina.* Philadelphia: University of Pennsylvania Press.

Kunreuther, H., R. Ginsberg, L. Miller, P. Sagi, P. Slovic, B. Borkan, and N. Katz. 1978. *Disaster Insurance Protection: Public Policy Lessons.* London: Wiley Interscience.

Kunreuther, H. and G. Heal. 2003. "Interdependent Security." *Journal of Risk and Uncertainty.*

Kunreuther, H., R. Hogarth, and J. Meszaros. 1993. "Insurer Ambiguity and Market Failure." *Journal of Risk and Uncertainty* 7.

Kunreuther, H., R. Meyer, and C. Van den Bulte. 2004. *Risk Analysis for Extreme Events: Economic Incentives for Reducing Future Losses.* NIST GCR 04-871. Philadelphia: The Wharton School.

Kunreuther, H. and M. Pauly. 2004. "Neglecting Disaster: Why Don't People Insure Against Large Losses?" *Journal of Risk and Uncertainty* 28.

———. 2006. "Anomalies in Insurance." *Foundations and Trends in Microeconomics* 1 (2).

Kunreuther, H. and A. Rose, eds. 2004. *The Economics of Natural Hazards.* Vol. 1. Cheltenham: Edward Elgar.

Kunreuther, H. and R. J. Roth, eds. 1998. *Paying the Price: The Status and Role of Insurance Against National Disasters in the United States.* Washington, DC: Joseph Henry Press.

Kunreuther, H., W. Sanderson, and R. Vetschera. 1985. "A Behavioral Model of the Adoption of Protective Activities." *Journal of Economic Behavior and Organization.*

Laderchi, C. R. et al. 2003. "Does It Matter That We Do Not Agree on the Definition of Poverty? A Comparison of Four Approaches." *Oxford Development Studies* 31.

Landesman, L. Y. 2001. *Public Health Management of Disasters: The Practice Guide.* Washington, DC: American Public Health Association.

Landesman L. Y., J. Malilay, R. A. Bissell, S. M. Becker, L. Roberts, and M. S. Ascher. 2001a. "Roles and Responsibilities of Public Health in Disaster Preparedness and Response." In Novick, L. F. and J. S. Marr, eds., *Public Health Issues in Disaster Preparedness: Focus on Bioterrorism.* Gaithersburg, MD: Aspen Publishers, Inc.

Landis, M. 1998. "Let Me Next Time Be 'Tried by Fire': Disaster Relief and the Origins of the American Welfare State 1789–1874." *Northwestern University Law Review* 92.

Landis, M. 1999 "Fate, Responsibility, and Natural Disaster Relief: Narrating the American Welfare State." *Law and Society Review* 33.

Laska, S. 2004. "What If Hurricane Ivan Had Not Missed New Orleans?" *Natural Hazards Observer* 29.

————. 2005. "The Role of Social Science Research in Disaster Preparedness and Response." Testimony before the U.S. House of Representatives Science Committee, Subcommittee on Research. (November 10).

Lecomte, E. and K. Gahagan. 1998. "Hurricane Insurance Protection in Florida." In Kunreuther, K. and R. Roth, Sr., eds., *Paying the Price: The Status and Role of Insurance Against Natural Disasters in the United States.* Washington, DC: Joseph Henry Press.

Lerner, J. S., R. Gonzalez, D. Small, and B. Fischhoff. 2003. "Effects of Fear and Anger on Perceived Risks of Terrorism: A National Field Experiment." *Psychological Science* 14 (2).

Lerner, J. S. and D. Keltner. 2001. "Fear, Anger, and Risk." *Journal of Personality and Social Psychology* 81 (1).

Lewis, C. and K. C. Murdock. 1996. "The Role of Government Contracts in Discretionary Reinsurance Markets for Natural Disasters." *Journal of Risk and Insurance* 63.

Lindblom, C. 1959. "The Science of Muddling Through." *Public Administration Review* 19.

Lindell, M. K. and R. W. Perry. 1992. *Behavioral Foundations of Community Emergency Management.* Washington, DC: Hemisphere.

————. 2005. *Communicating Environmental Risk in Multiethnic Communities.* Thousand Oaks, CA: Sage Publications.

Lipton, C. E., C. Drew, S. Shane, and D. Rohde. 2005. "Storm and Crisis: Government Assistance; Breakdowns Marked Path from Hurricane to Anarchy." *New York Times* (September 11).

Litan, R. 2005. "Sharing and Reducing the Financial Risks of Future 'Mega-Castrophes.'" Brookings Institute Economics Studies Working Paper. (November 11).

Loewenstein, G., T. O Donoghue, and M. Rabin. 2003. "Projection Bias in Predicting Future Utility." *Quarterly Journal of Economics.*

Loewenstein, G., C. Hsee, E. Weber, and N. Welsh. 2001. "Risk as Feelings." *Psychological Bulletin* 127.

Loewenstein, G. and J. S. Lerner. 2003. "The Role of Affect in Decision Making." In Davidson, R., K. Scherer, and H. Goldsmith, eds., *Handbook of Affective Science.* New York: Oxford University Press.

Loewenstein, G. and D. Prelec. 1991. "Anomalies in Inter-temporal Choice: Evidence and an Interpretation." *Quarterly Journal of Economics* 107.

Löfstedt, R. 2005. *Risk Management in Post-trust Society.* London: Macmillan.

Louisiana Coastal Wetlands Conservation and Restoration Task Force and the Wetlands Conservation and Restoration Authority. 1998. *Coast 2050: Toward a Sustainable Coastal Louisiana.* Baton Rouge: Louisiana Department of Natural Resources.

Louisiana Office of the Governor. 2005. "Overview of Governor Kathleen Babineaux Blanco's Actions in Preparation for and Response to Hurricane Katrina." <http://www.gov.state.la.us/assets/docs/PDFs/Gov.response.12.2.05 .pdf>

Luce, M. F. and B. E. Kahn. 1999. "Avoidance or Vigilance: The Psychology of False-Positive Test Results." *Journal of Consumer Research* 26 (3).

McAllister, L. S., B. E. Peniston, S. G. Leibowitz, B. Abbruzzese, and J. B. Hyman. 2000. "A Synoptic Assessment for Prioritizing Wetland Restoration Efforts to Optimize Flood Attenuation." *Wetlands* 20.

McDonnell, K. 2005. "What Is Martial Law?" *Slate* (September 2). <http://www .slate.com/id/2125584/>

McKerlie, D. 1989. "Equality and Time." *Ethics* 99.

McNamara, D. 2005. Paper presented at "New Orleans After Hurricane Katrina: An Unnatural Disaster?" (December).

McPhee, J. 1989. *The Control of Nature.* New York: Farrar, Straus, and Giroux.

Mallion, M. 2005. "After the Storm." *Institutional Investor* (November 10).

Manale, A. 2000. "Flood and Water Quality Management Through Targeted, Temporary Restoration of Landscape Functions: Paying Upland Farmers to Control Runoff." *Journal of Soil and Water Conservation* 55 (3).

Mank, B. C. 2000. "The Draft Title VI Recipient and Revised Investigation Guidances: Too Much Discretion for EPA and a More Difficult Standard for Complainants?" *Environmental Law Reporter* 30.

Mannarelli, T., K. Roberts, and R. Bea. 1996. "Learning How Organizations Mitigate Risk." *Journal of Contingencies and Crisis Management* 4 (2).

Manes, Alfred. 1938. *Insurance: Facts and Problems.* New York: Harper and Brothers.

Marks, G. and N. Muller. 1987. "Ten Years of Research on the False-Consensus Effect: An Empirical and Theoretical Review." *Psychological Bulletin* 102 (1).

Martin, M. W. and R. Schinzinger. 2005. *Ethics in Engineering.* 4th ed. New York: McGraw-Hill.

Masestri, W. 2002. Interview with American RadioWorks. <http://americanradioworks.publicradio.org/features/wetlands/hurricane2.html>

Mawson, A.R. (2005). "Understanding Mass Panic and Other Collective Responses to Threat and Disaster." *Psychiatry* 68 (5).

Mayers, D. and C. Smith. 1990. "On the Corporate Demand for Insurance: Evidence from the Reinsurance Market." *Journal of Business* 63.

Meade, R. H. 1995. *Setting: Geology, Hydrology, Sediments, and Engineering of the Mississippi River.* U.S. Geological Survey Circular 1133. Reston, VA: United States Geological Survey.

Mechler, R. 2003. "Natural Disaster Risk and Cost-Benefit Analysis." In Kreimer, A. et al., *Building Safer Cities: The Future of Disaster Risk.* Washington, DC: The World Bank.

Menon, G., L. G. Block, and S. Ramanathan. 2002. "We're at as Much Risk as We Are Led to Believe: Effects of Message Cue on Judgments of Health Risk." *Journal of Consumer Research* 28 (4).

Meyer, R. J. 2006. "Why We Under-Prepare for Hazards." In Daniels, R. J., D. F. Kettl, and H. Kunreuther, eds., *On Risk and Disaster: Lessons from Hurricane Katrina.* Philadelphia: University of Pennsylvania Press.

Meyer, R. J. and H. Kunreuther. 2005. "Earthquakes in the Lab: Evidence for Dysfunctional Learning About Mitigation in a Natural Hazard Simulation." Working Paper. Center for Risk and Decision Processes, University of Pennsylvania.

Michel-Kerjan, E. and N. de Marcellis. In press. "Public-Private Programs for Covering against Extreme Events: The Impact of Information Distribution on Risk-Sharing." *Asia-Pacific Journal of Risk and Insurance.*

Mileti, D. S. et al. 1999. *Disasters by Design: A Reassessment of Natural Hazards in the United States.* Washington, DC: Joseph Henry Press.

Millhollon, M. and M. Ballard. 2005. "Blanco Coolly Greets Bush." *Advocate* (September 6). <http://2theadvocate.com/stories/090605/new_blanco001.shtml>

Moberg, F. and P. Ronnback. 2003. "Ecosystem Services of the Tropical Seascape: Interactions, Substitutions and Restoration." *Ocean and Coastal Management* 46 (1–2).

Mongin, P. and C. d'Aspremont. 1998. "Utility Theory and Ethics." In Barbera, S. et al., *Handbook of Utility Theory.* Vol. 1. Dordrecht: Kluwer.

Monterey Institute of International Studies. 2001. <http://russnelson.com/why-red-cross.html>

Moore, D. A., D. M. Cain, G. Loewenstein, and M. Bazerman, eds. 2005. *Conflicts of Interest.* Cambridge: Cambridge University Press.

Morduch, J. 1994. "Poverty and Vulnerability." *American Economic Review* 84.

Morgan, M. G., B. Fischhoff, A. Bostrom, and C. Atman. 2001. *Risk Communication: The Mental Models Approach.* New York: Cambridge University Press.

Morgan, M. G., and M. Henrion. 1990. *Uncertainty.* New York. Cambridge University Press.

Morgenstern, R. D., ed. 1997. *Economic Analyses at EPA: Assessing Regulatory Impact.* Washington, DC: Resources for the Future.

Morrow, B. H. 1999. "Identifying and Mapping Community Vulnerability." *Disasters* 23.

Morrow, B. H. and W. G. Peacock. 1997. "Disasters and Social Change: Hurricane Andrew and the Reshaping of Miami?" In Peacock, W. G., B. H. Morrow, and J. Gladwin, eds., *Hurricane Andrew: Ethnicity, Gender, and the Sociology of Disasters.* London: Routledge.

Moss, D. 1999. "Courting Disaster: The Transformation of Federal Disaster Policy Since 1803." In Froot, K. ed., *The Financing of Catastrophe Risk.* Chicago: University of Chicago Press.

———. 2002. *When All Else Fails: Government as the Ultimate Risk Manager.* Cambridge: Harvard University Press.

Muir, J. 1911. *My First Summer in the Sierra.* Boston: Houghton Mifflin Company.

Myers, M. F. 1996. "Midwest Floods, Channel Reforms." *Forum for Applied Research and Public Policy* 11.

Nagel, T. 1991. *Equality and Partiality.* Oxford: Oxford University Press.

Nagin, C. R. 2005. Quoted in the *New York Times* (December 11).

National Academy of Sciences. 1996. *Understanding Risk: Informing Decisions in a Democratic Society.* Washington, DC: National Academy Press.

National Oceanic and Atmospheric Administration. 2005. "Storm Surge: A 'Rising' Concern Among Coastal Residents." *National Oceanic and Atmospheric Administration Magazine* (September).

National Research Council. 1983. *Risk Management in the Federal Government.* Washington, DC: National Academy Press.

———. 1989. *Improving Risk Communication.* Washington, DC: National Academy Press.

———. 1994. *Science and Judgment in Risk Assessment.* Washington, DC: National Academy Press.

———. 1996. *Understanding Risk.* Washington, DC: National Academy Press.

———. 2000. *Watershed Management for Potable Water Supply: Assessing the New York City Strategy.* Washington, DC: National Academy Press.

———. 2005. *Valuing Ecosystem Services: Toward Better Environmental Decision-Making.* Washington, DC: National Academies Press.

National Research Council and Committee on the Restoration and Protection of Coastal Louisiana. 2005. *Drawing Louisiana's New Map: Addressing Land Loss in Coastal Louisiana.* Washington, DC: National Academies Press.

National Weather Service Forecast Office Mobile-Pensacola. 2005. "Extremely Powerful Hurricane Katrina leaves a Historic Mark on the Northern Gulf Coast." <http://www.srh.noaa.gov/mob/0805Katrina/>

Newby-Clark, I. R., M. Ross, R. Buehler, D. J. Koehler, and D. Griffin. 2000. "People Focus on Optimistic Scenarios and Disregard Pessimistic Scenarios While Predicting Task Completion Times." *Journal of Experimental Psychology: Applied* 6 (3).

New York Times. 2005. "The Flu Moat." <http://www.nytimes.com/2005/12/10/opinion/10sat4.html?hp>

———. 2005. "The Perplexing Pandemic Flu Plan." (November 20).

Niehaus, G. 2002. "The Allocation of Catastrophe Risk." *Journal of Banking and Finance* 26.

Novick, L. F. and J. S. Marr, eds. 2001. *Public Health Issues in Disaster Preparedness: Focus on Bioterrorism.* Gaithersburg, MD: Aspen Publishers, Inc.

Nussbaum, M. C. 2000. *Women and Human Development: The Capabilities Approach.* Cambridge: Cambridge University Press.

O'Brien, M. 2000. *Making Better Environmental Decisions: An Alternative to Risk Analysis.* Cambridge, MA: MIT Press.

O Donoghue, T. and M. Rabin. 1999. "Doing It Now or Later." *American Economic Review* 89 (1).

———. 2001. "Choice and Procrastination." *Quarterly Journal of Economics.*

Office of Management and Budget. 2003. Circular A-4 (September 17).

Oliver, M. L. and T. M. Shapiro. 1995. *Black Wealth/White Wealth: A New Perspective on Racial Inequality.* New York: Routledge.

Olson, M. 1990. *The Logic of Collective Action: Public Goods and the Theory of Groups.* Cambridge, MA: Harvard University Press.

Palm, R. 1990. *Natural Hazards: An Integrative Framework for Research and Planning.* Baltimore: Johns Hopkins University Press.

———. 1995. *Earthquake Insurance: A Longitudinal Study of California Homeowners.* Boulder: Westview Press.

Pandey, S. K. and D. P. Moynihan. 2006. "Bureaucratic Red Tape and Organizational Performance: Testing the Moderating Role of Culture and Political Support." In Boyne, G. A., K. J. Meier, L. J. O'Toole, Jr., and R. M. Walker, eds., *Public Service Performance.* Cambridge: Cambridge University Press.

Parenti, M. 2005. "How the Free Market Killed New Orleans." (September 3). <http://www.zmag.org/sustainers/content/2005-09/03parenti.cfm.>

Passyn, K., M. F. Luce, and B. Kahn. 2005. "Effectiveness of Regret-Based Persuasive Appeals for Motivating Adaptive Coping Behavior." Working Paper, Department of Marketing, University of Pennsylvania.

Pasterick, E. T. 1998. "The National Flood Insurance Program." In Kunreuther, H. and R. J. Roth, Sr., eds., *Paying the Price: The Status and Role of Insurance Against Natural Disasters in the United States.* Washington, DC: Joseph Henry Press.

Peacock, W. G. et al. 1997. *Hurricane Andrew: Ethnicity, Gender and the Sociology of Disasters.* London: Routledge.

Penland S. et al. 2005a. "Changes in Louisiana's Shoreline: 1852–2002." *Journal of Coastal Research* 44.

Penland, S. 2005b. "Taming the River to Let in the Sea." *Natural History* 114 (1).

Perrow, C. 1984. *Normal Accidents: Living with High-Risk Technologies.* New York: BasicBooks.

Pew Center. 2005. "Two-in-Three Critical of Bush's Relief Efforts: Huge Racial Divide over Katrina and Its Consequences." Washington, DC: Pew Center for the People and the Press. (September 8).

Phillips, B. D. 1993. "Cultural Diversity in Disasters: Sheltering, Housing, and Long Term Recovery." *International Journal of Mass Emergencies and Disasters* 11.

Phillips, B. D., L. Garza, and D. N. Neal. 1994. "Intergroup Relations in Disasters: Service Delivery Barriers after Hurricane Andrew." *Journal of Intergroup Relations* 21.

Pielke, R. A., C. Simonpietri, and J. Oxelson. 1999. "Thirty Years After Hurricane Camille: Lessons Learned, Lessons Lost." *Technical Report,* Center for Science and Technology Policy Research, University of Colorado, Boulder. <http://sciencepolicy.colorado.edu/about_us/meet_us/roger_pielke/camille/index.html>

Pierre, R. E. and A. Gerhart. 2005. "News of Pandemonium May Have Slowed Aid: Unsubstantiated Reports of Violence Were Confirmed by Some Officials, Spread by News Media." *Washington Post* (October 5).

Pilkey, O. H. and R. S. Young. 2005. "Will Hurricane Katrina Impact Shoreline Management? Here's Why It Should." *Journal of Coastal Research* 21.

Pinter, N. 2005. "One Step Forward, Two Steps Back on U.S. Floodplains." *Science* 308.

Platt, R. H. 1982. "The Jackson Flood of 1979: A Public Policy Disaster." *Journal of the American Planning Association* (Spring).

Pojman, L. P. and R. Westmoreland. 1997. *Equality: Selected Readings.* Oxford: Oxford University Press.

Posner, R. A. 2004. *Catastrophe: Risk and Response.* Oxford: Oxford University Press.
———. Forthcoming. "Lessons of Katrina." *New Republic.*

Powell, D. and W. Leiss. 1997. *Mad Cows and Mother's Milk: The Perils of Poor Risk Communication.* Montreal and Kingston: McGill-Queens University Press.

President's Columns, Society for Risk Analysis. 2005. *RISKNewsletter* 25 (2–4). <www.sra.org>

Presidential/Congressional Commission on Risk. 1998. *Risk Management.* Washington, DC: Author.

Priest, G. L. 1996. "The Government, the Market and the Problem of Catastrophic Loss." *Journal of Risk and Uncertainty* 12.
———. 2003. "Government Insurance versus Market Insurance." *The Geneva Papers on Risk and Insurance* 28.

Prince, S. H. 1920. "Catastrophe and Social Change: Based upon a Sociological Study of the Halifax Disaster." Columbia University, Department of Political Science.

Qizilbash, M. 2002. "A Note on the Measurement of Poverty and Vulnerability in the South African Context." *Journal of International Development* 14.

Quarantelli, E. L. 1996. "Just as a Disaster Is Not Simply a Big Accident, So a Catastrophe Is Not Just a Bigger Disaster." *Journal of the American Society of Professional Emergency Planners.*
———. 1997. "Ten Criteria for Evaluating the Management of Community Disasters." *Disasters* 21.
———. 2005. "Catastrophes Are Different from Disasters: Some Implications for Crisis Planning and Managing Drawn from Katrina." <http://understandingkatrina.ssrc.org/Quarantelli/>

Quarantelli, E. L. and R. R. Dynes. 1972. "When Disaster Strikes (It Isn't Much Like You've Heard and Read About)." *Psychology Today* 5.

Quinn, R. 1996. "Floodplain Management Issues Against Losses." *Forum for Applied Research and Public Policy* 11.

Raghubir, P. and G. Menon. 1998. "AIDS and Me, Never the Twain Shall Meet: The Effects of Information Accessibility on Judgments of Risk and Advertising Effectiveness." *Journal of Consumer Research* 25 (1).

Rawls, J. 1971. *A Theory of Justice.* Cambridge, MA: Harvard University Press.

Read, D. and B. van Leeuwan. 1998. "Predicting Hunger: The Effects of Appetite and Delay on Choice." *Organizational Behavior and Human Decision Processes* 76 (2).

Read, D. and G. Loewenstein. 1999. "Enduring Pain for Money: Decisions Based on the Memory of Pain." *Journal of Behavioral Decision Making* 12 (1).

Reason, J. 1997. *Managing the Risks of Organizational Accidents.* Burlington, VT: Ashgate Publishing Company.

Rechtschaffen, C. and E. Gauna. 2002. *Environmental Justice: Law, Policy, and Regulation.* Durham: Carolina Academic Press.

Reddy, S. D. 2000. "Examining Hazard Mitigation within the Context of Public Goods." *Environmental Management* 25 (2).

Risk Management Solutions. 2004. "The Northridge, California Earthquake: A 10-Year Retrospective." (May).

Robert Wood Johnson Foundation (RWJF). 2005. *Benefits Outweigh Drawbacks When Medicine and Public Health Collaborate.* <http://www.rwjf.org/reports/grr/031706.htm>

Roberts, K. H. 1993. *New Challenges to Understanding Organizations.* New York: Macmillan.

Rochlin, G. 1996. "Reliable Organizations: Present Research and Future Directions." *Journal of Contingencies and Crisis Management* 4 (2).

Romano, C. 2005. "Opinion: New Orleans and the Probability Blues." *Chronicle of Higher Education* (September 14). <http://chronicle.com/free/2005/09/2005091402n.htm>

Romer, P. 2005. Quoted by T. Friedman. "It's a Flat World." *New York Times Magazine* (April 2).

Rose, A. 2004. "Defining and Measuring Economic Resilience to Earthquakes." In *Research Progress and Accomplishments 2003–2004.* Buffalo, NY: State University of New York at Buffalo, Multidisciplinary Center for Earthquake Engineering Research. MCEER-04-SP01.

Rosetta, L. 2005. "Frustrated: Fire Crews to Hand out Fliers for FEMA." *Salt Lake Tribune* (September 12). <http://www.sltrib.com/utah/ci_3004197>

Ross, L., D. Greene, and P. House. 1977. "The False Consensus Effect: Egocentric Bias in Social Perception and Attribution Processes." *Journal of Experimental Social Psychology* 13.

Roth, R., Jr. 1998. "Earthquake Insurance in the United States." In Kunreuther, H. and R. J. Roth, Sr., eds., *Paying the Price: The Status and Role of Insurance Against Natural Disasters in the United States.* Washington, DC: Joseph Henry Press.

Roy, A. D. 1952. "Safety-first and the Holding of Assets." *Econometrica* 20.

Roy, M. M., N. J. S. Christenfeld, C. R. M. McKenzie. 2005. "Underestimating the Duration of Future Events: Memory Incorrectly Used or Memory Bias?" *Psychological Bulletin* 131 (5).

Ryland, H. 2006. "Providing Incentives to Build Disaster-Resistant Structures." In Daniels, R. J., D. F. Kettl, and H. Kunreuther, eds., *On Risk and Disaster: Lessons from Hurricane Katrina.* Philadelphia: University of Pennsylvania Press.

Salopek, P. and D. Horan. 2005. "Gulf Coast Crisis: How Places of Refuge Went to Hell." *Chicago Tribune* (September 15). <http://www.chicagotribune.com/news/nationworld/chi-0509150211sep15,0,7268671.story?page=1andcoll=chi-newsnationworld-hed>

Samuelson, W. and R. Zeckhauser. 1988. "Status Quo Bias and Decision Making." *Journal of Risk and Uncertainty* 1 (1).

Sangristano, M. D., Y. Trope, and N. Liberman. 2002. "Time-dependent Gambling: Odds Now, Money Later." *Journal of Experimental Psychology, General* 131.

Scheffler, S., ed. 1988. *Consequentialism and Its Critics.* Oxford: Oxford University Press.

Schleifstein, M. 2005. "JP's Maestri said FEMA Didn't Keep Its Word." *Times-Picayune* (September 2). <http://www.nola.com/newslogs/breakingtp/index.ssf?/mtlogs/nola_Times-Picayune/archives/2005_09_02.html>

Schor, E. 2005. "Two Months After Katrina, Politics Tightens Purse Strings." *The Hill* (November 2). <http://www.hillnews.com/thehill/export/TheHill/News/Frontpage/110205/spread.html>

Schroeder, M. 2005. "Storms Rattle Federal Flood Insurer." *Wall Street Journal* (November 8).

Schwarz, N., H. Bless, F. Strack, G. Klumpp, H. Ritenauser-Schatka, and A. Simons. 1991. "Ease of Retrieval as Information: Another Look at the Availability Bias." *Journal of Personality and Social Psychology* 61 (August).

Schwarze, R. and G. Wagner. 2003. "Mandatory Insurance Against Natural Disasters: Why and How?" *Economic Bulletin, Deutsches Institut fuer Wirtschaftsforschung* 40.

Schweitzer, M. E. and J. C. Hershey. 1997. "Under-Contribution Bias in Health Care Spending Account Decisions." *Benefits Quarterly* 13 (2).

Seed, R. B. et al. 2005. "Preliminary Report on the Performance of the New Orleans Levee Systems in Hurricane Katrina on August 29, 2005." *American Society of Civil Engineers* (November 2). Preliminary report Report No. UCB/CITRIS – 05/01 <http://www.asce.org/static/hurricane/orleans_report.cfm>

Sen, A. 1982. *Poverty and Famines: An Essay on Entitlement and Deprivation.* Oxford: Oxford University Press.

———. 1988. "Family and Food: Sex Bias in Poverty." In Srinivasan, T. and P. Bardham, eds., *Rural Poverty in South Asia.* New York: Columbia University Press.

———. 1992. *Inequality Reexamined.* Cambridge, MA: Harvard University Press.

Shane, S. 2005. "After Failures, Government Officials Play Blame Game." *New York Times* (September 5).

Sheaffer, J. R., J. D. Mullan, and N. B. Hinch. 2002. "Encouraging Wise Use of Flood Plains with Market-Based Incentives." *Environment* 44 (1).

Silverstein, J. L. 2004. "Turbulence Times Three: Coast Guard Units Respond to a Trio of Deadly Storms That Hit the Southeast Coast." *Coast Guard Magazine* (October).

Simile, C. 1995. "Disaster Settings and Mobilization for Contentious Collective Action: Case Studies of Hurricane Hugo and the Loma Prieta Earthquake." Ph.D. Dissertation, Department of Sociology and Criminal Justice, University of Delaware.

Sjöberg, L. 2003. "Neglecting the Risks: The Irrationality of Health Behavior and the Quest for La Dolce Vita." *European Psychologist* 8 (4).

Small, D. A., J. S. Lerner, R. M. Gonzalez, and B. Fischhoff. In press. "Emotion Priming and Attributions for Terrorism: Americans' Reactions in a National Field Experiment." *Political Psychology.*

Smetters, K. 2004. "Insurance Against Terrorism: The Policy Challenge." In Herring, R. and R. Litan, eds., *Brookings-Wharton Papers on Financial Services: 2004.* Washington, DC: Brookings Institution Press.

Smith, L. M. and B. R. Winkley. 1996. "The Response of the Lower Mississippi River to River Engineering." *Engineering Geology* 45.

Smith, Michael. 1994. *The Moral Problem.* Oxford: Blackwell, 1994.

Stallings, R. A. 1996. *The Northridge Earthquake "Ghost Towns": Final Report to the National Science Foundation.* NSF Grant No. CMS-9416196. Los Angeles: University of Southern California, Department of Sociology.

Stallings, R. A. and E. L. Quarantelli. 1985. "Emergent Citizen Groups and Emergency Management." *Public Administration Review* 45.

State of Louisiana. 2000. *Emergency Operations Plan Supplement 1A: Southeast Louisiana Hurricane Evacuation and Sheltering Plan.* <http://www.letxa.com/katrina/EOPSupplement1a.pdf>

Stavins, R. N. and A. B. Jaffe. 1990. "Unintended Impacts of Public Investments on Private Decisions: The Depletion of Forested Wetlands." *American Economic Review* 80 (3).

Steinhauer, J. 2005. "New Orleans Is Still Grappling with the Basics of Rebuilding." *New York Times* (November 8).

Stone, G. W. and R. A. McBride. 1998. "Louisiana Barrier Islands and Their Importance in Wetland Protection: Forecasting Shoreline Change and Subsequent Response of Wave Climate." *Journal of Coastal Research* 14 (3).

Stone, J. 1973. "A Theory of Capacity and the Insurance of Catastrophe Risks: Part I and Part II." *Journal of Risk and Insurance* 40.

Strom, B. 2006. "Role of Public Health and Clinical Medicine in Preparing for Disasters." In Daniels, R. J., D. F. Kettl, and H. Kunreuther, eds., *On Risk and Disaster: Lessons from Hurricane Katrina.* Philadelphia: University of Pennsylvania Press.

Suhayda, J. N. and V. Aravamuthan. 2000. "Community Havens: A New Approach to Managing the Threat of Hurricane Flooding." Submitted to the Louisiana Office of Emergency Preparedness, Jefferson Parish OEP, Orleans Parish OEP, and the University of New Orleans. (July 10).

Sunstein, C. R. 1994. "The Anticaste Principle." *Michigan Law Review* 92.

———. 2002. *Risk and Rationality.* Cambridge: Cambridge University Press.

———. 2005. *Laws of Fear.* New York: Cambridge.

Sunstein, C. and R. Thaler. 2003. "Libertarian Paternalism Is Not an Oxymoron." *University of Chicago Law Review* 70 (4).

Suspect device. 2005. "Hurricane Pam: Where It All Started to Go Wrong." (September 6). <http://suspect-device.blogspot.com/2005/09/hurricane-pam-where-it-all-started-to.html>

Symposium on Equality. 2003. *Economics and Philosophy* 19.

Szabo, S. 1996. "The World Health Organization Quality of Life (WHOQOL) Assessment Instrument." In Spilker, B., ed., *Quality of Life and Pharmacoeconomics in Clinical Trials.* 2nd ed. Philadelphia: Lippincott-Raven.

Temkin, L. S. 1993. *Inequality.* Oxford: Oxford University Press.

Terris M. 1986. "Epidemiology and the Public Health Movement." *Journal of Chronic Disease* 39 (12).

Testimony of Peter Nicholson before the Committee on Homeland Security and Governmental Affairs. 2005. U.S. Senate. (November 2). <http://www.asce.org/files/pdf/katrina/testimony.pdf>

Thomas, E. 2005. "How Bush Blew It." *Newsweek* (September 19). <http://www.msnbc.msn.com/id/9287434/print/1/displaymode/1098/>

Thomas, P. 2003. *The Anthrax Attacks.* New York: The Century Foundation.

Thompson, L. L. 2005. *The Mind and Heart of the Negotiator.* 3rd ed. Upper Saddle River, NJ: Pearson Prentice Hall.

Tierney, J. 2005. "Magic Marker Strategy." *New York Times* (September 6).

Tierney, K. 2006. "Social Inequality, Hazards, and Disasters." In Daniels, R. J., D. F. Kettl, and H. Kunreuther, eds., *On Risk and Disaster: Lessons from Hurricane Katrina*. Philadelphia: University of Pennsylvania Press.

Tierney, K. J. 1988. "Social Aspects of the Whittier Narrows Earthquake." *Earthquake Spectra* 4.

———. Forthcoming. "Businesses and Disasters: Vulnerability, Impacts, and Recovery." In Rodriguez, H., E. L. Quarantelli, and R. R. Dynes, eds., *Handbook of Disaster Research*. New York: Springer.

Tierney, K. J., C. Bevc, and E. Kuligowski. Forthcoming. "Metaphors Matter: Disaster Myths and Their Consequences in Hurricane Katrina." *Annals of the American Academy of Political and Social Science*.

Tierney, K. J., M. K. Lindell, and R. W. Perry. 2001. *Facing the Unexpected: Disaster Preparedness and Response in the United States*. Washington, DC: Joseph Henry Press.

Times-Picayune. 2002. "Washing Away." (June 23–27). <http://www.nola.com/hurricane/?/washingaway/>

———. 2004. "In Case of Emergency." (July 20). <http://www.ohsep.louisiana.gov/newsrelated/incaseofemrgencyexercise.htm>

Tobin, R. and C. Calfee. 2005. *The National Flood Insurance Program's Mandatory Purchase Requirement: Policies, Processes, and Stakeholders*. Washington, DC: American Institutes for Research.

Towers Perrin. 2005. "Hurricane Katrina: Analysis of the Impact on the Insurance Industry." <http://www.towersperrin.com/tillinghast/publications/reports/Hurricane_Katrina/katrina.pdf>

Travis, J. 2005. "Hurricane Katrina: Scientists' Fears Come True as Hurricane Floods New Orleans." *Science* 309 (5741).

Trebilcock, M. 2005. "Journeys across the Divides." In Rowley, C. K. and F. Parisi, eds., *The Origins of Law and Economics: Essays by the Founding Fathers*. Cheltenham: Edward Elgar Publishing.

Trebilcock, M. J. and R. J. Daniels. 2006. "Rationales and Instruments for Government Intervention in Natural Disasters." In Daniels, R. J., D. F. Kettl, and H. Kunreuther, eds., *On Risk and Disaster: Lessons from Hurricane Katrina*. Philadelphia: University of Pennsylvania Press.

TRIA and Beyond: Terrorism Risk Financing in the U.S. 2005. Wharton Risk Center. (August 11).

Trope, Y. and N. Liberman. 2003. "Temporal Construal." *Psychological Review* 110 (3).

Trotter, P. S., G. A. Johnson, R. Ricks, D. R. Smith, and D. Woods. 1998. "Floods on the Lower Mississippi: An Historical Economic Overview." NOAA Technical Attachment SR/SSD 98-9 <http://www.srh.noaa.gov/topics/attach/html/ssd98-9.htm>

Tungodden, B. 2003. "The Value of Equality." *Economics and Philosophy* 19.

Turner, R. H., J. M. Nigg, and D. Heller Paz. 1986. *Waiting for Disaster: Earthquake Watch in California*. Berkeley: University of California Press.

Tversky, A., S. Sattath, and P. Slovic. 1988. "Contingent Weighting in Judgment and Choice." *Psychological Review* 95.

Tversky, A. and E. Shafir. 1992. "Choice under Conflict: The Dynamics of Deferred Decision." *Psychological Science* 6.

U.S. Army Corps of Engineers. *Engineering and Design—Design and Construction of Levees*. Publication no. EM 1110-2-1913. <www.usace.army.mil/inet/usace-docs/eng-manuals/em1110-2-1913/toc.htm>

———. 1974. *Final Environmental Impact Statement: Lake Pontchartrain, Louisiana, and Vicinity Hurricane Protection Project.*

———. 1984. *Lake Pontchartrain, Louisiana, and Vicinity Hurricane Protection Project—Reevaluation Study.*

U.S. Department of Commerce. 2001. *Hurricanes: Unleashing Nature's Greatest Fury. A Preparedness Guide.* Prepared by NOAA in conjunction with the American Red Cross.

U.S. Department of Health and Human Services. 2005. *HHS Pandemic Influenza Plan.* (November).

U.S. Department of Homeland Security. 2004. *National Incident Management System.* (March 1).

———. 2004. "National Incident Management System and National Response Plan: Overview." (August 2004). <http://www.txregionalcouncil.org/ep/training/nims_briefing.ppt>

———. 2004. *National Response Plan.* (December).

U.S. General Accounting Office (GAO) [now Government Accountability Office]. 1982. *Improved Planning Needed by the Corps of Engineers to Resolve Environmental, Technical, and Financial Issues on the Lake Pontchartrain Hurricane Protection Project.* Memorandum GAO/MASAD-82-39.

———. 1990. *Flood Insurance: Information on the Mandatory Purchase Requirement.* Washington, DC: General Accounting Office (August).

———. 1991. *Disaster Assistance: Federal, State, and Local Responses to Natural Disasters Need Improvement.* Washington, DC: General Accounting Office.

———. 1995. *Midwest Flood: Information on the Performance, Effects, and Control of Levees.* GAO/RCED-95-125. Washington, DC: General Accounting Office, Resources, Community, and Economic Development Division.

———. 2005. *Catastrophe Risk, U.S. and European Approaches to Insure Natural Catastrophe and Terrorism Risks.* Report to the Chairman, Committee on Financial Services, House of Representatives. (February).

U.S. Government Accountability Office. 2005. *Army Corps of Engineers—Lake Pontchartrain and Vicinity Hurricane Protection Project.* GAO-05-1050T. Washington, DC: Government Accountability Office.

U.S. Nuclear Regulatory Commission. 1975. *Reactor Safety Study: An Assessment of Accident Risks in U.S. Commercial Nuclear Power Plants.* Washington, DC: Nuclear Regulatory Commission. (WASH 1400 Report originally published by the Atomic Energy Commission).

Urban Land Institute. 2005. "A Strategy for Rebuilding New Orleans, LA, Executive Summary." <http://www.uli.org/Content/NavigationMenu/ProgramsServices/AdvisoryServices/KatrinaPanel/exec_summary.pdf>

van Asseldonk, M., M. Meuwissen, and R. Huirne. 2002. "Belief in Disaster Relief and the Demand for a Public-Private Insurance Program." *Review of Agricultural Economics* 24.

Van Boven, L., D. Dunning, and G. Loewenstein. 2000. "Empathy Gaps Between Owners and Buyers: Misperceptions of the Endowment Effect." *Journal of Personality and Social Psychology* 79 (1).

Van Boven, L., G. Loewenstein, and D. Dunning. 2005. "The Illusion of Courage in Social Predictions: Underestimating the Impact of Fear of Embarrassment on Other People." *Organizational Behavior and Human Decision Processes* 96 (2).

van Heerden, I. L. 2005. *Coastal Land Loss: Hurricanes and New Orleans.* Baton Rouge: Center for the Study of Public Health Impacts of Hurricanes.

Vaughan, D. 1996. *The Challenger Launch Decision: Risky Technology, Culture, and Deviance at NASA.* Chicago: University of Chicago Press.

von Winterfeldt, D. 2001. "Decisions with Multiple Stakeholders and Conflicting Objectives." In Weber, E., J. Baron, and G. Loomes, eds., *Conflict and Tradeoffs in Decision Making*. New York: Cambridge University Press.

von Winterfeldt, D. 2005. *A Risk and Decision Analysis Framework for Protecting New Orleans Against Future Hurricanes*. Technical Report, Center for Risk and Economic Analysis of Terrorism Event, University of Southern California.

von Winterfeldt. 2006. "Using Risk and Decision Analysis to Protect New Orleans against Future Hurricanes." In Daniels, R. J., D. F. Kettl, and H. Kunreuther, eds., *On Risk and Disaster: Lessons from Hurricane Katrina*. Philadelphia: University of Pennsylvania Press.

von Winterfeldt, D. and W. Edwards. 1986. *Decision Analysis and Behavioral Research*. Cambridge: Cambridge University Press.

Walsh, B., R. T. Scott, and J. Moller. 2005. "Bush, Blanco Spar over Military, Visit: Blanco Says Army Brought Attitude, Not Resources." *Times-Picayune* (September 6). <http://www.nola.com/newslogs/tporleans/index.ssf?/mtlogs/nola_tporleans/archives/2005_09_06.html#077199>

Walters, J. and D. F. Kettl. 2006. "The Katrina Breakdown." In Daniels, R. J., D. F. Kettl, and H. Kunreuther, eds., *On Risk and Disaster: Lessons from Hurricane Katrina*. Philadelphia: University of Pennsylvania Press.

Warrick, J. 2005. "Investigators Posit Levee Design Flaws." *The Boston Globe*.

Wecht, C. H. and V. W. Weedn. 2005. "Forensic Pathology." In C. H. Wecht, ed., *Forensic Science and Law: Investigative Applications in Criminal, Civil and Family Justice*. Sudbury: International Publishers.

Weick, K. 2001. *Managing the Unexpected: Assuring High Performance in an Age of Complexity*. New York: Jossey-Bass.

Weinstein, N. D. 1980. "Unrealistic Optimism about Future Life Events." *Journal of Personality and Social Psychology* 39.

Weinstein, N. D. 2000. "Perceived Probability, Perceived Severity, and Health-Protective Behavior." *Health Psychology* 19 (1).

Weinstein, N. D. and W. M. Klein. 1995. "Resistance of Personal Risk Perceptions to Debiasing Interventions." *Health Psychology* 14 (2).

Westrum, R. and A. J. Adamski. 1999. "Organizational Factors Associated with Safety and Mission Success in Aviation Environments." In Garland, D. J., J. A. Wise, and V. D. Hopkin, eds., *Handbook of Aviation Human Factors*. Mahwah, NJ: Lawrence Erlbaum Associates.

Westrum, R. 2004. "Letter to the Committee on Accident Precursors of the National Academy of Engineering." In Phimister, J. R., V. M. Bier, and H. Kunreuther, eds., *Accident Precursor Analysis and Management: Reducing Technological Risk through Diligence*. Washington, DC: National Academies Press.

White, K.L. 1991. *Healing the Schism: Epidemiology, Medicine, and the Public's Health*. New York: Springer-Verlag.

Wiest, R. E. 1998. "A Comparative Perspective on Household, Gender, and Kinship in Relation to Disaster." In Enarson, E. and B. H. Morrow, eds., *The Gendered Terrain of Disaster: Through Women's Eyes*. Westport, CT: Praeger.

Witt, J. L. 2005. "Strong Building Codes Protect Life and Property." *Miami Herald* (November 4).

Whoriskey, P. 2005. "Risk Estimate Led to Few Flood Policies." *Washington Post* (October 17).

Wikipedia. 2005. "Hurricane Frances." <http://en.wikipedia.org/wiki/Hurricane_Frances>

Wilson, T. D. and D. Gilbert. 2003. "Active Forecasting." In Zanna, M., ed., *Advances in Experimental Social Psychology*. Vol. 35. New York: Elsevier.

Winchester, S. 2003. *Krakatoa: The Day the World Exploded, August 27, 1883.* New York: Harper Collins.

Winchester, S. 2005. *A Crack in the Edge of the World: America and the Great California Earthquake of 1906.* New York: Harper Collins.

Winter, R. A. 1988. "The Liability Crisis and the Dynamics of Competitive Insurance Markets." *Yale Journal on Regulation* 5.

———. 1991. "The Liability Insurance Market." *Journal of Economic Perspectives* 5.

———. 1994. "The Dynamics of Competitive Insurance Markets." *Journal of Financial Intermediation* 3.

Wisner, B. et al. 2004. *At Risk: Natural Hazards, People's Vulnerability and Disasters.* 2nd ed. London: Routledge.

WHOQOL Group, The. 1998. "The World Health Organization Quality of Life Assessment (WHOQOL): Development and General Psychometric Properties." *Social Science Medicine* 46.

Worth, R. 1998. "Reinvention Lite: Why Al Gore Still Has a Long Way to Go." *Washington Monthly* 30 (9). <http://www.washingtonmonthly.com/features/1998/9809.worth.gore.html>

WRI. 2005. "EarthTrends: The Environmental Information Portal." <http://www.earthtrends.wri.org/>

Yaukey, J. 2005. "Federal Troops Should Be First Responders to Natural Disasters, Experts Say." *Air Force Times* (September 14) <http://www.airforcetimes.com/story.php?f=1-292925-1102914.php>

Yen, H. 2005. "U.S. Unprepared for Super-Flu Pandemic." Associated Press. (November 20). <http://news.yahoo.com/s/ap/20051120/ap_on_he_me/flu_us_preparedness>

Yezer, A. M. J. 2002. "The Economics of Natural Disasters." In Stallings, R. A., ed., *Methods of Disaster Research.* International Research Committee on Disasters.

Young, A. and S. Borenstein. 2005. "Experts: Focus on Terrorism Delays FEMA Response to Katrina." Knight Ridder Newspapers. (September 2). <http://www.realcities.com/mld/krwashington/12548203.htm>

Acknowledgments

This volume is the result of an extraordinary collaboration among colleagues at the University of Pennsylvania and beyond who were determined to develop a timely and thoughtful response to some of the key challenges posed by Hurricane Katrina to the way in which American governments and markets respond to the risk of natural disaster. To do this, we convened a major conference in Washington, D.C., entitled the National Symposium on Risk and Disaster. That conference was attended by more than 250 leading academics, business managers, community leaders, and policymakers. It took place on December 1, 2005: 100 days after Hurricane Katrina first unleashed its fury on the Gulf Coast of the United States.

Our decision to convene a national dialogue on risk and disaster in the aftermath of Hurricane Katrina was inspired by University of Pennsylvania President Gutmann's evocative call for societal engagement in the Penn Compact. At the core of President Gutmann's Compact is the idea that the intellectual resources of the University should be harnessed in the service of illuminating and shaping public debate on matters of national or international importance. The implicit assumption of the Compact is, of course, that ideas can shape public policy outcomes for the better, and there is no institution in society that is better suited to the task of generating and harnessing ideas for the public good than a university.

There is little doubt that the task of mounting this conference and publishing this volume in such a highly compressed time frame was a daunting challenge. Despite the challenges of this enterprise, however, we were heartened by the collective determination of everyone involved in it to ensure its success. And so, a number of expressions of gratitude and appreciation are required.

First and foremost, we need to give a heartfelt and special thanks to the contributors to this volume, who worked under extremely tight timelines but who clearly took great care in thinking through these issues, shaping their ideas and articulating a set of "best ideas" which they felt would help the nation mitigate the pain, suffering, and loss in future disasters. Thank you for working with us to move the dialogue on risk and disaster forward. We feel privileged to have had the opportunity to collaborate with you all.

We were also fortunate to be able to work closely with *Congressional Quarterly* and The Communications Institute in mounting this project. We thank David Rapp of *CQ* and Jack Cox, Saundra Halgrimson, and Marianne Cox of TCI for their efforts and support in organizing and convening the symposium in Washington.

We were also supported by a number of offices and individuals at the University who were dedicated and committed to the success of this enterprise. We would like to thank the deans of all twelve schools and their delegates who served on an overarching steering committee that originally conceived and structured this project. We also enjoyed the ongoing support of the University's Vice-President of Government Relations, Van McMurtry, and his Executive Director, Carol de Fries, as well as the support of our Vice-President of University Communications, Lori Doyle, and the Director of Media Relations, Ron Ozio. From the Wharton Risk Management and Decision Processes Center, we owe thanks to Robert Meyer and Hannah Chervitz.

A number of individuals in both the President's and Provost's Office deserve our thanks as well. We thank Stephen Steinberg and Jim Gardner from the President's Office for their invaluable assistance. From the Provost's Office, we are grateful to Ray Simon for stepping in to assist with the symposium.

We cannot thank enough Eric Halpern, Peter Agree, and the staff of the University of Pennsylvania Press. They also found for us one of the most tremendous development editors we have had the pleasure to work with, Edward J. Blum. Together, their efficiency, care, responsiveness, and commitment to this project were truly spectacular.

Finally, our final and greatest debt is owed to Lois Chiang, Executive Director of the Provost's Office. Lois was responsible for coordinating this project in every dimension. In her quiet and understated way, she provided the direction, energy, and persistence that ensured the success of our project. Put simply, we could have not done this volume without her leadership.

The views expressed in this volume are those of the individual authors and not those of our sponsor organizations.

Contributors

MATTHEW D. ADLER is Professor of Law at the University of Pennsylvania, specializing in the areas of constitutional law, administrative law, regulation, and legal theory. He is particularly interested in the application of rigorous philosophical techniques to problems of public law. Adler has published numerous articles and shorter scholarly works, in the Harvard, Yale, Michigan, Minnesota, Northwestern, Virginia, and the University of Pennsylvania law reviews as well as in the *Supreme Court Review, Journal of Legal Studies, Legal Theory*, and elsewhere.

VICKI BIER holds a joint appointment as Professor in the Departments of Industrial Engineering and Engineering Physics at the University of Wisconsin-Madison, where she has directed the Center for Human Performance and Risk Analysis (formerly the Center for Human Performance in Complex Systems) since 1995.

RONALD J. DANIELS, Provost of the University of Pennsylvania, is the author of numerous scholarly articles and books. His scholarly interests lie in the law and economics of the corporation and of the regulatory state. His current scholarship focuses on the challenges of building strong laws and legal institutions in developing states. His most recent publications include, as coauthor, "Rethinking the Welfare State: Government by Voucher" and "The Political Economy of Rule of Law Reform in Developing Countries." Daniels is active in public policy formulation and has contributed to several Canadian public task forces.

BARUCH FISCHHOFF is Howard Heinz University Professor in the Department of Engineering and Public Policy and the Department of Social and Decision Sciences at Carnegie Mellon University. He is past President of the Society for Risk Analysis and past President of the Society for Judgment and Decision Making. He is a member of the Institute of Medicine of the National Academy of Sciences, the U.S. Department of Homeland Security's Science and Technology Advisory Committee, and the U.S. Environmental Protection Agency's Scientific Advisory Board, where he chairs the Homeland Security Advisory Subcommittee.

KENNETH R. FOSTER is Professor of Bioengineering at the University of Pennsylvania. In addition to papers in his technical specialty, he has written widely on the social implications of technology, technological risk, and ethical issues related to technology. He is the author of two books on science and the law, including *Judging Science*. Foster is a Fellow of the Institute of Electrical and Electronics Engineers and former President of the IEEE Society on Social Implications of Technology.

ROBERT GIEGENGACK is Professor and Chair of Earth and Environmental Sciences at the University of Pennsylvania. He studies the history of climate change at selected sites around the world as a baseline from which we might be able to evaluate the threat of human-caused climatic change.

PETER G. GOSSELIN has been a reporter with the *Los Angeles Times* since 1999 covering national economics. He is author of "The New Deal," a continuing series on the economic insecurity of a growing swath of American working families.

AMY GUTMANN is the eighth President of the University of Pennsylvania, where she also holds faculty appointments in the Departments of Political Science, Communication, Philosophy, and Education. Gutmann came to Penn from Princeton University, where she served as Provost and the Laurance S. Rockefeller University Professor of Politics. Gutmann is a former President of the American Society of Political and Legal Philosophy, a Fellow of the American Academy of Arts and Sciences, the W. E. B. Du Bois Fellow of the American Academy of Political and Social Science, a Member of the American Philosophical Society, and a Fellow of the National Academy of Education. She has published more than 100 articles and essays and edited books in political philosophy, practical ethics, and education, which have been translated into many languages. Her most recent books include *Why Deliberative Democracy?* (with Dennis Thompson); *Identity in Democracy*; *Democratic Education*; *Democracy and Disagreement* (with Dennis Thompson); and *Color Conscious* (with K. Anthony Appiah). Her reviews have appeared in the *New York Times Book Review, Times Literary Supplement, Washington Post,* and other general publications.

SCOTT E. HARRINGTON is Alan B. Miller Professor, Health Care Systems and Insurance and Risk Management, at the Wharton School, University of Pennsylvania. A former President of both the American Risk and Insurance Association and the Risk Theory Society, he has published widely on the economics and regulation of insurance markets.

DONALD F. KETTL is Stanley I. Sheerr Endowed Term Professor in the Social Sciences at the University of Pennsylvania, where he is Director of the Fels Institute of Government and Professor of Political Science. He is the author or editor of a dozen books and monographs, including *System under Stress: Homeland Security and American Politics*; *The Global Public Management Revolution*, 2nd ed.; *The Politics of the Administrative Process* (with James W. Fesler), 3rd ed.; and *The Transformation of Governance: Public Administration for the 21st Century*. He is a fellow of the National Academy of Public Administration.

CAROLYN KOUSKY is a Research Fellow in the Science, Environment, and Development group at Harvard's Center for International Development (CID) and a doctoral candidate in the Public Policy Program at Harvard's Kennedy School of Government. Her current research examines the public policy of ecosystem services.

HOWARD KUNREUTHER is Codirector of the Risk Management and Decision Processes Center at the Wharton School of the University of Pennsylvania. He has a long-standing interest in ways in which society can better manage low-probability, high-consequence events as they relate to technological and natural hazards and has published extensively on the topic. Currently a member of the National Research Council Boards on Radioactive Waste Management and Natural Disasters, he chaired the H. John Heinz, III Center Panel on Risk, Vulnerability and True Costs of Coastal Hazards. He is Distinguished Fellow of the Society for Risk Analysis and has received the Society's Distinguished Achievement Award. He has written or coedited a number of books, including *Catastrophe Modeling: A New Approach to Managing Risk* (with Patricia Grossi) and *Wharton on Making Decisions* (with Stephen Hoch). He is a recipient of the Elizur Wright Award, given to the author of the publication that makes the most significant contribution to the literature of insurance.

ROBERT J. MEYER is the Gayfryd Steinberg Professor of Marketing at the Wharton School of the University of Pennsylvania and Codirector of the Wharton Risk and Decision Processes Center. His work has widely appeared in a number of journals in marketing, management, and transportation. He is a former editor of *Marketing Letters* and former associate editor of the *Journal of Consumer Research* and *Marketing Science*.

HARVEY G. RYLAND is President and Chief Executive Officer of the Institute for Business and Home Safety, which he joined after serving as Deputy Director of the Federal Emergency Management Agency (FEMA). While at FEMA, he helped develop a new strategy for emergency management in the United States, emphasizing loss reduction through mitigation. Ryland has also served as Executive Director of the Central United States Earthquake Consortium, whose mission is earthquake mitigation and preparedness in the New Madrid Seismic Zone.

BRIAN STROM, M.D., M.P.H., is George S. Pepper Professor of Public Health and Preventive Medicine, Chair and Professor of Biostatistics and Epidemiology, Professor of Medicine, Professor of Pharmacology, Director of the Center for Clinical Epidemiology and Biostatistics, Director of the Graduate Group in Epidemiology and Biostatistics, and Associate Vice Dean, all at the University of Pennsylvania School of Medicine. He is also Associate Vice President for Strategic Integration, University of Pennsylvania Health System.

KATHLEEN TIERNEY is Professor of Sociology and Director of the Natural Hazards Research and Applications Information Center at the University of Colorado at Boulder. Her research focuses on the social dimensions of hazards and disasters, including natural, technological, and human-induced extreme events. With collaborators Michael Lindell and Ronald Perry, she recently published *Facing the Unexpected: Disaster Preparedness and Response in the United States.*

MICHAEL J. TREBILCOCK is University Professor and Professor of Law at the University of Toronto. He has been a Fellow in Law and Economics at the University of Chicago Law School, a Visiting Professor of Law at Yale Law School, and a Global Law Professor at New York University Law School. He was awarded the Owen Prize by the Foundation for Legal Research for his book *The Common Law of Restraint of Trade.* He has also authored *The Limits of Freedom of Contract* and coauthored *The Regulation of International Trade*; *Exploring the Domain of Accident Law: Taking the Facts Seriously*; *The Making of the Mosaic: A History of Canadian Immigration Policy*, and *The Law and Economics of Canadian Competition Policy.* He serves as Director of the Law and Economics Programme at the University of Toronto.

DETLOF VON WINTERFELDT is Professor of Public Policy and Management in the School of Policy, Planning, and Development at the University of Southern California. He is also the director of USC's Homeland Security Center for Risk and Economic Analysis of Terrorist Events, a joint center of SPPD and USC's Viterbi School of Engineering. He is the coauthor of two books and author or coauthor of over one hundred articles and reports on these topics. He is a fellow of the Institute for Operations Research and the Management Sciences and of the Society for Risk Analysis. He received the Ramsey Medal for distinguished contributions to decision analysis from the Decision Analysis Society of INFORMS.

JONATHAN WALTERS is a senior staff writer for *Governing* magazine. He has covered state and local public policy for the past 20 years, with an emphasis on management and administration.

RICHARD ZECKHAUSER is Frank Plumpton Ramsey Professor of Political Economy at Harvard University's John F. Kennedy School of Government. He is author, coauthor, or editor of over 215 articles and 10 books. Much of his research focuses on issues of risk, uncertainty, and ignorance. Zeckhauser is an elected member/fellow of the Institute of Medicine of the National Academy of Sciences, the American Academy of Arts and Sciences, and the Econometric Society.